PENGUIN BOOKS
REPORTING PAKISTAN

Meena Menon is an independent journalist and former deputy editor of *The Hindu*. She has been a journalist since 1984, starting out in *Bombay Magazine*, and has worked for the United News of India, *Mid-Day* and the *Times of India*. She was chief of bureau with *The Hindu*, Mumbai, before being posted to Islamabad in August 2013, where she remained until she was expelled in May 2014. She was later based in New Delhi as the paper's environment correspondent till March 2015. She is the author of *Riots and After in Mumbai: Chronicles of Truth and Reconciliation* and *Organic Cotton: Reinventing the Wheel*, and co-author of *The Unseen Worker: On the Trail of the Girl Child* and *A Frayed History: The Journey of Cotton in India.*

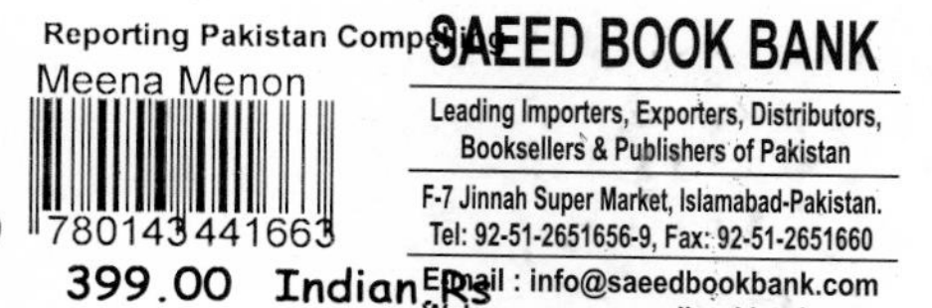

PRAISE FOR THE BOOK

'[Menon's] astute portrayal of the lack of professional freedom that she faced makes for a compelling reading for any journalist who wishes to write and understand Pakistan'—*The Hindu*

'Engaging and evocative'—*Open*

'This is what makes this book so special: rising above both the pride and the prejudice that often overwhelm our perceptions of [Pakistan], [Menon] unhesitatingly presents both the warts and the astonishing resilience of a people fighting fierce odds'—*Indian Express*

'Menon has done an extraordinarily detailed and in-depth job of documenting her experiences during her relatively brief stint as an Indian reporter in Pakistan'—*Herald*

'Exciting and informative'—*Free Press Journal*

'Through *Reporting Pakistan*, Meena Menon makes a convincing case for a much broader media exchange between the two countries. It is time to distribute the book widely in both India and Pakistan'—*The News*

'A fascinating narrative filled with sharp and witty observations' —Wire

'*Reporting Pakistan* is one of those rare books which introduces us to the unseen side of Pakistan'—Firstpost

Reporting Pakistan

MEENA MENON

PENGUIN BOOKS
An imprint of Penguin Random House

PENGUIN BOOKS

USA | Canada | UK | Ireland | Australia
New Zealand | India | South Africa | China

Penguin Books is part of the Penguin Random House group of companies whose addresses can be found at global.penguinrandomhouse.com

Published by Penguin Random House India Pvt. Ltd
7th Floor, Infinity Tower C, DLF Cyber City,
Gurgaon 122 002, Haryana, India

First published in Viking by Penguin Random House India 2017
Published in Penguin Books 2018

All photographs by Meena Menon

10 9 8 7 6 5 4 3 2 1

ISBN 9780143441663

Typeset in Adobe Garamond Pro by Manipal Digital Systems, Manipal
Printed at Thomson Press India Ltd, New Delhi

www.penguin.co.in

This book is for Ravi, the sunshine in my life

Contents

Acknowledgements

As Pakistan correspondent for *The Hindu*, I was stationed in Islamabad and not allowed to travel, thanks to visa restrictions, and so reported on most events in the country based in the capital. I thank *The Hindu* and its former editor Siddharth Varadarajan for nominating me as Pakistan correspondent. The paper's foreign desk with Srinivas Ghantasala, and later Prabhakar Subramaniam, apart from P.J. George and Hari Narayan, Suresh Nambath on the edit page, and Venkatesh Mukunth who handled the blogs were wonderful to work with, not to forget the news editor, P.K. Subramaniam. I also thank K. Sathyanarayanan and Harini from the accounts department. My predecessors in Pakistan, Anita Joshua and Nirupama Subramanian, made my job that much easier, as they had kept meticulous records and contact, and gave me valuable advice. My husband, Venkat Iyer, has always been there for me and was a great support during my posting, as also my family and friends. Islamabad was a comfortable place to live in because of the hospitable people, the media community and the friends I inherited and made. I am grateful to so many people, including many journalists and complete strangers who went out of their way to make me feel at home. I wish to thank Shoaib Sultan Khan, Shandana Humayun Khan, Amir Mateen, Anila Daulatzai, Mariana Babar, Arifa Nooor, Ayesha Siddiqa, Kishwar Naheed, Waqas Rafique, Lt. Gen. Talat Masood, Rustomshah

Mohmand, Brig. Ayaz, Raza Rumi and many others, as also some who do not wish to be named. The Pakistan high commission officials in New Delhi and government officials and ministers in Islamabad were always courteous and helpful. I would also like to thank all the officials at the Indian high commission and their families for their hospitality and concern about our well-being. I am grateful to the Asiatic Library, Mumbai, for some of the books which were difficult to find elsewhere. I thank the editors of Penguin Random House for publishing the book, and Kamini Mahadevan. The Mumbai Press Club was very supportive after my expulsion, as were many other organizations, including the Committee to Protect Journalists. The Mumbai Press Club has an exchange programme with the Karachi Press Club, enabling delegations of journalists to visit each other's countries. That's how I first visited Pakistan. It was a wonderful exchange and a great way of learning about each other.

As I wrote in *The Hindu* on my return to India after I was expelled in May 2014, there are two states of mind in Pakistan, two states in that nation and the twain may not necessarily meet. These are only my experiences and they are not universal. I am not a Pakistan expert; there are too many around.

Preface

Of the Many Pakistans and Borders

The border is a fearsome thing God wot!

—With apologies to Thomas Edward Brown

On one side of the 'border' was a cluster of shanties, and on the other, a hillock with ramshackle huts. A man in dark glasses, a Shiv Sainik, trying to be well meaning, pointed to the hillock, warning me not to go there. That is Pakistan, the mosques are full of bombs and guns, he said. Even before crossing the Wagah border, I was already there! That was the first of the many Pakistans I was to discover in Mumbai, miles away from the partitioned country. It was a few years before the demolition of the Babri Masjid on 6 December 1992, the first time I was at the 'border'. There were riots in Jogeshwari East, a suburb of Mumbai which has a long record of communal violence. I thought the man was joking; I had been to the other side of the 'border' and families were mourning their dead and injured. He looked shocked when I questioned him. He had meant it kindly, for my safety. Pakistan was synonymous with any large Muslim pocket and, in Jogeshwari, the scene of some of the worst violence during the December 1992–93 riots in Bombay (it was renamed

Mumbai in 1995), the 'border' was very well defined early on. Hindus and Muslims knew their geographical limits and stuck to them. The divide was sharpened after the riots when the few 'mixed' settlements emptied out. The devastating floods of 2005 in the city brought the communities together and Hindus and Muslims are now working to understand each other and overcome the past.

Behrampada, a slum outside Bandra station, in Mumbai, had a nefarious reputation and no one had ventured inside, not even to help the injured people during the communal riots of 1992–93. It was after an NGO went in and found people unable to get medical help and saw destroyed houses that the truth about this large Muslim pocket, which even today has Hindu families, came out into the open. In Mira Road, in Thane district on the outskirts of Mumbai, which many riot affected chose as their new home after the 1992–93 violence, the 'border' begins as soon as you step out of the suburban railway station. A large road divides the Hindu and Muslim sections of the suburb, and there are apartment buildings where only Hindus or Muslims or their subsects can stay. Muslims are not welcome everywhere, an estate agent told me. It is the builders who decide the convenience of religious groupings. Brokers brazenly advertise their anti-Muslim feelings here and in Mumbai. Another central suburb, Kurla, has a large Muslim population and once while waiting for a function, I asked a vendor where I could get something to eat. Don't go ahead, he warned, it's Pakistan. When I looked puzzled, he said it's full of Muslims, you won't get anything to eat there that you like.

An electricity bill was delivered to a locality—Chhota Pakistan—in Nalasopara (in Palghar district, originally called Tanda Pada); predictably, it did have a large Muslim population.[1] (The area was often referred to as Chhota Pakistan by the local electric utility office but inexplicably it was legitimized as a postal address in the bill.) In April 2013, I was invited to the power-loom town of Malegaon in north Maharashtra to speak on the media and Muslims. During the discussion on stereotypes, one of the journalists gave an example of shoddy reporting that in a way involved Pakistan. A Pakistani girl was reported to be among the over thirty killed in the bomb blasts in Malegaon in September 2006. Though journalists covering the blasts had found that she was from Islamabad, a mohalla in Malegaon, no correction was issued. They were proud that during Partition, 'not a single person from Malegaon [had] left for Pakistan'. Yet Malegaon, with all its history of fighting for Independence, and educational institutions, is labelled a terror hotspot. In reality, it is even more victimized. All nine men arrested for the same 2006 bomb blasts near the Malegaon mosque were acquitted after a decade in April 2016. There is an unshakeable belief that terror is perpetrated by Muslims alone, so the revelation that those from the majority community were involved in the blasts took a while to digest. All terrorists are Muslims but all Muslims may not be terrorists was a popular refrain of the Bharatiya Janata Party (BJP). After he heard that I was going to Islamabad, one of my friends from Malegaon jokingly said that he hoped it was to the place across the border.

*

Even before the line creating the two new countries was drawn by the Boundary Commissions headed by Sir Cyril Radcliffe, the subcontinent had convulsed with hate-filled violence and distrust. The spidery tentacles of the new border went right into people's hearts and minds, and stayed there. It became the line we drew inside us, separating the other. Pakistan became at once something dreadful and unpleasant, and travelling in Gujarat just after the Godhra train burning in 2002, my driver, a Muslim, asked me if it was true that all Muslims would be dropped at the border and asked to go to Pakistan. He refused to believe that it wouldn't happen. If an Indian says something that is remotely in favour of Muslims or against the so-called patriotic or nationalist notions of being Indian or 'anti-national', a chorus will start, 'Go to Pakistan', 'Send him or her to Pakistan', and so on. The legion of 'traitors and anti-nationalists' who have been summarily dispatched to Pakistan is constantly expanding. Pakistan is a repository of people traitorous to India and the enemy is clearly defined.

The border is like a Lego block—you can place it anywhere and create division; we don't seem to cross it easily and we don't need visas certainly but we never jump the fence for fear of finding out the truth. So the Shiv Sainik who warned me about the bombs hadn't actually been there, or the vendor who warned me not to go ahead wasn't sure himself, but they had an idea of Pakistan. There is an unshakeable feeling in the minds of many people that it must be a rotten place, anti-Indian, full of bearded men wanting to blow themselves up, and with guns and ammunition stored in mosques, burqa-clad women, and people straining at the leash to attack India. Pakistan, far from being the Land of the Pure, gives the opposite impression in India. The little pockets of 'Pakistan' that we have symbolize those fears. And the war and proxy war with India over Kashmir and terrorism have only made things worse. Terrorism is inextricably linked with Pakistan, and shadows all moves for peace. In Bombay the 1992–93 communal riots became the basis for 'revenge' in the form of twelve serial bombings on 12 March 1993. For the first time, terror came home to a city, already devastated by a prolonged orgy of violence. After the Babri Masjid was demolished on 6 December 1992, rioting started in Bombay that evening, and the violence escalated to claim nearly 1000 lives in the next two months, and injured many more. The bloodletting was capped by the first terror attack on Bombay. The perpetrators of the twelve bombings that day—Dawood Ibrahim and his henchman, Tiger Memon, along with his family, among others—were all in Pakistan, something that Memon's brother, Yakub, confirmed when he returned to

India in 1994. Yakub and 100 others were convicted, and he was among the eleven sentenced to death for financing the operation, for instance, by providing tickets to the men to be sent for arms training in Pakistan.[2] Yakub's testimony nailed the suspicion about Pakistan's involvement in the serial blasts which had already been publicized by India's Home Minister S.B. Chavan in Parliament in April 1993.[3] The charge sheet filed in November 1993 in the case mentioned that some of the accused had gone to Pakistan for training.

*

When I came to the city in 1975, it was called Bombay. Its name would change twenty years later when the Shiv Sena–Bharatiya Janata Party government won the elections for the first time riding on the wave of Hindutva euphoria after the Babri Masjid was demolished in 1992. By then, I had already reported on two major events that would strip Bombay of its cosmopolitan façade—the communal riots of 1992–93 and the serial bomb blasts of 12 March 1993.[4] After 1993, Bombay was under attack repeatedly, culminating in the 26 November 2008 strike. Each bombing intensified the animosity towards Muslims and Pakistan, but few will acknowledge that the ground for division and ghettoization was also paved well before that in the form of divisive and sectarian politics. The mini Pakistans or Muslim ghettos are no-go areas for many, and the stereotyped distancing is reinforced by suspicion.

The last terror attack on 26 November 2008 was a defining moment for Mumbai. The city which never slept was catatonic after ten highly trained armed men created havoc in posh South Mumbai. Everyone was baying for blood and demanding the public execution of Ajmal Kasab, the sole gunman caught alive by the police. Anti-Pakistan sentiment reached an all-time high. I was relieved to hear the strong condemnation of 26/11 when

I visited the Karachi Press Club three years after the attack, and heartened by the sympathy and protest.

There is a tendency by many to view Pakistan's war and proxy war over Kashmir as disparate from the political context in which it is happening. That the Kashmiris' right to self-determination is the crux of the matter slips into the background; and in the cacophony of jingoism, with each country asserting ownership over Kashmir, its people are forgotten. Yet politicians who find it so easy to say that 'restraint' becomes difficult in the face of this constant provocation from Pakistan make no attempt to resolve the problem.

It is always easier to simply blame 'the enemy' than to separate the elements perpetrating such monstrous attacks from ordinary people in the other country who, for the most part, don't endorse them. Families who have lost their loved ones to terrorism or wars cannot understand the calls for friendship between the two countries. After 26/11 in the clamour for the public execution of Kasab, there were few dissenting voices. Between war and terrorism on the one hand, and calls for friendship or peace on the other, lies an unforgiving chasm. That sense of belonging because we were once undivided quickly changes to bloodthirsty revenge after repeated bombings or attacks. The weary discussion on the state and non-state actors leads to blurred lines of blame.

The stereotype of a Muslim as a back-stabber is transferred to a Muslim nation. After the Kargil intrusion was detected in 1999, Prime Minister Atal Bihari Vajpayee is reported to have told General Pervez Musharraf, 'You have stabbed us in the back!'[5] In an interview to journalist and editor Raj Chengappa during his exile in Saudi Arabia in February 2013, Nawaz Sharif used this phrase to describe what his own army chief of staff had done to him.[6] Coming on the heels of Vajpayee's historic bus trip, it seemed like a monumental deception by the Pakistan Army. So Pakistan in our hearts is not a neighbour but a huge blot.

As *The Hindu*'s correspondent in Islamabad, I had to contend not only with the Pakistani establishment but also my readers back home, many of whom had set ideas about Pakistanis and also on what I should be writing about. But amazingly, I got very favourable responses to most of my stories, including my last piece. There was only one bitter critic of my stories who said he was happy that I was kicked out and even called it poetic justice since my stories favoured Pakistan. He was the only one I replied to—after many months. I wrote to him saying he had a warped mind. Others were resentful I hadn't written much about Hindu persecution in Pakistan. This armchair carping notwithstanding, those who visit the country are pleasantly surprised. An Indian business delegation to Islamabad was relieved to find Dunkin' Donuts, a spanking highway between Lahore and the capital, and women wearing jeans and also driving, instead of cowering at home, shrouded in a burqa. Even the IT parks were a revelation for them.

We persist in our desire for peace and friendship, however big or small the constituency may be, even as hostilities continue on the Line of Control (LoC) and on the icy peaks. Kashmir is still the prize for both countries and there can be little doubt that we are enemies. But I was surprised at the reactions when I moderated a discussion in Mumbai on Christophe Jaffrelot's new book on Pakistan, *The Pakistan Paradox*,[7] in 2015. During question time, an Indian gentleman asked why India could not do more to help Pakistan instead of the reverse. There are good feelings on a person-to-person level, disregarding the hype and propaganda, and there is an understanding that the state and the people function on different levels.

Most people were amazed that I came back home in one piece and asked me in hushed tones: How was it to live there? Not everyone in Pakistan was carrying a bazooka, I said, and yes, they seemed quite normal to me, just like us. Though the usually safe capital had its shock moments and terror did surface, with suicide bombings at the district court near my house, and a blast in a marketplace, apart from other incidents, the capital was largely spared the regularity and intensity of sectarian killings.

Patriotism is the last refuge of scoundrels and we in India and Pakistan invoke it to our detriment. The 'borders' and Pakistans in India are a reflection of that misplaced sentiment. Student leaders from Jawaharlal Nehru University (JNU) in Delhi were charged with sedition because of a meeting held on Kashmir and on the hanging of Afzal Guru where some people allegedly shouted anti-India slogans. Over decades, the few rational voices in our countries who can take the debate to a sane level where solutions, instead of the blame game, can triumph have been drowned out by a hawkish narrative.

I make no claim to being an expert on Pakistan, and this book is about my experiences as a journalist in Islamabad. I was curious about the country and how things worked there since it is often opinion and not facts that dominate our relations. As eminent educationalist Professor Krishna Kumar points out, 'Both countries tend to rely on retired diplomats and journalists when they need information about the other. It is usually not knowledge that is sought; opinion suffices to keep the machinery of tension working.'[8] We have little scholarship or expertise on each other, though this book is not an attempt to fill those gaps. While there are many similarities between India and Pakistan, comparisons, though inescapable, are odious as we know. As sinister plots, spy games and terrorism continue, cloaked by attempts at bonhomie, the stories there centre on life, about ordinary Pakistanis and are not always about firing on the LoC or the Taliban, brinkmanship and the mud-slinging which has become a national sport in the two countries. The minute you write something about Pakistan as an Indian it is presumed both in Pakistan (and India) that you are passing some kind of judgement or there is a hidden agenda, though there are exceptions to this. There will be statements along the lines of 'why is an Indian writing this?' Or there is a feeling that 'it's the same in India too, so it evens out' (and we are equally—if not more—prickly in India). The danger of harping on similarities is that often one ends up in a nostalgic rut. Covering Pakistan doesn't imply doing stories only on peace moves or trashing the country. At every point you are painfully conscious that you are an Indian and treading on eggshells, and can at any moment overstep hidden limits. Is it possible to criticize Pakistan without it being misunderstood as an anti-Pakistan tirade or a Research and Analysis Wing (RAW) operation? There were surprises, disappointments and red lines. As a journalist, what mattered was that it was a rare opportunity for an Indian to live in Islamabad, with all its attendant pleasures and a few discomforts, and report on events at close quarters.

1

Oh, for a Visa!

Till the early 1990s, *The Hindu,* the *Times of India, Hindustan Times,* All India Radio and the Press Trust of India had correspondents in Pakistan. That was when two journalists from the *Times of India* and *Hindustan Times* were sent back and the visa was whittled down to three cities from the all-country multiple-entry visas. In the end, only the Press Trust of India and *The Hindu* were permitted to have correspondents in Pakistan. The Press Trust of India's Snehesh Alex Philip and I were expelled in 2014, but the Press Trust of India's coverage continues as it has stringers in most cities in Pakistan.

After months of waiting for a visa, it finally came through suddenly—and one for my husband as well—in record time with just one visit to the Pakistan high commission in New Delhi. My husband had to give a written undertaking that he would not indulge in any journalistic activity there. I had left New Delhi when the high commission officials called to ask me if I wanted a visa for my husband so that he could travel with me. They allowed my dear friend Preeti Mehra to collect and deliver the passport and papers. I was already charmed! All rules could be bent if they so desired. When I met the officials for the first time, they were pleasant enough and the high commission office had a beautiful exterior, the minarets and small tile work adding an exotic touch. I was asked about my views on the Pakistan General Elections in 2014 which had just been held. I had followed it on Twitter and in the news. It was an exciting election even if I was far away, and they also wanted to know about the books I had written. It seemed like friendly banter but there was a seriousness to it.

It would be an understatement to say that Pakistan is a coveted posting for all journalists; it is also an undeniably challenging country to live in, write and report on. For an Indian, there will always be the overhanging baggage of Partition, and the cloud of hostility and suspicion has not diminished over the years. An American foreign correspondent who arrived at the same time as I did in Islamabad, complained that she merely had a three-city visa. I was astounded—here I was stuck in one city and she was complaining about three whole cities. She later told me that her visa had been extended to the entire country except for some restricted areas. Increasingly though, Americans are not in favour for various reasons, and more so after the war against terror. The *New York Times*'s Islamabad bureau chief, Declan Walsh, was given a seventy-two-hour notice to leave the country in the middle of the night in May 2013. Despite the highest interventions, Walsh has not been allowed back.

Travelling outside Islamabad was not even an option. I kept up a flow of applications to visit places. After some months, the external publicity officer in charge of our visas and also our point of contact in Pakistan, snapped at me, 'Why are you making so many applications when your visa itself may not be renewed?' It was the first indication that my stay here would not be for long. That was the other thing about the visa: it was not renewed after the initial three-month period. I was told by the suave and helpful officials at the Pakistan high commission in New Delhi that my three-month visit visa would be changed to a journalist's visa once I got there. Nothing of the sort happened. As with visas, so it was with identity cards which were issued for three months provisionally. The first visa extension happened three months after the expiry and in the second instance, it was never renewed. We were given visas for a few days in May 2014 to leave Islamabad. The concession was that I was allowed to travel home via Karachi to Mumbai.

That was the norm, at least for Indians, as my colleagues from *The Hindu* who were posted there before I was, explained to me—they had been without valid visas and expired identity cards for several months at a time. The only kindness was that the overstay charges which were nominal were waived, though some correspondents were charged. While the authorities constantly suspected us of subversive activities, ensuring that we were followed everywhere, holding up our visas and identity cards was another form of harassment. Also, living without a visa, or with a single-entry visa, meant that you couldn't rush back home in an emergency! Innumerable visits to the visa office and filling countless forms became an unhappy routine. It was a take-it or leave-it attitude—and we took it. When we were expelled, we were warned to be quiet about it by the authorities and some Pakistani journalists so that future correspondents were not affected by the bad publicity. People, even my own colleagues and my newspaper, were worried if a replacement for me would be permitted!

Living in a country, even if it was for nine months (too short a time to understand Pakistan, I am often told rather dismissively), is more valuable than short trips. Both countries revelled in babudom and paperwork. Among the many commonalities was the need to fill forms and everything about them had to be official, including seals. And the seals had to be round. I was perplexed when the telephone company and others asked for my organization's seal to be stamped on each letter or application. I had to ask for bunches of letterheads from my head office in Chennai which obliged, but I hadn't thought of bringing a seal. Finally I had to get one made with my office address and name on it, and I stamped away to glory on every letter or application I made. The obsession for letterheads and seals notwithstanding, I read to my amazement that the historic Simla Agreement signed between President Zulfikar Ali Bhutto and Prime Minister Indira Gandhi in July 1972 didn't have the official seals of the respective governments, because it almost didn't happen and everyone had nearly given up. As a result, there was no stationery or even a typewriter at hand; the Pakistani seal had been sent off with other luggage to Chandigarh.[1]

All my applications, stamped and sealed, requesting permission to travel out of Islamabad came to nothing. I wanted to visit Gah, the birthplace of former Prime Minister Manmohan Singh and do a story, as also Bangay, Bhagat Singh's home. There was silence over an application to visit the ancient city of Taxila—you see, there is an ordnance depot nearby. In fact, the spooks (spies, or the guys who would follow me around at the behest of the Pakistani establishment) who got to know of my applications asked the official with whom I had lunch if he had given permission for my visit to Taxila, as if that was a crime. Rawalpindi was out of bounds anyway since it had the mighty Pakistan Army general headquarters, and I didn't even apply! So a visit to the historic Murree Brewery, also in Rawalpindi, the garrison city as everyone called it, was out of the question, but I did manage to do a story on the wonderful brewery.

*

I met a Pakistani journalist who was posted in India and he had warm memories of it and made it a point to tell me so at a party. Some Pakistani journalists I met had complaints, and one of them had his passport taken away and he never wanted to go back to India. The levels of harassment were often petty and unimaginable; there is no low both countries cannot stoop to. The Pakistani high commission officials in New Delhi were cut up about not being allowed to travel even to Agra to see the Taj Mahal or to visit the Aligarh Muslim University, which is unfortunate. But the Indian government does take Pakistani media delegations around the country for exposure, and one hilarious meeting they had was with Delhi Chief Minister Arvind Kejriwal (a very inspirational figure in Pakistan) who coughed into his muffler and didn't seem to know much about Pakistan when the journalists questioned him.

Pakistan also obliges some with visas quite frequently. Many writers go for various literary festivals, and journalist Jatin Desai was a frequent visitor. I met delegations of journalists from India (there were two while I was there—one from the Mumbai Press Club and another from Kolkata), MPs, social workers and other people in the Pakistan–India friendship circuit, apart from writers like A.G. Noorani, Shobhaa De and Ritu Menon, and activists like Sushobha Barve. While Pakistan is fussy about visas, and restricts travel to some areas, India, too, displays similar tendencies and some areas like Kashmir are difficult to enter for human rights groups; more recently, NGOs who have taken on the government are at the receiving end of official petulance. This can be in the form of court cases, frozen bank accounts and scrapping of foreign-aid permissions. When it comes to suppression of rights and access to troubled areas, both India and Pakistan can function rather regressively.

In fact, while I was allowed to cover the Pakistan Parliament and go regularly to the foreign office, I learnt from Pakistani officials that their journalists were not always granted this leeway in India. A Pakistani official posted in New Delhi returned with unhappy memories of her stay and turned into a complete hawk thanks to the Indian media. It was difficult for her to even rent a place to stay. Yet this official was kind enough to plead for an Indian journalist whose visa was rejected and made sure she could come for a track-two meeting. She also intervened when an Indian journalist was attacked in Karachi while covering the 2014 elections.

India and Pakistan have not had the best relations, and yet Indian journalists have lived and reported with a fair degree of comfort and acceptance from Pakistan. *The Hindu* has a fine tradition of correspondents, all of whom are well-remembered much after they have left and who have been critical of the governments, and reported on various issues, even during the military regime of Musharraf. *The Hindu* correspondent Amit Baruah, even if he was not allowed to go to Kandahar to cover the hijack in 1999, when he was posted in Pakistan between 1997 and 2000, wrote about the events leading to the military coup by General Musharraf, and lived in Islamabad during the Kargil war, inside enemy country. Nirupama Subramanian who reported for *The Hindu* in Islamabad between 2006 and 2010, covered the lawyers' agitation against Musharraf in 2007, interviewed the Baloch leader Akbar Bugti, and wrote on other major political events. She was given permission to go to Rawalpindi at the last minute to cover Benazir Bhutto's historic rally where Bhutto was assassinated. This, despite the paranoia that Indians, especially women, are RAW agents sent to entice Pakistani men, which is laughable (I was the third woman correspondent posted there). My predecessor, Anita Joshua, was invited by the Pakistan Army to visit the site of the avalanche in Gayari sector which killed 140 people, the bulk of them soldiers, apart from civilians.

There was an inborn courtesy everywhere and a desire to change the status quo by some intrepid officials that ran on a different track from the suspicion about Indian journalists which was also very real. The ministry of interior made generous allowances for other journalists, and lovingly provided them with an armed escort to go to Waziristan (though *The Hindu*'s correspondents were permitted to enter Muzaffarabad—B. Muralidhar Reddy who reported from Chakothi in Pakistan Occupied Kashmir on the historic visit of the All Parties Hurriyat Conference delegation and later covered the launch of the Muzaffarabad–Srinagar bus service and its political implications, both in 2005, and Sandeep

Dikshit in 2010 who was part of a team of eight Indian journalists accompanied only by a Pakistan Army captain in Bajaur tribal agency—an instance of rare openness at a time when the Pakistan Army was chasing the Tehreek-e-Taliban out of the region and sustaining huge number of casualties). As soon as I got there, a story on women fighter pilots in the Pakistan Air Force appeared in a British paper, and my editor wanted a follow-up. I did make a request to the Pakistan armed forces' PR wing, Inter Services Public Relations (ISPR), to which, unsurprisingly, there was no reply till I left. That story spoke of the women pilots who were likely to bomb Indian targets!

There was a democratically elected government in Pakistan, the second successive one in its military-rule dominated history, but the people and the government were up against a more decisive force, which sets the agenda ruthlessly when it comes to India. The spooks didn't spare their own countrymen who interacted with Indian 'spies'. During lunch with a government official, the dour duo tailing me sent the waiter to ask who he was. They sat across from us, glaring in disapproval. It was so laughable that they didn't even recognize him and later when we left, they stopped his car and asked for his identification papers.

After 2011, there is no Pakistan correspondent in New Delhi, and there is talk of a bilateral agreement which stipulates that each country can have two journalists posted in the other. I checked on this agreement and didn't come up with anything concrete—it seems to be more of an informal agreement to keep the good faith. From a three-city visa, when it came to Anita Joshua (2010 to 2013), her visa was restricted to Islamabad and it was single entry. She could not visit any other city in Pakistan except for two official trips to Quetta and Gayari. Mine was a visit visa for three months and again single entry. The buzz was the Pakistani establishment felt that since no journalist from that country was in New Delhi, why should visas be given to Indian journalists? Better sense prevailed after a lot of efforts by some journalists and Pakistani bureaucrats, but 'the attack of nice' obviously did not last long. A journalist who was visiting Islamabad from India hissed in my ear, 'Do you know who didn't want to give you a visa . . . it was the army which doesn't want you here, don't you see?' I had other people telling me the army wants Indian journalists there. Everyone seemed to be an expert on who wanted and didn't want Indian journalists, but their opinions mattered little. Despite all this cloak-and-dagger stuff, the ISPR included me in their media list and kept sending regular email and SMS updates. I was on the mailing list of most offices, including the PMO. The ISPR media-in-charge even sent a nice message to me, in response to mine, when I was leaving. Once he even called me up to guffaw at my pathetic Urdu, when I asked for a clarification.

Successive Indian journalists in Pakistan have for many years been taking a number of restrictions in their professional stride without complaint. I was already warned that I would be tailed and spooks would be stationed right outside my house. Phones, too, would be tapped. 'You will be thought of as a RAW agent whatever you do,' a colleague had warned.

The paranoia that prevails about the Indian or Pakistani state cannot go away if there is little media interaction and exchange. While the usual tenure for a journalist is three years, in my case I was asked to leave after nine months, with no reason given. In Islamabad, friends asked me what I had done to be expelled and I really didn't have any answer because I didn't know. I was grilled by a senior official after my op-ed interview with Mama Qadeer Baloch, who outdid Mahatma Gandhi's Dandi march by travelling on foot for over 3300 kilometres from Quetta to Islamabad to focus on the missing young people in Balochistan. The official's take was that I should be writing on art and culture and not on political movements; did I write on Kashmir, for instance? he snarled.

Some government officials went out of their way to be helpful but they came up against a wall. A senior journalist and writer told me he wished he had the power to revoke the cancellation of my visa, but he could do nothing. The authorities seemed to have some problem with me and I heard that efforts were made to try and get them to retain the Press Trust of India's correspondent, Snehesh Alex Philip, whose visa had also not been renewed. His wife had already gone to India for a wedding and couldn't return, as her visa was not reissued. In the end, Snehesh and I were both asked to leave by 18 May 2014 without being given a reason. Since 2011, Pakistan has not posted a journalist in India. Earlier they had two nominees from Radio Pakistan and the Associated Press of Pakistan (APP). Javed Jadoon was posted in India for Radio Pakistan from 2008 and he left in 2011 while Sadiq Toor was the last APP correspondent who left a few years earlier. I had met both of them in Islamabad and they seemed to have nice things to say about their stay. Now neither India nor Pakistan has journalists from each other's countries, and on their scorecard of pettiness, it's quits. A balance has been achieved, however unbalanced that may be.

When I was expelled, in response to protests on Twitter, someone I think from Pakistan tweeted that granting a visa is a country's sovereign right and I had to respect that. As if I had a choice. The visa is used as a deterrent by both countries. It is a reality that common people understand easily. On one of our many hikes in the Margalla Hills in Islamabad, Trail 6, my husband and I were almost at the top taking a break (not the time the spooks were after us), and we saw a young man heaving up, tired and breathless. He saw us and stopped to say 'hello, how are you? in a fake American drawl. We replied with the traditional Urdu greeting. But you don't look Pakistani, he said, astonished. We are Indians, we said—waiting for a reaction—and it was not entirely unexpected: he was ecstatic. He called out to his companions and they all greeted us like long-lost friends. All of them had given lots of money to agents for an Indian visa and it was a country they wanted very much to visit. They were from Gujranwala in the Punjab in Pakistan, and had come there for a

Sufi saint's fair at Golra Sharif in Islamabad. One of them asked if Pakistan was like India, and his friend was annoyed. He didn't wait for my answer and said of course it's similar. He explained that this visa denial is a ploy to keep us apart and never discover the truth about each other!

While on a personal level there is enthusiasm, as nations we remain daggers drawn. We can't even get magazines or newspapers from each other's countries. I met a retired brigadier who wanted so much to read *India Today*. The Pakistani TV channel Zindagi was hugely popular in India, as are all the Indian soaps in Pakistan. Actor Fawad Khan's sweeping Indian conquest must outrank all wars and diplomacy, but his popularity didn't save him when Karan Johar's film *Ae Dil Hai Mushkil* (in which Fawad had a role) was targeted for being 'anti-national'. In the wake of the attack on Uri cantonment in Jammu and Kashmir on 16 September 2016, the Maharashtra Navnirman Sena (MNS) threatened to disrupt the film screening, and Johar finally broke his silence in October 2016,[2] to give an undertaking that he would not use Pakistani stars in future films. So, on one level there is no pretence of even a moderate friendship. Cordiality can crumble at a touch, and all the noise and protest after we were expelled resulted in nothing. No one seemed to mind that journalists from each other's countries couldn't report without the tag of suspicion. Despite the many platitudes in support of an unfettered media from leaders in India and Pakistan, the basic issue was that there was no free media exchange or reporting. This shows a lack of openness and maturity, and the hollowness of the professed commitment to freedom of the press in both countries. Instead of strong protests, there were stories that we were spies and carrying out unfriendly activities.

There is little debate about this lack of media exchange, and it seems to have faded from public memory in any case. Even the exchange between the Karachi and Mumbai press clubs seems fraught with uncertainty.

With the stinginess over visas, there are only a few Indians in Islamabad other than the diplomatic community, and they are in a severe minority. Often, you are the only Indian in a meeting—for instance, at the launch of a book on Indian nuclear deterrence, the author kept saying that China was not really a threat to India, insinuating that Pakistan was the target of India's stockpiled weapons. It seemed to me very unhealthy that such events were so one-sided and lacked any deeper understanding or a broader picture. I attended a meeting of parliamentarians in Islamabad who were enthusiastic about friendship with India; everyone displayed detailed knowledge of India and her politics. A woman parliamentarian, who spoke favourably of Indians, suddenly asked, with evident anguish, why did Indians always stab you in the back? Another person who had just made a positive speech about relations with India agreed with the first woman and said, yes, the Indians were small-minded (*unke chote dil aur dimag hai*)— they needed to be a little more generous. I tried to keep my annoyance to myself, but later I rationalized and attributed such statements to stereotypes, a lack of adequate exchange between the two countries and opportunities to meet more often and clear the air. Pakistani officials told me that if you show Indians a beautiful painting, they will find a blemish in some corner! Such are the stereotypes that exist. Sometimes I felt it was the form to be nasty about Indians just as there were preconceived notions about Pakistanis, going by the many vicious Pakistani jokes that are quite popular in India.

Among most of the population in India and Pakistan, peace moves are greeted with catcalls of derision and often after a terror attack in India, the brunt of this animosity is borne by Pakistani artists, singers and even cricketers who are much loved all the same in India. Post-Partition, the hostility stems from Pakistan's suspected involvement in terror attacks on Indian soil and Pakistan, too, blames the RAW for various operations aimed at destabilizing the country. The arrest in 2016 of a suspected

RAW agent, Kulbhushan Jadhav, by Pakistani authorities and his summary trial and death sentence announced on 10 April 2017 has brought the relations between the two countries to a fresh low.

Even before Partition, a disgusted Jinnah who was leaning towards the two-nation theory, referred to Congress as the Hindu party and Gandhi as the Hindu leader. President Mohammad Ayub Khan said, 'Freedom as far as we were concerned, meant freedom from both the British and the Hindus.'[3] Hindus are often portrayed as deceitful people who have no fighting acumen, though I didn't come across any such remarks directed at me. There is, however, a stereotype that Indians tend to haggle too much or undercut prices and that we are not a generous people.

The peace process between the two countries takes place on different tracks, and continues despite the odds. Candlelight vigils on the Wagah border have become a firmly entrenched activity and also the frenzied daily tourist trips to the border from Amritsar. Diplomatically, there are many backchannel efforts and often a handshake between two leaders or a statement can be the result of many strenuous efforts which are not widely written about or photographed. These backchannel negotiations have been significant contributions to the peace process. My perception about diplomats changed somewhat when I met many of them in Islamabad. They seemed to be rather honest and not all of them lied for their countries! I could be wrong, of course, on both counts! When I ran into the former Pakistan high commissioner to India, Salman Bashir, he said I was a very important person to have in his country. I don't know if he was being polite. There are many well-meaning track-two efforts by institutions like the Jinnah Institute, Pugwash, the Sustainable Development Policy Institute (SDPI) and the Institute of Strategic Studies, Islamabad (ISSI), which take place with great regularity and both Indians and Pakistanis have an opportunity to clear the air and discuss bilateral issues in an unfettered manner. These meetings often issue strong statements on resolving the impasse between the two countries. And, people-to-people exchanges are increasing despite the hostility, but peace efforts dented by terror and proxy war come up against the armies of the two countries, the rising fundamentalist forces, and political expediency.

Like a seesaw our relations go back and forth. Former Pakistan Foreign Minister Khurshid Mahmud Kasuri's book *Neither a Hawk Nor a Dove*[4] had a controversial launch in Mumbai in October 2015. The organizer from the Observer Research Foundation, Sudheendra Kulkarni, had his face painted black by the Shiv Sena to protest against the event. Before that, singer Ghulam Ali's concert in Mumbai was cancelled after protests and threats from the Sena to disrupt it. Cricket ties between the two countries are often snapped by dips in relations. However, a T20 match did take place at Eden Gardens on 19 March 2016 in Kolkata, with Imran Khan and other celebrities in attendance.

Even before Narendra Modi was elected prime minister, there was a lot of hope from a BJP government at the Centre; the Pakistanis remembered Vajpayee's overtures and the famous bus trip to Lahore in 1999. It is the BJP and not the Congress which seems to give Pakistanis hope. I sensed a lot of support for the BJP since Vajpayee's time and there is a feeling that this party can do something to change the relations or resolve Kashmir, even if it may not necessarily be true.

Just when everyone had given up on talks being revived and the dreary brinkmanship seemed to have reached a dead end, Modi did one better with a stopover in Lahore in December 2015 on his way from Kabul to greet Sharif on his birthday. There was a brief revival of cordiality with a proposal for comprehensive talks in December 2015. Soon after came the Pathankot terror strike, creating another storm of accusation, though this time it resulted in a 'joint investigation'. But the Pathankot airbase attack in January 2016, blamed by India on the terrorist group Jaish-e-Mohammed, and later on 18 September, the terror strike on an army camp in Uri, snuffed out whatever little chance there was of peaceful negotiations. India responded with surgical strikes across the border in September 2016, the details of which were not publicized till a press conference by the director general of military operations (DGMO), Lt. Gen. Ranbir Singh, on the morning of 28 September 2016. Before that, in March 2016, Pakistan had caught a major prize—an alleged flesh-and-blood RAW agent and spy accused of creating trouble in Balochistan. Our relations seem characterized by overtures which are half-hearted and the pas de deux is somewhat strained. So a liberal visa regime has to wait in the wings once again.

2

Islamabad, Unreal City

A midnight welcome

We didn't have time to savour the fact that we had landed in Pakistan, in Lahore, a city I couldn't visit. Ignorant of visa restrictions, people would ask me in amazement—have you not visited Lahore? As if it was so easy for me to just pop across. Yes, yes, I know if you haven't seen Lahore, you haven't lived, etc., and this was repeated to me with great condescension. I had to stay content with Asghar Wajahat's play, *Jis Lahore Nai Dekhya O Jamya Nai* in JNU which I had watched while on a visit to Delhi.

My husband, Venkat, and I had just enough time to board the connecting flight to Islamabad. The twin-engine aircraft looked incapable of even taking off but the small cabin was cosy and we could see the lights as we flew low over the countryside. We touched down in the capital in less than an hour—it was that easy. On the flight from New Delhi was journalist, writer and activist Beena Sarwar whom I hadn't met for a long time and we were glad to see each other. The Press Trust of India correspondent, Snehesh Alex Philip, and his wife, Ruchira Hoon, also a journalist, were travelling with us. It was almost midnight when we got into Islamabad, and we stopped for water at a medical shop near the house where we were to live. Aurangzeb (the driver), whom we nicknamed Emperor, was quite a personality with his round Chitrali cap, had been waiting to pick us up. My predecessor as *The Hindu*'s Islamabad correspondent, Anita Joshua, had, with some difficulty, rented a house for two years, so I didn't have to go through what could have been a painful process of finding a place to stay, since it was not so easy.

Shops are open late and the salesman, looking at us, wanted to know where we were from. On hearing that we were Indians, he smiled warmly and said, 'Welcome to Pakistan.' Finally, I had crossed the real border. The only two people I knew from Islamabad were journalists who were with me on an environment-related trip in Kathmandu. At that time, we had never thought we would encounter each other again. I didn't feel even for a moment I was in a strange country—a neighbour who was friends with my colleagues invited us for tea at midnight when we reached home, but we were tired after the long journey from Mumbai and it was an offer we had to refuse.

Home was a huge four-bedroom one-storeyed bungalow with a small lawn in front and a porch to park the old beat-up Suzuki sedan, Margalla, bought by Amit Baruah in August 1997. After he had bought the car with a 'normal' registration number, the vehicle registry department sneakily got the number plate changed to a yellow one with the number 27 used to identify Indians. It was a like a beacon proclaiming our identity. I didn't know that this number plate would get me into trouble, but it did, with my yoga-cum-Pilates teacher. On the mornings when I went for class, the car would be parked outside her house. One day, some policemen asked her tall security guard who always scowled at me, what the car was doing there. The teacher, who tried to be nice, asked me to park my car elsewhere. But after a month I realized she was not too keen on having me. I had a great time there and met some charming women from the city, including some expats. She had a sunny terrace, a portion of it enclosed with glass which was heated mercifully for our classes, and served us chilled juices after the one-hour workout. Her lovely furry grey-and-white cats would sneak into the warm room at times. It was too good to last.

When I sold the car, the buyer was in a great hurry to change the dreaded number plate on the same day. He said he knew my colleague B. Muralidhar Reddy who had been posted there. I had asked my editor for a new car and I was thankful for not having had to go through the legwork of buying it. Earlier, a friend familiar with the politics of car stealing had advised me against buying a new car. He said if you can get from place A to place B with this old Margalla, don't change it. Car robbery was rampant in the city, with the Taliban assisting an organized mafia to steal the cars and take them to Afghanistan and sell them in the two countries.[1] When I went for lunch to his house, the direct route from the main road was lined with concrete roadblocks, the kind which you can't move easily. I had to take a roundabout road to get there. There was a perfectly logical explanation. It was to deter car thieves. He also told me a hilarious story. A man who owned a fancy car had parked it outside a building where he had work. When he came out, he couldn't see his car. He asked someone hanging around if he had seen a black car, and the man said no. The anguished owner went to file a police complaint. Meanwhile, the car thief who had blithely fobbed off the owner, took the cover off the new car and drove away. By covering the car, he had made sure it wouldn't be seen! Simple yet effective, and difficult to beat in terms of ingenuity.

Pakistan's best-kept secret

Nothing quite prepares you for a sojourn in Islamabad. You realize that it is not among the top-ten tourist destinations in the world and while I did read the perfunctory descriptions of it on the Net, I had to rely on my colleagues posted in Islamabad who told me about the beautiful capital, its hills, and the hospitality. Even so, everything was a big surprise. It is, after all, Pakistan's best-kept secret! The hills, the sprawling bungalows, tree-lined avenues, the posh markets give it a distinction above most cities in the subcontinent. It's all new and the absence of colonial architecture sets it apart from Karachi or Lahore. The buildings are concrete and squat, somewhat low on aesthetics, not architectural marvels but modern and spacious. The mushrooming suburban sprawl is hidden from the main city and the squalor of the slums is not immediately visible and neither are the poor, unlike in Karachi. Writer Shobhaa De said the capital reminded her of a small European city, even Bonn. Islamabad is also a city of gardeners. My neighbours obsessively cut and pruned their hedges to resemble flowers or animals—topiary. On the many green strips, you would see men in salwar kameez at all hours of the day, trimming leaves, cutting grass, pruning flower beds. When I first heard I was to have a gardener, I was amused. The man who came to work in my house in his free time was dedicated to tending the small lawn and the plants, watering them lovingly and planting whatever I wanted. In the leafy, well-tended lanes of Islamabad, you can be lulled into thinking all is well, and it's difficult to believe that some distance away, young boys are being trained to become suicide bombers, and the country is ravaged by bombing and sectarian killings. The anomaly lurks in the background—a leisurely green capital, with its elegant drawing rooms. I was reminded of T.S. Eliot: 'In the room the women come and go / Talking of Michelangelo.'

So I should not have been surprised when the sylvan calm was shattered one winter morning by staccato gunfire and the sound of at least two deafening blasts. The huge glass panes shook fearfully and I thought my house would collapse. It was past 9 a.m., the TV was on as usual and I was in my 'office' searching the Net for news. There was nothing, no news, I tweeted. Soon the ticker started playing out a horror story—the district court complex behind my house was under a bomb attack. Even the capital wasn't as safe as it was made out to be—charming Islamabad was under attack, not for the first time and certainly not for the last. For a moment, life stood still as I waited for more sounds, and they kept coming, while the windows trembled. I would soon venture out across the street to see the bloody aftermath of the suicide bombing and gun attack that I could report on without any permissions and applications. More on that later.

A capital on a plateau

It's a carefully created capital with its neatly laid-out sectors, each with its own market, and every tree planted in its chosen place. It is difficult to imagine that once this was a plateau, with 'natural terraces and meadows'[2] and a few trees. The tall kachnar blooms in winter and its stubby pink flowers can be sautéd into a delicious dish. Towards spring, there are plenty of blue-purple jacaranda. In winter, the trees turn into shades of russet. The long avenues are dotted with brightly coloured flowers. Compared to the bustle of Karachi and its myriad cultures, the capital can seem a little soulless and sedate like the bureaucracy it is meant to house. Far from the madding crowd as President Mohammad Ayub Khan wanted it to be, the low-ranging Margalla Hills, on the outskirts of the Himalaya, lift it from a certain mundaneness.

On a clear day, Islamabad shimmers in a glowing haze from Monal, a popular restaurant perched on the edge near the highest point in the Margalla Hills, a little before the pass that drops into Abbottabad. You can see the spiralling roads below and the capital city beyond. On the way is a memorial to the 152 people killed when Airblue flight 202 crashed into the hillside on 28 July 2010. The first evening we went to Monal, there was a sudden thunderstorm and we had to move to an inner table so that the downpour didn't drench us. The inky night was serrated by lightning and jagged bolts fell all around us. We preferred the continental section and the food was outstanding. Often on Sundays, we would trek up the many trails in the hills and traverse to Monal to dig into a well-earned breakfast. In winter, a light fog would blanket the city and we could see very little of it.

In the now touristy but ancient village of Saidpur, next to an empty old temple and gurdwara, is a hall with black-and-white pictures of Islamabad being developed into the capital of Pakistan. In the evenings a man comes to play the rebab for visitors. There was something sad and appealing in his music, and we sat in the verandah and listened to him for a while. Saidpur village was given a facelift some years ago and is full of restaurants, and one of them was recommended for its Indian food. Sadly, it didn't live up to its reputation. In the pictures, I was surprised to see the vast empty terrain which had since been converted for habitation. Islamabad is designed by a Greek architect, C.A. Doxiadis, and in the photographs, President Ayub Khan is showing the plans to a number of leaders, including Indian Prime Minister Jawaharlal Nehru, and Chinese Premier Zhou Enlai is planting a tree. It was President Ayub Khan's idea to create a capital in a more salubrious place than Karachi which he said had an enervating climate, along with unhygienic conditions which wore out the administration. He was worried about the intense political nature of the city and the corrupting influence of business.[3] The location of the capital on the Potwar plateau ringed by the Margalla Hills was chosen by a commission under General Yahya Khan. The capital narrowly missed being named after Ayub Khan, and Zulfikar Ali Bhutto's classmate from Mumbai and friend, Piloo Mody, takes some credit for the naming:

> That evening I wrote a small footnote to Pakistan's history. I was talking to President Ayub Khan and I told him how happy I was that they had decided to build a new capital for Pakistan, but that to make a city like that a living thing, it was necessary to give it an inspiring name so that it could fire the imagination of the people; it was no good just talking about a 'federal capital for Pakistan'. I remember this very distinctly. It was a Sunday

> night. On Monday I returned to Bombay, and on Wednesday morning, I read in the Bombay papers that Pakistan had named its new capital Islamabad. At the time I dismissed it as a remarkable coincidence but later I learned that Ayub had been taken up with my idea. On Monday the cabinet had moved to Rawalpindi. On Monday afternoon there was a circular that a Cabinet meeting would be held on Tuesday morning—no agenda. When the cabinet met on Tuesday, Ayub informed them that he had met me and that I had suggested that the capital should be named immediately. Several suggestions were made including Ayubabad, then somebody mentioned Islamabad, and Ayub said that's right—and so the capital of Pakistan was named. For weeks thereafter Ayub told the story, so I hear, to several people at social gatherings.[4]

Mody, a classmate of Zulfikar Ali Bhutto who was then a minister in Ayub's Cabinet, was in the thick of things those days.

Settling in

In the winter mornings, the tree pies would hop around in the branches blurred by mist. Through the tall glass windows, while having my morning coffee I could see the magpie robin or the hoopoe flitting across the smooth lawn, lovingly tended to by Jan Mohammed. A thick cluster of white bougainvillea and tall pine trees screened off the road outside. The house was close to the market, in a quiet, leafy corner of the sector. Early mornings were precious, often it would be the only peaceful time of the day.

My entire flat in Mumbai would have fitted into the large, well-appointed drawing room, with glass doors opening into a dining area and a swing door concealing the kitchen. The day after we arrived was a Sunday and Aurangzeb, despite it being his weekly day off, kindly agreed to drive us to the *Itvar*, or Sunday Bazaar, for supplies. After a quick breakfast—Sajida the cook-cum-help had left bread and eggs in the fridge—we left for the bazaar near Peshawar Mode for supplies. It was a large, sprawling market with second-hand goods and everything under the sun, including fresh vegetables, cold-pressed oils and other provisions. There were long rows of stalls neatly demarcated with sections for vegetables, snacks, pickles, dried fruits, fresh fruits, clothes, furniture, and even at times, home linen. There were people who sold large, blue plastic bags in case you forgot to bring your own carrier bag, and trolleys for the big buyers, with helpful men who would wheel them around; but we carried our own bags. The vegetable vendors didn't like us to choose the stuff; they would snap at us, but soon we learnt to work our way around their bad tempers and found some nice stalls. The freshly pressed oils, especially coconut, were a treat, and in winter we managed to buy some natty jackets for a song. Instead of ready-made bed sheets, you could buy yards of cloth, and there were tailors who stitched them up for you. Compared to the upmarket shops in the various sectors, this was more down to earth and accessible to everyone. It was a colourful place with a rustic air, as people from the nearby villages also shopped there. The parking area was jammed with cars, and if you didn't go early, the policemen would direct you to a place a little far off. Nurseries alongside the main road sold the prettiest and most exotic flowers, and I bought up a whole lot in winter to line the pavement outside the house and to skirt the lawn. They looked bright and fresh when I left thanks to the tender care of the gardener.

The regular pilgrimage to the external publicity office began the day after I arrived, and in the evening the prime minister was to make his first official address to the nation. I thought I would file a story for the paper, though I was advised to take it easy and not rush into filing it. My Urdu was never good and Sharif's speech didn't make it easy for me. A contact helped me with the speech and translation, and bingo, I had my first story out. There was no dearth of stories to be filed and no time for rest, not even on Sunday—that's when something always happened. If I was at home, the TV would be on all the time till past midnight when the deadline was over. I would switch it on first thing in the morning, while also checking for any updates on Twitter as well as on newspaper websites. A thick bunch of newspapers would be delivered every morning, along with several magazines, and I had to plod through them. I loved *Friday Times* and some of the magazines, but Sundays were particularly daunting with fat glamour supplements full of women wearing outrageous clothes—each one worse than the other. Off-the-shoulder, diaphanous, ethereal and utterly unwearable. There would be pages of glazed-over socialites posing for pictures at some party or the other. Even the covers would be ultra-glamorous, with heavily made-up, racoon-eyed women dressed in bizarre costumes, provoking me into giggling fits in the morning. I wish I had kept some of these glossies, they were as unreal as the capital.

Thankfully, I was spared spooks outside my house and for three months no one followed me, or so I thought. We had to wait a week for our goods coming from Mumbai and I had to go to the customs office at the airport. The official had to okay the consignment and he wanted to 'see my face'. Soon the house was a sea of cardboard cartons, and while my husband and Sajida helped, every evening I would have to unpack my own things and keep them in order. There was plenty of room, though things tend to expand with the available space and soon all the wardrobes and kitchen shelves were full. Even my silver and junk jewellery which I had packed arrived intact. Not so while returning when I hastily put everything into the cartons, and then found out some valuables were missing, including a thick silver necklace and a lovely silver-and-marcasite butterfly-shaped ring. A friend and I had gone to shop and when I saw the ring, I liked it so much, but didn't have enough money. The salesman from Swat said I could take it and give the money later. He said he couldn't guarantee it would remain if I left it at the shop. I was so happy; I took it and gave him the money after a few days. But I seem to have no luck with jewellery. I had dropped a gold ring in a taxi in Islamabad one day, but managed to get it back.

It was the winter that I was dreading, coming from a city which was once a cluster of islands in the sea. I had to buy a fat duvet which I later used in Delhi where it was also a boon. There were a bunch of heaters in the basement which I had to get inspected and okayed for use. They were all gas heaters and would warm the large rooms in minutes. I was petrified of using gas as I had read horror stories of people sleeping with closed windows and dying of the fumes. I never left the heater on at night and once when the bedroom was being warmed, something happened and there was a fire; luckily, I saw it in time and managed to douse it, but the walls were blackened and the smell of smoke stayed in the house for days. The cold marble floors were freezing and getting from one room to the other was a challenge. I had to install a small heater for Sajida in the kitchen, since it was too cold to work there otherwise.

Permit versus bank account

The other joke about Islamabad is that it is not really a part of Pakistan, and one of my friends explained that it was an unreal façade to the country. One email from Karachi in response to my farewell article said Islamabad was considered to be fifteen kilometres away from the country! It's a place where getting a liquor permit is easier than opening a bank account if you are a non-Muslim that is, and the services sector can sometimes shock you with its courtesy and efficiency. They replaced a wireless router on a Sunday without complaining and repaired my phone for free. Contrary to popular belief, Fridays were only a half-day holiday, or with time off for prayers at 1 p.m.; the official weekly holiday was Sunday (though shops or tradespeople sometimes closed on Fridays and worked Sundays). The Indian and Pakistani business communities have been asking for banking norms to be eased, and while that is taking time, it was a revelation for me that the liquor permit which I decided to get as a test, was a cinch. The irony was not lost on a Pakistani minister who has been campaigning for MFN (most favoured nation) status to be fully realized with India and has been working to improve banking norms. When I told him the permit was so easy, he joked that this must be headline news! The excise department office was near my house and all one had to do was fill out a form. I was asked to return with my passport in three days and was handed the licence for six units of alcohol per month for six months after which it had to be renewed. It was that simple, no questions asked, and the officer only looked up once to check me out before signing the sheet of paper. If he was surprised I was a woman, he didn't show it. There were two or three five-star hotels which sold Murree products, the only legally available liquor, but it was the best really in terms of beer. There was every vodka flavour imaginable and even whisky. Sadly, Irish cream had stopped being manufactured as it didn't have many takers in a country where hard liquor was the norm. I had to regretfully leave behind several cases of beer. Most days, there were no stocks of beer and the black market thrived. Bootleggers would deliver the required brands at your doorstep for a price, though I didn't need to use them. Funnily I found that Pakistanis favoured imported beer like Carlsberg or Heineken when their own country made such excellent stuff.

Prohibition and calling liquor 'haram' had not reduced its popularity and the well-concealed shop would be thronging with men, many waiting outside for the rush to clear. The entrance is innocuously located next to a laundry at the back of the hotel, where the burly security guards would leer at me because they knew where I was going. One of them asked for money but I pretended not to understand. The salesmen were very nice; I only saw one other woman once, and she was white; otherwise, the boxy room was always full of policemen, security guards or bootleggers.

Opening a bank account, on the other hand, took over a month and I almost ran out of money. No bank was willing to let an Indian open an account. One foreign bank openly said that there was no question of letting an Indian journalist open an account. The only place we (Snehesh and I) managed to open one was where a guy sweet-talked us into opening the account without telling us we could withdraw money only in Pakistani rupees. We really fell for his oily charm and talk of Bollywood. So my salary had to be sent back and the account closed till finally we asked the Indian high commission to intervene so that we could open an account in the 'diplomatic enclave' and operate it outside since entering the enclave entailed security clearance two hours in advance. Finally, after a month of dithering, my bank account was opened, and there was a branch near my house. The staff couldn't have been nicer!

Unreal city—power issues

It was the low, thundering sound that puzzled me at first. There was an inverter in the house, so I didn't realize that power cuts were as often as every alternate hour when I got there in August 2013. The rumbling came on often and I connected the two—it was the powerful diesel generators kicking off in the bungalows with several rooms, each with their obligatory air conditioners. It is not uncommon to have a large drawing room with three or more ACs. Everything seemed large and lavish in Islamabad, an unreal city with its massive houses and exaggerated emphasis on lawns and gardens. The regular power failures were at least real.

Not many had inverters even though diesel generators were prohibitive. I was told it could cost PKR 6000 a day for an average house. While I didn't notice any neighbours on one side, there were a few men who lived in a large house and they spoke noisily all the time. When there was power, I could hear the sound of multiple ACs, and I wondered about the point of keeping them all going in an empty house. I did have some conspiracy theories! My friends back home couldn't believe there was such an acute power shortage. I also learnt that the Tatas were once keen on building a power plant near the border and supplying electricity, but the army vetoed it.

Outside the soft, grassy lawns of a big hotel, I saw women and children picking up twigs and bundling them up. They were from a nearby village. It is not uncommon in Islamabad to see people carrying bundles of wood or twigs on their heads or men breaking branches in the leafy parks for the much-needed fuel supplies. The long, snaking queues of vehicles would choke traffic and the wait for that elusive CNG could be endless and frustrating. Gas powers both cooking and vehicles, and there is an acute shortage. The last sixty-five years of the country's history only totted up a capacity of 17,000 MW. With stagnant power generation for nearly a decade and excessive reliance on independent power producers, Pakistan, according to the National Power Policy 2013, faced a yawning supply–demand gap of up to 4500–5500 MW. In summer, load-shedding could cross twelve hours across the country, and while the rich have inverters or diesel generators, the poor shivered through the harsh winter by wood fires. Acute gas shortages meant that gas would only be available for cooking and not heating in the freezing winter. That year in 2013, for three months there was no gas for CNG vehicles. In June 2016, the country had achieved a record 17,350 MW of power generation but that didn't curb power cuts.

After the new Nawaz Sharif government took over in 2013, it placed increasing power generation on an equal footing with combating terrorism. The country's fuel-import bill in 2013 was hovering at $15 billion per annum. The policy said that the inefficiencies were costing the taxpayers additional PKR 2.70 per unit over and above the cost of generation at PKR 12, and the water and power ministry had estimated the true cost of delivering a unit of electricity to the end consumer at greater than PKR 15.60.

The Economic Survey of Pakistan said that in 2011–12 about $4.8 billion or 2 per cent of the GDP was lost due to power sector outages. The textile industry had taken a beating and some of the factories moved out.

One of the big questions then was the completion of the Iran–Pakistan pipeline, and Iran was dead set on fining Pakistan for not completing its share of the pipeline. I wrote about an SDPI report,[5] which said that the gas purchase agreement and pricing should be renegotiated or else the project could be a death sentence for the country's economy. The report said the price of the gas under the Iran–Pakistan pipeline project is linked to crude oil prices, and it was unfortunate that the country blatantly ignored the energy dynamics and its pricing while going for this deal. The SDPI report started a debate about gas pricing and whether the pipeline was at all feasible. I interviewed Petroleum Minister Shahid Khaqan Abbasi who said that till the US sanctions on Iran were lifted, it would be financially difficult to build Pakistan's share of the pipeline. I did a few stories on the pipeline which was of great importance and there was also talk of sourcing gas from India. While Pakistani officials did go for meetings in India, the gas price was still too high. The Iran pipeline has hope now after the US sanctions have been lifted, and China has offered to build the Pakistan section of the pipeline, originally called the 'peace pipeline' since India was a part of it.

Apart from making stopgap payments to tide over circular debt, the government did embark on a much-needed capacity expansion programme. The Pakistan Muslim League-Nawaz (PMLN) is working on a twenty-five-year energy plan to add 21,000 MW electricity to the national grid in the next eight years. Like India, Pakistan has turned to nuclear energy, and its Nuclear Energy Vision 2050 envisages nuclear power generation of about 40,000 MW by the year 2050. It was during an earlier tenure of Sharif that the contract for Pakistan's first nuclear power plant at Chashma—of Chinese origin—was signed. Two huge nuclear power plants were coming up in Karachi, but as one journalist I spoke to said, the people in that violent city had more worrying things on their mind.

Different strokes

After the teeming streets of Mumbai, to walk on real pavements without trampling someone or stepping over vendors was a joy, much as I support the hawkers. That was the other thing about the city—it was so planned that you couldn't just stop anywhere and buy things from random roadside shops like I was used to in Mumbai. Everything had its own place. Dedicated fitness freaks preferred the open spaces, including a large, round cricket ground for their walks against the scenic backdrop of the Margalla Hills. Driving past it one day, a puzzled Aurangzeb asked me why people went round and round the same place, and we laughed a lot over that. The Fatima Jinnah park in sector F-9 was a large, rambling place to walk, and in the evening people sometimes drove cars or bikes around which was unfortunate. Still it was lovely with four tall imposing gated entrances, plenty of trees and shrubs and careful landscaping.

The city had a quiet air about it; though its markets were full of people, sometimes there were very few women around in the not-so posh places. The air was crisp and unpolluted, except for some dust storms, and the traffic was usually smooth. You got to most places within fifteen minutes or so and that took a while for me to get used to. There was no need to leave hours in advance, and the airport was one of the farthest places, Chaklala air base, a forty-minute drive from the city at the most.

What was different from my own country was the attire of the men. Most of them wore the loose salwar kameez, popularized by Bhutto who wore it to proclaim his identity with the working class, and later by General Zia-ul-Haq in his Islamization drive, and that set them apart from Indians. There weren't too many women in saris either, and long, flowing kurtas with cigarette pants or the loose palazzos as they are called, were the style statement of that time. Few women wore the burqa; they just covered their heads with a dupatta or shawl. Once I was surprised to see posters put up all over the city: 'A woman modestly dressed is like a pearl in its shell, I love Hijab.' I couldn't see who had put them up from the car.

Many things seemed different. When we wanted to make a spare set of keys for the house, Venkat went to get one made from a key maker near the petrol pump close by. He asked for the address and also a copy of Venkat's passport. In India you could so easily get a duplicate set made without all this fuss! Another time he went to a hardware shop to buy hammers and screws, and he refused to accept a plastic bag since he had, as we usually do, taken a cloth bag. The shopkeeper said you can't be from here since people ask for a plastic bag even if they want to buy a tiny screw. Venkat said he was from India and the shopkeeper said no wonder!

Islamabad was a sea change from Karachi and Hyderabad, the two cities I visited in 2011 (as part of an exchange programme between the Mumbai and Karachi Press Clubs). Friends from Karachi called the capital a cold and soulless city. What was striking and quite different were the paintings on trucks, which is now a popular art form in Pakistan. On the drive to Hyderabad, truck drivers were happy to pose for pictures in front of their large and brilliantly coloured vehicles festooned with black balls of wool to keep off the *nazar* (bad eye). My particular favourite is a large pheasant-like bird, probably a monal, in pastel hues (the book cover photo). In Islamabad I met this lovely artist from Lahore who made expensive but exquisite truck art on metal. But the flashy colours are best seen on enamel which is available everywhere. At Lok Virsa (on the outskirts of Islamabad), I found the garish truck art painted on to everything that can be imagined—lanterns, kettles, plates, mugs—only that you couldn't let water touch it, said the old man from Rawalpindi who was selling them.

After the sedate pace of life in Islamabad, its wide streets and lush gardens ringed by the Margalla Hills, I realized what set Karachi apart is perhaps its sense of uncertainty and bustle, its all-night eating joints, a vibrant art scene, and a liberal press and student community. Coming from Mumbai, a city with a high rate of crime and criminal gangs, I was horrified at the daylight robberies and killings, and I was told even the rich who clustered together in Clifton or Defence Colony areas, own cheap mobiles. People are robbed at gunpoint, and if your car is held up, it makes sense to give up the keys and walk away. Suicide bombers targeted the shrine of Abdullah Shah Ghazi, the patron saint of Karachi, while we were there—the police chased them to an open piece of land near a popular seaside restaurant where they blew themselves up. We had eaten at that very restaurant the night before! I read that the shrine was now being walled off and pushed to obscurity for some exclusive modern complex which was being built for Karachi's elite.

Karachi was not a safe city and we were advised not to travel alone or carry expensive mobiles or money, and the only time we escaped vigilance was when we went off on our own to buy some books and shop around. We stayed at PILER, the Pakistan Institute of Labour Education and Research (on the outskirts of Karachi in the sleepy locality of Gulshan-e-Maymar). The organization is led by the left-wing Karamat Ali and the redoubtable B.M. Kutty, a fellow Malayali, who migrated to Pakistan. My early morning walk became a security problem, with friend and journalist Jatin Desai who was chaperoning us and a policeman riding up beside me on a bike as I was chatting with a young boy on his way to work in a bakery. I was given a stern warning never to walk alone again. The stout policeman with a bushy moustache said he had to keep an eye on me and so I could only walk within fifty feet of his sight. He clearly disapproved of women walking.

On the last day of our stay I didn't go for a walk and when I came down for coffee, I found the policeman standing there. He looked miffed and said, '*Aaj mai aapke liye jaldi aya tha, aur aap aye hi nahi* (I came here early for you today and you didn't turn up).' I found this really funny and told him that it served him right for being so rude to me all the time. Journalist Yogesh Naik from *Mumbai Mirror* said let's take a picture, but the policeman rebuffed him and said, 'I don't pose with women.'

Striding on the road one morning with a shawl thrown over my shoulders, I met two women in flowing burqas who watched me come up to them with amazement. 'Mashallah,' they said, 'you are a woman', and dissolved into a giggling fit. I, too, joined the laugh riot I had unwittingly provoked, but there was nothing more eventful during my walks other than that for the week I was there. The city, however, was reporting murders and robbery with regular intensity, and it was shocking that a young woman was killed in daylight because she refused to give up her car keys. Much later I reported on an attack on a Sufi shrine in this locality.

My eyes searched for the foreign element in Karachi. After all, we needed a visa and there was endless waiting before we could get here. The more I saw, the more it reminded me of home. I took pictures from the bus we travelled in, of people, of the streets, women sitting outside a closed shop, men on scooters, an old Fiat, and in Ibrahim Hydari, donkey carts, children and the huge boats with fishermen repairing nets. Unlike Islamabad, men didn't always wear the salwar kameez there and the women were casually dressed. Some parts of Karachi reminded me of the old city in Mumbai. It looked and felt like a city of migrants and there was a mishmash of communities and localities, each with its own peculiarities. Compared to the cleanly laid-out, artificially organized capital city, Karachi was haphazard and intriguing in a sense. We squeezed in a quick visit to the Holy Trinity church, with its triple-stained glass panels and wooden pews, consecrated in 1855, and its memorials to soldiers killed in the First World War, and where Jinnah attended a service. Two days after Partition, 'the Anglican archdeacon had arranged for a special service of prayer and thanksgiving in Holy Trinity Church, the Anglican Cathedral in Karachi. The archdeacon had also composed a special prayer, in which the Quaid was mentioned. When Jinnah heard of this, he asked that he might be allowed to attend the service, in State.'[6] Since it was a whistle-stop tour we couldn't see much really, but we paid a visit to the cottage industry showroom to buy souvenirs. It was a cavernous, dark and dingy place, and everything was dusty. The salespersons showed a marked reluctance, not because we were Indian—they didn't know that—but they seemed to be lethargic as a rule. So we took out the things we wanted to buy, like Harappan seals, terracotta statues, tiles and beautiful earthen bowls from Sindh (though they were chipped, we bought them). They didn't have too many of any item and we bought up the one or two remaining pieces. Along with the mounting Ajrakh shawls, we were gifted an agate chess set in a velvet box which weighed a ton. I was among those who had to pay excess baggage on our return, even though the kind woman at the PIA counter said she was giving me a concession. Pakistan's Oxford University Press had a lot of books on which they gave me a discount and that had added to the luggage.

Before the influx after Partition, Karachi was different. Piloo Mody writes: 'When I visited Pakistan in 1959 and 1960 I found Karachi—which by all accounts had grown abnormally in the last decade and had become unmanageable—very clean and orderly, almost like a European city.'[7]

With thousands of Mohajirs and over 150 temples, some of them endangered by development, and churches, Karachi has a multicultural dimension. People proudly told us that women drove cars and at that time the art scene was dominated by women who ran the city's top six galleries. I briefly met the writer Husain Naqvi thanks to the writer and journalist Naresh Fernandes (part of the Mumbai Press Club delegation) who took me along with him to his house and later for an art exhibition. On display was a mix of sculptures and the installations were bold and evocative of the times—bullets were part of the theme and the uncertainty of life in general. So apt for a city like Karachi.

Over the years, from a liberal cosmopolitan city, Karachi has been under attack from extremist elements that are threatening co-education schools and Sufi mosques, and creating an atmosphere of fear and terror. People being robbed at gunpoint of their cars and mobile phones is not uncommon, and as Ghazi Salahuddin, a senior journalist, whom we met on that trip, wrote in the *News*, 'Pakistanis are hostage to a society that is infested with religious extremists on the one side and with violent crime on the other. We all feel extremely vulnerable. The breakdown in law and order is more serious a threat to our survival than any conspiracies in a political context.'

Unlike Islamabad, the pavements were crowded with people and lined with small markets. Everything seemed to be cheaper than in India. In fact, some shopkeepers gave us concessions because we were Indian. Women were everywhere in scarves, while a few wore burqas. As we drove through the posh Clifton and Defence colony areas, much as in the rest of the subcontinent, I realized the huge divide between the lives of ordinary people and the secure, guarded lives in elite housing localities. We drove past 70, Clifton, the famous house of the Bhuttos, and some of us wondered if we could go inside. I did meet Fatima Bhutto in Mumbai before she had become a famous writer, but I cannot claim any real acquaintance.

Murtaza Razvi was our self-appointed friend and guide. We ran into him while visiting the Avari Hotel and he took it upon himself to chaperone us around the city in the breaks between our official functions, and also entertain some of us at his home. Murtaza was a senior journalist with the *Dawn* newspaper. He was outspoken about the growing terrorism in the country and the intolerance. He had a column, and became rather unpopular for calling Imran Khan the poster boy of the Taliban, and often joked that every country needs an army but in Pakistan it is the army which needs a country. We were amazed by his open denouncement of what was going wrong. He told us that he couldn't enter his daughters' school without the round blue-and-yellow sticker on his car. The school was heavily guarded and fenced with barbed wire and it insisted on identity cards for parents. Co-education schools are under threat in the city, like Sufi mosques. Razvi was energetic, friendly and acerbic, and when I heard of his death in bizarre circumstances a couple of years after I met him, I thought of his charming wife, Sherezade, and their three lovely daughters and wondered what they would do without him. One more person I met on that trip, Masood Hamid, also of *Dawn*, and a frequent visitor to India, also died in strange circumstances in 2015.

Avari Hotel is quite an institution in Karachi, and then the only place where we got some decent coffee. Its owner, Dinshaw Avari, took us to the top of the seventeenth floor to give us an aerial view of the city. Over a disused racecourse, and an empty swimming pool, the city shimmered in the hazy afternoon sunlight up to the distant hills and the orderly slum of Orangi beyond. Dinshaw's parents had won the gold in Enterprise class sailing in the 1982 Asian Games for Pakistan, and his brother Xerxes had represented the country in sailing. The Avaris are part of a small Parsi community in Karachi which has lost much of its cosmopolitan flavour over the years. Like the Goans, many of them have migrated to Canada and other places. It was a pity that Naresh Fernandes couldn't carry a couple of bottles of feni (liquor brewed from cashew, a speciality of Goa) for his relations in Karachi who were justifiably heartbroken that he had to leave them behind. It was probably their only chance to have a taste of that much-loved yet forbidden spirit!

A visit to Karachi cannot be complete without visiting the home of the Muttahida Qaumi Movement (MQM) founder Altaf Hussain at 'Nine Zero', and as we entered the narrow house in a crowded locality, there were scores of people around us, all supporters shouting slogans. Before that, under a large tent we had been treated to snacks as we waited to hear a live broadcast from London of the exiled leader. We were given bag loads of material on him and all of us were made to wear Sindhi caps and shawls, again. The MQM calls itself a secular party with considerable middle-class support. At Nine Zero we climbed narrow staircases to see a most impressive media room where a number of TV sets had been arranged, all showing different channels. News was monitored round-the-clock by the efficient media managers of the party. The MQM is often accused of being supported by RAW, and once some Indian-made weapons were said to have been recovered from a police raid on one of their offices in Lyari. In fact, right from the hijacking of an Indian Fokker aircraft called Ganga, in January 1971, to the Bangladesh war, the unrest in Balochistan and violence in Karachi or the Taliban bombings, there is little that does not seem to have a RAW hand in Pakistan.

A day trip to Hyderabad

As we approached Hyderabad city, a few hours' drive from Karachi, we crossed the Indus and there were the usual stretches of plastic garbage that you see in any Indian city. The crowded streets too were very similar. Large posters of Benazir Bhutto were everywhere looking down at you, smiling benignly at times, and there was Katrina Kaif flashing her teeth for a soft-drink advertisement. At the entrance of the Hyderabad Press Club was displayed a large panel with a quote from Jinnah on the condition of the press in India in a speech from 1918, especially significant in the light of diminishing press freedom. We had the usual affectionate exchanges, and the business meeting showed a keenness for trade between the two countries. The hospitality was crushing and all the women were gifted with boxes of bangles and shawls. A retired Supreme Court lawyer was our host, and a singer whose name I forget, but whose golden voice I remember, entertained us all evening, with the finale being '*Damadam Mast Qalander*', which she sang even better than the famous Runa Laila. There was much dancing and singing that evening, though while returning, the news of a bomb blast in Karachi did suppress the merriment a bit. While sectarianism was gaining ground, Farheem Mogal, then a member of the Sindh provincial assembly, told us of the liberal Sufi traditions of Sindh and protest marches against the killing of three Hindus in a riot.

A part of the day trip to Hyderabad was a boat ride on the Indus, and for many of us it was the first time we set our eyes on the river. The serene waters and the barrage gilded by the setting sun formed a backdrop to fishermen in colourfully painted boats casting their nets around. While returning, we saw a bus with people sitting on top, and two women in creamy, billowing skirts, shirts and dupattas got off and walked into the sunset.

The city has the wonderful Hasrat Mohani library, a tasteful brick building set in green lawns with elegant interiors full of books in high-ceilinged halls, formerly Holmstead Hall reconstructed at a cost of PKR 26 million in 2008. The crowded locality where L.K. Advani, former deputy prime minister and BJP leader was born, was another stop in Hyderabad, and the area had some remnants of the colonial-style buildings of the past rubbing shoulders with ugly modern construction.

Social life, undercover restaurants and Kabul

I usually woke up early, having slept only after midnight, and then walked or—if it was too cold—read all the newspapers and magazines. The first thing even before I had coffee would be to put on the TV and the computer, and quickly scan for any breaking news. I made it a point to walk or work out, and briefly joined yoga-cum-Pilates (my teacher used to call it 'yogilates'!) classes. Work kept me busy all day, filing three or four stories into the evening, and then reading or watching films if I wasn't going out. It was hectic and there was very little time to relax except when we were doing the hiking trails or watching films. I also tried to do what we call special stories or op-eds which took up a lot of time.

I used to see my next-door neighbour driving in an old, red Toyota. She would say hello and was friendly but we didn't get around to visiting each other. She used to think I was a diplomat since I appeared on TV sometimes. On the other side I didn't see too many people. Behind the house lived some young men who played cricket, and often the ball was hit inside my compound and they would pester Sajida for it. On my walks, I mostly saw security guards who spent their lives guarding huge bungalows from tiny concrete cubbyholes built outside the gate.

Islamabad is a friendly city and doing stories was not too difficult since most people were forthcoming. I had already been warned about my appearance by my friends at home. Clothes were important and make-up. A friend had advised me to 'dress well', as otherwise I would appear shabby in comparison with the elegant Pakistanis. I was gifted dupattas and kurtas so that I would not be a disappointment, and I thought I got along fine till a make-up man in a TV station scolded me for my simplicity! In Mumbai, casual dressing was the norm for journalists and that was also one of the reasons I liked my profession, but here I was vastly out of sync with the prevailing mode. I refused to be made-up before a TV talk show, and the make-up man was aghast that I didn't even wear lipstick. He insisted on some light powdering, and proceeded to give me a short lecture on how I should be conducting myself. He said such simplicity would do me no good and people wouldn't take me seriously if I didn't up my glamour quotient! By then, I had a fair idea of my shortcomings, and worse was to come. Friends in Islamabad were often surprised that I didn't use make-up. Appearances clearly mattered even if you were a journalist.

I was advised against celebrating festivals in an obvious manner. Since I didn't do that back home, this wasn't difficult.

Unlike in India with its noisy festivals, the only sound of crackers I heard was during Diwali celebrations within the high walls of the Indian high commission. I read reports in the papers of muted celebrations for Indian festivals. When Bakri Id approached, again I was warned by friends against going out, saying that there would be blood on the streets. I could hear the goats bleating in the houses around me and TV shows were full of programmes on *Qurbani*, and there was a particularly awkward episode where the TV anchor spoke of how they tried to kill a camel and it bolted and they had to stick a knife into it or some such thing. While I didn't see anything as gory, the street outside my house was wet after washing off—I'm guessing, blood. I woke up on Id morning to hear a dull thudding sound, like that of wood being cut. I looked out and between the bushes I could see my neighbour's garden where the carcass of a stretched-out goat was being chopped. I didn't look out after that. Everything was closed for a few days and people outside their gate would clamour for meat.

While I didn't get any top-secret information (quite damaging for the spy I was thought to be), I could walk around, buy the things I wanted, I could get fresh farm produce and meet nice people. Social life in Islamabad is full of diplomatic dinners and get-togethers and they mostly end early at 9.30 p.m., except once when a visiting Indian dignitary refused to be sent off at that rather early hour. Parties are the norm and from day one we were invited to dinner. A friend invited me to a party and when I said I didn't know anyone, he said you will, once you get there. It was a birthday celebration of a senior politician who treated me like his long-lost daughter. The friend had said he would come and pick me up around 9 p.m. and I had to be ready to leave in a flash. Leaving home was not easy; I had to lock so many doors, plus the gate, and it was too cold to wait outside, so I was on tenterhooks when his call came. I rushed out to find the small lane leading up to my house jam-packed with jeeps and huge cars, blinding me with their bright headlights. Carloads of gun-toting security personnel were behind a black, sleek vehicle, and I heard a sharp voice asking me to jump in quickly while I locked the gate. In the darkness, I couldn't see this important personage who was escorting me and I had to wait till I reached the party to find out. The evening was full of Punjabi poetry and songs, Scotch and excellent food, and very male. For a while I was the only woman around. The friend who had invited me forgot about me and left the party. It was very late and thankfully, a kind politician whom I knew, wondering why I was standing outside, quite lost, dropped me home

Journalist and now TV anchor, Amir Mateen, was my closest neighbour and he would often call me up to meet many of his friends—newspaper editors, human rights activists and politicians—who were friendly and off guard, and almost all of them were clued into the happenings in my newspaper and my country. We would have long conversations lasting till late in the evening and if the mood and occasion dictated, there would be music. Amir's man Friday, a shy but charming young man called Adnan, would ply us with food and snacks, while his dog would bark all the time as it was confined to a small area in the compound. Keen to showcase his Punjabi culture, he once invited me for a relative's wedding he was hosting, complete with all-night singing.

Amir played my guide in the National Assembly and often he would pick me up and drop me back when I didn't have a driver. He would tell me about all the politicians and I would read his column the next day in the *News*. He wrote as if he were talking to you, so it was engaging and quite funny at times. The first time, we were seated in the long press gallery—and later always in the same place—he pointed to the ornate ceiling and joked that the calligraphy was verses from the Koran, in case I thought it was graffiti. I spluttered in anger, saying I knew that much and he guffawed. He was really helpful while I learnt the ropes about covering both the Parliament and Senate, and who was who. We spent long hours in the canteen waiting for sessions to start and that was where we met more politicians and journalists. If the celebrated Geo TV anchor and journalist who had interviewed Osama bin Laden, Hamid Mir sat with us, there would be a crowd of people who wanted photographs with him—he seemed to have a huge following. A few of us went for movies together, or met for small parties or lunch, and the Centaurus mall was walking distance from where I lived. Coffee at the Kohsar Market—Islamabad's equivalent of Delhi's Khan Market—was a regular ritual, but sometimes we had to leave in a hurry due to filing stories and deadlines. Asmatullah Niazi from Pakistan TV (the state channel which is in English) was most helpful with almost anything. Many other friends too were part of my life in the city and at times we hung out together. Having a car and driver, and the short distances made things so easy as the available public transport in the city was not a great way of commuting.

I got to know a few people really well and was invited to their homes. The first thing that strikes you when you enter Brigadier Mohammed Ayaz Khan's flat is a framed photograph of a handsome, blue-eyed young man: his son Salman, a police officer, who was killed while nabbing kidnappers in an operation some years ago. It is a wrenching loss that the family tries to bear with dignity, but in their eyes, you can see a deep sadness which overshadows their lives. Brigadier Ayaz drove from his fort in Swabi to bring fresh vegetables to the weekly farmers' market in Kuch Khaas, a café and arts centre much favoured by expats, which has a huge front lawn where the market takes place. That's how I met him. A tall, burly man, he was cheerful and friendly like the rest of his lovely family, especially his two grandchildren, Suleiman and Momina, who would stand behind a small table with fresh produce every week at the market. I was a dedicated customer for the large, golden Lisbon lemons, honey, oranges and fresh vegetables. Soon I would phone Brigadier Ayaz every week before he set off for Islamabad with my weekly order and he would bring it home to his flat. He often regretted the hostile relations between our countries and the fact that he couldn't read Indian magazines; he really liked *India Today*. Once I showed him how to read it online on my iPad, but he still wanted hard copies.

Suleiman was an ardent fan of Imran Khan and he asked me to get an autograph for him from the cricketer-turned-politician. Khan obliged after a crowded press conference by signing a piece of paper. Suleiman said he would frame it and hang it on the wall! I used to meet Brigadier Ayaz at think-tank meetings and he would often despair about how India and Pakistan couldn't get on better. He often invited me to Swabi, but there was little chance of my being given permission to see his sprawling fort—but at least I could see the photographs.

In his flat in Islamabad, there would be a large tray of dry fruits on the table in the centre of the large hall and I found this was quite the norm in many houses I visited. When some friends came over, they would bring quantities of pine nuts which were cheaper there and other lovely stuff. I got addicted to munching dry fruits and always had a bowlful on my dining table after that. We used to go to the local Aabpara Market to buy dry fruits which were cheaper and of excellent quality.

There would always be some excuse for a get-together, and a farewell for an Indian diplomat, a very popular one at that, in charge of visas, led to a large round of farewells. Some Indian diplomats who were given repeated farewells and stayed on, provoked statements on the lines of 'now no more farewells for this person', but inevitably there would be a few more parties.

A friend of a former correspondent invited me for a lavish brunch on his return from the USA after surgery, and often at these gatherings, there would be newspaper editors, retired army or government officials. The hosts would sometimes carefully select people who could be important and useful. Journalists and sometimes politicians also would invite us over, and once I went to a friend's house where the table groaned with many dishes, even though to begin with it looked as if there would be nothing to eat.

Food was top of the agenda and it was delicious. Another friend told me about a restaurant which had an 'all you can eat iftar' during Ramzan, and people ate it all up, prompting a hasty closure.

Unlike in Mumbai or even Karachi, there was not much of a nightlife in Islamabad. On New Year's Eve, there was a private party in a restaurant we went to for dinner, and that seemed to be the norm. While a few of the Indian high commission officials' parties were dry, the EU and the USA had elaborate parties; the EU national day was hosted on the lawns of a five-star hotel, complete with drinks, music and dancing, and very good food. Many parties were held at the Indian high commissioner's house and in the extensive grounds. The only time I was invited to the US embassy deep inside a walled, secluded area was to the home of the then US ambassador, Richard Olson, when a delegation of the Committee to Protect Journalists (CPJ) and its trustee, Kati Marton, was visiting. The precautions and high security seemed doubly necessary after the rampage on the old embassy in November 1979, coinciding with the Iran hostage crisis which must have left some bitter memories.

Anita had kept a stack of takeaway menus for us, and in the first week of our stay while settling in, we would order from a new place every day. Pakistani food was meat, meat and more meat, and even chicken was considered vegetarian. A friend once asked me what was for dinner, and when I said cabbage, he made a face. Obviously, it was fodder! Once at a restaurant when Ruchira ordered a vegetarian dish, it had chicken. When she pointed this out to the waiter, he looked shocked. 'It's only chicken,' he said, as if it was a common vegetable! While the kebabs and naan were great, the Chinese food was a disappointment; the noodles were thick and oily, and the gravy very Punjabi and red. The restaurant scene in Islamabad is limited, though there was Japanese and Chinese food as well, and not being a great meat eater, I didn't really go to the lesser-known and tastier joints. There was a popular eatery for biryani, kebabs, and it had nice kheer as well. There was one named after Bombay but it had very little of the food from the city.

We met the owner once who was keen on learning how to make dosas. Later, we found that some enterprising Chinese had opened 'undercover' restaurants with delicious food and secret bars. The long, green beans with sesame were a particular favourite. It was one more memorable birthday in Pakistan, this time, dinner with Snehesh and Ruchira at one of these Chinese restaurants, with Ruchira generously baking an orange-flavoured cake for me.

There was a huge controversy over one of these open secret restaurants, La Maison, run by a Frenchman which disallowed Pakistanis, and put up a board outside saying so. The Frenchman said he didn't intend it that way and it was because he used pork or ingredients like wine in his cooking that he had put up the board. But the outrage from Pakistanis closed his restaurant for a while, though I think it opened again. It was rather crude of him to put up such a notice, however fine the dining may have been. The Chinese restaurants were quiet and didn't have signboards; the one we liked was a house where a few tables were set in two rooms. The owner's child would sometimes wander into the rooms. It was like eating in your own house; often, we would get an entire room to ourselves.

A favourite haunt was Kuch Khaas (where, as I mentioned earlier, the weekly farmers' market took place), with its secluded Lime Tree café on the main Margalla Road owned by Poppy Afzal Khan who sadly passed away later. It was a centre for arts and performances, and had many events, apart from being a good place to meet people. The lawns were framed by dense bushes and trees all around, and the café was cosy inside. The food was good and the coffee, particularly, was excellent. On winter evenings, electric fires kept you warm while you ate the delicious barbecued meat. The place was managed by the feisty Khaleda Noon who was always fretting about ensuring the quality of food and service.

I also discovered a neighbour who made wonderful jams, bread, couscous and hummus. Then there were large-scale farmers, some of them ex-military men, who had farms on the outskirts of Islamabad that sold cheese, milk, fruit and crisp vegetables. One

Children in the Afghan refugee camp on the outskirts of Islamabad.

Graffiti outside the Karachi Press Club in 2011 praising Malik Mumtaz Qadri who murdered Punjab Governor Salman Taseer for opposing the blasphemy law.

Shoaib Sultan Khan admiring a picture of himself relaunching a programme in Rae Bareli with Rahul Gandhi.

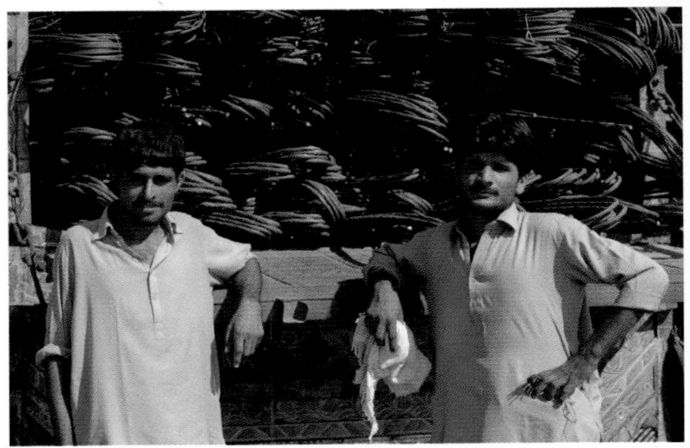

Two truck drivers who insisted I photograph them—during a stopover in Hyderabad from Karachi (2011).

Filling water can be a precarious and dangerous mission for these children in Islamabad's *katchi abadi*s.

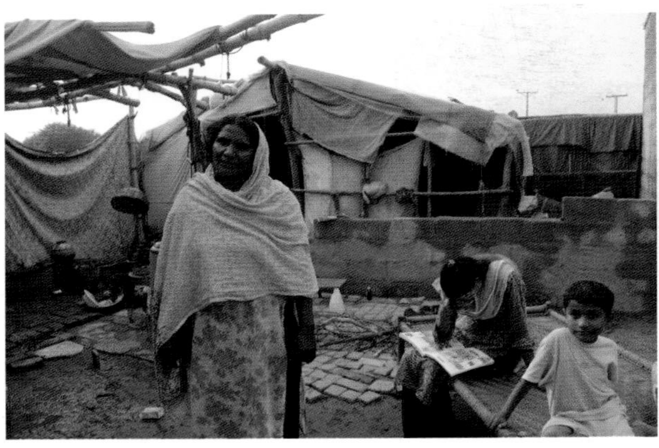

The Christians who fled Meherabad live in a tent colony very unlike the rest of the leafy and clean capital (2013).

Firewood collection is not an uncommon sight in Islamabad.

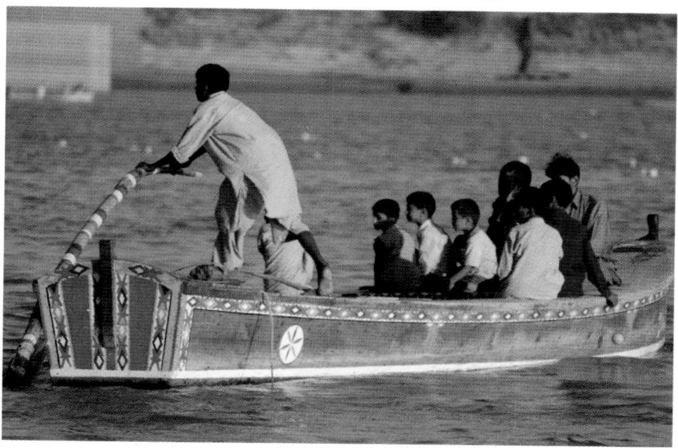

Boating on the Indus River near Hyderabad.

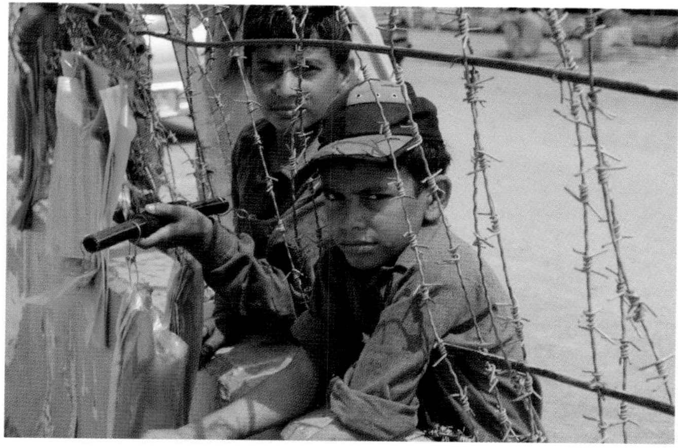

Young boys selling plastic bags outside the Bari Imam mausoleum in Islamabad.

A view of Karachi city from the top of Avari Hotel, with Jinnah's tomb in the distance

A poster in the Karachi University campus (2011).

Stranded Malayalis in Karachi.

Sugra (right) and her mother bemoaning their fate. Sugra's father, a fisherman, was arrested for straying into Indian waters and never seen again.

Hafiz Saeed's rally in 2013 at D-Chowk opposite the National Assembly in Islamabad.

A tribute to Salman Taseer at Kohsar Market on his death anniversary.

A policeman cleaning up after the suicide bombing in the Islamabad district court complex in March 2014.

A view of Islamabad from the Pakistan Monument.

The scene after a blast in the capital's fruit market.

Journalists outside the Islamabad Press Club protesting the attack on Geo TV anchor Hamid Mir.

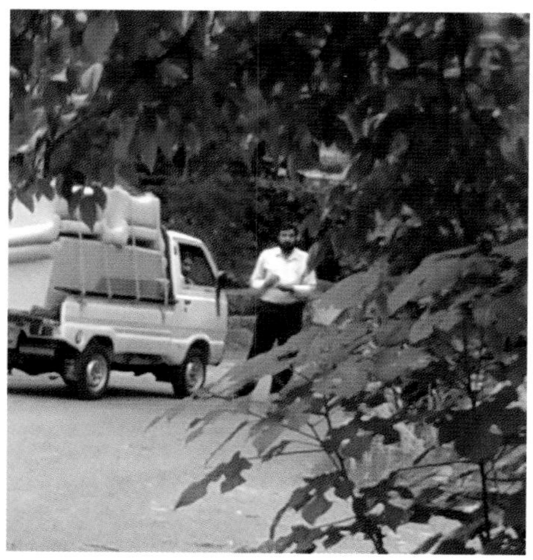

My spook, Beard, making notes about the tempo leaving with furniture that I sold, outside my house in Islamabad.

Venkat hiking up Trail 6 in the Margalla Hills.

A view of Islamabad and Rawal Lake from the traverse along the ridge of Trail 6.

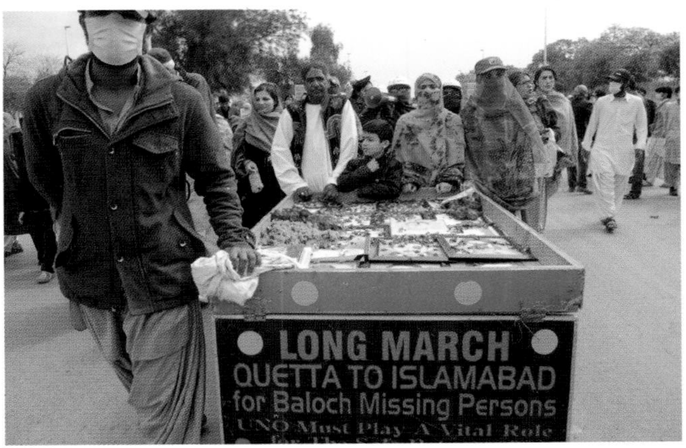

Mama Qadeer Baloch and his small band of youngsters wheeling their cart with pictures of the missing people from Balochistan.

Faisal Mosque with the Margalla Hills in the backdrop.

was owned by a couple whose daughter was married to General Musharraf's son. I didn't mention that I knew this to the couple who were friendly and sold some really good dairy products and vegetables. In fact, I had bottled milk delivered to my house every morning. When the tempo driver realized we were from India, he asked my husband to get him some hair oil he had read about which had magical restorative properties. Every time he met me he would ask, has your husband come back, where is the oil? He was probably the most distressed of all Pakistanis to learn I was going away. His dreams of having a lush crown of hair disappeared with my expulsion.

At Kuch Khaas, I was delighted to find *bagara baigan*, and even the South Indian *murukku* made by a charming lady who lived in Madras (Chennai) a long time ago, and had learnt the recipes. But things can be overpriced; once a farmer from Peshawar tried to sell me a lemon tree sapling for Rs 500, sparking outrage from a chain-smoking army officer's wife who had a stall there. Then there was a friendly woman who made pink Kashmiri tea, and even gave me a free bottle once. You had to boil this concentrate with milk and add nuts and bits of biscuit—it was a meal almost, and I had it as often as I could in the cold evenings. Columnist Zahrah Nasir with her trademark sun hat and myriad bead necklaces drove down from her farm called La La Land every week. She made the most delicious jams, even rosehip jelly, among other exotica, which she brought all the way from the hill station where she lived, which was cut off in winter. I also planted apple mint thanks to her, and it thrived in the cold weather. Ordinary mint grew wild in my garden and I felt a little foolish when, after buying a large bunch soon after I arrived, Sajida showed me what a little forest I had at the back of the house.

Sometimes Ruchira hosted fabulous lunches and dinners; at the farmers' market, she would cook using the ingredients sold there, and soon became very popular with her innovations. Ruchira also introduced me to *shakshuka*—a Mediterranean dish of spinach, vegetables and poached eggs—which became my favourite since it was so easy to make on Sundays when Sajida had her day off. A neighbour made the most delicious couscous and once I gave her some dosa batter which she liked, having lived in New Delhi. I was sad to learn that Kuch Khaas and the café have now been closed.

It was at Kuch Khaas that I first saw Indu Mitha when she was teaching dancing on the lawns, and wondered who this youthful grey-haired lady could be, as she moved gracefully on the grass, dressed in a cotton sari with a white churidar beneath. When I met her, she groaned and said you are not interviewing me again—since she had already been profiled by Nirupama in a charming story. She ran the dance class discreetly in a house, and didn't advertise it. I chatted with her and her students for a while. Later I got an invitation for a performance by her students but, sadly, I couldn't make it. There were quite a few who learnt Bharatanatyam from her and it was wonderful to know that despite all the extremist tendencies, an ancient Indian dance form, could—if not flourish—at least have a presence here, and it seemed quite popular. (Kuch Khaas also had classes in Indian classical music, but there was no time for me to attend them.) Indu Mitha came from a 'well-known Christian family from Lahore' and always dressed in her favoured cotton saris. Her father, Professor Chatterji, was with the famous Government College in Lahore before Partition, but later lived in India. Married to the late Major General A.O. Mitha, who was from a wealthy Memon family which once lived in Lands End in Mumbai, Indu still teaches Bharatanatyam to enthusiastic Pakistanis. Maj. Gen. Mitha's book *Unlikely Beginnings*[8] is a riveting account of his life in the new country of Pakistan, which he adopted in 1947 while his parents remained in India.

The Centaurus mall was a place to meet friends and it was usually full, with people eating burgers and pizzas, a favourite activity of families. Just as in India, it was fast food that everyone stuffed their faces with. I once had a dosa in a Karachi mall and regretted it; but I hate fast food and that was the only option. Served me right, I guess. The best *nalli nihari* (lamb slow-cooked for a long time in gravy) and biryani I had was when a friend dragged me to an all-male lunch, a weekly ritual into which I gatecrashed. I didn't regret it but I don't know about the poor host. The food was fabulous and there was some awesome kheer to round off the meal. That was the first time I had the huge Afghan naans, and vowed to get them often. The *chapali kebab* was a favourite and in Khiva restaurant, you could sit in the open under heaters while the staff served you cinnamon tea and kebabs on a platter. The different breads, some with raisins, were also a treat. There were caged birds though, which I tried hard to ignore but otherwise it was a warm place to visit. The ice cream place Hotspot, which I was told was also a favourite of Benazir Bhutto's, had many fruity flavours which I enjoyed.

We often went to Karam Lebanon for the excellent Mediterranean food there. It was a house done up warmly in red and wood panelling, and was quite close to where I lived. The Kohsar Market, with its upscale cafés and outdoor seating, was another hang-out, and they even had ghostly pumpkins for Halloween! Very unreal. The lovely handicrafts shop-cum-café Behbud had nice food, and the person who ran it would always ensure you got exactly what you wanted. It was run by a collective of women and had the most attractive crocheted and hand-embroidered table linen and clothes. It was here I attended the first of journalist Mariana Babar's famed chapali kebab parties, this time a farewell for a rather popular Indian diplomat. She would get the kebabs, large, flat, crisp and spicy, all the way from Peshawar, and there were strict rules for the party. You just had to add salad and bread, nothing else, or no one would eat the chapali kebab, she would say. Once when this took place at another friend's house, he had the audacity to make some *sarson ka saag* and *makki di roti*, and the sparks flew. Mariana herself didn't eat these offending dishes, but had it packed up for her dinner. The only time I had a formal lunch for friends was also a chapali kebab event, and Mariana warned me to get only the naan and salad, which was easy. She even heated the kebabs her way as she didn't trust anyone else. That was the fag end of the kebab parties season since it was difficult to get them from Peshawar in summer. The indomitable writer and poet Kishwar Naheed, like Ayesha Siddiqa, author of *Military Inc.*,[9] threw a lot of parties which were informal and warm gatherings. Complete strangers would invite me for brunches or dinners, and it's not for nothing that the Punjabis and Pashtuns are famed for their hospitality. They treat you like a long-lost friend and lavish every attention on you. Often at Kishwar's place, the food was brought by various people. My friend Shandana sometimes took me to the Islamabad Club on Sundays for swimming and brunch—and that's how I spent my last day in the capital. The club was well laid out and lush green, and had two pools, a large outdoor one (with a Ladies Time specified on a board outside) and an indoor one for women. It was superb and on that last day, it rained while we swam. The brunch was a huge spread of all kinds of food imaginable, and people turned up elegantly dressed to savour it. We ate without guilt; all that swimming can make you very hungry.

The markets in Islamabad are big, glitzy affairs, with glass-fronted buildings and huge shops. Apart from the Centaurus mall, there was another obscenity which was opening just when I was leaving, rather airily called Safa Gold Mall. There was a lovely mithai shop near the OUP Pakistan outlet in Islamabad's central 'Blue Area' which sold hot gulab jamuns and carrot halwa, which my husband loved. Often he would go straight there while I bought books. I liked the smaller places, samosas at Bengali Market, and especially Kabul restaurant run by Afghans. It had a superb bakery where the man at the counter would prevent me from buying the tempting baklava, saying it was 2500 calories a piece. It has the best cinnamon bread in the world, among other delectable stuff, like the large 'skateboard' Afghan naan, which my friend Anila learnt to bake in Kabul. 'Skateboard' is her term. That and the delicious chicken kebabs with blobs of fat stuck in the heavy iron skewers made for a most appetizing meal washed down with golden kahwa and little, round sesame sweets. In fact, I ended up buying the big naans often since I found the wheat in Islamabad inedible. I thought this was the Punjab with its large wheat fields, but the flour was like chaff. Sajida used to knead the dough and freeze it, but the result was cardboard-like chapattis. Hers tasted better because she made them thick and fat. I got tired of the wheat, and ended up eating brown rice or breads. I suspect some of that wheat was imported. Also, like in India, we couldn't buy wheat everywhere and get it ground. In the market near my house, there was one *chakki* (flour mill), but the guy had only one type of wheat and you didn't have a choice. The ready-made wheat flour was a disaster.

The other difficulty was finding coconuts. I wasn't very fond of coconut-based gravies, but after a few months in Islamabad I craved for home food. That's when I learnt to make *aviyal* (a South Indian dish with vegetables and ground coconut), but buying coconuts was not easy. I hate cooking but I was hungry for something familiar. Soon I made dosas and even sambar. My mother-in-law had given me packets of all kinds of home-made powders. The Indian diplomats' wives were all very good cooks, and some of them were South Indian; so I was very grateful for a regular dose of some of my favourite food. The Kashmiri vendor near my house would promise to get coconuts, and inevitably delay it for several days but I found a supermarket where they were available. I also bought ready-made *bhel*, something which I detested, but I found myself eating it with great relish, and papad too.

I didn't find freshly ground coffee or fresh milk in any shop, as everything was in Tetra Paks. The market nearby had milk imported from Austria or Australia, and we had to wait till evening for cow's milk from some faraway country to arrive. The fresh supply from Simli farms was life-saving. Kohsar Market had some expensive shops full of imported stuff, and I mainly went there for the sesame oil—again hard to get. Olive oil was available in plenty. Locally they seemed to be using canola oil, which I didn't like at all. There was a lot of brown rice and noodles which I often bought, and organic wheat flour, a slight improvement on the local stuff. There was some local brand of butter which didn't taste good, so we often had to rely on imported brands for butter and cheese, of which there were plenty. Imported goods filled the shops for those who could afford them.

The shelves looked so tempting, full of colourful, and for me, useless cartons of stuff I never ate or drank, like juices, chips and whatnot. Friends warned me against American coffee; don't touch it, they said, so I settled for Lavazza. People favoured tea here, especially from teabags, for reasons I never fathomed, and green tea after every meal even as late as midnight was something that was the norm.

Water supply was scarce and came from bore wells. I was advised against drinking that water and had to buy twenty-litre Bisleri cans and heave them up the kitchen platform. So used to drinking boiled water back home, this reliance on bottled water took me a while to get used to. In terms of water, power and transport, the city was way behind, though I hear that now there is a new public transport system and the power situation is improving.

Luckily for me, *kadi patta* (curry leaves which no one used there) grew at home, and I tried planting *dhania* (coriander) as well. But finding mustard seeds was a challenge—the only stuff available was microscopic red seeds which were tasteless and often didn't sputter. Finally, I had to settle for that and despite searching in many markets, I didn't have any luck. There was no sign of raw bananas which were among my favourite vegetables—sautéed with onions. I didn't see some of the vegetables I used back home, like the many varieties of beans and gourds we have. But to make up, fruits were in plenty. In winter, fresh strawberries grew in the fields of Bani Gala. Small carts piled up with the lovely fruit would line the roads, and strawberries in any form became the order of the day. When I got there, giant and juicy peaches from Swat were in season, which passed soon to my regret. Compared to the ones back home, these had a delicate rosy tinge to the golden yellow, and were huge—eating one of them was almost like a meal.

Outside the Kabul bakery, there was an old man who sold flowers—they were *nargis*, the small yellow-and-white fragrant flowers in winter, or later the orange-and-red roses. I was a regular customer and I suspect he overcharged me, but it was too tempting to pass up those beautiful flowers. Their gentle fragrance came back to me in Delhi's Khan Market where they were similarly kept on the pavement in thick bunches. The bakery had a small showcase outside which advertised real guns—a 1917 Webley revolver, Mark 6, was priced at $1000 while a 1913 Enfield rifle with what looked like a bayonet cost $1300. There was another more expensive rifle below. They didn't seem to have any buyers since I saw the guns there for a long time. The F-8 market had a shop for guns and ammunition as well.

Of Mehrans, robberies and katchi abadis

The well-planned city had no public transport worth the name then. When the driver had his day off, I had to rely on the expensive private taxis or radio cabs which were very efficient. The cheaper way of rattling about was the Suzuki Mehrans. Islamabad had no metred taxi system and the fares were random. The Mehran rundowns moved strictly on willpower—they often had every part loose, no brakes, and poor wheel alignment; it was a big risk to travel by one of them though they were the cheapest option if you could bargain for a while.

Aurangzeb was a fount of information and gossip. He knew everything—he was the one who told me about the robbery at the house of an Indian high commission official who was away on vacation. Even his large alcohol stash was filched and his silver. Later, the house in which Aurangzeb was living, where his wife worked as a maid, was robbed. The house was also that of an Indian diplomat's. The thieves entered through the terrace, which was not locked properly, and took away all the gold jewellery, and even the passports. After the incident, we were summoned to the high commission for a short lecture on security. We were advised to keep our doors locked and even the bedroom door had to be locked at night. They stopped short of advising us to have security guards posted outside our houses, which my driver said would attract unnecessary attention and in any case, he said that these men almost never fought with attackers. Ironically, the expected robbery did take place, not in Islamabad but in my flat in Mumbai after I returned. Nothing happened while I was away but a couple of days before I left for New Delhi (in June 2014) where I was posted, I came home after a visit to a doctor to find my cupboard ransacked and all the jewellery I had, mostly gifted by my mother and mother-in-law, gone. Someone had broken the lock, and they took my husband's phone but mercifully left behind our passports, money and my iPad. One of the policemen who swarmed all over my house boasted that he had solved a robbery in actor Hema Malini's house a few days ago. I knew then that nothing would happen and since I wasn't a celebrity, the police couldn't even trace the cell phone.

In the Islamabad house there were no grills or iron bars, so I had to be content with the wooden doors and hope no one tried to break and enter. On the first floor, the terrace had a glass door with a wire mesh cover, both of which were flimsy. These houses were not built with security in mind; they were friendly in a way, not fortresses. It was bucolic, and the lawns, the trees, all added to that feeling of cosiness. Sadly, for such a city, the garbage and dried leaves were usually burnt on the road or in the compound in my neighbourhood, and no one seemed to mind. The lovely streams below the road would have plenty of garbage, and the small slopes would glow with burning refuse. There was some move to have a garbage dump but there was no centralized garbage clearance, just as in Delhi where the garbage piled high into little mountains on the outskirts.

My friends at home would worry if I was safe and how the spooks were treating me. My veteran colleagues from *The Hindu* had warned me about spooks, who were going to be a part of my life. Some had them stationed outside their homes too. There would also be jokes about the ISI (Inter-Services Intelligence), and one of my friends in his 'direct messages' on Twitter would always say 'Hi' to the ISI and a note saying I know they are reading this! I must say that Islamabad is safer than Karachi, and walking around, though few do, is kosher. It's a city for the well heeled, with its capacious bungalows fronted with lawns. Its quiet, leafy lanes will see few people except for the drivers hanging around and maids who travel long distances crushed in uncomfortable vans. Nowhere is the divide between the very rich and poor more evident than it is in the capital. Much like New Delhi, the poor are herded together in slums. People tend to use cars even for minuscule distances. The rains are scarce—nothing like the wretched downpour in Mumbai which I am used to—and it does get cold. My friends laughed when I asked about rain shoes and umbrellas. No one used them.

The capital is charming with its wide roads, but the poor public transport meant that those who didn't have cars had to wait for the shared vans which were erratic in their frequency. Sajida who lived near Bari Imam would reach home late, and sometimes she had to walk a long way for the shared vans. The red-bricked katchi abadis—where the poor lived are bigger than the small rooms in Mumbai slums and spacious, but are just as sordid as in India in terms of basic amenities, cleanliness and overflowing gutters. Poverty, as much as it was hidden in Islamabad, was acute. People had to collect firewood for their fuel needs, food security was low, and the power sporadic. When I was leaving, I offered the large fridge to Sajida as a gift. She refused to take it. Her son said that since there was no power, it could end up as a storage cupboard. I insisted she should anyway use it when there was power, but she didn't budge. But after I sold the fridge on the last day she looked very sad. She said she wished she had listened to me, but really it would have been difficult to keep that fridge. Sajida was so honest about the whole thing—anyone else would probably have taken it and sold it, since there seemed to be a demand for second-hand stuff.

While the economic situation of the country is far from happy and the wealth is concentrated in a few families, Prime Minister Sharif has done well for himself as the richest elected representative, with assets of PKR 1.82 billion. His election affidavit, uploaded by the Election Commission of Pakistan (ECP) in December 2013, shows that he owns vast tracts of agricultural land and property worth well over a billion Pakistani rupees, some of it inherited or gifted, in Lahore and Sheikhupura, while his wife Kulsoom Nawaz owns two properties in Murree. He also has investments in sugar, textile and engineering companies, and owns four vehicles, a 2010 Toyota Land Cruiser, two old-model (1991 and 1973) Mercedes-Benz cars and a tractor. His son also sends him money from London. The only other billionaire is the minister for petroleum and natural resources, Shahid Khaqan Abbasi. Imran Khan, the chairperson of Pakistan Tehreek-e-Insaf (PTI), has assets worth over PKR 29 million, while Punjab Chief Minister Shehbaz Sharif has a modest PKR 424 million, making him the richest chief minister in Pakistan. Only an Independent member of the National Assembly, Jamshed Dasti, declared no property or assets except his salary as a people's representative.

Stone carvers, truck art, books

I wasn't allowed to visit Taxila, but I met a stone carver from that great centre of learning and art at a handicrafts fair at Lok Virsa, a folk art and history complex on the outskirts of Islamabad. Usually the stuff tended to be tacky, but I got lucky. He made exquisite Buddha figurines in the Gandharva style. He even gave me his card and said I could call him for more. He was a young man who had started carving at an early age and the two small figures I bought were of stone and made with great delicacy. My predecessor in Islamabad, Anita, had bought a lovely sofa from a second-hand furniture-cum-antique shop which agreed to take it back for a small cut in the original price. Since I wasn't taking it back, it wouldn't have fitted in my small home, I sold it. The shop in the city had a courtyard where furniture was being refurbished and there were some unique articles on sale, like blue pottery jugs, beer mugs, carpets, lacquer coasters and Sindhi window frames.

I had interviewed Mohammed Ilyas, the only slate carver from his village Bail near Haripur. Slate was used for doors, window frames and tombstones which used to be intricately carved. If it was a woman who had died, there would be a necklace or something to indicate that. With marble replacing slate as tombstones, people like Ilyas rely on their wits. It is difficult to get slate and few people know the craft. He is an innovator though, and has introduced calligraphy—he carves Koranic inscriptions on houses in slate. A modest man in his fifties, he was hard at work when I met him at the Satrang art gallery, run by the gracious Asma Khan. Looking at the displays in the gallery, he said it took him two years to make all of them. 'Isn't it foolishness?' he asks. Ilyas has transformed slate art into everyday articles, like trays, wall hangings, clocks and coasters, but the precision carving with a small chisel was masterly. I watched him patiently chip away at a design of a mosque using a fine chisel. It's as strong as an iron hammer. He used an iron pencil to draw the design on the slate before carving.

In the elegantly arranged art gallery, there was plenty of his work—some of them huge cabinets and tables (dressing tables, side tables), clocks—and the grey slate added a touch of class. I had never seen such beautiful carving on a stone which we used to scribble on in school, and most people don't even know what slate is now. From dull roofs and tombstones, he had managed to give life to this nondescript grey stone. I bought some slate art, the small trays and plaques, one of them with a rose carved on it, as souvenirs. He was amused by all the questions I asked him, but replied with great patience. His visiting card said 'Chitrakar'; he peered at me over his glasses and told me that's Hindi for painter in your country, isn't it?

The other place I loved to visit was Saeed Book Bank, almost an institution in the capital, with an amazing collection of non-fiction on Pakistan, India and Afghanistan. The salesmen would show me books they thought I would like, and they were good at finding stuff. And the discount coupons made you want to buy even more. Once they went out of their way to get me a copy of Maj. Gen. A.O. Mitha's book, *Unlikely Beginnings,*[10] which wasn't available anywhere. The Oxford University Press also had a well-stocked shop with wonderful books and discounts, and I was a regular customer. There were some second-hand book shops in the same market where some rare books were available, but searching in the musty shelves made you sneeze all the time.

This is Pakistan

Just before I left, Khaadi, which was one of my favourite shops, offered me loyalty points. I wanted to tell him, 'Hey, wasn't I supposed to be enemy number one!' I had to regretfully refuse and say I was being sent back to India, and that loyalty points from a cloth store didn't count any more. The salesman looked puzzled and I didn't offer an explanation.

The lawn sale before summer set in was quite an event and if you were not savvy, you could end up as collateral damage. The crowds put me off and I waited out the sale. I wasn't very fond of the really fine fabric which people seemed willing to die for.

Islamabad also has a dedicated Facebook page appropriately called Islamabad Snob where you can post about events in the city. I did post once on a Parsi businessman from Mumbai who often travelled to the capital to sell Indian goods like saris and jewellery. I met him at a guest house; he had brought his mother along and she sat in a plush chair in a corner, while people came and looked at his exotic Indian clothes and jewellery.

The capital may seem unreal and detached, but it is a city which also witnessed furious and prolonged protests by lawyers when the then Supreme Court chief justice, Iftikhar Chaudhry, was removed, along with other judges summarily in 2007 by General Musharraf. It may not have the bustle and culture of rallies and crowds that Karachi has, but people did take to the streets often, especially after the church bombings, the Shia attacks and the attempts to terrorize journalists and media houses. The lawyers' protest was, in a way, a major one, coming as it did after so many years of repression, and people are still proud of that phase in Pakistan's history. I had not realized the mark it had left till I saw the procession on Justice Chaudhry's last day in office. I was at PTV that day for an interview and couldn't leave as the gates were shut. Outside, Justice Chaudhry was being taken out in a procession—there was much shouting and sloganeering, and we ran to the wall surrounding the PTV headquarters opposite Parliament to watch. In the darkness all I could see were cars moving slowly and white-shirted lawyers shouting. The PTV journalists were impressed; they told me, 'This is Pakistan—this won't happen anywhere else.'

'Bollywood film hai, ticket milega?'

The city's first mall, Centaurus, had just opened before I arrived and it had a multiplex cinema which was a bonus (there were no other cinemas, in case you are wondering). I loved movies, and though DVDs were an option, there's nothing like the big screen. In fact, thanks to my friends there, I ended up seeing very bad Hindi films which I would have avoided. (I preferred to see movies on my own in Mumbai, since most people tend to chatter all through.) Sitting in that packed hall, I could feel a buzz of approval for Bollywood, and no matter how terrible the films were, they ran to full houses, and people loved every minute. I seemed to be in the minority. In fact, they didn't even want to know anything about the film before watching it. Once when I went to buy tickets, I heard a woman asking, *'Bollywood film hai, ticket milega?'* I count among the worst films I ever saw *Main Tera Hero*, which, to my astonishment, was highly appreciated. Even my friend who was the one who wanted to see it, said it wasn't so bad! People loved the locales, especially if it was Mumbai, which looked great on screen, much better than it did in reality. They would be awestruck by the sea and Marine Drive, and I rose in esteem because I came from this city of dreams and glamour. In fact, moviegoing became a regular activity. I went alone to see the Pakistani film *Waar* which was praised for its high production values, and I sat in a hall full of clapping Pakistanis, and squirmed at the stereotypes—the Indian agent, Lakshmi, had set a honey trap for a Pakistani businessman (how predictable) and there was much vocal appreciation for her role; since she fitted in with a stereotype of an Indian woman spy enticing a poor Pakistani, the Taliban was full of Indian agents, and so on. It was tacky, clichéd and the English dialogue often bordered on the hilarious. I did read some real criticism of this film and was happy to find I wasn't alone in my distaste. I concluded that the young people sitting next to me were indiscriminate; by the interval, they seemed enchanted—I heard them say it was fabulous, and they were ecstatic that such a film was made, and Pakistan had never seen anything like this. I couldn't believe we were watching the same film. There was much clapping and hooting, especially when the Indians were exposed but that was not the reason I didn't find anything to like in the film. I don't know if Pakistanis reacted similarly to *Sarfarosh*, which also has stereotyped agents, but at least it was a slicker film with some decent acting. I also watched bad Hollywood. *Gravity*, with Sandra Bullock uttering guttural sounds in bluey 3D outer space, was exasperating and not redeemed by George Clooney. There was another theatre in nearby Bahria Town, which was off limits, so watching Naseeruddin Shah in *Zinda Bhaag* had to wait till I got a bad copy in Delhi. The soundtrack was, however, available at Kuch Khaas, and the highlight was a superb *qawwali* by Rahat Fateh Ali Khan.

In fact, most Pakistanis internalized Bollywood so much they almost believed that Holi was celebrated exactly as it was shown in the movies, with *pichkaris* and colours, and long, flowing outfits. I tried telling people I knew that Holi was dreaded in some parts of the country and synonymous with balloon throwing, blinding people, and the licence to molest women. It was a festival I avoided, and in Mumbai, I would even prefer to leave the city for a few days to avoid being doused with water balloons on the way to work. Suburban trains were targeted, especially the women's compartments—Holi had assumed criminal proportions. There were cases of women going blind, thanks to water balloons being thrown at them. Besides, those balloons didn't always have water. The colours were toxic and caused allergies. It was a day to be spent indoors. But I was wasting my time telling this to my friends in Pakistan—they thought I was making it all up. On the other hand, Basant, the kite festival that takes place in March every year, was banned in Lahore; one of the several reasons being that the use of the *manjha*, or the glass-coated twine used to fly kites, led to too many accidents, with the lethal string cutting the throats of innocent passers-by. In fact, I once got a message that Holi was going to be celebrated at a secret venue in Islamabad, but I didn't reply since the source was anonymous and sounded like a hoax.

Bollywood reigns supreme

While we were in Hyderabad city in Pakistan (during my visit in November 2011), Aishwarya Rai, Bollywood actor and model, had just given birth to a baby girl. That was the day we had a meeting with business leaders, and at lunchtime while we tried to get interviews, TV crews hounded us, the women in the delegation, asking our views about this event which they thought was breaking news and momentous. I asked them why only the women were questioned and they, the breathless, bright-eyed and bushy-tailed (that's definitely something we have in common) TV reporters said they were wondering if we would be upset if it was a girl and would we say so on camera! We were speechless with indignation! That didn't earn us too many brownie points and for some moments Indo-Pak relations tottered on the brink!

In Pakistan I found that even the most serious journalists, and there were many, would take the trouble to come and introduce themselves and ask you about the political scene quickly before launching with great deliberation on their favourite subject. Not being a big Bollywood fan and not even clued into filmi gossip, I would dread these encounters and fob them off by asking about things that interested me in Pakistan. Two years later when a delegation of the Karachi Press Club visited Mumbai, a meeting was arranged with actor Aamir Khan. One of the journalists said after the meeting that he didn't have anything more to wish for in his life! (*'Bas ab aur koi kwaish nahin raha!'*) This amused me no end, as I hadn't suspected this serious sports journalist of such a weakness.

Indian TV serials are popular and the dresses the women wear in them are much sought after. In Islamabad, a journalist craved the bindis the women wore and I gave her the only packet I had. My husband's encounter with a security officer when he was returning home via Lahore was enough to make him swear off that route again. He was buttonholed by the officer while he was locked up in a room in transit waiting for the next flight to Delhi. No fancy transit lounges there. On learning that he was an Indian, the officer spoke of how addicted he was to Indian soaps and he was in a hurry to go home to watch the next episode of some TV serial which Venkat had never seen. In fact, he had rescheduled his shift in such a way that he would never miss the episodes. He was anxious about what would happen and when Venkat was non-committal and couldn't conceal his lack of interest, the officer asked him, first, if he had been to Salman Khan's house and then why he and the whole country couldn't prevent a breakup between Salman Khan and all his girlfriends. He felt no one in India was doing enough to ensure that Khan got married, and beseeched Venkat to seek the highest intervention. Salman Khan's wedded bliss being of little or no interest to Venkat, the conversation petered out into a monologue which only ended when the flight to Delhi was announced—a period which my husband said felt like a decade. Traumatized by being locked up in that stuffy room, smoking with an official droning on about Bollywood, TV serials and broken love affairs of stars, the next time he visited, Venkat returned via Karachi where he could stay in a hotel.

Lots of goodwill but no real change

For the cynics who groan and don't get carried away by Pakistani hospitality, I must say that this unconditional affection and warmth is overwhelming. For instance, during my first visit to Pakistan, when I went to Karachi, groups of people with rose garlands were waiting for us at the airport. Our delegation of Indian journalists was clearly unprepared for the effusive welcome and the unending receptions and felicitations and being honoured with the traditional Sindhi black, white and red Ajrakh shawls of which we amassed a large collection by the time we left.

We had come to Karachi three years after the brazen 26 November 2008 terror attack on Mumbai, and most of us in the delegation were not only from Mumbai, but had reported and lived through it. While the 'composite dialogue' was all but shot to pieces after that, there were consistent attempts by people across the border to forge better relations. There was widespread condemnation of the Mumbai attack and it was felt that this must never be repeated. Karachi itself witnessed two blasts while our press club delegation was visiting, and much like Mumbai, the people seemed shaken but stoic.

There was much bonhomie and nostalgia but quite a few present at the first meeting in the club felt a sense of déjà vu and said it had to go beyond that and result in tangible gains. There were some sensible suggestions from people tired of these successive feel-good sessions without any results. One came from Muhammed Badar Alam, editor of the *Herald* magazine, who clearly said that the problem with interactions between the people of India and Pakistan is that often they tend to become emotional and that was not surprising since they shared the same history and culture, and were divided later. Visits generated instant goodwill without any tangible benefits, and it is important to create constituencies of peace within a society.

The lack of a free media exchange meant that during the 26 November attacks, no Pakistani journalist was allowed to visit and report the attacks, except for the two permitted in India. Eternal optimists like Karamat Ali and B.M. Kutty hoped that the momentum for change would continue. We visited some official institutions and the University of Karachi, where women outnumbered the male students by 70 per cent. Tensions between liberal and conservative students were visible in the colourful posters, some calling for rock music parties while others put up by the conservative Islami Jamiat Talibat (girls' wing, IJT), the student wing of the Jamaat-e-Islami (JeI), spoke of how the students' hearts were in the West while they lived in the East.

Karachi University has perhaps contributed more to the language of peace with confidence-building measures (CBMs) and people-to-people contact programmes which has changed the vocabulary of bilateral talks. It also runs a popular course on CBMs. Peace between the two countries can improve academic relations and research possibilities, and the university has a number of collaborations with Indians, leaving aside political differences. Academically, at least, peace is the motto.

The play's the thing

The theatre scene is rather non-existent in the capital and so the few plays staged ran to capacity. It was exciting to watch *Sawa 14 August*, a play written by Anwar Maqsood and directed by Dawar Mehmood, at the Pakistan National Centre for Arts, an elegant brick complex, where they don't let you in till a few minutes before the show. So everyone had to freeze outside and the queue kept getting longer, full of people muttering in anger. Once we got inside, the place was overflowing and people were sitting on the staircases and aisles. It was one of the few significant cultural events in the city and people made the most of it. The play was a take on the political situation in Pakistan and the legacy of Jinnah and Bhutto. The actors smoked real cigarettes I think, and in the stuffy hall it made people cough. But it was a live theatre experience which I enjoyed and it made you laugh while questioning the current situation by taking you through history and the erratic political leadership.

Other entertainment included a bowling alley where we went once to celebrate a friend's birthday; it seemed to be popular and was fun, though I can't imagine it becoming a habit. I didn't know I had latent bowling skills. There was also a large trampoline and a mini golf course—in a desolate play area by the lake. Another game involved wearing special clothes and shooting paint at each other. It didn't entice me in the least.

Since there wasn't much by way of entertainment, films were the cheap way out. I was advised not to bring CDs or DVDs, and so had to buy everything in Islamabad. I bought a simple music system and a DVD player. Fortunately, copyright was taken to mean the right to copy, and music and films, all kinds were available easily. I didn't see any original films or CDs, and managed to get a large collection of copies of old Hollywood films which were expensive elsewhere, and watching movies at night was the norm if I had nothing else to do. Similarly with music; I wasn't sure if I could bring CDs from home, so I bought copies of a lot of music, including the best of Pink Floyd, Pashto pop, classical music, both Indian and Western, jazz and rock, as well as the Coke studio albums which were among my favourites. I found very good copies of most of the albums I used to listen to at home. Pink Floyd kind of grew on me and I didn't know what it was but the haunting music and the lyrics seemed so appropriate there, and I always switched it on when I entered the house. Pink Floyd and Pakistan would remain connected in my mind. One had to be 'comfortably numb' to survive sometimes.

3

On Being a Foreign Correspondent

It was my first posting outside India. I was a foreign correspondent in a not-so foreign country. Things were at once easy and difficult. From the word go, people were helpful and it was easier than I thought. You had to be grateful for things you could access and also accept that some things would remain out of bounds—which later came to include the whole country! One of my colleagues was told that my stories were too critical of the country. At some level, like most countries, there is an 'if you are not with us, then you must be against us' attitude.

Before leaving for Islamabad, I had long discussions with Anita and Nirupama, the two colleagues who were posted in Pakistan before me. I was saved a lot of the spadework about setting up the house, and so on, and learnt many dos and don'ts. One of the things I was warned about was speaking politely. I was from Mumbai, and our Bambaiya Hindi was not known for any degree of formality or correctness. Unlike Hindi, which has a strict grammar with masculine, feminine and a neutral gender, our imperfect slang has no such demarcations—we women can get away with saying '*mai ata hoon*' and other atrocities. Words and sentences were short and to the point; no niceties were observed and everyone was as rude as they liked. Swearing was the norm.

I found that since Pakistanis were addicted to Bollywood, the slang was familiar to them but I didn't try it out.

Most of the time we spoke in English but when I switched to Hindi or Urdu, I had to remember to say the right things, keeping the correct gender in mind and also the Urdu greeting and the reply. Not knowing Urdu can be a severe handicap, even though I liked poetry and ghazals. And the fact that I was a South Indian didn't help. There was a comical bias against 'Madrasis' (all the South Indians are called this in India too, so it's a bias not restricted to Pakistan), and the stereotype included the belief that we were some uncultured, dark louts, not used to the freezing northern climate and bundling up in excess for the cold. In fact, once someone in Delhi on a freezing winter morning heritage walk, remarked that I was dressed like a 'Madrasi'. Many people I met joked about our lack of appreciation of Punjabi which I didn't know in any case. Once at a party when Punjabi poetry was being recited, I asked for a translation and was soundly ticked off. I concluded that Punjabi pride is as great as the hospitality, and my asking for a translation had kind of insulted the great language—or so the politician who was reciting it said. The loss was mine!

So I had to think carefully and frame sentences fully before I spoke; it took me twice as long to say anything politely but I learnt how to. Once when I posted Ghalib's poetry on Facebook, my Punjabi friend (I really didn't think of him like that) was shocked that I knew it. I told my friend that just as the 'Madrasis' are vilified, the Punjabis, or Punjoos, are stereotyped as ostentatious, loud people in India who have lavish weddings. I found them a warm, hospitable community, proud of their language and culture, and often clashing with the equally proud, hospitable and charming Pashtuns. It was quite funny at a harmless, friendly level but nationally, it was the basis of a serious political divide. Once when a lawyer spoke in Punjabi to a Pashtun friend, she snapped at him and asked him to speak to her in a language she could understand! Even in our circle of friends, there would be these fights which became very serious at times.

Spooks on my trail

A lot of people ask me if I volunteered to go to Pakistan. That was not the case. I didn't imagine I would ever be a correspondent there and was surprised to hear I was nominated. When I was asked by Siddharth Varadarajan, then editor of *The Hindu,* whether I would like to be posted in Islamabad, I didn't think twice before saying yes. After my visit to Karachi and Hyderabad in 2011, I was excited about going to the capital even if it meant getting stuck there with little hope of travel. I realized it was a much-envied posting, and one of the more memorable reactions came from a former journalist and foreign relations expert who was so excited that she asked me to leave all my clothes at home and get them all done there! The exquisite tailoring in Pakistan had a reputation of its own. I admit this was the last thing on my mind, as generally I find it tiresome to run around to tailors, though I did get some stuff stitched there.

Initially I was lulled into a sense of well-being because of the warmth of people and the comfort of living in Islamabad. It was the end of the summer when we got there and soon the temperatures dropped, and we didn't even need fans. The first question that many would ask me was: 'Are you being tailed?' or 'Where are your friends'?' It was during a routine visit to the visa office in January 2014, with its corridors reeking of urine, that I realized that I was really being tailed. Two men literally walked into me, it could not have been an accident—a bearded creature in a salwar kameez who tried to leer all the time while trying to look grim and failing; and a younger man, chubby, and awkward about what he was doing. I will name them Beard and Chubby. That same evening they walked into a café where I was waiting to meet someone for an interview. I was sitting in a plush sofa near the door when Beard pushed open the glass door and stopped suddenly on seeing me. Satisfied that he had 'terrorized' me, he shut the door abruptly and walked outside. I sometimes wished their intelligence could be put to better use, for instance, stopping young men blowing themselves up in public places or preventing them from wrecking churches, courts and marketplaces. The first time I went to the house of an Indian diplomat, we got out hesitantly from the car and a burly red-moustached man was there to welcome us; he announced my name with satisfaction. I was impressed he knew my name and was so welcoming, but the diplomat laughed and said that they were his 'friends'. Some well-meaning people went to the extent of telling me that these guys were meant for my safety and that they could be quite helpful; one Britisher said they helped his parents get a rickshaw in Lahore when they were struggling with the language. I was relieved to hear that spooks were tailing people from other countries as well. To the credit of Pakistanis, they knew I had this baggage, but they would rarely refuse to meet me or entertain me in their homes, and often it was a subject of much laughter and jokes. My driver, too, was constantly pestered for information and he was quite savvy about the goings-on in the capital. Even if they obviously didn't follow me everywhere, they would know where I went and land up there and grill people endlessly on why I was meeting them, what I wanted to know, and whether I asked any 'sensitive' questions.

How was I supposed to do stories without getting around? Only one NGO didn't allow them inside where I was to attend a meeting—otherwise they came everywhere. They would pounce on my friends and ask them for information—if I had discussed defence matters (very funny) and if I had wanted any secret information. And once when a friend was particularly dogged about not talking, they invoked the patriotic question and said that she must tell them what I had said in 'the name of Pakistan'. That did it for her and she really tore them apart and told them off about lecturing her on her national duties. They also felt free to stand outside the walls and take pictures or intrude into houses and ask questions. They seemed to have a carte blanche and nothing and no one could stop them.

Spooks are seemingly bumbling and inept but can annoy you, a little like flies buzzing around. Only you can't swat them. I was told to pretend that they didn't exist which was difficult, but possible and even amusing. They looked very silly tailing my husband and me on a hike, right from when we left our house. It's walking distance to the trail and they got off their bikes a little before Faisal Mosque. Every time I stopped to take a picture, Beard would stand in front of me and speak loudly into the phone. By then my anger had turned into amusement and most of the time, I was stifling my giggles and concentrating on my frame (the auto focus helped), and as the hike progressed they must have realized how pointless it was and that there was no deep plot to uncover. The Margalla Hills have six main trails and Trail 6 is behind Faisal Mosque. We weaved in and out of the Sunday crowd, with little boys selling pink candyfloss and fried papads. While I was taking pictures, Beard was standing close enough for me to hear his drivelling commentary on my movements. I stopped deliberately to change lenses, to shoot the top of the rocket-like minarets and the giant, burnished crescent on Faisal Mosque. A young boy selling papad was perplexed by this semicircle of attention—I was taking pictures, my husband was next to me, and Beard was jabbering into the phone. It was ludicrous. We had been trekking in the hills for a while, and this was our third time on this trail, and the only time we were so closely followed. I must be grateful that I was not stopped from hiking, though that seemed to be the general idea, with all this intimidatory tailing and furious chattering into the phone. The Margalla Hills had been off limits for Amit Baruah while he was posted there, but luckily no one stopped us (Nirupama also trekked a lot in the hills and in fact, I met a friend of hers by coincidence while he was hiking on Trail 5). Trekking was a passion for both my husband and me, and we used to trek often in the Sahyadris in Maharashtra, with its wide range of hills and forts, and even in the Himalaya. We couldn't believe our luck with the Margalla Hills, and used to joke that it was like having the Sahyadris in our backyard. I kept reading about a proposed tunnel through the hills to connect to a new city in Abbottabad, and there would be periodic protests by environmentalists. It is a precious ecosystem in the capital and it would be a pity if it were damaged.

It was 26 January 2014, our Republic Day, a cold and blue morning, and we were kitted out for a long haul. Not so Beard and Chubby. Dressed in tight, uncomfortable clothes and pointed leather shoes, they heaved up the hill with no food or water, and kept asking the odd person on the trail if there was another way of going down. At the beginning of the leafy trail, every time I looked back they would dodge into the bushes on the side. When we stopped to rest at a lovely rocky pool fringed by palms, Beard and Chubby watched us eat apples and drink water. When I moved on the rocks to take pictures, they moved too. At a particularly narrow path, I almost stepped on Beard's pointed leather shoe but he didn't flinch and sat there like one of the many rocks. That was too close for comfort but I refused to be put off by their stupid tactics. Once I had to ask Chubby to move from my camera frame as I didn't want my picture spoilt by a spook in a muffler. He grinned and moved. Beard was already featured in an earlier shot, looking gloomily into the distance. At one point I could hear him speaking to someone loudly and telling him nothing was happening. The joke was on them. They sat down before the last climb over a bare portion of the hill, waiting for us to come down. The top was lovely with a canopy of trees and a single house. A few other trekkers were lying flat on the ground, looking up at the beautiful sky. It was all so glorious—the trees, the skies, the breeze rustling the leaves. Nothing could spoil it for us. Someone needs to tell whoever is sending these poor guys that hiking is a pleasurable pastime, quite distinct from spying. They didn't know we Indians are experts at finding shortcuts too! At the top we found a traverse to the other side and trudged a couple of hours, with the route circling the edge of the hills, offering excellent views of Rawal dam and lake. It was doubly exhilarating. And we walked down to the restaurant at Kuch Khaas, for a much-needed meal. It was a cheap thrill, and didn't last. (That the spying can have a crassness about it, I found out on the last day in the country.) The next morning I went for a business visa meeting organized by the Indian high commission at a five-star hotel, and walking into the lobby, I saw Beard and couldn't stop myself from greeting him with a bright 'good morning'! Secretly I wondered what happened after they waited for us on that hilltop. Beard was not amused, he replied with a grim 'okay'. That was the only exchange we ever had.

Once on a trail behind the golf course which was supposed to lead up into the hills, which we didn't find, we came across an old village, including an old and disused haveli. The women had the most extraordinary pink cheeks, and they were amused that we were looking for some trail early in the morning. The village opened out into a clearing with the hills at the back and we didn't have the energy to look for the trail leading up. Finally we walked around and emerged on a road somewhere near a secured defence area. We kept our heads down and walked fast, worried we would be picked up for snooping.

The top of the Margalla Hills was ridged with tall trees, even pine in some places, and in the rains we were told the waterfalls were furious. The easily negotiable paths had small rock pools and rocky traverses which didn't test your stamina. There was one route on Trail 5 with a wooden board pointing downwards saying 'Dangerous Trail' and we took that once to find it was steep all the way up to a place where it joined the main trail just before the rocky outcrop at the top. It was a wonderful climb with great views of the hills, but no place to rest. Another trail led us to Daman-i-Koh which has a terrace to view the city. It's very crowded on holidays, with families on their outing having ice cream. The view is much better from Monal or from any of the traverses on the trails. We preferred hiking to the many social events, but they were a place to meet people and it was fun in some ways. I did not emulate some of my earlier colleagues who threw a lot of parties, and this difference was painfully pointed out to me many times. I was even accused of that stellar crime '*kanjusi*', or miserliness, and a lack of generosity. Friends of former colleagues from my paper would rave about the parties they had attended, but I didn't quite see myself in a hostess avatar.

But Beard and Chubby were a pesky end of the spectrum, and their masters, the sinister side of it. Kindness was the norm and not the exception. I soon ran out of passport-size photographs for various forms and ID cards, and went to a shop near my house. Each time I applied for a pass to cover the National Assembly or Senate or for the visa, I had to provide fresh pictures. The owner of the studio was amazed that I was from India. He shyly confessed that it was the first time he had set eyes on an Indian and was full of admiration. He didn't suspect me of being a spy, and happily gave me a hefty discount and enough photographs to last me for a couple of years. That morning the Mumbai Press Club delegation was set to meet the foreign secretary, Jalil Abbas Jilani, but I was told we couldn't go along. The external publicity officer was stern in refusing us permission. He clearly told me I wouldn't be allowed to accompany the delegation. It was another matter that Jilani had sent a very welcoming mail to my former editor asking me to be comfortable during my stay, which I was. The visiting delegation met the President and other important people, while the two Indians stationed in Islamabad were mostly refused such requests.

The distance between our countries was not great; it was shorter than some Indian cities but the chasm in our minds was cavernous. Thankfully, the best propaganda had not killed the natural instinct of a human to trust another. While buying DVDs at a music shop, the salesman was so thrilled I was from Mumbai, his dream city, that he gave me a free DVD. He was very solicitous and promised to record any film I wanted which he didn't have on his list. Once after a TV discussion on business and MFN,[1] the charming anchor laughingly told me off-camera that all this hostility and suspicion would end if I brought Kareena Kapoor and other Bollywood stars to the border. A retired general on the show, usually affable, bristled and said, 'We have so many beautiful women in Pakistan including you [meaning the anchor].'

Once I dropped my phone in the toilet, causing much mirth, and it was soaked for a while before I found it. The Samsung service centre went out of its way to repair it in record time. I had no hope of getting my numbers, many of which were newly added, but it was a miracle that they repaired the phone. And because I was an Indian, it was free, they said, and even offered me a cup of tea. Of course, my doubting friends said they must have downloaded all my data and I shouldn't have left my phone with them. In fact, visiting Indian friends cribbed that they were always shortchanged and overcharged!

Many people asked me how I managed as a woman and if there were any safety issues. I also got some requests asking me to explain how to be a foreign correspondent. I was the third woman to be posted in Pakistan by *The Hindu*, and by now I thought this question 'Oh, how can a woman manage alone?' should have been answered satisfactorily. The curiosity was not only about how I managed as a woman, but as a woman in 'enemy' country. 'How can you live in such a place?' was the usual reaction from people. Some male colleagues believed that women were unsuited for being posted in Pakistan, though Nirupama disproved that early on. This is largely to do with our perceptions of Pakistan as a country since not enough Indians get to travel there, though the number of visitors is increasing. The same worry wouldn't be there for people from other countries, say the USA or London, though there are risks. Pakistan has dreadful connotations, and someone going to live and report in that country becomes at once enormously courageous or foolish. There are people who tend to draw similarities with soldiers fighting the enemy. A politician I knew joked when I met him in New Delhi: 'Why did you go to Pakistan? To fight a war?' Some people even wanted to shake my hand for surviving for nine months. There are several forces at play in Pakistan which is grappling with a feudal past, fundamentalism and terrorism, and this colours most of our perceptions, with much of the media portrayal reinforcing the image of a backward and failed state. It is little wonder then that visitors are pleasantly surprised when they see glimpses of a country that is different from what they think it is. That is not to say that Pakistan does not have several problems, as it is shackled by an unequal society, huge income disparities, a shaky economy and sectarianism and terrorism. Viewing it through a hostile lens, a country which is fighting a proxy war with India, and is held to be responsible for the many terror strikes, adds to the contradictions. And so, in the midst of all this, if someone is actually living and reporting from there, it becomes quite a job! You can be admired or denigrated.

Work kept me busy most of the day, filing stories through the evening. Reporting is often a lonely job and over the years, I found I was happiest being on my own. Solicitous Pakistanis would often drop in and check if I was okay and they sometimes mistook my preoccupation with work as a slight. The charmed circle in the capital which met for dinner at 7 p.m. found it difficult to understand that it was our deadline time, and often I would file stories or answer queries from the desk in the middle of social gatherings. The half-hour advantage in Islamabad was a relief at times. The day when I attended a rally on Defence of Pakistan Day in September 2013, Ayesha Siddiqa had invited us for dinner. The rally finished at 10 p.m. and I was filing my story on the phone. I got to her place in Bani Gala very late and for some reason the story vanished from my email and was not sent.

My evening was ruined, though Ayesha tried to be helpful and said I could resend the story on her computer. It just didn't work. The next day my editor said he didn't want a routine news story, and I needed to rework it and so it all ended quite well. Once, just as I was going out, the government was returning Sarabjit Singh's (the suspected Indian spy who died in jail in Pakistan) belongings, and I had to make a few calls and type the story immediately.

Everyone oozed charm and concern and that can be disconcerting sometimes if you are used to being left alone. Despite war, deep suspicion and hostility I made friends, and I didn't quite feel I was living in an 'enemy' country for most of the time, except when the presence of spooks became hard to ignore and any victory over India was celebrated with unholy glee.

I was foolish enough to think I could work on a book on the history of cotton with a friend who is a cotton expert, back in India; and in my little spare time I tried to focus on it, but without any success. In Mumbai, other than political party dinners or get-togethers which was for work, social life was really at a minimum, since we worked very late and travelled long distances. Parties were impromptu and there was no calling important people home and socializing. It was mostly close friends who got together, at least in my case. I think Islamabad would probably gasp if it didn't get that dose of parties and social gatherings.

One place we felt quite welcome was the foreign office and I rarely missed the weekly briefing by the spokesperson. The thick carpets with floral designs and the elaborate chandeliers which hung from high ceilings gave it an old-world, warm feeling. The delicious hot and crisp samosas with paneer and spinach stuffing were worth coming a little early for; otherwise, you had to settle for the potato ones, which were almost as tasty. We met the then spokesperson and later Foreign Secretary Aizaz Ahmad Chaudhary who was warm and welcoming. He was one of the few officials who would respond to text messages and was forthcoming, like his successor Tasneem Aslam despite diplomatic guardedness.

It was a good place to meet people and also a way to get clarity on any new developments, though after a while, the diplomatic answers got on your nerves. The spokesperson was patient, and answered everything as best as he or she could.

I arrived in August 2013 and the euphoria of a second democratically elected government in Pakistan had not died down. There was a breathlessness about the smooth transition, though Imran Khan kept up a high-decibel campaign of claiming the results were rigged and he went right up to the Supreme Court with his accusation. Prime minister for the third time, Nawaz Sharif was seen as favourable to India, and the Pakistanis were fond of repeating that the election campaign was devoid of India bashing. The new mantra was that the Pakistan government was all for peace with India. Sharif, in his first address to the nation, emphasized the importance of Kashmir, referring to it as the jugular vein of Pakistan in a time-honoured manner. Indians called it an inalienable part, or '*atoot ang*' (literally, a limb which cannot be broken) in Hindi. My friends in the media in Islamabad often joked about this 'atoot ang'; it was Hindi they couldn't understand. For some time after Vajpayee visited Lahore, this reference to 'atoot ang' had stopped. The Kashmiris were squeezed between being the jugular vein and 'atoot ang', and a syncretic culture fell apart. Young men crossed the border to become terrorists or freedom fighters depending upon which side you were on; the mujahideen trained in Pakistan wreaked violence in the name of liberating Kashmir; the threatened Kashmiri Pandits fled fearing for their lives—those who were not killed that is; and tourists trampled over the valley's sorrow.

Sharif, who rose to power with army and religious sections backing him, now wanted to change things. Some said he was the one who was in favour of giving us Indian journalists our visas. He has roots in Kashmir and many of his aides are from that region. There are many stories of his penchant for Kashmiri food or food in general, but people told me that unlike

Asif Zardari who was perceived to be a forgiving person, Sharif was not likely to forget his humiliation of exile in a hurry. So it was providential for him that General Musharraf chose to return to his country.

Between victory and defeat

Early on in my stay, I was puzzled by news of Victory Day streaming on news bulletins, and then the accompanying celebrations. There were reams of photos of young men killed in action. The government channel, PTV, was full of discussions and programmes on those days and I realized that even if Pakistanis had not really won a single war, the government commemorated each ceasefire as a victory. You could be fooled into thinking that it had emerged victorious in all the wars it had embarked on, starting with sending mujahideen fighters into Kashmir in 1947, on to Operation Gibraltar in 1965, the Kargil operation in 1999 and, most important of all, 1971, when it lost East Pakistan much to its eternal chagrin.

The sixth of September, Youm-e-Difa, or Defence Day, marked the 1965 war, a cause for much celebration. I thought the war ended in a UN-brokered ceasefire and I was a little puzzled. Hostilities were sparked off by Operation Desert Hawk and later Operation Gibraltar, but going by the Pakistan media, one would think that India suddenly attacked, causing this brave defence. I watched the celebrations on TV, the tribute to the martyrs, and I was genuinely perplexed. I thought I had got it all wrong. But then I realized that this was one of the many wars won by Pakistan and it had never lost one with India right from 1947. War and the blowback from terrorism had cost Pakistan heavily. I met many Pakistanis who didn't support this need for a security state, and there were many voices for peace. Later (in 2014), I attended a candid discussion on Kargil at the Islamabad Literature Festival. Journalists and top diplomats said that it was an avoidable adventure, and lessons should be learnt from it for better coordination between the civilian government and the military.

Tensions on the LoC were ongoing and a mandatory item of reporting, but I never managed to go beyond the official press releases from the ISPR. Firing from both sides of the border, sometimes resulting in injuries and fatalities to civilians, had to be reported, even if sketchily. Some years back, during a visit to the Rann of Kutch, the Border Security Force (BSF) had hosted us and they showed us the border fence, which we easily crossed over through a gap into Tharparkar. It was a shrubby desert and the officer showed us a place marked with white where the flag meetings were held. Camels often crossed over and one of the issues discussed was these lost animals.

It wasn't so peaceful on the LoC and the discussion tackled more serious issues than stray animals.

Being a woman but not Barkha Dutt

I came to realize I had a grave deficiency. I was not Barkha Dutt (for the minuscule minority who may not know her—a celebrity TV journalist who has reported on leading events in India and who, till recently, hosted a popular show). I didn't think this was a drawback till a friendly official in the Prime Minister's Office apologetically told me that an interview with Nawaz Sharif was difficult precisely because I was not Dutt. You see, Sharif had an old equation with her and he was not comfortable giving interviews to people whom he didn't know, or something on those lines. I agreed and fully sympathized with Sharif's discomfort. It was, I told the official, next to impossible for me to reincarnate myself at this late stage, and we both laughed about it. This was in response to a written request for an interview with the PM. Later, I learnt that another TV journalist was not granted an interview with Sharif. I was relieved to be in exalted company.

It was a season of refusals. In the end I didn't get an interview with the President or the prime minister. The request for the President's interview, routed through the external publicity office was rejected, while for the PM, it was just kept pending due to the reasons in the above paragraph. The PM's adviser on foreign affairs and national security, Sartaj Aziz, who was usually happy to accept interview requests was reluctant, even though a close friend had introduced me and I promised him that he could see the transcript. But Aziz brushed aside my assurances and was non-committal about the interview. As I mentioned before, access was granted to a visiting delegation of the Mumbai Press Club to both the President and the foreign secretary—at that time, Jalil Abbas Jilani—and I didn't hear the end of it from my friends who were able to travel to Lahore, Karachi and Islamabad, and meet so many people who were inaccessible to us. The charm is unlocked selectively and for obvious effect. As Indian journalists stationed in the capital on a shoestring visa, we didn't count as important, and we were at the mercy of the powers that be.

Pakistani leaders have, however, been quite open with the Indian press. *Tribune* editor, Raj Chengappa, has interviewed Nawaz Sharif in exile and had flown into Rawalpindi to meet Prime Minister Shaukat Aziz and then General Musharraf. In 1972, Dilip Mukerjee from the *Times of India* visited Pakistan after he was granted an interview with President Zulfikar Ali Bhutto. In his book, Mukerjee quotes from that interview which seemed to be a frank chat on the events after the Bangladesh war of 1971. Bhutto admits that he was having trouble with Yahya Khan and his services chiefs were of no help, which eventually led to him replacing them.[2] The veteran Kuldip Nayar, too, has bagged interviews with Bhutto, Sharif, Benazir and others, and has visited Pakistan repeatedly and written several books. Nayar went to Pakistan after the war in 1971, and he wrote, 'When I entered Pakistan, as an Indian, I felt as though I had walked into the lion's den. But there was no hostility, though curiosity greeted me wherever I went.'[3] Nayar goes on to say, 'The two things uppermost in the people's minds were the POWs [the 90,000 prisoners of war in India after the Bangladesh war] and Bhutto,' said Nayar. Towards India, the attitude of the 'average' Pakistani was one of hostility, he wrote. A typical remark thrown at him was that India was out to destroy Pakistan.[4] However, writer Shobhaa De told me in an interview during the Islamabad Literature Festival that there was no hostility, only hospitality!

Many enduring friendships exist across the border, and a famous example is that between politician and architect Piloo Mody and Zulfikar Ali Bhutto. 'That our friendship has lasted through innumerable quarrels, the partition of the country and four wars, to some extent demonstrates the universality of human nature and the relative insignificance of governments, nations and even nationalism.'[5] The small band of peaceniks believes it can overcome in an atmosphere full of spitfire and suspicion. But not too many Indian leaders have given interviews to the Pakistani journalists and so Indian journalists must be denied. It is after all a tit-for-tat game and we must stoop as low as we can. My editor and colleagues had told me not to bother with interviews since they were rarely granted.

I had to deal with some strange characters who pretended to know you and wanted to take you around. After I made some inquiries about one particular pest, I realized no one knew him and he had no credentials as a journalist. He wanted for some reason to take me to the eating joints near the Quaid-i-Azam University (QAU) which sounded a little shady to me. He once stalked me at a press meeting and stood next to me waiting for an introduction to the people I was with. I didn't bother and he glowered at me. He was a big, beefy man and my friends thought he was going to get violent. The other nuisance was callers wanting to know your name and a lot of other things. I used to save these numbers as Creep 1, 2, and so on, and some were persistent till it got to a point where I had to ask an official to intervene and get the numbers blocked. There was one particular man who was insistent and I had to explain to him on email that I really was not interested in his unflattering attention. My phone had a useful mechanism to reject certain numbers, but the calls were unending. I once told them that this was a police station but they got back and said they knew it wasn't. I then had to hastily disconnect many calls or not take them. It got to a point where it became harassment.

Still, being a woman was the least of my problems while living there. I didn't come across men ogling at me or pawing me (though journalist Kim Barker had some terrible experiences) or people humming songs and making vulgar noises behind me. Moreover, my house was in a relatively safe place. Even though Bollywood masala was hugely popular, fortunately, it didn't penetrate to baser levels of mimicking most Indian filmi heroes who have exalted harassment and sexism into a fine art. That is not to say that sexism or violence against women doesn't exist. Pakistan is as feudal and patriarchal as India, and many horrifying cases of violence are reported regularly. Every day, the *Express Tribune* newspaper would have a crime graph, with locations on the city map and I would anxiously pore over it for cases of robberies and rape. While rapes were few, at least the reported ones in the capital, a large number of robberies took place. One journalist I met in Parliament told me that often the robbers would eat up everything in the house.

The fact that I was an Indian worked against me at one level, though equally and happily, it was also the reason most people went out of their way to help me. The line between me as a journalist and the fact that I was an Indian often tended to blur. Everything was seen and weighed according to whether it was anti-Pakistan, and it had to be, coming from an Indian. So if I interviewed Mama Qadeer Baloch, I must certainly be working against Pakistani interests. When I posted pictures of Islamabad's slums on Facebook, someone took umbrage that I was posting such pictures since I was from India, also a poor country. In fact, in that sanitized city of Islamabad, the slums were the one thing that stuck out for being close to any reality. Everything had to be black and white. My colleague's warning that whatever you do, you will be taken for a RAW agent, came home to me. I was relieved to read Pakistani journalist Raza Rumi's evocative book[6] on New Delhi and he, too, had the same 'unhealthy' curiosity about slums and visiting Dalit *basti*s in the capital.

The Aam Aadmi Party effect

I found that two politicians fascinated Pakistanis. One was Narendra Modi who seems to have quickly replaced Vajpayee in popular memory, and the other was Arvind Kejriwal who had won the Delhi assembly elections then. First it was Arslan-ul-Mulk from Gujranwala whose Aam Aadmi Party (AAP) was registered with the Election Commission of Pakistan (ECP) and then a former foreign services officer and lawyer, thirty-four-year-old Adnan Randhawa had applied to the ECP for registering his Aam Aadmi of Pakistan Party (AAPP).

He was formerly deputy secretary in charge of central information of the PTI led by Imran Khan, a party which has often been likened to the AAP in India. Yet, Randhawa had become disillusioned with the way things were going and the turning point came on 3 March 2014 when he saw the district court being fired at and bombed from his office overlooking the complex. He expected a strong statement from his party which was not forthcoming and it was still harping on a rapprochement with the terrorists. That's when he decided enough was enough and quit his party. He found it difficult to defend his party's stand on terrorism and he felt an out-of-the-box solution was needed.

A diplomat-turned-political worker, he was posted in China for two years before becoming a protocol officer in Pakistan. Like Kejriwal, he too wants to appeal to the educated middle class and end the corruption of the ruling elite. He has studied the AAP phenomenon in India and felt that it had given a voice to the voiceless, and winning the Delhi assembly, a major power centre, was remarkable. Kejriwal symbolized honesty and credibility, and that's what he wanted to emulate in Pakistan. His new party was to bear a resemblance to both the AAP in India and the PTI. He hoped to draw from workers of the PTI who were not status quoists and were sincere. I don't know what became of his venture.

Finding my feet

Before I knew it, I was writing on events around me which had formed a leitmotif of sorts during my stay. One of them was the tension on the LoC, the others were drone strikes, release of Afghan militants, talks with the Taliban, hostility between India and Pakistan, and the unending bombings and attacks on minorities. A few issues would shadow the coverage, and Kashmir was not the only one. Lashkar-e-Taiba founder Hafiz Saeed, a much-wanted man in India, would pop up like a bad penny every now and then; there was the uncertainty of talks or no talks between India and Pakistan, and the focus on army–civilian relations. The eight-point composite dialogue between India and Pakistan was stalled after the 26/11 terror attack. The change of guard in the army, too, was an important event, with Sharif opting for an officer junior to two others in rank despite his public statements that seniority would be the criterion. That was not the first time he was doing that; there was another famous exception he lived to regret. The incumbent chief of army staff, General Ashfaq Kayani, was not given another extension and the new chief, General Raheel Sharif, was reported to be very close to the prime minister. He was the former ISPR head Major General Athar Abbas's batchmate, and I spoke to the latter for my story. Pakistan also had a new President; when Asif Zardari's term expired, I had to write a small piece on his exit and suddenly Mr Ten Per cent, as he was disparagingly known for his corrupt deals, became the great unifier. The talks with the Tehrik-i-Taliban Pakistan (TTP) which meandered aimlessly, the MFN status not given to India in toto, attacks on the media, drone strikes, and the high treason trial dominated the news. Once the high treason trial began, General Pervez Musharraf occupied most of my time, and we had to be in court by 9.30 a.m. or earlier. I did squeeze in some other stories—on polio, textbooks, and on the left parties regrouping. Sharif was hell-bent on the treason trial which was to backfire on him soon. The trial was mired in legal proprieties and even assuming it was a historic decision to prosecute a former dictator, there was a sense of foreboding, and soon everywhere retired generals held meetings to support General Musharraf. It was not easy to take on the army in Pakistan, and Sharif was to be taught a lesson soon. I was not there to see the huge protests launched by Imran Khan's PTI and Tahir-ul-Qadri, a cleric, and the Blue and Red areas, a high-security zone, with restricted entry, were jammed for weeks with these anti-Sharif protests.

I was also offered an interview with Dawood Ibrahim, quite by chance, but nothing came of it. Evidence given by Yakub Memon, who was hanged in 2015 for his involvement in the serial bomb blasts of March 1993 in Mumbai, points to Dawood Ibrahim and Yaqub's older brother Tiger Memon living in Pakistan, which had given them refuge. Pakistan has repeatedly denied that Dawood or Tiger Memon are in residence and there would be surges of evidence surfacing in the media in the form of taped conversations and Dawood's addresses in Pakistan. So far, he has been untraceable, though the Indian government firmly believes he is a guest in Pakistan. At a party I attended in Islamabad, I met a man who asked me if I wanted an interview with Dawood Ibrahim. I said yes, thinking it was a joke. Later when I mentioned this to some friends, they said Islamabad was full of people ready to get you an interview with Dawood.

The main stories coming out of Pakistan were usually about terror, bomb blasts and the 26/11 case, and before coming to Islamabad I used to read the updates on the case by the Press Trust of India's Rezaul Hasan Laskar who was posted there from 2007 till 2013. For an Indian journalist stuck in Islamabad with little hope of travelling anywhere else, I had to be innovative, and learn to make do with the limited possibilities in the capital. My editor had told me glibly that I would get to know everyone there was to know within three months. There was plenty to do, I found, the least of which was meeting people. I aimed at meeting at least one new person a day, a maxim from one of my friends, and things seemed to be going well. There were many resources at my disposal; people even came up with suggestions which were constructive, and my journalist colleagues and contacts from my predecessors' time were very helpful and obliging with information. So when one TV journalist I knew was questioned by the ISI or whoever, after he had coffee with me and another reporter, it became a joke. They asked him if I wanted to know anything about the defence installations or the army. He told them that even if I wanted that information, he was the last person I would have asked. There is a persisting undercurrent in their notion about Indian journalists—we are seemingly always on the lookout for classified information which we can pass on to our 'handlers' in New Delhi. When officials in the Indian high commission had once asked me to tell them what I was filing on a daily basis and even send the copy to them, I had refused to do so. All they had to do was read the newspaper, and all my stories were usually used first online almost immediately, and in the newspaper the next day. There was nothing hidden about my reports or activities, contrary to the suspicions voiced in the Pakistani media after the visa was not extended. Some of the Indian officials were helpful with stories and confirmed or denied matters, especially in connection with Indian fisherfolk or prisoners, and all of them were friendly and extremely hospitable, always hosting us for lunch or dinner. That didn't mean I was spying for them.

Apart from meeting people, covering day-to-day political events involved going to the National Assembly or Senate, attending press conferences, the weekly foreign office briefing, the Supreme Court, or the special court once the Musharraf trial started. Political parties, too, had press conferences, like the PMLN or the PTI, the Jamaat-e-Islami, the Jamiat Ulema-e-Hind, and the Pakistan Muslim League (Quaid) (PML[Q]). There was an openness about certain things—I attended special committee meetings of Parliament. I grew to like the Parliament canteen and the open terrace outside where it was a pleasure to sit in the evenings. The food was good and the kebabs and fish were particular favourites. It was a place where I could meet journalists and many parliamentarians who were very friendly even if they made anti-India statements on granting MFN and other issues in the House. The Parliament library was well stocked with shelf after shelf of all the records of Indian parliamentary proceedings since Independence, which the friendly librarian proudly showed me.

Islamabad was a seminar city and every day there were several events, some of which were interesting and yielded stories and useful contacts. Some, of course, were deathly boring but I attended most of them in the hope of getting story ideas and meeting new people. The Sustainable Development Policy Institute, the Jinnah Institute, the Institute of Strategic Studies, the many UN organizations and government departments, too, had events open to the press. Ministers and their office staff were usually helpful and happy to meet and talked frankly about issues. The ministry of interior had many press conferences at the lavish Punjab House on top of a hill which reminded me of one of the royal outhouses in Versailles with its opulent archways and lush lawns, and fountains. Below elaborate chandeliers and in elegant interiors, with intricate floral screens and lace-covered chairs, the minister would hold forth on inelegant subjects. From Punjab House you could see the whole city stretching out in front of you, glowing dully in the dusk. Compared to the 'houses' of other provinces, this was the most lavish, and the winding road to the top was lined with gorgeous blue-purple jacaranda. The interior minister, Chaudhry Nisar Ali Khan, was not a man of few words and his preamble could easily take an hour. He was a bit theatrical and much to our despair, he would always call a press meet on Sunday at 6 p.m., making everyone groan. Despite his long-winded speeches, he would say something important which had to be filed and there would be a scramble to get home. I would usually start typing the story on my phone while listening to the recording so that I didn't miss the deadline. Especially memorable was the press conference after TTP leader Hakimullah Mehsud had been killed. Chaudhry Nisar thundered against the US for the drone attack that killed Mehsud just before he was to join the peace talks. Short of wringing his hands, he did everything to demonstrate his despair—but in any case, the peace process had been torpedoed from the start. In fact, a senior and extremely well-read politician had a quiz for some of us at that time—which Shakespearian character did Chaudhry Nisar resemble? Despite being an English literature student, I couldn't guess the answer and we gave up. It was Lady Macbeth—I am not sure it was appropriate but it seemed amusing at that time. Chaudhry Nisar would sometimes choose the same person to ask the first question, but was forthcoming with all of us at times. I had even sent him questions for an interview, but predictably it didn't happen. At the press conference, there were these men who were very familiar with you, journalists whose visiting cards boasted of civilian honours, but were believed to be linked to the ISI. They would ask you provocative questions which you as a rule didn't answer.

Other than on the cricket field, the only time I saw Imran Khan up close was after Benazir Bhutto had been killed in December 2007. He was in Mumbai and held a press conference at the late socialite Parmeshwar Godrej's house on the beachfront in Juhu. When we got there, a huge press corps was waiting outside the closed gates of the Godrej bungalow, the security of which was unused to press conferences. We had to give our names and wait outside till we were called one or two at a time, leading to rising tempers and slanging matches. When we were let inside, through the glass doors we could see Godrej leaning towards Khan, giving the final touches to his appearance before he came out to speak to us. The conference was packed and everyone had questions which he patiently answered. The first thing he would do, he said, after going back would be to meet Sanam, Bhutto's sister, now the only surviving member of the ill-fated clan. Like most people he, too, was shocked by the turn of events and the political upheaval this portended for his country.

In Islamabad, too, he had full attendance, and the pressers were usually on the lawns of his party office. He would be flanked by Shireen Mazari, a feisty parliamentarian perceived to be anti-Indian; she was knowledgeable though on nuclear energy and bilateral issues. Or there would be former Pakistan Foreign Minister Shah Mahmood Qureishi, and sometimes Asad Umar, a young parliamentarian. Only once did I go up to his office at Bani Gala up a long road which stopped at a cliff's edge. It was quite a view from there, but I never got to see his mansion with the millennium swimming pool, though he did say yes to an interview when I had asked him. A TV journalist said till he actually sits in front of you, don't believe him, and that's exactly what had happened. The first time I saw Khan in Islamabad, the cricketing hero for millions and for yours truly, was at the Supreme Court where he was being hauled up for contempt in August 2013. It was strange to call him 'Mr Khan' when for years everyone in India simply called him 'Imran'. He drove up in an SUV and a small band of PTI supporters waving party flags greeted him. The Supreme Court, despite issuing a notice to him, didn't press the contempt charges, but pulled him up for lack of remorse in making offensive remarks against the judiciary. In a press conference in July 2013, Khan said he had used the word '*sharmnaak*' (shameful) to describe the conduct of the four returning officers in constituencies which had bogus voting, and he had filed a petition about this in the apex court. Khan offered no apology but said he never meant any offence to the judiciary or the judges, and that his remark was misconstrued. There was much argument on what sharmnaak actually meant and the court was not satisfied with Khan's reply that he was campaigning for an independent judiciary. The court was offended by such a comment coming from the frontline leadership of a political party. Pakistan, it said, was passing through a phase where the majority of the institutions had collapsed—there were sixteen judges hearing 19,000 cases. It also said that if Imran did not mean what he said, then there should be some indication of remorse in the detailed reply he had submitted, which was absent.

That was the first time I was at the Supreme Court; it's an unusual modern building, with its stress on angles and straight lines. So used to colonial, gargantuan buildings, I found its clean lines very un-court-like in appearance. Even the prime minister's secretariat had more character. The courtroom was large and spacious, with mikes thankfully, but there was limited space for the media. Khan was known for his off-the-cuff remarks and being wishy-washy as a politician, though he still cut quite a dash. His cricketing popularity and appeal to youth was not good enough for him to win the General Elections as Sharif swept the polls. His party was already losing support and some of the PTI contacts I called up had left to join other parties. Some were upset with his alleged proximity to the Taliban.

For the Pakistan People's Party (PPP), I usually spoke to Farhatullah Babar who was press attaché to the President till he retired. He was friendly and knowledgeable, and always accessible on the phone. General Musharraf's party, the All Pakistan Muslim League (APML), had Aasia Ishaque as spokesperson, and she was important for all matters related to the general, even his cases and health issues which were increasingly in the news after the treason trial was launched. I met politicians in the National Assembly, including Farooq Sattar of the MQM, Ramesh Kumar Vankwani (the only Hindu elected parliamentarian) from the PMLN, Rehman Malik (now senator), Aitzaz Ahsan and many others. When my visa extension was in doubt, the information minister, Pervaiz Rashid, assured me that it would be extended as he had spoken to Nisar (the interior minister). Rashid usually came to the National Assembly press room and smoked non-stop while chatting with journalists. That was when I managed to ask him, but his assurance didn't help. Journalists used to walk out of Parliament in protest against attacks on the media which happened often, and gather outside on the main road. The media was under grave threat and for every journalist, honest reporting could come at a price. Traffic would stop for a while and furious speeches would be made. There was a sense that the government would do nothing to stop these attacks, though Mr Rashid would be besieged with demands to protect journalists.

S.A. Shamsi of the JeI would often call and invite me for press conferences of their chief, Syed Munawar Hassan, which I attended in a small, cramped office opposite the Holiday Inn hotel. I did meet Hassan who told me that he would let me ask questions in future since I was from India. Often I would be the only woman journalist there and outrageous statements were the norm. Hassan would later be in the news for his statement that the TTP chief, Hakimullah Mehsud, who was killed in a US drone strike was a martyr which offended the army satraps no end. The PMLN office was closer to my house and the spokesperson often reminded me of the lavish parties thrown by one of my earlier colleagues. I don't know if I was being given a hint, but I didn't take him up on it. He was cordial, and his wife, a TV journalist, was helpful in news coverage. There would be some desultory press meets on the Kashmir issue for which we would be invited, but little else. The prime minister didn't have a press meet while I was there, and his joint 'stake-outs' and national addresses were televised. I was on the MQM mailing list which was busy with a lot of press statements and reactions. The PPP invited both the Indian journalists to cover their infamous Jiye Sindh celebration at Mohenjo Daro, and had made all arrangements. I did apply early enough, but as usual there was no response. So when there was a chance for us to cover art and culture, which I was advised to later, we were not allowed to go there either.

It was important to be on the mailing list of embassies and high commissions, and most people obligingly added me except for the Chinese embassy. After repeated calls, I spoke to a Mr Liu who didn't understand what I wanted. When I finally managed to explain to him that I would like to be added to the mailing list and be invited for press meets, he sounded shocked, and after a pause, he said, 'There is no precedent.' Indians were never on their mailers, but he said he would consider it. Obviously, he didn't because I was not added to their list.

A lot of time was spent in meeting people and filling out forms for identity cards and permission to cover the National Assembly and Senate. Soon after I arrived came the news of the thirty-three-year sentence of Dr Shakil Afridi being overturned by the Frontier Crimes Regulation Commission in Peshawar. Dr Afridi was suspected of helping the CIA track Osama bin Laden in Abbottabad in 2011, while being part of an undercover polio vaccination drive in the area. His lawyer, Samiullah Afridi, was most helpful over the phone and first insisted on telling me that my name in Persian means 'love'. Dr Afridi's case went through many twists and turns, and I reported each one of them, thanks to his friendly lawyer, but a year after I returned, Samiullah was killed. He was already facing threats while I was there and had almost decided to give up being Dr Afridi's lawyer, and there were reports he had left the country, which is what a lot of people facing death threats and who have the means to, seemed to be doing.

In the first week of my arrival, LoC tensions were increasing, with the chief of the Pakistan Army staff, General Ashfaq Parvez Kayani, going to ground zero, and statements from Sartaj Aziz, the prime minister's national security and foreign affairs adviser, one of the longest-serving politicians in the country, whose candid memoirs[7] I enjoyed reading.

That was also the time India and Pakistan were planning to hold talks at the upcoming UN General Assembly meeting in New York. There was much speculation, which formed the basis for many news stories, and I was soon bored with this kind of reporting based on statements and press releases, though that was the norm. I visited a tent colony in the capital, of Christians who had fled from Meherabad, where the young girl Rimsha Masih, convicted of blasphemy used to live, till she was forced to leave the country. Another development was the arrest of a Kashmiri teenager Mohammed Shoaib who was the nephew of Syed Asiya Andrabi of the banned Dukhtaran-e-Millat in Srinagar. Events happened thick and fast—there was the All Party Conference on 9 September 2013 on talks with the Taliban and the impending release of Mullah Baradar who was a close aide of Afghan Taliban leader Mullah Omar.

The new Pakistan government wanted to help in the peace process and there were endless platitudes on how it wished to facilitate the process, while there would be barbed comments coming from the Afghan side. Before the elections, the Afghanistan High Peace Council (AHPC), led by Chairperson Salahuddin Rabbani, visited Pakistan in November 2013, to meet the released Taliban commander Mullah Baradar in a visit that was not much publicized.[8]

Covering Parliament

I applied for and got passes for Parliament, and unlike India where the sessions are predetermined, here the President could summon both Houses at short notice. So every time this happened, I had to apply and I learnt a lesson not to go through the external publicity office which ranks high on both hospitality and red tape, and thanks to friends who put me in touch with the right people, I had no difficulty in getting the passes regularly. Only once was I stopped at the entrance by a guard who wondered if Indians were allowed inside the Pakistani Parliament.

The first time I went to the National Assembly, a burly security guard in charge, dressed in a salwar kameez, asked me a lot of questions after checking my identity card. He was friendly, yet there was a steely glint in his eyes; but he never once asked to see my pass after that. I later met him at the special court for Musharraf's trial. The parking was a little away and we had to walk the short distance to the entrance or go through the basement. The women security guards who searched my bag while chattering incessantly on their phones, would break off to ask me about India, and once they even spoke about the fine Indian cotton and how much they wanted it, especially the whites.

The National Assembly was quite grand and a little bigger than our own Lok Sabha which I was still to visit—that happened when I was posted to New Delhi after I was asked to leave Pakistan. The printed schedule for the day was kept outside, where there was also a small place to pray. Fridays were particularly memorable. If you didn't leave before prayer time, it was next to impossible to get out and once I had to apologetically leave with Amir who kept telling me to hurry past people and not to look down, which was difficult if you were trying to make a quick exit, gingerly stepping between rows of people bent in prayer. I realized I was the only woman and I could hear angry muttering. After that, I resolved to leave early if I went to the National Assembly on Fridays. Once I had gone to meet an official in the interior ministry and again it was prayer time. People were kneeling in front of his office and I was unsure as to what was to be done. I stood there uncertainly, till one man sharply told me to stand in the corridor, away from the praying men. I was clearly intruding.

The National Assembly sessions were a lot more casual than our own Parliament's. People chatted, sometimes sitting in groups, even with their backs to the Speaker, and went around greeting each other as if this was a social occasion. The speaker, Sardar Ayaz Sadiq, a mild-mannered man, once rebuked them saying if everyone spoke less loudly, they could hear what was being said. The women were mostly dressed conservatively, with their heads covered, except for Shireen Mazari from the PTI whose short, cropped hair was dyed in vibrant colours—I definitely saw red and green apart from white. It was easy to spot her from the press gallery with her colourful coiffure, as she bobbed up and down the aisle or talked animatedly with her back towards us. I attended some of her talks on nuclear energy and found that she was all for civil nuclear cooperation between India and Pakistan. I also remember another memorable line from her when people often fondly talk of India and Pakistan and their innate oneness. She snapped that only the Punjab and to some extent Sindh was close to India, Balochistan was not, it was closer to Iran in a way, and neither was Khyber Pakhtunkhwa which was closer to Afghanistan!

These sessions never began on time, and there was an interminable wait. During a heated debate, the MQM's Farooq Sattar asked for the discussion to be continued during the prayer break, which the speaker refused. Only once I remembered pin-drop silence and that was when the prime minister made one of his rare appearances in Parliament. One of the main themes for those covering politics at that time was whether Sharif would come to Parliament or not, and if his press aides were in the gallery, that was an indication of his imminent arrival. The late Raja Asghar, with his elegant crown of white hair, would always sit in the same place in the media section, and write perceptively and accurately about the proceedings. It was a pleasure to read him in *Dawn*. I met him at parties and he had the most amusing stories to tell.

We could even sit with our legs crossed in the media section, something which I found the Indian Parliament disallows—there is strict vigilance on how you sit and minders would tell you to sit straight, feet together! And, of course, everyone smoked in the press room outside the Pakistan assembly's media gallery.

I quite liked this casual approach in Parliament where we could chat and giggle with impunity. I went there regularly to check on stories. At that time, the MFN status was about to be granted; it didn't happen but it was interesting to hear the reactions from the House which were almost always against granting the MFN to India.

For the first time in the history of Parliament, there was a boycott, and Senate sessions were held outside on the lawn inside white tents. Spearheading this revolt, Senator Chaudhry Aitzaz Ahsan, author of *Indus Saga,*[9] had some fun at the government's expense. It was the interior minister's statement on 30 October 2013 on the number of deaths due to terrorism that led to this protest.

Attendance was never full in both Houses, but during the nine-day boycott, the Senate hall which was just across from the National Assembly in the same corridor was almost empty. Quickly under a makeshift tent, the mock sessions got under way, with some members sitting on the ground while others had chairs. There was an impromptu visitors' gallery as well, and a presiding officer. Interior Minister Chaudhry Nisar Ali Khan kept saying the figures he provided were correct for the drone strikes and terrorism-related deaths.

Senator Ahsan from the PPP demanded an apology for the wrong figures. Chaudhry Nisar said that 136 incidents of terrorism were reported from Khyber Pakhtunkhwa between June and October 2013, killing 120 people. However, Ahsan and others said the figure was 187 or so. Already on 30 October, the interior minister had created a controversy when he told the Senate that only sixty-seven civilians and 2160 terrorists had died since 2008 in 317 drone strikes, fourteen of them in 2013. Despite protests from the Opposition and a standoff in Parliament, the minister was indignant. He maintained that his figures were correct and later clarified that the Opposition had issues with only one small portion of his answer, which concerned the number of deaths in Khyber Pakhtunkhwa. The interior minister blamed a drone strike for killing Hakimullah Mehsud, as if he was some ambassador of peace, the senators said. But unity was lacking in Parliament, with the leader of the Opposition, Syed Khursheed Shah, regretting that a 'small issue' was holding up the Senate proceedings. I ran into former Interior Minister Rehman Malik who kept insisting he had met me earlier, and he, too, was firm about the protest till the government clarified.

Bold and brave

Journalism in Pakistan has been bold and brave despite the many threats, and between the security agencies and the terror groups life hung on a thread for many professionals. Less than a month after I was there, I wrote about Ali Chishti, a journalist from *Friday Times*, who was forced to leave his home in Karachi. I did an interview over the phone with Chishti when he came to Islamabad. Despite his ordeal, he hadn't lost his sense of humour and he told me that when he was blindfolded by his kidnappers, he was partly relieved. 'I knew then they wouldn't kill me,' he said. But before he was released by his tormentors, he was tortured and abused for several hours, and asked why he was writing on national and security issues and on the MQM.

This incident in Karachi, a city consumed by violence and terror, stood out among the many things that were wrong there. Chishti may have got off lightly compared with what happened to Baloch journalist Abdul Razzak, who lived in Karachi's Lyari area. He had been missing since March 2013 and his body was found in August that year. It was so badly mutilated that his family could not identify him when they first saw it. In the end, only his arms and legs were sufficiently intact to enable identification, according to the Human Rights Commission of Pakistan (HRCP). I met many journalists who wrote about Pakistan, like Kathy Gannon, Victoria Schofield whose book[10] on the Bhutto trial I enjoyed reading and the *Washington Post*'s Pamela Constable who relaunched her book[11] in the capital, almost apologetic that Pakistan was an over-analysed country. It was shocking that Gannon was shot at while covering the elections in Afghanistan, while the photographer Anja Niedringhaus was killed. Reporting in those regions sometimes had a finality to it. Pakistani writers and journalists were always accessible, and had written many books which helped me understand their country. There was Imtiaz Gul, Ayaz Gul, Babar Ayaz and Ahmed Rashid (who has written most comprehensively about Pakistan, Afghanistan and the Central Asian region); Ayesha Siddiqa, too, for her admirable book *Military Inc.* Apart from this, I had many friends whom I met daily while reporting and they were always helpful and kind. I am not going to name them as some were harassed even while I was there.

On most days I would walk to Faisal Mosque, and it was a lovely path with russet trees and the hills on one side. There was a small deer enclosure, with spotted deer and one big nilgai. In the morning a vehicle would stop by with grass bundles. The nilgai and her baby ran around in the small enclosure, stifled and possibly unhappy. Few people even stopped to admire them. I saw very few 'walkers', but once there was a man on a beautiful horse on the path.

While current events or politics and the usual sabre-rattling press releases or press conferences were the order of the day, I looked for other interesting issues. People were helpful and spoke freely even in situations which were dangerous for them. For instance, the Ahmadis who spoke to me, the witnesses in the Shahbaz Bhatti (the former minister who was shot dead) case, were all forthcoming. Without the frankness and cooperation of such people, all the stories I did would have been difficult going, and credit must go to them first. Even in the case of the Afghan refugee camp, the UNHCR provided me an escort to visit the camp, which would have been tough otherwise.

One of the stories I could not do justice to from a long distance was the situation in Karachi which had reached a point of no return. The city was always in the news, if not for murder and arson, then for terror strikes, and one January afternoon in 2014 for the death of a policeman often referred to as Dirty Harry in news reports. It was on a day when Chaudhry Aslam Khan did not have a bomb-proof vehicle. Khan, the Karachi superintendent of police and also heading the counter-terror operations in the city, was killed in a suicide bombing on the Lyari Expressway, along with his gunman and driver. It was not the first time he was targeted. He survived his house being bombed in 2011 which killed eight persons. His statement that he was not going to be scared by such tactics and the terrorists had in fact 'put their hand in a lion's mouth' had got a lot of publicity. That was one of nine attempts on his life, but his luck ran out that day on 10 January 2014. Before his death, he had launched an operation which killed three Taliban militants in the Manghopir area which he spoke about in a press conference. For the man who dressed simply in white, with a reputation for being trigger-happy, death brought more fame and accolades. Predictably, the TTP claimed the killing.

Pitched battles, murders, looting and arson were the norm. In Lyari many Kutchis had to flee their homes fearing violence. In Karachi alone, 3218 people were killed in violence, up 14 per cent from 2012, according to the HRCP in its annual report of 2013. Over 40,000 cases of crime were reported. Chaudhry Aslam, not widely respected among his peers, was only the latest of more than 200 police and security personnel who had lost their lives.

4

Covering Terrorism

I. Minorities in Terror

A place of worship

The prayers were almost over. It was a cold Friday afternoon. People with drawn faces were making quick getaways in their cars, trying to pretend they weren't there. It could have been any corner of the capital. The road was leafy and quiet, and the trees lightly burnished by the winter sun. There were random yellow barricades placed half-heartedly, and there was a police vehicle or two. When I went up to the barricade, a young man appeared out of nowhere to ask me what I wanted. I gave him my visiting card and said I wanted to meet the priest in charge. He came back and said it was not possible and asked me to try again next Friday. I stood on the roadside watching people: the women had their faces covered with only the eyes exposed, while the men looked straight ahead and drove off quickly. A week later I had better luck and I was allowed up to the entrance of the building. On the high walls above, there were thick rolls of barbed wire all around. This was some place of worship. The gate was heavily barricaded and next to it there was a small cubicle. Someone handed me a receiver through the barred windows and a voice at the other end asked me to identify myself and my purpose. I repeated my request. While speaking, I could see the gates open narrowly to let out people who had finished prayers, and again there was this quiet urgency to leave. The tension radiated from the stiff circles of barbed wire, down to the barred gates to the young men who were grim but courteous. The man said they were not allowed to speak to anyone and I certainly could not enter the place. Disappointed, I thanked him and walked away. I turned back to see the parking lot nearby emptying out.

The law had pulled a veil over their existence and they were mere shadows. Constitutionally, the Ahmadis or Ahmadiyya or Qadianis had no right to be called Muslims. They could do nothing other Muslims could. They were heretics, according to the law, and could pray only in 'a place of worship' which could not be called a mosque. The Ahmadis are followers of Mirza Ghulam Ahmad, a self-styled leader from Qadian in Gurdaspur district of Indian Punjab whose interpretation of Islam has invited the ire of some who perceive him to be an upstart prophet. Ahmadis are often taunted as agents of Israel or Western imperialists, and it is held that their belief in their leader amounts to apostasy. The anti-Ahmadi riots of 1953 led to martial law in the Punjab, and Maulana Maududi of the Jamaat-e-Islami got the death sentence for his role in the riots, though it was later commuted.

It was with help from a friend that I found one such place of worship. It was surprisingly close to a popular marketplace and I went there on Friday, as instructed. It was not easy to locate it since obviously there was no sign advertising its existence. This was before Beard and Chubby started following me, so I was free to walk and check things out near the place. I had to regretfully abandon the story, till one day in December 2013, I got a call from a stranger who said he had got my card from the 'place of worship'. He knew that I had been there a couple of times and was ready to meet and speak to me. He even said I could use his real name. But I am not doing that. He will be X for the purposes of this story. It was in early January 2014 that we arranged to meet at a popular café, and as I was waiting, seated in a plush sofa, the two spooks who had careened into me that morning at the visa office decided to stage a comeback. It was Beard trying to look sinister; he pushed the glass door open and shut it on seeing me. That was to make sure I knew I was being followed just in case I had any doubts. I called X and found he was waiting downstairs. He was a chartered accountant and travelled widely. He seemed well-to-do but that didn't mean he could escape his identity or the lack of it. He was open about it; he told everyone who he was and went on with his business. 'We would never pass any remark against the country. We also never asked anyone for help after the constitutional amendment. God is with us. The majority of the Islam community is not against us, only the mullahs,' he said. The million Ahmadis in Pakistan are not allowed to pray in mosques. Three months before I met him, his relative had put up a small board, saying 'Subhanallah'[1] over his new house. He was immediately asked to take it down. He did so in front of the protesting community and the police so that there would be no case afterwards.

'Anybody can kill us any time and no case will be registered,' X said matter-of-factly. He had a narrow escape in Lahore some years back during prayers when the 'place of worship' was bombed. That's when he saw death up close and what it meant to be a 'heretical' minority. Over ninety people were killed in the two bombings, and he relives it almost every day. He said religious persecution started with the Ahmadis and when that was successful, with the government doing all it could to declare them non-Muslims, other communities were targeted, like the Hindus, Christians and Sikhs. X promised to give me a detailed interview after he returned from his travels abroad, but it never happened. I left some months later and lost contact.

Most Ahmadis huddle together in a town in the Punjab called Rabwah, renamed Chenab Nagar, which was constantly under threat. They are peace-loving and don't believe in protest which is why they have to suffer so much, said X. Like the blasphemy law which is often used to cook up cases and jail people, it can take very little if you are an Ahmadi to get you killed. The community lives on a razor's edge. The promise to safeguard the interests of the minorities remains only on paper.[2] In November 2015, a fire destroyed a Christian cable TV station in Karachi. Gawahi TV employees were certain that this was a deliberate act. There were two attacks on churches in March 2015 in Lahore, and a factory and mosque of the Ahmadis were burnt after allegations that workers had set fire to the Koran in Jhelum, and the army had to be called in to restore the peace. Ahmadis were excommunicated by the second amendment to the Constitution in 1974. A special house committee of the National Assembly had debated the issue secretly for nearly four months before that. Those proceedings of the secret sessions are not available in the Parliament library in Islamabad, and the librarian said the report was not yet declassified. However, copies are online, according to a book I read.[3] What I did manage to get was the debates on the issue in the National Assembly and the passing of the resolution on 7 September 1974 which declared Ahmadis as non-Muslims. I was shocked when I met a journalist from this community who had been forced to leave his house and decided to write about it. I didn't realize how difficult it would be, and despite my research, I didn't get around to doing a story. Few people are willing to stick their necks out and even friends who helped me were unwilling to go on record, and reminded me not to publicly call their mosques by the name and to always remember to use the phrase 'place of worship'. Not even Dr Abdus Salam, Pakistan's first Nobel Prize winner, could escape his Ahmadi identity.

On 30 June 1974, the National Assembly appointed a special committee to discuss 'the status of Islam of persons who do not believe in the finality of the Prophethood of Mohammed'. Abdul Hafeez Pirzada, then law minister, said that he didn't think such a committee would be opposed. On 13 June the same year, Prime Minister Zulfikar Ali Bhutto, in his broadcast to the nation, had said the issue of the finality of the prophethood and the consequential matters that have arisen out of it, shall be taken by him to the National Assembly for an effective, just and final solution. Pirzada was also confident that the Opposition would not speak up against this committee. He said, 'And there is one other aspect. There has been any amount of speculation in the Press. It has been said the issue is going to be put in the cold storage. The issue is not going to be put into the cold storage.'[4]

And so, on that day, Maulana Shah Ahmed Noorani Siddiqui was allowed to move a resolution on the status of the Qadianis (Ahmadis):

> Whereas it is a fully established fact that Mirza Ghulam Ahmad of Qadian claimed to be a prophet after the last prophet Muhammed, and whereas his false declaration to be a prophet, his attempts to falsify numerous Quranic texts and to abolish Jihad were treacherous to the main issues of Islam and whereas he was a creation of imperialism for the sole purpose of destroying Muslim solidarity and falsifying Islam, his followers by whatever name they are called, are indulging in subversive activities internally and externally by mixing with Muslims and pretending to be a sect of Islam, now this assembly do proceed to declare that the followers of Mirza Ghulam Ahmad, by whatever name they are called are not Muslims and that an official Bill be moved in the NA to make adequate necessary amendments in the Constitution to give effect to such declaration and to provide for the safeguard of their legitimate rights and interests as a non-Muslim minority of the Islamic Republic of Pakistan.[5]

Sahibzada Ahmad Raza Khan Kasuri was one of the twenty-two movers of this resolution. I was to meet him when I covered General Musharraf's treason trial; he was part of the defence team and vociferously endorsed the ban.

That House committee was the last nail in the coffin for the Ahmadis. On 7 September 1974, the report of the 'special committee of the whole house on the Question of status in Islam of Persons who do not believe in the finality of Prophethood of the Holy Prophet Mohammed', was adopted and the Constitution sanitized accordingly. Abdul Hafeez Pirzada, once again at the helm of affairs, said the entire National Assembly converted itself to a special committee to discuss this matter. All the sittings of this special committee were held in camera. In the entire three months of the sittings there was consensus and unity, said Pirzada in the National Assembly. The special committee even called in witnesses, including the heads of Sadr Anjuman-Ahmadiyya, Rabwah, and Anjuman-i-Ahmadiyya Ishaat-Islam (Lahore), before approving a new clause in Article 260 which would define a non-Muslim.[6]

Speaking after the report was adopted in Parliament, Prime Minister Bhutto said:

> I do not want to make political capital when I say that this is a unanimous decision of the entire House. We have had elaborate discussion with all members of the House representing all shades of opinion and all Parties in the National Assembly. And the decision which has been reached today is a national decision. It is a decision of the people of Pakistan. It represents the will and the aspirations and the sentiments of the Muslims of Pakistan. I would not want the government to take any credit for it. I would not want any individual to take any credit for it. I would say that this difficult decision, and in my humble opinion in many respects the most difficult decision, would not have been taken without democratic institutions and with

> democratic authority. This is an old problem. The problem is 90 years old, and with the passage of time it has become more complicated. It has aroused much bitterness, much division in our society and to this day it has not been resolved.[7]

The anti-Ahmadi riots in 1974 (there were riots earlier in 1953) and the need to placate fundamentalists put pressure on Bhutto, though he denied it and he defended this decision in Parliament by saying that it was both a religious and secular decision. It was Pakistan's achievement, he said, and the National Assembly met in a secret session since it wanted to approach the problem in the spirit of finding a final solution to it. 'It was important for the NA to meet in secret session. If the NA had not met in secret session, do you think Sir that all this truth would have come out? That people would have spoken as freely and as frankly as they did because it was the secret session of the House,' he said.[8] There was also the usual noise about guaranteeing constitutional rights, which if you see what happened afterwards, don't exist for the Ahmadis. The second amendment was passed 130 to nil. The Speaker made a plea for secrecy of the sessions over four months to be maintained and that mandate has not been lifted, though Bhutto did say it would be revealed in the fullness of time[9]—bureaucratic-speak for never.

Bhutto also defended this decision in his appeal before the Supreme Court in December 1978 against his death sentence by the Lahore High Court. Outlining what he had done as a good Muslim, he included the decision on the Ahmadis. He countered aspersions that he was a Muslim only in name and defended his good Muslim-ness by saying he had 'solved the 90-year-old Ahmadi problem'.[10] He and his tormentor, Zia-ul-Haq, left behind a trail of continuing persecution against the community.

> In 1984, the military government of General Zia-ul-Haq, via a Martial Law Ordinance, added sub-clauses 298B and 298C to Section XV, Article 298A, of the PPC [Pakistan Penal Code].

> Under the amended law, Ahmadis have been prohibited from proclaiming themselves as Muslims, referring to their beliefs as Islamic, preaching their faith, terming their places of worship as 'mosques', practising their faith in non-Ahmadi worship places, including public prayer areas, performing Muslim call to prayer, publicly quoting texts of the Holy Quran, and saying Muslim greetings in public, among other restrictions. These 'crimes' are punishable with imprisonment of up to three years, with a fine.[11]

Despite the antipathy towards the Ahmadis, when it came to a situation of having little choice, Bhutto did appoint a member of the community as head of the air force. Some months after Bhutto took over from Yahya Khan after the 1971 war, the air chief, Rahim Khan, was replaced by Air Marshal Zafar Ahmad Choudhary. Indian journalist Dilip Mukerjee writes that Choudhary might have been passed over for the top job but for Bhutto's drastic reshuffle.[12] The armed forces, as a rule, remained free of such prejudices, but Major General A.O. Mitha points to the contrary. The Ahmadi officers were gradually replaced under General Ayub Khan's orders.[13]

We will never know how the Quaid-i-Azam, Mohammed Ali Jinnah, who stood for secular values would have taken this. The man whose idea it was to create a separate homeland for Muslims was also not spared this excoriating sectarianism. The public funeral of Jinnah, an Ismaili who converted to an Isna Ashari (also spelt 'Ithna Ashariyya') Shia (or Twelver Shia, a sect of Shias believing in the twelve Imams),[14] was according to Sunni ritual. His sister, Fatima, who died in 1967 was also given a private Shia funeral before the public one according to Sunni rites.[15]

> There was an initial Namaz-e-Janaza at her residence in Mohatta Palace in accordance, presumably with Shia rites, then there was a Namaz-e-Janaza for the public at the Polo Ground. There an argument developed whether this should be

> led by a Shia or a Sunni; eventually, Badayuni [a Shia priest] was put forward to lead the prayer. As soon as he uttered the first sentence, the crowd broke in the rear. Thereupon he and the rest ran leaving the coffin high and dry. It was with some difficulty that the coffin was put on a vehicle and taken to the compound of the Quaid's Mazar, where she was to be buried.[16]

In his Nobel Prize-winning speech in 1979, jointly awarded for Physics, Dr Abdus Salam said, 'Pakistan is deeply indebted to you for this.' But his country has chosen to obliterate his memory because he was an Ahmadi. In a famous exchange with Bhutto, when Salam resigned as scientific adviser, Bhutto tried to placate Salam and said, 'This is all politics. Give me time, I will change it.' Salam asked Bhutto to write down what he had just said on a note that would remain private. 'I can't do that,' replied the master politician.[17] Dr Salam's memory is not allowed to garner pride, though he was given the highest civilian honour, Nishan-e-Imtiaz, by Zia-ul-Haq, after winning the Nobel Prize.[18] Fraser writes that the highest-ranking Pakistani official present for his funeral was a superintendent of police.

The word 'Muslim' (the inscription on his grave had said the 'first Muslim Nobel Laureate') was removed by court orders. As a journalist wrote, 'This son of Jhang is less known in his own country today than the terrorist Lashkar-e-Jhangvi, even though he had founded and led an abler lashkar (brigade) of some 500 Pakistani physicists and mathematicians over the years whom he arranged to send to UK and US universities on scholarship for higher studies.'[19]

In the end, this 'secular' constitutional amendment vilified men like Dr Salam despite the guarantee to respect the rights of the minorities. Gordon Fraser[20] writes of how Pakistan's Foreign Minister Mohammed Zafrullah Khan, an Ahmadi, was a target for criticism, though Jinnah had resisted demands to remove him from the cabinet. The anti-Ahmadi protests spun out of control into violence in the 1950s and Abdus Salam was caught in this vortex of hatred when he returned from Cambridge in 1951. When Bhutto amended the Constitution, Salam's diary entry for that day said, 'declared non Muslim, cannot cope'.[21]

'My kids don't have a future'

'My younger son was beaten up one day. He wanted to complain to the police. I told him to forget it. My son is eighteen, they were playing snooker and some kids from the madrasa near my house told him he was a Qadiyani [Ahmadi], why are you playing here? They thrashed him and his friends badly. His friends said your father is a journalist, call the police. I told my son to go home and drink water.'

The identity of this person has to be kept anonymous. It was difficult to get him to tell his story and his eyes were gleaming with tears. I had to wait for occasions to meet him and it was quite by accident that we met twice and he could complete his story. It's not easy to get Ahmadis to speak up, most of them are afraid and tend to keep a low profile so that they are not killed. After the incident, Hameed (name changed) decided to move house. The threats to his son continued and he was tense all the time. He has two sons and a daughter. Every time his phone rang, he would expect some intimidation. He sold his house—it was a house he had built, and he had saved every paisa over the years to build it. He wanted to leave the country, his wife, too, was keen on leaving but he didn't have that kind of money. He says, 'I want my children to live in a free society. My son works so hard, he does his MBA.' He himself holds two jobs, starting the day at 7 a.m. and getting home very late. At fifty-six, he is tired of juggling jobs, worrying about his safety and that of his children. 'I am tired now and my kids don't have a future. It's difficult for my son to get a job since the fact he is an Ahmadi is in his CNIC [Computerized National Identity Card].[22] You also have to sign a declaration that as a Qadiyani you cannot be taught the Koran. While Musharraf gave the Ahmadis the right to vote, we can only vote for the minorities. We don't accept this discrimination, we are not non-Muslims. I keep a low profile and I use my contacts for my protection.' But he knows that no one really can protect him.

I met Ahmad Raza Kasuri who was defence lawyer for General Musharraf during his treason trial, and asked him about the Ahmadi question. He fully endorsed it, he said, and was part of the National Assembly when the amendment outlawing Ahmadis as Muslims was passed unanimously. There are many who condemn it, and the two articles I have quoted—one by Adil Najam and one by the late Murtaza Razvi—are examples of this public dissent on the plight of the community. But the Constitution has not been amended in their favour despite cases in court.

The Hindu question

'Of all minority groups, Pakistani Hindus have borne the brunt of stigmatization as a consequence of biased school textbooks that paint them as evil, anti-state and untrustworthy. In 2015, there were numerous incidents of forced conversions, rape and attacks on places of worship targeting members of the Hindu community.'[23] There has been no let-up in the attacks on minorities, and the Jinnah Institute documented 351 incidents of violence in the period 2012–15. When I came back from Pakistan in May 2013, I read some comments on my farewell article that I didn't mention the oppression of the Hindus. I got long emails on what was going on in the Sindh province and how Hindus were being tortured and fleeing the country. If it was Pakistan, then it must be the Hindus who were oppressed. First of all, I couldn't travel anywhere, much less to Sindh, and the people from the Hindu community I met in Islamabad, some of them were from Rawalpindi, did not tell me that they were oppressed or that they wanted to leave the country. However, places in Sindh and Punjab were showing an increase in the number of cases of human rights violations against Hindus, causing an exodus. There were pressing issues for the Hindus in and around the capital. They were agitating for a temple in Islamabad; the only one was in Saidpur, part of an old gurdwara, and it did not have an idol. They also wanted a crematorium in Islamabad since there was only one in Rawalpindi. Some of them were leaders of the community in successful businesses and would present their demands to top politicians. There was also a group of shopkeepers from Rajasthan who had migrated from the Thar many years ago, who had a row of shops selling woollen clothes and handicrafts in a premier shopping area. They were happy to meet an Indian and even offered to host 'a vegetarian lunch' for me. They didn't speak of oppression and torture, and seemed very well-to-do. One of them had built a new house and was having a celebration of sorts.

No one can deny there are grave human rights violations against Hindus who are under threat in some areas, and they are severely under-represented in the National Assembly (like all minorities), and Ramesh Kumar Vankwani is the only one from the ruling PMLN. The Pakistan Hindu Council does regularly take up issues of temples under threat and girls being married off or converted, and Vankwani himself faced death threats during the local bodies' elections.

I met the small Hindu community in Islamabad and Rawalpindi, which came to show solidarity with the Christians after the Peshawar suicide bombing on the All Saints Church in September 2013. There are about 115 families in Islamabad and about 400 families in Rawalpindi, and they are all original residents of the area and have not come as migrants from India. Security is not on their agenda yet and they perceive little threat in the twin cities. But there is unhappiness over the list of demands which the government has not fulfilled.

Pandit Channalal from Rawalpindi said that while the Hindu community was not targeted in any way, the government had not agreed to any of its demands for a temple, a community centre and a crematorium in the capital. While Hindus elsewhere in the country, especially in Sindh, are under threat and there have been 'forced conversions', the community is highly integrated in Rawalpindi, the members said. Rawalpindi has a Krishna temple but in Islamabad, despite repeated requests, the government was not taking a decision on handing over a temple near the Rawal Lake to the community for active worship. Professor A.K. Tanwani had even met the former President and prime minister, but their demands were pending. 'We live on hope that it will happen one day,' he said.

In fact, when I was there, the Pakistan Hindu Council did take up the issue of the rising cases of kidnapping of Hindu girls and forced conversion and marriage. There was the case of Rinkle Kumari which went right up to the Supreme Court, though the apex court left it to the girls to decide their future. Sometimes the media and activists do ensure that the girls are restored to their families, as was the case with Sapna Rani from Peshawar. The Sindh government had set up a committee to examine the forced marriage of Hindu girls, and there were reports that there were twenty such cases every month, which I did write on. After coming back, I get regular updates from the council on the many kidnapped girls and how it was difficult for them to return to their families. Vankwani remains, along with the Human Rights Commission of Pakistan, the most vociferous and active in highlighting crimes against Hindus.

The Hindus who come to India don't want to go back to a situation where their identity is being almost erased. There were only two instances when I wrote about Hindu institutions: one, when a dharamshala in Larkana in Sindh was attacked, and there was a huge uproar from the civil society which came together to celebrate a joint Holi as a testimony to their harmonious relations; the other incident was in Peshawar when one morning, a security guard outside one of the Hindu temples in Peshawar was shot dead. I called the local police to confirm this, but they couldn't tell me which temple it was—there were two temples in the city. When I asked the policeman to name the temple, he could only say it was a Hindu temple. I had to leave it at that for the story I filed.

The Hindu dharamshala in Larkana was set on fire just before Holi in 2014. This time I did get specific details from the local police. There were reports of a burnt Koran outside a Hindu man's residence and when people found out, they burnt the dharamshala. It seemed or was made to look like a quid-pro-quo crime. A room next to the dharamshala was damaged and the government stepped in to announce it would rebuild it soon. The police appointed two members from the Hindu and Muslim communities to oversee the investigation. The situation snowballed into violence in other areas of Larkana and Sindh, and there were protests and shops were shut, and police had to call meetings of the two communities to keep the peace. Sharif issued a statement saying it was the government's responsibility to protect minorities.

There were elaborate temples in Karachi, some of them ancient, and the city's development has posed a threat to some of them, but the courts have taken a stand or there have been interventions by the public. There have also been cases when ancient temples like Katasraj were restored by earnest government officials on their own initiative. But the situation can't be too happy, and festivals in places like Rawalpindi have a muted quality, and the temples and members of the Hindu community avoid ostentatious displays. Basant, even though it wasn't a specifically Hindu festival, was popular in Lahore, till it was banned for various reasons. And to think it was a festival for both Hindus and Muslims in possibly happier times with week-long celebrations in eighteenth-century Delhi.

The HRCP intervened to try and save the more than 150-year-old Sri Ratneswar Mahadev Temple, which was going to be affected by some proposed underpasses and flyovers near Clifton in Karachi. The temple, which is visited by thousands of Hindu and Sikh devotees, was located in a cavern within a few metres of one of the underpasses. The HRCP wrote a letter to the chief justice of the Supreme Court saying that business interests in complicity with officials of the Karachi Metropolitan Corporation (KMC) had started construction of multiple flyovers and underpasses around the Clifton seafront without any prior notice. There was no environmental impact assessment (with public hearings) mandated by law, and the HRCP said the Hindu community in Sindh had been experiencing escalating human rights violations over the past few years. The Laxmi Narayan Mandir, located at Native Jetty near the Jinnah Bridge on M.A. Jinnah Road, had its access, privacy and environs severely affected a few years ago by another commercial project, Port Grand.

Art of Living

I didn't realize that Art of Living (AOL) was popular in Pakistan till I heard about one of its centres being burnt down in Bani Gala in March 2014. I went with Shahnaz Minallah who had a lovely home, which was gutted, on the banks of the Rawal Lake. She was the co-chair of the AOL Foundation in Pakistan and only escaped because she was away for an advanced training course in Nankana. Bani Gala is where the rich have huge houses, including Imran Khan who seems to have occupied an entire cliff side. The AOL headquarters in Islamabad was protected by a flimsy bamboo gate. The two security guards were tied up and one of them had a gun held to his head by a group of people who went on to set fire to the office, the guest rooms and Minallah's residence with petrol.

The advanced training course with an Indian teacher was to be held there which was why the guest rooms were in readiness with pristine white bedcovers. Minallah was an ardent practitioner of AOL and became a disciple of Sri Sri Ravi Shankar when he visited Pakistan in 2004. She put all her money to build the complex on her own land. The centre was formally inaugurated by Sri Sri Ravi Shankar in 2012. 'In 2004 it was sheer chance that Guruji visited us and I don't know what drove me to follow him. We do courses mostly in three cities and from twenty-odd people the number has swelled to over eighty per training session,' she said.

Even without any marketing or publicity, people would come for the training sessions. The small campus had a meditation hall, an amphitheatre and guest rooms, apart from Minallah's house. She was mystified as to why the centre was a target and said that people have had the most extraordinary experiences there.

When Minallah bought the land, it was a swamp and she worked hard to make it what it is now—a serene meditation centre. Her house and all her belongings were destroyed in the fire, including all her documents and photos. I remember her standing in the middle of a blackened front room looking at bits of old photos. There had been a TV programme some days earlier where her co-chair, Naeem, was interviewed and grilled on the funding for the centre. 'They had said it would be about the Art of Living course but instead they asked pointed questions about our funding and didn't wait to hear our answers,' she said. A lot of motives were imputed to the AOL centre. The arson attack came after that. 'I have nothing to hide, I am an open book—anyone can walk in and see what we are doing,' she said. I ran into her once after the story appeared in the paper and she said her friends asked her why she had taken an Indian there or something to that effect.

To be a Shia

When I first met a Shia journalist, he seemed nervous. We were guests at a diplomat's house. He told me that if there is some trouble, 'it is I who will be shot not you as an Indian and a Hindu'. That's how much the Shias were hated. And there would be regular attacks on Shia pilgrims and on the *imambargah*s.

I later met another Shia journalist who joked that he would always watch his back for fear of being stabbed. I realized this was not a joke. For this community, there was everything to fear and no one would help, despite brave attempts by the HRCP to highlight their situation and issue strong condemnations, or stage public protests. Over 50,000 Shias have been killed in the proxy war between Iran and Pakistan. The coffins on the road had become a symbol of defiance for the Shia Hazaras who were often bombed on their way back from pilgrimage in Iran. In January 2013, 100 of them were killed, and in protest the community sat with their coffins outside, refusing to bury them. A year later, the coffins were on the street again to protest one more bombing. I went for a protest outside the Islamabad Press Club where a handful of determined people raised their voice.

The new year of 2014 brought a sense of déjà vu to many Shia Hazaras after a bus in Mastung in Balochistan was blown up, killing over twenty pilgrims returning from Iran. Across the country there was solidarity for the protests in the freezing cold at Alamdar Road in Quetta. In Islamabad, protestors were up all night. Once a seasoned journalist asked me if the same twenty people protested against everything in Mumbai and it was regrettably true of Islamabad. Activists Rehana Hashmi of the Sisters Trust Pakistan and Tahira Abdullah were among those who sat up all night in outrage and grief. In 2013 too, Abdullah was among those who guarded the coffins for four nights of the 100 killed in Quetta. There was a helpless rage against these attacks which no protest could mitigate. I met some Hazara Shias who had fled Quetta to make their home in the capital. Even a simple act of going to buy things or sending children to school was fraught with anxiety, as Faisal (name changed), a shopkeeper from Quetta, pointed out, and it was so difficult to live with this daily threat of death. He sold his shop and came to the capital to earn a living. In Quetta the community is confined to Hazara Town and Alamdar Road. Over eleven years, the Hazaras have been reduced to a miserable condition, as one of the protestors said: 'They are psychologically ill, socially isolated, and economically finished.' There was no sense of security and during a major blast at Kirani Road in Quetta in 2013, a tanker full of explosives had made its way through six check posts. Even though people covered their faces in public or wore dark glasses, they were still targeted.

A young student who was injured in a bomb blast in a university bus in Quetta had to leave the city to complete his studies. 'People target you if you are a Hazara,' he said, their Mongoloid features making it easier for them to be identified. I met a Hazara waitress from Bamiyan in Afghanistan who was waiting to go abroad after her family's appeal for refugee status was approved by the UNHCR. There was no way she could ever go back to her beautiful home, now ravaged by the Taliban.

To die is to sleep no more

It was his word against another's and the courts ignored the fact that he was a paranoid schizophrenic. Blasphemy laws are used conveniently against the minorities and Muslims too, to evict them or take revenge, and Mohammed Asghar, a mentally challenged man, was a victim. Initial news reports on Asghar, a sixty-nine-year-old British Pakistani who was sentenced to death for blasphemy, made no mention of the fact that he was suffering from schizophrenia. The government prosecutor in the case, Javed Gul, told me that Asghar had come to Pakistan in 2010 and he was accused of printing visiting cards in the name of Prophet Mohammed. Police had also seized some letters he had written where he wrote that he was the Prophet. Handwriting experts had testified in court that the letters were written by Asghar. When asked to say something in his defence, Asghar confessed that he was indeed the Holy Prophet, Gul said.

The real story is a bit different. When Asghar who lived in Edinburgh with his family, came to Rawalpindi in 2010, he was shocked to find one of the two properties he owned there occupied by a notorious land grabber. He filed a complaint against him before leaving for the Haj pilgrimage, but it was Asghar who was arrested on his return. Predictably, all the evidence, including the letters, was handed over to the police by the complainant, who had many anti-corruption cases against him. Section 295C of the PPC says: 'Whoever by words, either spoken or written, or by visible representation or by any imputation, innuendo, or insinuation, directly or indirectly, defiles the sacred name of the Holy Prophet Muhammad (peace be upon him) shall be punished with death, or imprisonment for life, and shall also be liable to fine.' Sections 295 to 295C of the PPC are generally referred to as the 'blasphemy code'. The punishments for offences under these provisions include death (under Section 295C), life imprisonment, imprisonment for various periods, and fine.

The trial court threw out Asghar's legal representatives who were working with him from October 2013, and appointed a state counsel. Asghar has a long and well-diagnosed history of schizophrenia which started in 1993. His stroke resulted in him walking with a limp. Even in Edinburgh, he had been detained under the Mental Health Act, in February 2010, as he suffered from paranoid delusions, and was later admitted to the Royal Victoria Hospital. It was diagnosed that he suffered from paranoid schizophrenia. His defence lawyers obtained his medical records in March 2011 from the National Health Service in the UK and an affidavit from Dr Jane McLennan, the consultant psychiatrist at the Royal Victoria Hospital in Edinburgh. The judge ordered a medical examination on the basis of all the documents.

In the affidavit to the court, Dr McLennan had warned that the probability of him attempting to take his own life was significant and might increase if he remained in prison, while recommending a comprehensive treatment and rehabilitation plan. Sure enough, Asghar tried to commit suicide, on 8 January 2012, and had to be hospitalized. While he was recovering, a hastily constituted medical board with one psychiatrist was sent to evaluate him in hospital. The doctors received threatening calls and the hospital wanted to send Asghar back to jail. The medical report said he suffered from 'major organic affective depression'. Under law, a mentally ill person cannot be convicted.

By then the judge had changed and the new person did not hear the evidence. For the final judgment, Asghar's legal team was not even informed. The lawyers feared homicide and that's what happened in October 2014 when a policeman shot Asghar in the back, injuring him. There have been many appeals by his daughter, and signature campaigns to release Asghar. While awarding the death sentence on 23 January 2014, the sessions court which conducted the trial in Adiala Jail in Rawalpindi disregarded his medical records from Scotland.

This was not the first case where a mentally challenged person had been convicted for blasphemy. Young Rimsha Masih was sentenced to death for blasphemy, though she was finally acquitted by the court in 2012 and granted asylum in Canada. I met her Christian neighbours who had been forced to flee their homes in Meherabad, and who now live in a precarious condition in Islamabad. Rimsha Masih's persecutor, a cleric, was acquitted in 2013; he had been accused of filing false charges.

Former US Ambassador Sherry Rehman faced threats after she proposed a bill banning the death penalty for blasphemy. Media reports estimate that over 1200 people had been charged with blasphemy from 1986 till 2010. The Human Rights Watch (HRW) World Report 2014 says that abuses are rife under the country's blasphemy law, which is used against religious minorities often to settle personal disputes. Dozens of people were charged with the offence in 2013. At least sixteen people remained on death row for blasphemy, while another twenty were serving life sentences.

The HRCP in its report on the state of human rights in 2012 says that while Pakistan did not execute anyone under Section 295C, many of the accused were killed by extremists outside the courts or in prisons. The HRW World Report of 2015 estimated that since 1990, at least sixty people had been murdered after being accused of blasphemy.

Sawan Masih, a conservancy worker, was sentenced to death for blasphemy soon after Asghar. The case against him was filed after an argument with a neighbour where he was accused of defaming the Prophet. A mob attacked Joseph Colony where he lived, in March 2013, and nearly 100 homes and some churches were torched. According to his lawyer, Masih said that the attack on the colony was a move to evict the residents from the area. The case against over a 100 arsonists filed in an anti-terrorism court doesn't seem to be getting anywhere and it is unlikely that his appeal will get quick results. After Masih, it was the turn of a couple in Toba Tek Singh to be sentenced to death. Again a bizarre case. Shafqat Masih, who was paralysed from the waist down, was thrown out of his wheelchair and made to confess that he had misused the Prophet's name. He and his wife, Shagufta, who was also sentenced to death, were accused of sending text messages against the Holy Prophet, and a case was filed against them by a lawyer and a cleric. Farrukh H. Saif, the executive director of World Vision in Progress which is defending them, said the organization was looking after the couple's four children—three sons and a daughter between the ages of twelve and six. All of them were in custody initially. The case was filed by some local cable operator who had a dispute with Shafqat, and the latter was forced to confess to his crime after being tortured. The couple earlier lived in Gojra and had to be moved to Toba Tek Singh after there were huge protests over the alleged blasphemy incident.

Opposing blasphemy laws can be fatal. It's the smiling, unrepentant face of Malik Mumtaz Qadri that crops up when it comes to a lack of remorse for hate crimes. Qadri gave himself up after pumping over twenty bullets into Salman Taseer at Kohsar Market in January 2011, and in 2015, the Supreme Court reaffirmed his death sentence and he was executed. The execution could be thought of as an honour for Taseer's killer, not a punishment, going by the multitudes who reportedly came out in his support. Taseer had spoken up against blasphemy laws and defended Aasia Bibi who was the first woman to be convicted under it, in 2010. Friends told me that no one was willing to read the funeral prayers for Taseer, and his own party members didn't support a condolence motion in Parliament, and went and sat in the visitor's gallery. While Aasia Bibi was finding it difficult to get legal help, Qadri was celebrated with rose garlands and processions in the streets. (Though she finally got a lawyer, when her appeal against her death sentence came up in the Supreme Court in October 2016, Justice Iqbal Hameed-ur-Rehman recused from the bench because of a 'conflict of interest'.) There was a mosque named after him in Islamabad which became public news after a tweet in 2014. More recently, in February 2017, a mosque in Maryland, USA, eulogized Qadri on his death anniversary, provoking much protest.[24] A library in the Lal Masjid, after all, has already been named after Osama bin Laden.

A small minority of journalists, human rights activists and other individuals struggle to keep the country sane by raising their voices against extremists, terrorism, the plight of the minorities, the curbs on freedom, and rising crimes; but the fight is unequal. In 2014, I attended a small memorial service for Taseer with his family in attendance at the very spot where he was killed under a large tree at Kohsar Market. The judge trying Qadri had to leave the country, and I read there were support marches taken out to mark the day Qadri killed Taseer. At that time there was little hope of justice.

In 2011, apart from Taseer, a former federal minister and Roman Catholic, Shahbaz Bhatti, was killed for opposing the blasphemy law. Two eyewitnesses to Bhatti's murder faced death threats from some terror groups after they appeared in court. Bhatti, who founded the All Pakistan Minorities Alliance (APMA), was killed in the I-8 sector of Islamabad in March 2011; his car was stopped and he was shot. Bhatti had stood up in defence of the

Christian community and spoke out against both the blasphemy law and Aasia Bibi's death sentence.

In September 2013, two suspects, Hammad Adil and Umer Abdullah, were arrested in the Bara Kahu area and later charged with the murder of Bhatti. Adil was picked up after a car full of explosives was found at his house. He later confessed to being involved in Bhatti's killing. On 22 January 2014 at the trial in Adiala Jail, the two eyewitnesses claimed that they saw the two accused, one of them was driving the car, and the other was throwing pamphlets on the road after Bhatti had been shot.

Over a week later, when one of the eyewitnesses came to his office, there was a printed letter signed by the Lashkar-e-Jhangvi, an extreme sectarian group, and the TTP threatening the two witnesses and their families with death if they continued to give evidence. A case of criminal intimidation was registered and they were given some security, but they skipped one hearing, fearing for their lives.

Worse was yet to come. In April 2014, Rehman Rashid, a lawyer defending Junaid Hafeez, a blasphemy accused, was shot dead in his office. Before his death both Rashid and another lawyer, Allah Dad, were threatened for defending Hafeez in Multan Central Prison. Rashid was threatened in open court by three persons who said: 'You will not come to court next time because you will not exist any more.' Rashid, HRCP's Multan Task Force coordinator, drew the judge's attention to the threat but the judge is reported to have remained silent, according to an HRCP statement. The killing drew strong condemnation and protests from the HRCP and lawyers across the country. Rashid was a committed human rights activist and lawyer, and associated with HRCP for over twenty years.

Living in tents

It was some Christian activists who spoke to me about a tent settlement in the capital. They refused to escort me there and I went on my own. I couldn't believe such a place existed in the capital—it was tucked away in a remote sector, unseen and unwashed. This was a colony of about 400 Christian families who were forced to flee Meherabad after the infamous Rimsha Masih case. They lived as refugees in their own country. Though the mentally challenged girl was acquitted in November 2012 of all charges after it was found that the cleric who filed the case against her had planted evidence, the residents of her former neighbourhood were terrorized and forced to leave.

While she and her family have found asylum abroad, the cleric was acquitted of all charges. The state was unlikely to appeal, said Masih's lawyer Tahir Naveed Chaudhary. That isolated tent camp in many ways, spoke of hate and discrimination. Its people were running scared and willing to live in squalor and anonymity. There were no walls there, only bed sheets and old clothes strung up for privacy. Mosquitos were everywhere, and many residents suffered from malaria. The whole place was full of stagnant water and wet mud. There was a small bore well for water, and a giant red cross in a square of sorts where the people plan to build a church. Everywhere bright-coloured cloth was used to screen off houses.

Bilkis Bibi was standing outside a muddy pool in front of her tent house. When I went up to her, she invited me inside and was open about the pitiful nature of her life. In her forties, she moved here a year ago after Rimsha Masih was falsely accused of burning the pages of the Koran. She said she was threatened and the men in her family were beaten. The landlord suddenly hiked the rent to PKR 5000 a month and the electricity charges as well. They had no choice but to leave. Her daughter dropped out of school, and Bilkis's husband sold vegetables to survive. Her elder daughter and grandchildren had come back to live with Bilkis after her (the daughter's) husband left her. There was no light or cooking fuel, and toilets were the nearby forest. Living in Meherabad had become impossible after the constant abuse. The shopkeeper used to throw things at them, and once the landlord threw all their belongings on the road and ordered them to leave. The residents complained to the police who did nothing. The Capital Development Authority (CDA) agreed to resettle them in another sector but the local people didn't even allow that. The signal was clear—they were not wanted anywhere.

Bilkis would weep every day in her new home. She had lived in Meherabad for fifteen years and worked as a house help. She was weakened by Hepatitis C. Her tent had a single low bed and behind it, there was a pile of sodden beds and bedclothes drenched by the rain. Her daughter was washing vessels in what looked like muddy water. I walked around the colony talking to people. On one side of the tents was another small row of makeshift homes. Outside one of them, sitting in the slush, another resident, Maria, was cooking rice on a wood-fired stove. She, too, had run away from Meherabad and was surviving on a pension after her husband died. She had five daughters, and one of them sitting next to her, Rubina, suffered from cancer. There was no money for treatment, she said.

Nadeem used to be a sanitary worker in a private company. He was sacked after the Rimsha incident and didn't have a job. His child had to drop out of school. The CDA was also threatening the eviction of the colony. People who moved here find it difficult to get work, like Shamim, a tailor. Arif John who claimed to be Rimsha's neighbour, said she was a poor girl who was mentally challenged; she did not burn anything and it was all false. Arif was clear that the Muslims wanted to evict the Christians from the area, and they had even announced it once during prayers in Meherabad. Before that, they had attacked a Christian convention and broken the mikes. Arif and the others tried to look for houses to rent but everywhere they were refused. In this untidy settlement, they could pray safely. In Meherabad, they were not allowed to play music during the prayers and once some people tried to burn the church.

Social activists said that Christians were discriminated against in jobs, promotions and housing. In the eleven slums, or *kachchi abadi*s, as they are called in Islamabad, where mostly Christians live, there was no water or light, and sanitation was non-existent. In one of these kachchi abadis, Hansa Colony, water was a big issue and schoolchildren could be found filling cans in their free time. Standing on a slippery slope next to a deep and fast-flowing gutter, Saima and her brother Haroon filled plastic bottles, watched over by their father. Not surprisingly, some children would fall into the gutter.

Faisal Zulfiqar's classmates roundly abused him at school after the Danish cartoons on Prophet Mohammed. In the government schools, Christian children were called the children of '*chudus*', or sweepers. Many of the Christians were converts from the Dalit community and they were still outcaste in some ways. Salamat Masih worked as a sweeper, but the day I met him, he was standing outside his house, chopping huge logs for the day. Sometimes he wandered around to fetch firewood. Many Christians had also moved from Sialkot, Narwal and Gujranwala, fearing persecution. Here in Islamabad, they took odd jobs and lived in a relatively safe environment. You could see people filling small cylinders with LPG from a strange contraption in a most unsafe manner, for PKR 100 at a time.

Some attempts were being made by activists in Hansa Colony to improve matters and there was some bonhomie with the local Muslims who gifted a water cooler to the church; there would also be joint iftar parties. But lasting peace or even justice for the community could be elusive. It was not the case that only Christians were persecuted under the blasphemy law, but it was a handy tool. Pastor Boota Masih was conducting choir practice in the new Pentecostal church. A handful of people were singing in that small, damp room with a big cross. He had kept the church going since 1991, unfazed by threats and the murder of Christians.

In April 2014, while launching the HRCP report on the state of human rights in 2013, veteran activist I.A. Rehman said the condition of minorities was worsening and it was nearly impossible for those accused in blasphemy cases to have a trial in Pakistan. The HRCP's Kamran Arif said that human rights was in a state of regression and 2013 was no exception. Sectarian clashes were on the rise and the administration of justice was far from satisfactory. There was a heavy backlog of cases across all tiers of the judicial system, and the report said 20,000 cases were pending in the Supreme Court alone.

Sectarian violence claimed the lives of over 200 Hazara Shias in Balochistan in the first few weeks of 2013. The report documented more than 200 sectarian attacks, which killed 687 people. Seven Ahmadis lost their lives in targeted attacks and in the deadliest assault ever against Pakistan's Christian citizens, over 100 people were killed in a Peshawar church. A Muslim mob torched a predominantly Christian neighbourhood in Lahore after a Christian man was accused of blasphemy; 100 houses were burnt as residents fled. Individuals charged with offences relating to religion included seventeen Ahmadis, thirteen Christians and nine Muslims.

In November 2013, the HRCP released a report[25] that assessed the improvement in the level of respect for the political rights of minority religious communities, especially in relation to their participation in the elections as voters and candidates. The General Election of May 2013 was the third one since the abolition of separate electorates in 2002 and except for the Ahmadiyya community, everyone else had equal rights to vote or seek election to general seats. The HRCP chose six constituencies in Sindh for observation which had a substantial minority presence. The constituencies are located in Mirpur Khas-Umarkot, Tharparkar and Lahore—the last has a sizeable Christian population. The minority group in the area under observation was Hindu, and both voters and candidates faced discrimination because of this.

A large number of the Hindus worked as daily wagers in the farms of the feudal landlords, and most followed their employer's diktat. The report found some positive outcomes—despite their failure to win a general seat in the National Assembly in the past elections, members of religious minorities continued to stand, and in five constituencies in Sindh, there were eleven minority candidates in 2013 as against five in 2008. Majority community candidates, who, in the past, had largely ignored them, actively sought their votes and even asked them to manage their campaigns in some cases.

However, there were serious issues of security. A minority community candidate in Mirpur Khas-Umarkot felt threatened by religious pressure groups and was too scared to name his tormentors. The report said that almost all minority community candidates complained of being asked by the returning officers, during the scrutiny of the nomination papers, questions they thought were derogatory to their faith. Voters from the minority community were also deterred by deliberately asking them to register as voters in far-flung areas or by registering members of a single family in different polling stations.

While women voters from the minority community turned out in large numbers in Sindh, often outnumbering Muslim women, there were problems in places. In the Mirpur Khas-Umarkot constituency, the only non-Muslim candidate, Santosh Kumar, got just sixty-five votes even though there were 85,000 voters who were non-Muslim. Kumar told the HRCP that during the campaign, he feared attacks by religious groups, but was scared of naming anyone.

In a National Assembly constituency in Tharparkar, during the May 2013 General Elections, a pamphlet was circulated warning Muslims against voting for an 'infidel' or a candidate belonging to a religious minority. While ten seats of the 342 in the National Assembly are reserved for non-Muslims, only one non-Muslim candidate was elected from the 272 general seats. Minorities were not accorded protection during elections, and complaints were not taken seriously. They lost out in the democratic process as well after being deprived of their fundamental rights.

Minorities formed 25 per cent of the population at the time of Partition; this figure had dwindled to 5 per cent or less. The rights and secular ideals envisaged by Jinnah have been consumed by violent sectarianism. Jinnah defended the only Ahmadi member of his Cabinet but the sect was outlawed by the Constitution itself. There is clear and present danger for religious minorities, including the Hindus who are escaping to India, fearing conversion and having their daughters kidnapped and forced into marriage. And the law takes its own time to deliver justice. Even if there are rational voices of protest and condemnation, hatred is a powerful force. Often leaving the country seems to be the only option for those who can afford it.

II. Covering Bomb Blasts, the 26/11 Case, Drone Strikes . . .

Terror and the Taliban

The blowback for supporting and training terror groups to fight the Soviets and later to infiltrate into Kashmir has been borne by ordinary Pakistanis and the security forces. Some of the radicalized tribal groups morphed into the TTP in 2007, which was bent on creating an Islamic state in Pakistan and imposing the Sharia. A decade previously, sectarian terror groups, including the Lashkar-e-Jhangvi and Sipah-e-Sahaba, were active in the Punjab with the support of the Taliban; one of them even attempted to assassinate Nawaz Sharif during the time of his first tenure as prime minister in 1998. Sectarian strikes targeted at Shias, Christians and Ahmadis, and at marketplaces and cinemas soon became the norm; in bombings that took place over a decade from 2000 onwards, nearly 60,000 fell victim, including a number of armed forces personnel.[26] 'By 1998 Pakistani Taliban groups were banning TV and videos in towns along the Pashtun belt, imposing Sharia punishment such as stoning and amputation in defiance of the legal system, killing Pakistani Shia and forcing people, particularly Pakistani women to adapt to the Taliban dress code and way of life. Pakistan's support for the Taliban is thus coming back to haunt the country itself, even as Pakistan leaders appear to be oblivious of the challenge and continue to support the Taliban,' writes Ahmed Rashid.[27] The bombings intensified after General Musharraf supported the USA in the war against terror after the 11 September attack in New York, and endorsed drone strikes against terrorists.

Terror comes in many forms in Pakistan, and suicide bombings are unending. Islamabad, known to be a safe capital, was struck twice when I was there, one attack very close to where I lived. In 2002, attacks did take place in the capital when the Protestant International Church in the diplomatic enclave was attacked. A school run by Christians in Murree and a church attached to a hospital in Taxila were also targeted by the terrorists. The shocking attack on a public park in Lahore on Easter in 2016 was yet another monstrosity perpetrated by a faction of the TTP which splintered after the killing of its leader Hakimullah Mehsud on 1 November 2013.

The sectarian attacks in the Punjab have spread to other parts of the country and few are spared in this war. Civilians, minorities, army personnel, government officials, politicians and the media, too, have been victims, and in the chapters to come, some of the incidents I reported on are discussed in this context. The talks with the TTP went nowhere—they were destined to fail from the start, and the army launched Operation Zarb-e-Azb (the Prophet's Sword) to bomb the terrorists in Waziristan towards the end of 2013, creating another massive civilian exodus. Terrorism and safe havens are still the subject of discussions among the US, Afghanistan and Pakistan, and Pakistan certainly does not seem to have given up its much-desired 'strategic depth'[28] policy in Afghanistan. The Haqqani Network, for instance, does not seem to be hampered in its activities in any way in spite of repeated requests from the US to Pakistan to stop backing the Haqqanis. Despite the TTP being in disarray and the Afghan Taliban weakened by the death in 2013 of their long-time chief, Mullah Omar, and later that of his successor Mullah Akhtar Mansour, who was killed by a US drone strike in Pakistan in 2016, there seems to be no let-up in Afghanistan. Sirajuddin Haqqani is now the second in command in the Afghan Taliban. The Haqqanis, once favoured by the CIA (Central Intelligence Agency), are now facing American wrath for targeting its armed personnel in Afghanistan. There is the overhanging threat of the Islamic State, though Pakistan denies it exists there. The Taliban's spring offensive in April 2016 was launched with a bombing in Kabul, and the suicide attacks continue in 2017 with depressing regularity. Increasingly, more areas are coming under Taliban control in Afghanistan.

While the government offered the TTP an olive branch, the spate of bombings, starting with the church in Peshawar in September 2013, showed that the terror outfit thought little of peace. The capital was rocked by two bomb blasts in March and April 2014, and there were incidents all over the country—a teenaged boy died fighting a suicide bomber and a young politician in Khyber Pakhtunkhwa was killed on Bakri Id in his *hujra* (a place outside the house where men meet). Terrorists die or go unpunished for the most part, but Pakistan is trying the perpetrators of the 26/11 Mumbai attack, and this is a trial which is keenly watched in India.

Shrapnel for a souvenir

I met some of the families targeted by the suicide bombing of the Peshawar church. One of them showed me a small plastic box with a piece of shrapnel with congealed blood on it. It was from Arsalan's neck, his mother explained. She clasped it in her hand like a treasure. In the end that's all she had left of the boy. It was a bright Sunday morning on 22 September 2013, and I was hoping nothing would happen to disturb my holiday when I saw the flash on TV a little after 11.45 a.m. It was the All Saints Church in Peshawar and the twin suicide bombers were the first to strike in that week-long orgy of violence which ended with a third blast the following Sunday. It was a stunning attack and took place when the congregation stepped out to enjoy some food after the service. Putting aside shock and horror at the event, on a professional level, I was in helpless despair as I couldn't get anywhere near the blast site and cover it from the ground. So I had to resort to a mix of Internet, TV interviews and some quick phone calls to put together a story, as was often the case with my reporting from Pakistan. Two weeks later I did meet some of the families of the survivors at the Pakistan Institute of Medical Sciences (PIMS) in the capital.

It was not the first church strike in Pakistan and it wasn't going to be the last, but the intensity and boldness was chilling. In September 2012 in Mardan, sixty kilometres from Peshawar, a protest against a 'blasphemous' film—news reports indicated only that the US-made film was anti-Islamic—turned violent, resulting in the burning and ransacking of St Paul's Church and the school, the library, the vicarage and two other houses inside its premises. All Saints Church is located in Kohati Gate, an inner city area of Peshawar, and at least eighty-one people were killed and over 100 injured (137 was the official figure, with ten of them critical); many of them were women and children. One of the suicide bombers reportedly carrying six kilograms of explosives entered the church while the other detonated himself outside the compound where around 600 people were milling around.

Missionary schools decided to close down for three days in protest, but it was only when I went around the churches in Islamabad that the fear and insecurity came home to me. One of the places I would have liked to visit was the Lady Reading

Hospital in Peshawar, which seemed to be in a perpetual state of emergency. It managed admirably with the limited resources at its disposal to deal with the unending bombings; later, some of the critically injured were moved to the PIMS in Islamabad and the Combined Military Hospital in Peshawar. An eyewitness who lived close by saw one of the bombers blowing himself up sometime after 11 a.m. and felt the shattering effect of the two blasts. The All Saints Memorial Church has the distinctive Indo-Saracenic style of architecture favoured by the British, and it opened for service in December 1883. In a statement online, for which I was grateful, the Rt Revd Humphrey S. Peters of Peshawar, condemned the attack and said it reflected the total failure of the new government in Khyber Pakhtunkhwa (KPK) led by the Pakistan Tehreek-e-Insaf, to provide security to the minorities in the province. He had spoken to one of the parish members who lost his aunt and nephew in the bombing. Among the dead were a number of Sunday school children and members of the church choir.

In Peshawar, one of the few people I could depend on for reliable information, other than a few journalists, was Shiraz Paracha, a former journalist and then spokesperson for the Khyber Pakhtunkhwa chief minister. Even for Peshawar, often in the centre of a storm, this kind of attack was unprecedented, Paracha said. A multitude of protests erupted in the country and the PTI was under fire for not doing enough to secure institutions such as churches. All over the country there was mourning and condemnation.

The Peshawar diocese was created in 1980 and it is one of the largest in the country. The total number of Christians living in the KPK province is around 100,000, out of the provincial population of around 17 million, according to the diocese website. For the prime minister it was unfortunate that the incident happened on the day he was leaving for New York to attend the United Nations General Assembly session, and it was a strange coincidence that every time he was going abroad there would be a 'situation'. There were calls for greater security for churches and more protection for the minorities, but the next day after visiting two of the main churches in the capital, I realized how vulnerable they were to attack.

A lone policeman with a sub-machine gun sat outside St Thomas Church, one of the two big churches in Islamabad. There were many small churches in the slums, often in small rooms with makeshift crosses and tiny groups of people praying. Here, the branches of the tall fir trees almost covered the warm red-brick church and a certain stillness and fear permeated through the closed maroon gates painted with golden crosses. Built in 1992, the church had installed CCTVs a few months ago for safety. Policemen on motorcycles patrolled the roads once in a while.

I wasn't allowed to go inside, and apart from the policeman, I saw a man standing outside and he turned out to be someone who had a close connection with the All Saints Church. This parish member and retired government employee was in tears. His nikah ceremony had been held there in 1978. Soon after the incident he got in touch with his old Bible study coordinator in Peshawar, who had lost his wife and daughter. His relatives were all in hospital having suffered serious injuries, and the interview ended in a welter of fresh tears. The church had asked for increased security in the past and on Sunday there were usually two or three policemen. But he looked up and said, 'We leave security to God.'

At the Roman Catholic Our Lady of Fatima Church, built in 1979, Father Rahmat Michael Hakim was discussing security with a senior officer when I was allowed inside after my passport was checked. The churches had to be very careful. Father Rahmat reminded the policeman gently that the Sunday mass began at 7 a.m. Outside, a Kalashnikov-wielding policeman lounged in a chair. There are 4000 Catholic families in the Islamabad Capital Territory. The Islamabad and Rawalpindi dioceses have about 200,000 Christians. The church was planning to install CCTVs but for now, Father Rahmat said the razor fencing would have to do. Churches have become soft targets after mosques. Father Rahmat and others were helpless against forces which hate so much that they were prepared to kill themselves.

The TTP claimed responsibility for the attacks, and coming after the All Parties Conference endorsing talks with the terror outfit, hope faded fast of any reconciliation as the TTP was not giving up on suicide bombings and terror strikes. The national flag flew at half mast and outraged protestors took to the streets in many parts of Pakistan. In Islamabad too, nearly 2000 people marched on the streets shouting slogans against the Taliban, demanding justice. Posters said 'Save minority rights, be a true Pakistani'.

There was a protest at D-Chowk, opposite Parliament, where candles were lit, and religious and political leaders said this was a mourning (*matham*), not a protest, for those who were 'martyred' in the bombing. There were spontaneous actions from ordinary people outraged by the latest suicide attack. Farida Choudhry, a nurse, and her young son, who had come carrying placards, said that there should be no religious discrimination and this terrorism should end. Many women from the Christian-dominated slum colonies joined the protest, beating their chests in sorrow. Nageen Hyat of the Women's Action Forum felt it was not a matter concerning the minorities alone and that all progressive people were under threat. Minorities like the Hazaras and the Kalash from Chitral also came all the way to lend support. Pakistan has several dynamic activists like eminent lawyer Asma Jahangir and activist Tahira Abdullah, and the National Human Rights Commission is helmed by the venerable I.A. Rehman. I met human rights activist Farzana Bari who said the country was moving towards chaos because the state was failing to provide security, while Khawar Mumtaz, the chairperson of the National Commission on the Status of Women, said this was part of the militant agenda—and the church was a soft target. In the past, it was bazaars and crowded places. I often met many activists in the small progressive circle and they were calm, reacting like rational people, helpless against the macabre violence. A few of them bravely took part in open demonstrations denouncing government policies or attacks on minorities, and faced great danger.

A little after the church blasts, I read about some Peshawar survivors who were admitted to PIMS, and decided to go there. At least this public hospital was accessible: a sprawling place with low buildings and many barricades. The broad road leads to the casualty ward while the burns ward where the three children were admitted, is located at a little distance behind. The oldest of them, eight-year-old Arsalan, didn't return home. I went to the ward where I met his mother, Raziabibi, and uncle, Akram. A bed sheet was spread out in the corridor with some belongings on it and they excitedly showed me a small taped plastic box with a bloodied lump in it, possibly ball bearings congealed in flesh and blood, removed from the side of Arsalan's throat.

Arsalan went to church every Sunday with his father, who suffered a fracture and was in a hospital in Peshawar. 'Every home that day had at least four funerals,' Razia said. She didn't know at that time that she would lose the youngest of her five sons.

Arish, a first-year college student was accompanying his sister, Simran, who had extensive injuries, her body spattered with shrapnel; only her face was spared. She'd had two operations already. His younger sister, a six-year-old, was in hospital in Peshawar. They all loved church and they went to Sunday school with great enthusiasm.

For Asma and her family, the bombing would leave a bitter mark forever. She had celebrated her twenty-fifth birthday the night before. The young schoolteacher lost her father and brother, Imtiaz, in the bombing. 'I can't speak about it and I can't forget that scene. I couldn't do anything for them,' Asma said, trying to control her grief. She was amazed that I was from India, but was welcoming despite the grim situation she was in. Her niece, three-year-old Mehek, had a head injury and was in a critical condition in the burns unit, while Asma's younger brother, too, was in hospital at that time.

She had to come to Islamabad as Mehek's mother was coping with her husband's death. Asma said her brother, Imtiaz, had joined the police recently and he was killed in the attack. Her father had stepped out from the church to the compound where food was being served. That's when the bombs went off. Asma was still inside and found it difficult to get to her father in the stampede and smoke.

That was only the first of the bomb blasts that week in Peshawar and in less than a fortnight the number had gone to five. After the All Saints Church, that Friday a bomb went off in a bus carrying government employees, killing nineteen of them and injuring over forty. Then, for the third time in a week, Peshawar was brought to its knees. This time it was a powerful 225-kg bomb in a car parked near a police station in the historic Qissa Khawani Bazaar, which killed over thirty persons and injured over 100 on Sunday. Just as shops were opening at around 11 a.m., the crowd, with many women and children, was stunned as the bomb detonated, causing another cylinder explosion in a nearby car. The market was engulfed in thick black smoke as cars and shops caught fire while panic spread.

A white Toyota was fashioned into a bomb, and a crater was formed at the site of the blast. Firefighters had to climb up to the shops lining the road to douse fires, and the whole area was in a shambles. There were a number of handcart vendors on the road who took the brunt of the blast which came after the PTI chairperson, Imran Khan, suggested that the Taliban be allowed to open an office in the country for talks, for which he was roundly criticized. Qissa Khawani Bazaar is historically known for the massacre of the Khudai Khidmatgars, the legendary freedom fighters led by Khan Abdul Ghaffar Khan, the Frontier Gandhi. In April 1930, the Khudai Khidmatgars were gunned down by the

British Army during a non-violent protest. It was also the place where a soldier of the Garhwal regiment refused to fire on unarmed people, yet today innocent lives are the target.[29] A popular place, it was made famous by Kipling as the market of storytellers, and once caravans from far away used to find a resting place there. It is also the birthplace of Mohammed Yusuf Khan, better known as Dilip Kumar, an icon of Indian cinema. Qissa Khawani Bazaar has more macabre tales to tell now and they won't be about the caravans from afar or Frontier Gandhi.

In the rest of Pakistan the pace of events was so rapid—unlike the somewhat sedate capital which chugged along at a different speed with its active think-tank seminars and formal social events. Peshawar seemed to be lurching from one bombing to another, and this frontier city reminded me of Mumbai and its bomb blasts which happened at one time with unfailing regularity. I also read the all-too-familiar stories of resilience in Peshawar, just as we eulogized Mumbai as an unbreakable city. I wondered if the Lady Reading Hospital was like the King Edward Memorial Hospital with its huge infrastructure or like the JJ Hospital. Both hospitals in Mumbai did a marvellous job each time there was a crisis.

Far from resilience, in the eyes of the people I met, there was only anguish. Arsalan's mother kept wondering why the church was bombed and she told me that her son was getting better. There were other stories related to terrorism and while I couldn't visit those places, I tried to report them as best as I could. One was about a teenager who saved his school. Nearly eleven months before the brutal Army Public School bombing in Peshawar in 2014, a chubby teenager had stopped a suicide bomber outside the gate of his government school in Hangu (in Khyber Pakhtunkhwa), garnering international attention. Young Aitizaz Hussain, a student of class nine, grappled with a bulky stranger that morning of 6 January 2014 and died when the bomber blew himself up. He had asked the man to stop and even threw a stone at him.

In a country inured to violent death, his story tugged at the hearts of everyone, and he was an instant martyr and hero. The young boy was immediately given the highest civilian honour and received accolades from another celebrity terror victim, Malala Yousafzai. Aitizaz saved hundreds of his schoolmates from death, and drew out a statement from the prime minister's office. His school is in Ibhrahimzai, a Shia-dominated area, and the government decided to name it after the boy who saved it from destruction.

When death came smiling

On the face of it, it was just another suicide bomb attack, but this time it killed a young politician and several others sitting near him. When Khyber Pakhtunkhwa Law Minister Israrullah Khan Gandapur walked a few steps to greet one of the many visitors in his hujra at Kolachi on Bakri Id, he didn't think it would be the last thing he did. It was one of the bizarre incidents I wrote about thanks to a chance encounter with someone who knew the family. The Gandapurs were an old political family from Dera Ismail Khan district in KPK, and no one knows the real reason which eventually led to this handsome young minister being blown up. Israrullah Khan exchanged greetings with his young visitor who was wearing new clothes, who embraced him and then detonated the bomb strapped to his body. It was the first day of Bakri Id and they were gathered in the hujra outside his residence at Kolachi in Dera Ismail Khan. The minister was killed on the spot, along with seven others, while his older brother, Ikramullah, survived. Later we knew that the suicide bomber was between twenty and twenty-two years old and had spoken to the minister in the local language. Coming after the many suicide bomb attacks in KPK, this one added to the existing insecurity, and media reports suggested he could have been killed by a little-known terror outfit in connection with the sensational jail breaks in Dera Ismail Khan, but that was only one of the many speculations.

Faisal Karim Kundi, a PPP politician from Dera Ismail Khan and a former deputy speaker of the National Assembly, was one of the few people to meet him before he died. 'It was the custom to go to greet people who come to visit you on Id day and Israrullah walked eight to ten feet to greet his visitor before it all ended.' Married in 2006, Israrullah is survived by his wife, an infant daughter and a son.

The thirty-nine-year-old held a master's in political science, and started his studies in Kulachi before completing them in Peshawar. That was his third term in the provincial assembly which he contested as an Independent, and later joined the PTI. He took to active politics after the death of his father, Sardar Inayatullah Khan Gandapur, a former chief minister of the North-West Frontier Province and a strong influence. The family has a close relationship with Maulana Fazl-ur-Rehman of the Jamiat Ulema-e-Islam (JUI-Fazl-ur-Rehman faction) and they backed each other during the elections. In a by-election in Dera Ismail Khan and Tank area for the National Assembly, even though the Pakistan Tehreek-e-Insaf and the others had ranged themselves against the maulana's party, Israrullah supported the maulana's son, Asad Mehmood, who lost.

Israrullah did get some threats since 2012 and there had been an attempt on his life in April 2013 too. Hours before his death, he had sent a text message to a friend asking him to come and meet him that evening before it was too late, said Shiraz Paracha, on whom I had to rely once again. Everyone was talking about this message and whether it was a premonition of sorts. That seems unlikely going by a photo taken before Israrullah was killed. It showed a smiling, relaxed politician meeting people.

Paracha knew him for a few months and said he was one of the finest members of the provincial Cabinet in terms of his extensive knowledge about constitutional affairs and his understanding of the rules of business. He had a grasp of governance issues and in a short period of time he had become one of the shining stars of the

PTI government. He called him a 'thorough gentleman' and said that he would come prepared for meetings and put the bureaucrats on the back foot. There was a perception, unfortunately, in KPK that politicians were not up to scratch but this young man was an outstanding exception.

Unlike his father, Israrullah was known for his simple lifestyle. He mingled with people and met them easily. Paracha rued that he was so accessible, and that could be one of the reasons for his death.

I was keen on reconstructing the picture of the man who was killed in this wanton fashion even though there were many such incidents, and the country moved in a daze from one numbing tragedy to another. I didn't even know this man, and couldn't even visit his home, but the casual and everyday quality of greeting a visitor during Id had acquired a gruesome and chilling turn. It was an incident that replayed in my mind like a stuck record.

A safe capital

The Islamabad district court complex in F-8 Markaz, which also houses the Regional Transport Office (RTO) and the excise department, was a far cry from any district court I have seen. The rooms were low-ceilinged, poky and crowded. Once my husband, who loved to potter about in the narrow by-lanes walked into a court in session, startling everyone including the judge who asked him what he was doing there. Venkat, conscious for the first time that he had meandered into the unknown, replied he was strolling around and didn't think this was a serious courtroom. The judge soundly ticked him off. It was rather difficult to believe that courts could run in this ramshackle complex, which was across the road from where I lived. It also housed the Anti-Terrorism Court (ATC) where the 26/11 trial was under way. I had gone there one morning to meet the special public prosecutor. It was so nondescript and easy to target as it had none of the security trappings, like CCTVs or monitored gates.

A week after the minister for interior had declared Islamabad safe, there was a deadly attack (3 March 2014) on the court complex. It was not the neatly arranged legs of a suicide bomber or the bloodied, narrow lanes that stayed in my mind, but the calm, almost everyday actions of gloved policemen picking up pieces of flesh and putting them into a plastic bag. The first blast shook the glass windows of my house and I thought everything was going to collapse. I tweeted helplessly; there was nothing on TV. And soon the news came in and I heard another deafening explosion; then the firing continued in staccato bursts. It was a sound I'd heard before—during the riots back home in 1992–93 and the same staccato bursts during the 26/11 terror strike while standing outside the CST in the darkness when Kasab and his companion were raining bullets on travellers in the train station. It was a sound I would never forget.

My first thoughts were relief that my husband was back in India and he was not pottering about in those wretched by-lanes. He knew many of the people by name and asked if the man who sold samosas had survived the blast when I called to tell him. I waited for things to calm down before I ventured across the road. I thought the area would be sealed off but just as in India where there is no sanctity to a crime scene, I realized everyone was walking around unhindered. There was yellow tape on the main road, guarded by policemen, and I waited hesitantly before I saw a TV journalist ducking under the tape and walking across. I followed him—all the shops were closed and there was silence everywhere. I walked past the ATC and to the narrow lane full of blood and a thick layer of broken glass. The courts, judges' chambers, lawyers' offices, Xerox centres and shops were packed into the thin lanes now emptied of the routine crowd. Not a single shop or courtroom was untouched; there was blood in big and small puddles, and pieces of flesh; soon I reached the courts where one of the suicide bombers had blown himself up. Being a reporter in Mumbai had exposed me to a lot of violence and blood since 1992–93. We had to visit morgues regularly and scenes of communal carnage and blasts. There were quite a few sights I wish I hadn't seen. We had actually done a body count, visiting the city morgues after the December 1992 riots, and after the blasts on 12 March 1993. But now after many years, I felt I had seen enough for a lifetime. I took pictures of the horrifying scenes before me with my cell phone, but that mechanical action didn't reduce the horror of what I saw.

People were bursting with stories: that morning a group of five to ten young men (there were varying versions) dressed in salwar kameez with shawls draped over them, walked into the court complex and started firing, throwing grenades, and two of them had lethal vests. It was that easy, no one stopped them; there was a calm, almost casual quality about these terror attacks. This was the new guerrilla tactic, the opposite of surprise—no surprise. Walk in with guns and people will notice only when you start firing and by then it's too late. We saw that in Mumbai too.

Policemen were picking up pieces of flesh from here and there and putting them into plastic bags. They would be then deposited into a large brown carton-like paper bag. Police and officials explained the scene patiently to us. These grim men were equally horrified but, like me, were trying to do their job. These were once people, I thought, as I peered into the bag. After that, I couldn't eat blood oranges, which were then in season, though I loved the fruit. The spooks I had seen during Mama Qadeer's march were milling around and I grinned at them. Beard and Chubby were absent, or so I thought. They had a way of knowing everything I did though (through GPS tracking, I learnt later).

There was a small crater where one of the suicide bombers had blown himself up. One policeman had climbed up a ladder to retrieve a large lump of flesh stuck high up in the electric wires.

A bloody portion of the wall screened by a white cloth was where the suicide bomber's head had left a mark. It had been blown that high. A pair of legs lay neatly arranged nearby outside the chamber of the additional sessions judge, Rafakat Awan.

Lawyer Khalid Mahmood was going back to his office when he saw five young men in their early twenties, bearded and wearing salwar kameez, carrying AK-47s and grenades, with bags slung on their shoulders. His white sleeves were stained with blood as he had helped carry the victims to hospital. He had removed nine bodies. At 9.19 a.m. he called the then Islamabad inspector general of police, Sikandar Hayat, who said he didn't know about the firing. An outraged Mahmood kept showing me his cell phone to show the time of the call.

The gunmen shot a senior lawyer Rao Rashid Iqbal Khan and moved to Gilani Hall near the canteen. Another judge, Adnan Jamali, was also shot at. Lawyers had complained a week before that the court was vulnerable as it had no CCTVs or a proper security mechanism in place. Rana Abid Farooq was sitting in his lawyer's office when the gunmen fired through the glass windows. Abdul Ghaffar lay on the ground under a chair to escape the firing. He took me to the small, narrow office and I wondered how he had managed to survive even if he hid under a chair. There were two suicide bombers who were killed and two of the gunmen managed to escape—that's what officials on the site said. Orders to search for the men who escaped were given in hushed tones. I looked around half expecting a sniper or another bomber. Everyone seemed clueless.

Mohsin Akhtar Kayani, who headed the Islamabad High Court bar association, had a narrow escape but his associate, young Fizza Malik, was killed and so were two of his staff. Almost everyone knew the additional sessions judge, Awan, and said that he did not try to escape when he was told about the attack—and he paid for it with his life. Twelve people were killed and twenty-eight injured in the attack which lasted for about thirty to forty minutes. When I went to the Supreme Court which took suo motu notice of the attack a week later, angry lawyers said the police refused to fire, saying that their guns were not working or that if they fired, then the terrorists would come towards them. Only one brave policeman defied this pattern and fired at a suicide bomber, it was said, who fell down and blew himself up. The policeman, too, was killed.

The court was critical of the contradictory statements by the police. 'When will you understand how to tackle terrorism?' Justice Azmat Saeed Sheikh asked, adding that they needed to go to a bookshop and read up. I saw the helpless judiciary trying to instil some order into the investigation but with little effect. There seemed to be no SOPs even though the country had been fighting terror for over a decade. The police were bumbling and fearful, and the lack of security and warnings were to prove costly as there was another blast soon.

A lethal carton of guavas

A month after the district court bombing, it was the turn of the Sabzi Mandi in sector I-10. A powerful bomb went off during the busy auction time around 8.05 a.m. in the sprawling fruit and vegetable market in the capital, killing at least twenty-four persons and injuring close to 100. The five-kg bomb was planted in a carton of guavas. Thousands of people throng the Sabzi Mandi from 5 a.m. for the auction. Dilawar Khan, a commission agent, said the auction was under way when the bomb went off just 100 feet away from him. He didn't give himself any time to recover, but started helping the injured people into cars. He kept thanking Allah for his miraculous escape.

Naqash, a TV cameraman, reached there soon after 8 a.m. to find a scene of devastation. He saw bodies lying all around, and private cars ferrying the injured. Some bodies were piled up in a pickup, and the ambulances were yet to arrive. Ripe guavas lay everywhere and there was a small crater in the place where the auction had been taking place which was cordoned off with yellow tape. As teams of police stood around, scared workers and commission agents stood in the stalls, at a distance, watching the scene in silence. Gul Mohammed, a commission agent, was having breakfast when he heard the loud explosion in his house opposite the market. His wife thought a wall had collapsed, but his son called him to say it was a bomb blast.

The Sabzi Mandi is the central market for the Punjab province where all the fruit crates are unloaded, auctioned and transported to other parts of the country. Gul recalled a bomb blast nearly fifteen years ago in the fruit market and that too had a high casualty count. He said it was the season for guavas and that was why the auction was so crowded. At the office of the Anjuman Wholesale Fruit Commission Agents, an umbrella group of agents, near the market, there was a furious debate on the need for scanners and more security. Tahir Ayub, its general secretary, explained that the auction usually began at 5 a.m. every day and this was the biggest market in the region, with fruits coming in from all over the place, including India by way of the LoC, as well as China and Kabul. The auction was almost over when the bomb went off. While I was talking to the men in their office, one of them asked me who I was reporting for, and the minute I said *The Hindu* and India, the bomb blast was forgotten; they insisted I have tea and said wonderful things about my country. They wouldn't let me leave and I had a difficult time explaining that I couldn't sit and chat with them as I had to go to the hospital to check on the injured for my news report. They let me go after much pestering but it's something that always amuses me when I think of the unhappy relations between the two countries.

The market, spread over twenty-five acres, was a security nightmare. There was no compound wall and the security guards were not even armed. There was no system to scan the trucks or the goods, and the volume of business was very high. There were 300 firms dealing in fruit and an equal number in vegetables. At least 100,000 people visit the market daily and it had been working almost round the clock since 1983 when it was moved here. It was mostly poor vendors and daily wage labourers who were killed or injured.

Terror and trial

For the first time in a terror attack in India, a perpetrator, Ajmal Kasab, was caught fleeing the police at a beachfront in Mumbai. His accomplice was shot dead by a band of Mumbai policemen, some of whom had never fired a gun before, while Constable Tukaram Omble who held on to Kasab's gun, became an unwitting martyr. The Dadasaheb Bhadkamkar Marg police were the unassuming heroes of that encounter. I had interviewed some of them after the incident and they didn't know that a routine *nakabandi* (or a stop-and-check operation) would result in actually catching a terrorist who had killed dozens of people in the city at random, including some top police officers.

Before carjacking a silver Skoda, Kasab and his accomplice were photographed by AFP's Sebastian Fernandes at the CST. He was later interrogated by Rakesh Maria then the joint commissioner of crime, Mumbai Police; for some reason, extensive recordings of the interrogation of Kasab were played on television, and if I recall correctly, Maria ended the grilling by asking Kasab if his 'friends' (who were all dead) got the promised number of virgins in heaven.

Kasab, it turned out, was from Faridkot in Okara district of the Punjab. A news report confirmed his parents lived there, and his father even identified Kasab from Fernandes's famous photograph, amid denials from Pakistan. For the first time, the Indian government which had been pointing fingers at its neighbour for sponsoring terror strikes since 1992, said it had what it called 'hard evidence'. It also had voice recordings, which BBC's Channel 4 broadcast in its film on the terror strike where you could hear voices egging on the men with guns in the Chabad House and the other places they attacked. But apparently, this evidence was not enough—at least that's what the lawyers for the accused said. However, the evidence from the phone calls was presented to Pakistan, and seven persons, including one of the masterminds, Lashkar-e-Taiba Commander Zaki-ur-Rehman Lakhvi, were arrested after the attack. To the Indian government's consternation, Pakistan steadfastly refused to acknowledge that the Lashkar-e-Taiba founder, Hafiz Saeed, was involved in 26/11. The trial was something I was keen on tracking since I had covered the attack in some detail and followed Kasab's fate at home. India had sent dossiers to Pakistan as evidence and there was a feeling that this time the culprits could be nailed. In Mumbai the high-profile trial of Kasab was held in a prison, and the media personnel needed special accreditation with biometric fingerprinting for attendance. There was a special cell connected to the court built for Kasab at a cost of Rs 2 crore, and security was tight. Ujjwal Nikam was a star special public prosecutor and used to give bites to the media every day. There was daily coverage of everything about the trial—the evidence, the cross-examination, the charges, how Kasab looked, what he said, how he cried or didn't cry, what he ate. Nikam's statements, some of which he has confessed to making up for effect (for instance that biryani was fed to Kasab)[30] were played up widely. He was an authority on the trial and people hung on to his every word.

I foolishly thought the trial would be on similar lines and open to the press in Pakistan. It was high security all right, but no one was allowed to attend the proceedings, and from the ATC it moved to Adiala Jail in Rawalpindi. In addition, public prosecutors were under threat. The ATC in the district court complex had none of the security trappings of our own court. In May 2013, Chaudhry Zulfiqar Ali, the earlier Federal

Investigation Agency (FIA) special public prosecutor, was shot dead in his car while on his way to Rawalpindi. The new FIA special prosecutor, Chaudhry Muhammed Azhar, a grey-haired man, was friendly on the phone and said I could meet him on the date of the next hearing. I arrived at the district court complex before 9 a.m. to wait for him and he wandered in accompanied by some casual-looking security guards in blue who didn't stop me as I went up to him. We spoke briefly and he said I couldn't attend the hearing since the media wasn't allowed. I later went up the stairs to see the small, wooden furnished court which was empty. He was helpful and after every hearing, I would call him for updates. There was no media buzz and no one even knew him at the court, unlike our own Nikam.

There were fresh delays in the trial after the court rejected the findings of the Pakistan Judicial Commission following its visit to Mumbai in 2011 since it was denied permission to cross-examine four witnesses. In September 2013, the Pakistan Judicial Commission visited India for more interviews with witnesses and officials in Mumbai, and they came back 'highly satisfied'. Their initial dates for travel were changed twice and there was much speculation in the media that India wasn't giving them visas—which was not true. We tried in vain to dispel this myth, and eventually the commission did travel and get its work done. This time the commission could cross-examine two witnesses, a doctor who carried out the postmortems of the nine terrorists who had been killed in the attack and the investigating officer of the case, Ramesh Mahale. In 2012, the ATC judge had rejected the report of the commission since he couldn't cross-examine some witnesses or meet the two doctors who had conducted the postmortems of the nine dead terrorists.

India has been demanding a speedy trial in the case and says it has sent all the relevant evidence to Pakistan. Talks between the two countries ceased after this attack. While I was there, the trial was coming up with more and more evidence but suddenly the defence lawyers were changed, and Rizwan Abbasi and his team were presented to the media at a flashy press conference coordinated by an event management agency.

On the fifth anniversary of the Mumbai terror attacks, 26 November 2013, the new defence team addressed a press conference on the case. Abbasi would now represent the seven accused in the case, including Zaki-ur-Rehman Lakhvi. He felt the case was already prolonged and he would approach the high court for expediting the trial, and he said that India had delayed matters by not submitting proper evidence. Invitations for the press conference were also sent out by the Jamaat-ud-Dawa, a front organization for the LeT. The event was managed by a public relations firm, Aye Tee, and had large banners raising ten questions on the Mumbai attacks which had not been answered by India.

Abbasi said no concrete evidence had been provided against any of the seven accused in jail. He said Indian courts did not allow the Pakistan Judicial Commission to meet or cross-examine Kasab or question his confession which had been retracted. His clients were in jail based on that single confessional statement and it was not tenable in law since it was not subjected to a cross-examination by the defence, Abbasi said. In addition, there was no proof that the handlers whom Kasab had named were from Pakistan and neither was this substantiated by phone call records. India, apparently, did not provide timely evidence and only sent dossiers which are not admissible in a court of law. Dossiers are just information, not evidence, he remarked. He said that evidence of photographs of Kasab or supporting statements relating to it were not sent to Pakistan. It was not possible for ten people to just walk into a city and conduct a terror strike, he added. (All of us thought that, but it was evidently possible.)

While reporting, whenever I called, Abbasi was forthcoming and even helpful at times, though he wouldn't give away anything specific, and the media didn't always report proceedings since the trial was being conducted at the Adiala Jail where Lakhvi and six others were housed.

Before that, in mid-November 2013, the defence lawyer for Lakhvi dropped out of the case, citing personal reasons. Riaz Akram Cheema told me that he had taken a decision that from 13 November 2013, he was no longer concerned with the case and did not wish to continue defending Lakhvi and the two other accused. He cited personal reasons, mainly that his mother was suffering from blood cancer and he wished to devote more time to her care. Cheema was the defence lawyer right from 2009 when the case was filed. He had earlier assisted defence lawyers Khwaja Sultan Ahmed and later Khwaja Harris Ahmed who had also stopped appearing in the case four months before. Cheema's assistant, Fakr Hayat Awan, was asked to discontinue when the Pakistan Judicial Commission returned after its second visit to Mumbai in September 2013.

On the other hand, Chaudhry Azhar brimmed with confidence. There was enough evidence in the case and some new witnesses were to be produced soon, he said. Among the witnesses were those who had obtained deep-sea fishing licences for the boats used by the ten terrorists to sail to India. Two witnesses, Saifullah and Omar Daraz, fishing harbour contractors who ran a company that procured licences for boats and also provided crew, gave evidence. Two boats, *Al Hussaini* and *Al Fouz*, had been licensed from the company for the attacks. Saifullah was the accountant for the company and Daraz the owner. They got the papers for the boats in question from the competent authority. More than thirty-two witnesses were examined at that time and more had been summoned. There are over 100 witnesses in the trial which began in February 2009.

For four weeks after the suicide attack on the Islamabad district and sessions court on 3 March 2014, the trial of the seven accused in the Mumbai terror strike was held up. It was then heard in the Adiala Jail in Rawalpindi, and security concerns were voiced by the judge, Atiq-ur-Rehman. Abbasi made an application to the law secretary to enhance security at the jail since the accused could not be transported outside. Later, the ATC was shifted to sector G-11 in Islamabad, and Abbasi moved an application for the accused to be exempted from appearance. The ATC used to hear the matter every week. The prosecution had earlier said there were several witnesses left to be examined and they also had a list of some people whose testimony had to be recorded. The accused were LeT operations head Zaki-ur-Rehman Lakhvi (who has been out on bail since April 2015)—named by Kasab in his confession as Zaki uncle—Abdul Wajid, Mazhar Iqbal, Hammad Amin Sadiq, Shahid Jameel Riaz, Jamil Ahmed and Younus Anjum.

Three of the ten terrorists who attacked Mumbai are believed to be from Okara, including Kasab. The district electoral officer from Okara provided evidence from the voters' list that linked one of the terrorists who was killed in the attack, to his family in Pakistan. Just before I left, there was an interesting development. One of the prosecution witnesses, a teacher, in May 2014, when cross-examined, said that Kasab studied in the Okara municipal primary school. But he was not the one hanged in Pune's Yerawada Jail. The teacher seemed to have turned hostile during the cross-examination. There was some confusion about this whole testimony and it all seemed fishy. The prosecution could declare the witness hostile and had asked permission to re-examine him, but wasn't confident of being allowed to do so. I don't know what happened to this witness.

Also interesting were some bank transactions which came to light. A bank manager from 'Azad' Jammu and Kashmir was cross-examined in connection with this. Some money had been transferred to the account of an accused in Karachi, ostensibly for the operation. The manager of the Muslim Commercial Bank in Islamabad was cross-examined. He had testified earlier that a sum of PKR 200,000 was transferred to the account of Hammad Amin Sadiq, an accused in the case. A police inspector, Mohammed

Ashraf, was also cross-examined by the defence. Ashraf was the person who was present at the time of the arrest of four of the seven accused in the case and also responsible for the recovery of some material from them. While I was getting all this information, I was shocked when in January 2014, Chaudhry Azhar who had always been so gracious, suddenly asked me to stop calling him. He said my reports were getting him into trouble. I had only quoted him with his permission, but there was a sudden cooling off. I realized that the government probably didn't want much news of the trial going out, and also did not like that an Indian was reporting it, though Pakistani journalists did report on it sporadically. Even the national security adviser, Sartaj Aziz, when I asked him about the trial, was on the defensive and said that he didn't consider Hafiz Saeed to be an offender and in fact, the courts had cleared him. On India's demand that Pakistan take action or hand over some of the alleged masterminds of the Mumbai attacks, including Hafiz Saeed, Aziz said that was ruled out. Belatedly, Saeed has been placed under house arrest in January 2017 and charged under the Anti-terrorism Act. It remains to be seen if the case will be taken to its logical end.[31] India has asked for a reinvestigation of the case and for Saeed to be tried for the attack. This was in response to Pakistan's request for recording the statement of twenty-four witnesses in the trial in India.[32]

India complains that Pakistan has been doing too little to bring the culprits to book, and the latter often retaliated by raising the Samjhauta Express blasts case and saying India wasn't sharing information. In any case, the trial lacked any transparency, though Chaudhry Azhar said there was enough proof and new eyewitnesses, and was confident of a favourable verdict. In April 2015, the Islamabad High Court set a two-month deadline for the completion of the trial. Little has happened in the last seventeen hearings (till March 2017), going by news reports, and the trial seems to be going on forever with repeated adjournments and laments that India hadn't given enough proof.

III. Talking to the Taliban, Drone Strikes and Other Stories

The tedium of talks with the Taliban

True to form, Major General Sanaullah Khan Niazi, the general officer commanding 17 Division (Swat), spent the night before he was killed with his troops in the Bin Shai sector, perched at 10,000 feet on the Pakistan–Afghanistan border. On his way back a little after noon, an improvised explosive device (IED) blew up his vehicle near Gatkotal village, Upper Dir, in Khyber Pakhtunkhwa. Lieutenant Colonel Tauseef Ahmad and Sepoy Irfan Sattar also died in the blast. Coming a week after an all-party conference had endorsed talks (in September 2013) with the TTP which owned up to the blast, this was a prelude to disaster. The three soldiers were the latest in the form of collateral damage in Pakistan's vicious cycle of terror and counterterror. A classmate of Maj. Gen. Niazi, Lt. Col. Shafqat Saeed, mourned his loss but said that the government should not pull back from talks, though there should be some restraint on the TTP. The government needed a plan to take the talks forward, but this wasn't in sight. He was deeply shocked by the death of his 'friend and good soldier', but Maj. Gen. Niazi would not be the first army casualty since the parleys with the TTP had been announced.

In the backdrop of terror attacks, there was a misplaced zeal about the desire to have all parties endorse a move to talk to the recalcitrant TTP. The TTP was not an outfit that believed in negotiation or talks; it was determined to set up a Sharia state in Pakistan by any means. On the whole the peace talks with the TTP were all sound and fury, signifying nothing—with people flying off to meet the TTP shura at an undisclosed destination, the confusing aspect of changing members of the committees, and the demands and counter demands; the reportage was more about all these details rather than on any substantive progress. Despite Sharif's well-meaning intentions to end bloodshed and offer an olive branch to cold-blooded murderers, in the end the army went in for Operation Zarb-e-Azb, an offensive which scythed through terrorist hideouts in Waziristan, and displaced millions of people once again.

The initial scepticism about the talks was reinforced by events every passing week. After the three army men's deaths, it was the suicide bombing of the All Saints Church in Peshawar, and there were two other bombings that week. Yet the government persisted with its efforts with the TTP, and the minister for interior, Chaudhry Nisar, claimed that mediators were flying out to meet the TTP chief, Hakimullah, with a letter when he was killed in a drone strike on 1 November in North Waziristan. It did seem a little odd that the TTP chief would actually want a letter of formal invitation—anyway, he didn't live to see it. Of course, no one in the government would confirm if it was really Hakimullah who had been killed and I finally had to rely on a reporter from *Dawn* who spoke to the TTP spokesperson, Shahidullah Shahid. It was frustrating to get the same non-committal replies from most government sources, and I realized that local journalists, too, were looking to the TTP's spokesperson for details. A week later, at a dramatic press conference on a Sunday, the interior minister chose to throw a tantrum over the US strike rather than share any important details of the strike or names of those killed. He even called for cutting off all ties with the US, something which is easier said than done.

The *Dawn* quoted Pakistani intelligence officials as having reported to their higher-ups that the Pakistani Taliban chief was leaving from a meeting at a mosque in the Dande Darpakhel area of North Waziristan when the drone targeted their vehicle. Five Taliban, including close aides of Hakimullah—Abdullah Bahar Mehsud and Tariq Mehsud—were killed, and two others were injured. The Dande Darpakhel area is five kilometres north of Miramshah, the main town of the North Waziristan tribal region. The ministry of foreign affairs issued the usual template condemning the US drone strike: 'These strikes are a violation of Pakistan's sovereignty and territorial integrity. There is an across the board consensus in Pakistan that these drone strikes must end.'

Untrue reports of Mehsud's death had appeared periodically before this, and the government was not taking a chance by confirming his death this time—at least that's what one official source said. Hakimullah had assumed leadership of the TTP in August 2009 after the death of Baitullah Mehsud in a drone strike. He carried a reward of $5 million on his head as a most wanted terrorist. The drone strike pulverized the ongoing talks with the TTP which many were sceptical about in any case. The terror outfit which seemed to have an excellent media reach was putting it out that it was keen on the talks with the government, and while bombs were going off everywhere, it kept denying it had anything to do with those incidents, putting the blame on its factions like Jundullah.

A BBC interview was quoted everywhere, with Hakimullah saying he was keen on talks, though no one had approached him. It seems in retrospect like an elaborate charade, with the government plodding on, keeping up the illusion of inclusion and democracy.

Hakimullah's death provoked disproportionate reactions from Pakistani authorities and Imran Khan's PTI. Interior Minister Chaudhry Nisar Ali Khan vented his anger against the US, calling for a review of all ties. Imran vowed to block NATO (North Atlantic Treaty Organization) supplies to Afghanistan from 20 November 2013 onwards. Nearly 1450 civilians had been killed in similar drone strikes, according to figures presented in the Peshawar High Court. Hakimullah was declared a martyr by right-wing groups and the government seemed to forget the huge casualties inflicted by the TTP in Pakistan.

Soon, in December 2013, helicopter gunships bombed terrorist hideouts in North Waziristan in what was described as 'surgical strikes' by the interior minister. In January 2014, terrorists struck with a rocket attack on the Bannu cantonment, killing twenty, and in a market near the sacred GHQ in Rawalpindi. No one expected the government to persist with talks but in a stunning move, on 29 January 2014, Sharif appeared in the National Assembly to give peace another chance. On a day marked by another suicide attack, this time on the Rangers' office in Karachi, instead of the much-expected green signal for a military operation, he announced a four-member committee to further the peace process, and this time it included the special assistant to the prime minister and columnist, Irfan Siddiqui, a former ISI operative involved in Operation Midnight Jackal,[33] Major (retd) Mohammed Amir, a senior journalist based in Peshawar, Rahimullah Yusufzai, and Rustom Shah Mohmand, former Pakistan ambassador to Kabul, who was nominated by the Khyber Pakhtunkhwa government, and who was part of the first committee as well. The ISI, excluded from the earlier committee, muscled in on this one. Mohmand, whom I met a few times, was optimistic for a while. The TTP was willing to negotiate within the ambit of the Constitution; it was not insisting on the enforcement of the Sharia and it had called for a ceasefire, to which the government, too, had responded. These were positive achievements and the committee felt the government would have to have a new group of people from the army, the ministry of interior and other agencies who would take the dialogue process decisively forward—which is why another committee with bureaucrats was formed in March 2014.

The TTP openly admitted to attacks on Shia pilgrims at Mastung, and also other bomb blasts in public places in KPK. It continued attacking the army, military convoys, polio teams, schools, media personnel and just about everyone. The talks hit a roadblock after 16 February 2014 when the chief of the Mohmand TTP faction, Omar Khalid Khorasani, issued a statement claiming the beheading of twenty-three Frontier Corps men held in custody since 2010 from a check post in Shongari. This prompted a minister to say that even India had not beheaded its Pakistani prisoners of war after 1971. The TTP said it was responsible for a bomb blast targeting a police bus in Karachi, in which thirteen policemen were killed; the Peshawar TTP chief had claimed the attacks on Shias in a hotel in Peshawar and said that Mast Gul of the Hizbul Mujahideen had been in charge of that attack. The government team was not willing to take any more after Khorasani's claim and decided not to meet the TTP nominees. A little later, the TTP first called for a month-long ceasefire (on 1 March 2014) and urged all its factions to stick to it, and a day later, the interior minister called a halt to the almost daily air strikes in North Waziristan and Khyber Agency, in which dozens of terrorists were reportedly killed. In April 2014 the TTP nominees travelled once again to Tank to meet the Taliban shura in Waziristan for the second time. The TTP submitted a list of non-combatants it wanted released, and the government wanted some high-profile captives like the late Punjab Governor Salman Taseer's son and former Prime Minister Yousuf Raza Gilani's son released (both were released in 2016). There were issues relating to foreign militants and matters regarding compensation and rehabilitation to be thrashed out, apart from dealing with the TTP factions which didn't agree to peace. While the talks became something of a joke, Pakistan Interior Minister Chaudhry Nisar Ali Khan after a cricket match, suggested the Taliban play cricket and stop fighting. The TTP put the onus of the ceasefire on the government which wasn't backing off from air strikes, and the whole thing collapsed like a derelict building in a cloud of dust.

Earlier in February 2014, the first committee comprising Professor Ibrahim Khan and Maulana Yousuf Shah had travelled to Miramshah to meet the TTP leaders. Even the first two committees entrusted with peace negotiations, one government-appointed and the other by the TTP, had had a standoff over the issue of ceasefire, and any kind of peaceful settlement seemed distant. Maulana Samiul Haq of the Jamaat-e-Islami, spearheading the TTP side, was the one who mediated and tried to break the deadlock. For a man whose Darul Uloom Haqqania madrasa at Akora Khatak had spawned some top-rung Taliban leaders, including Hakimullah Mehsud and members of the Haqqani Network which gets its name from here, it was paradoxical that he should now be in charge of peacemaking. The TTP kept making unreasonable demands—it wanted a peace zone so that talks could be held without the fear of being targeted. While both the government and the TTP had called for a ceasefire in March 2014, this didn't prevent the suicide strike on the Islamabad district and sessions court on 3 March. The TTP said it was not responsible, and another group called the Ahrar-ul-Hind claimed responsibility. Interior Minister Chaudhry Nisar said there could be half a dozen non-TTP factions, and within the TTP about thirty-seven or thirty-eight groups, which liked to believe they were united. He claimed some were not serious about the peace talks and there were non-TTP groups involved in ceasefire violations. The government then released several non-combatants from the Mehsud tribe.

All along, the Pakistan Tehreek-e-Insaf kept harping on the need for dialogue despite all the bombings. Imran claimed at a press conference that the army would only have 40 per cent chance of success in a military operation against the terrorists, and the government had not actually initiated talks. In the face of continuing attacks, there was little support for dialogue and the government was being criticized for its paralysis in tackling the TTP. Nawaz Sharif paid an unusual visit to the hilltop residence of Imran who endorsed the peace process. Imran was even nominated by the TTP to be on its committee for talks which he had the grace to refuse.

After Hakimullah's death in November 2013, the new TTP chief, Maulana Fazlullah, ruled out talks. The TTP factions were in disarray and there were some who broke away and formed new groups. There was no one to talk to. Even before Hakimullah's killing, the minister for interior, Chaudhry Nisar Ali Khan, had declared in the National Assembly that the talks with the TTP had broken down and as long as the drone strikes continued, there was no point in a dialogue.

A fresh controversy erupted when the Jamaat-e-Islami chief, Syed Munawar Hassan, called Hakimullah a martyr. This drew sharp reactions from the Pakistan armed forces which demanded an unconditional apology. Calling dead terrorists martyrs was an insult to the thousands of men killed in combat, the army felt. And before that, another right-wing leader had said Hakimullah was a martyr because he fought the Americans and even a dog killed by the US would be considered a martyr.

The government tabled its long-awaited National Internal Security Policy in the National Assembly towards the end of February 2014 and clarified that there was no operation, only surgical strikes, amid confusion that the military was going in for the kill. The government persisted with the mirage of talks, dividing the good Taliban and the bad. These peace deals had been coming a cropper since 2004 when Nek Mohammed was killed in a US drone strike after the Shakai pact. Despite all the surgical and other strikes, the TTP continued to rule the roost. The Pakistan Security Report of 2013 by the Pakistan Institute for Peace Studies (PIPS) said the major actor of instability in 2013 was the TTP and despite the killing of some of its top leaders, the operational capabilities of the group remained intact. Six new groups emerged on the terrorism landscape in 2012, the report pointed out, adding that four of them were part of the al-Qaeda–TTP alliance.

In 2013, there was a 39 per cent increase in suicide strikes, and militant, nationalist, insurgent and violent sectarian groups carried out a total of 1717 terrorist attacks, killing 2451 people and injuring over 5000. The National Action Plan and the constitutional amendment to authorize military courts to try terrorists were the outcome of a society trying to fight terrorism with more and more draconian measures. The Protection of Pakistan (Amendment) Ordinance of 2014 gives expanded powers to security and law-enforcing agencies, paving the way for longer detention and arrest. The HRCP was among the few voices that spoke against this and said it violated constitutionally guaranteed rights, and legitimized illegalities. The HRCP said that there were far too many things in the ordinance that rights-respecting individuals would find difficult to stomach. 'The main concerns include giving the authorities the power to withhold information regarding the location of any detainee, or grounds for such detention; detention of a person in internment centre instead of ordinary jails; creating new classifications of suspects such as "enemy alien" or "combatant enemy"; extending the preventive detention period for any suspect; and legitimising illegal detention and enforced disappearance through giving retrospective effect to the law.' While laws provide a framework to punish the guilty, serious questions remain over the dismantling of terror networks and the training camps.

The talks with the TTP seemed hollow from another viewpoint. The committees didn't have representation from the people of the Federally Administered Tribal Areas (FATA), a group of seven tribal agencies which underwent vast changes after the Soviet invasion of Afghanistan. It comes under the direct authority of the President. Battered by three cycles of war, everyone forgets that there are people living in these areas who are displaced after every military operation. At a seminar organized by the Institute of Strategic Studies just before the first round of talks with the TTP, author Ahmed Rashid observed that the region was suffering from the blowback of extremism and terrorism. He said it was unfortunate that the current debate was centred around whether to send the army or not instead of talking about bringing FATA into the fold of the state and making its people citizens. The issue of the status of FATA had disappeared from the Pakistan agenda.

With the Taliban gaining ground in Afghanistan and fingers pointing to the Haqqani Network in the various blasts there, FATA will continue to be a haven for terrorists. Its people have never mattered. However, things are looking up after the federal Cabinet approved steps in March 2017 to bring FATA into the mainstream, a precursor to its merger with the KPK province. The people of FATA can elect a representative to the KPK assembly, and the outdated and over 100-year-old Frontier Crimes Regulation will be replaced.[34] I did run into some members of the Mehsud tribe who were staging a protest outside the Islamabad Press Club to demand facilities for their area. One of them, a lawyer, was pleased I was from India and insisted on me meeting members of a large circle which sat on the grassy meadow outside the club. I hung around for a few minutes and escaped, not sure what the Mehsuds were up to.

The Haqqani muddle

For some time, the US had been demanding that Pakistan act on the Haqqani Network and its training camps. The Haqqanis count as the 'good' Taliban, and are backed by the ISI, but this is, of course, strenuously denied. A little after Hakimullah's killing in November 2013, the Haqqani Network's financier, Nasiruddin Haqqani, was shot dead in the capital on a Sunday while returning from a mosque at Barakahu on the outskirts of Islamabad. Once again it was the TTP which was quick to confirm that Nasiruddin was killed, and his funeral took place at Miramshah in North Waziristan. Some from the media knew he was living in the capital and used to interact with him, and they were not surprised. The fact that terror network leaders live in Pakistan is an open secret, though the powers that be are in a state of denial, especially about the most famous one who was killed by the Americans in Abbottabad in 2011. Many Pakistanis feel it was not Osama bin Laden and the US was making it all up. Mullah

Omar is another case in point: he died in Pakistan on 23 April 2013, but this was kept a secret till July 2015 due to 'military' reasons as that was the year when the NATO forces were pulling out. The Taliban's new leader Mullah Akhtar Mansour was killed in a May 2016 drone strike near the Pakistan–Afghanistan border in Balochistan, provoking fresh outrage. It is no secret that the Quetta shura (a council of top Taliban leaders who take decisions) is all-powerful and the Afghans have been protesting against the freedom of movement the Taliban has in Pakistan. The operations of these terror networks are tightly controlled and information leaks are made with a purpose. The deputy commander of the Afghan Taliban is Sirajuddin Haqqani who started running the Haqqani Network after his father and founder of the network, Jalaluddin Haqqani, suffered a stroke. In fact, the new head, Maulana Haibatullah Akhundzada, seems more of a prop.

Nasiruddin Haqqani, said to be in his thirties, was the eldest son of Jalaluddin. He was reportedly arrested in 2010 at the behest of the US and was kept in a safe house for interrogation. The TTP had alleged that security agencies were behind the killing. He was on the UN Security Council (UNSC) sanctions list of individuals whose assets were frozen and against whom there was a travel ban and an arms embargo as well. He was also a fundraiser for the outfit and travelled often to the Middle East.

The Afghan-led Haqqani Network, from the Zadran tribe, is based in North Waziristan, and the US maintains that the dreaded outfit was responsible for some major terrorist strikes in Afghanistan on the CIA and the siege of the US embassy. While the Pakistan government reacted furiously when the drone strike killing Hakimullah scuttled the peace talks with the TTP, there was no high drama and outrage after Haqqani's death. In 2011, the then chairperson of the US Joint Chief of Staff Committee, Admiral Mike Mullen, had told the US Senate Armed Services Committee that the Haqqani Network acted as a 'veritable arm' of the ISI. While Pakistan denied it supported the Haqqani Network, the US persisted with its contention and demanded action against the Haqqanis, something reflected in the Consolidated Appropriations Bill which was signed by President Obama on 17 January 2014. It linked funding to Pakistan's actions related to terrorism with the release of Dr Shakil Afridi who is in jail for helping the CIA track down Osama bin Laden in 2011. There are provisions to withhold $33 million unless Dr Afridi is released and cleared of all charges.

Pakistan reacted with disappointment over the withholding of funds till Dr Afridi was released. The other issues related to preventing cross-border terrorism are equally vital. The PTI's then blockade of the NATO supply lines to protest against the drone strikes invited the ire of the US, and Secretary of Defence Chuck Hagel, during his visit to Pakistan in December 2013, 'requested' the government to ensure that land routes were kept open. He reviewed 'shared concerns' regarding the activities of terrorist groups, including those of the Haqqani Network, on Pakistani territory.

Hubs of terror in the capital

Islamabad had a seamy side to it and there were hubs of terror being uncovered there. Terrorism was not confined to the remote regions of North or South Waziristan. Hakimullah Mehsud was killed in a tribal area, but Nasiruddin Haqqani was shot dead a week later in the capital in November 2013. A retired army officer said this was a huge embarrassment to the government. Comparisons were drawn to the US raid in Abbottabad which killed Osama bin Laden. Both the Bara Kahu and Tarnol areas are the developing parts of Islamabad, and do not have neat, well-tended sectors like the main city. The urban sprawl has spilled on to these outskirts, which are controlled by the land mafia and criminal elements. In August 2013, a Shia mosque was targeted by a suicide bomber who was killed by a guard, but after that a huge stash of arms and ammunition was found in a vehicle in the Bara Kahu area within the Islamabad Capital Territory. The owner of the vehicle was arrested and the police also raided the house of a Kashmiri family, the Gilanis, in Tarnol, and arrested the teenaged nephew of the Dukhtaraan-e-Millat founder-chairperson, Syed Asiya Andrabi.

Kashmiri family as terror suspects

It was in the district court complex that I saw young Mohammed Shoaib Andrabi who was arrested on 7 September 2013 after a raid in the Jammu and Kashmir Society in G-15 sector, twenty-two kilometres from the main city. On that day in court, his head covered with a scarf, the short, bespectacled and dishevelled Shoaib was produced in court, which had turned down the police request for five more days of physical custody of the teenaged suspect. He was charged with attempted murder, abetment and for possession of arms and explosives.

Ostensibly, he was caught with a cache of arms hidden in his house called Gilani Manzil. His brothers were missing, suspected to be in the custody of some security agency. There was a silence at House no. 563 on street 21 in the Khayaban-e-Kashmir Jammu and Kashmir Society in Tarnol. Except for two security guards, the place was desolate. Gilani Manzil looked prosperous and the big, light-brown one-storeyed house, with its flashy mirror windows and pretty blue floral awnings, was predictably locked. There were fields nearby, but nobody was around. Located in a developing colony, there was much rubble and half-constructed houses. On one side, the narrow strip of lawn had been dug up and that was where the police had found the drum with arms and explosives. Andrabi was being investigated for terror links and his brothers reportedly were with the al-Qaeda. Outside too, the lawn had been dug up, showing that the police were taking no risks.

I couldn't get much out of the neighbours or security guards, and everyone was tight-lipped about what they saw or heard about the midnight raid on 7 September 2013. The entire street was jammed with police cars. According to the first information report,[35] Inspector Mohammed Ajmal Khan rang the doorbell and Shoaib opened the door. Another person, later identified as Irtiyaz-un-Nabi Gilani, alias Sarfi, fired at the police as he escaped from the house. Shoaib showed the buried cache in the lawn—inside a plastic drum with sub-machine guns, pistols, detonators and ammunition. Some explosive devices were defused by the bomb disposal squad.

Shoaib was the first son of Asiya Andrabi's brother, Zia-ul-Haq Andrabi. Irtiyaz, an aeronautical engineer, was Asiya Andrabi's sister Rehana's son. Irtiyaz and his younger brother, Mujahid Gilani, a paediatric surgeon, lived in the house. Dr Mujahid had a practice in the neighbourhood market. Their elder brother, Zulqarnain Gilani, a captain in the Pakistan Army, was an occasional visitor at Gilani Manzil.

Shoaib was the one, says the FIR, who led the police to the drum buried in the lawn in front of the house. The police had already noticed the suspicious hump on the lawn as they entered the house. While only Shoaib was arrested and charged, Irtiyaz and Mujahid were missing. There was no information on their whereabouts.

A senior police official I spoke to said curtly that it was part of official record that the Gilani brothers were part of the al-Qaeda and they were testing spy planes. If the links are established and proved, it will be the first time that Kashmiris are involved in a terror plot in Pakistan, possibly involving the al-Qaeda. This was the first time a Kashmiri leader's relative had been arrested. My colleague at that time in Srinagar, Ahmed Ali Fayyaz, helped me with information from Asiya Andrabi who was quite shaken by the events and who repeatedly sought information on the whereabouts of her nephews. I didn't follow up on the case as there were too many events which had to be tracked. I wonder if they let off young Shoaib.

The curious case of Dr Shakil Afridi

In the bitter and rather humiliating aftermath of the US Navy Seals' raid on Abbottabad in May 2011, there was fresh angst for Pakistan. Dr Shakil Afridi, a doctor who was part of a USAID immunization team, had allegedly helped the CIA in getting DNA samples from the bin Laden household to confirm his presence. There is a serious tussle between the US and Pakistan over Dr Afridi who continues to be jailed even though his thirty-three-year-old sentence was overturned by the Frontier Crimes Regulation (FCR) commissioner in August 2013. His lawyer, Samiullah Afridi, a kind and helpful man with whom I used to have long phone conversations, was shot dead in March 2015 after repeated threats to stop defending his client. The Jamaat-ul-Ahrar which had split from the TTP and later rejoined it, claimed responsibility for killing the lawyer in Peshawar. Ehsanullah Ehsan tweeted that he was killed for helping the 'crusaders' in killing 'our beloved Shykh Usama' (bin Laden). Revenge and then to tweet proudly about murder comes naturally to the Taliban. They kill and boast about it in complete anonymity and with impunity.

On 29 August 2013, things briefly looked up for Dr Afridi who had been charged with links to the banned terror group Lashkar-i-Islam led by the dreaded Mangal Bagh. An FCR commissioner in Peshawar set aside his trial and the thirty-three-year sentence. It was Samiullah who gave me all the details, thanks to a local journalist who gave me his number. A fresh trial was to begin within a month's time in the court of a political agent authorized by the FCR. The order came after an appeal against the trial. The assistant political agent of the Bara subdivision, Iqbal Durrani, who had passed the judgment had no authority to try the offence or pass sentence, it was ruled, and it would have to be tried by a political agent in a sessions court who must act as assistant judge. However, Dr Afridi would remain in the Peshawar central jail. While he was arrested in 2011 in connection with the Abbottabad incident, the charges in his case did not refer to that matter; instead, the FCR was invoked which has stringent provisions, including suspension of fundamental rights. Samiullah was clear that this was done to keep Dr Afridi in jail and that it was a false case. He wanted the case tried by a sessions judge. Since British times, the FCR meant for the tribal areas has had a different system where the political agent is a judicial functionary.

There was to be no respite for Dr Afridi who was slapped with another charge—that of medical negligence, in November 2013. The trial was scheduled to begin in December. It was a case of 2006–07 where he had operated on a boy in a private hospital in Bara, who died. The complaint was filed by the boy's mother. Before Dr Afridi's lawyer was killed in 2015, the FCR Commissioner Sahebzada Anees-ur-Rehman—who overturned his sentence—died in a mysterious fire and explosion in Islamabad in October 2013. In December, a three-member tribunal disposed of his review petition demanding a fresh trial by a sessions judge by asking for clarification from the FCR commissioner on whether the trial should be held by a political agent or a sessions judge. He did get some relief from his sentence once again when it was commuted by ten years to twenty-three years in March 2014. The FCR commissioner, Munir Azam, directed the political agent of the Khyber agency to adduce evidence with the help of intelligence agencies and prepare a case against Dr Afridi and file it in an appropriate court. Instead of ruling on the plea for a retrial, Samiullah explained that the commissioner called for framing of charges.

By then, Samiullah was getting death threats for defending his client. It was not new but this time they had set a deadline for him. When I spoke to him on 10 May 2014, a week before I left Pakistan, Samiullah said some unidentified people had come to his office and threatened him—if he didn't back off from this case, they would attach a magnetic bomb to his car. He was one of the few who dared to take up the case and the threats were coming from the start, but now he'd had enough and wanted to back off. He said other lawyers would take up the matter.

The Pakistan government was on the back foot after the foreign office spokesperson made a faux pas in her weekly briefing. On 8 May 2014, Tasneem Aslam, the foreign office spokesperson, in response to questions on travel advisories after the high number of polio cases in Pakistan, said 'a fake campaign of vaccination was conducted in Pakistan in which the UN agencies were also used. I am referring to Dr Shakil Afridi's case. This further reinforced the negative perception about the agenda behind the polio eradication campaign. We have been trying to overcome that.' The WHO immediately took up the matter and issued a clarification that the UN agencies or WHO were not involved in Dr Afridi's actions.

After the US proposed to withhold $33 million because of Dr Afridi's imprisonment, the foreign office in an outraged statement said that Dr Afridi was accused of violating Pakistani laws and that his action had also caused immense damage to the polio campaign in the country. The statement said that his case was sub judice and that he remains entitled to due process under the law. Consequently, any linkage of US assistance to this case was not in keeping with the spirit of cooperation between the two countries. The government also reiterated that there was no possibility of releasing him at the request of the US.

Dr Afridi's case looks bleak—the judicial commission on Abbottabad, too, had demanded he be tried as per the law of the country. As a suspected undercover agent for the CIA, many believe he has little chance of justice—an assessment shared by his late lawyer.

Terror and polio

There was a time in December 2012 when Pakistan could have been polio free. But that was not to be. It was an outbreak in Syria that was traced to Pakistan in 2013 that drew me to write on the issue of polio. I interviewed WHO's Dr Elias Durry, the emergency coordinator for polio eradication in Pakistan, for the story. Sitting in his small, well-guarded office, Dr Durry showed me large, colourful maps on the wall with dots to indicate the polio cases. He was an optimist about polio eradication in a country where giving a child immunity can mean death for the vaccinator or the policemen guarding the teams. Unlike in India where women can freely go around from house to house, in Pakistan in some places, it is too dangerous. India has managed to be polio free and has celebrities endorsing the campaign. I didn't see anything on those lines, though the government spoke with great sincerity and concern about the situation.

While the anti-polio campaign was launched in 1994, it was not until 2011 that it was taken seriously when Pakistan formulated a National Emergency Action Plan, making district deputy commissioners directly accountable for the polio immunization programme. From ninety-eight cases in 2011, the intensity of the virus was curbed and environmental surveillance of sewage samples which used to show a high incidence of the virus was recording new lows. The last low season was December 2012, and that would have been a good time to intensify efforts, Dr Durry said. The rush of optimism ended with nine vaccinators killed in two days in Peshawar, Karachi and Charsadda, which inevitably disrupted the entire campaign.

Official sources said that from 2012 to January 2014, thirty-three polio workers had been killed, as also eleven security personnel, while nine were injured in the attacks. The Taliban had issued a warning against polio vaccination and these attacks were believed to take place in areas where they had a base. The number of deaths has gone up by now. Vaccination rounds are held under tight security and in some parts of the country, policemen keep a lookout for terrorists while children are given the doses. The army, too, was roped in to ensure protection for vaccination.

The attacks on polio teams began on 17 July 2012 in Gadap Town, Karachi, during a polio drive when a doctor attached to the WHO was injured when gunmen opened fire on his vehicle. His driver, too, was hurt. The next day, on the second day of the immunization programme, a polio worker, Ishaq, was shot dead in the same area. In Quetta in October 2012, one worker was killed during a campaign in Alizai Town.

In four attacks in Karachi in December 2012—three in one day—five persons, including four women—two of them in charge of the area programme—were killed, and two were injured. The polio programme is driven by optimism and bravery. Apart from areas in FATA, Machar Colony in Karachi city is off limits for polio teams and that's where some of the team members were killed. Except for FATA, all other provinces which had a high rate of polio have virtually eliminated the virus by 50 to 100 per cent. The mobile population of Pakistan is also targeted at permanent transit-point vaccination centres at key places in the country involving 200,000 government lady health workers. The WHO maintains that polio in Pakistan poses a significant risk to neighbouring countries, including the border areas of Afghanistan which are polio free.

Pakistan, along with Afghanistan, remains the two polio endemic countries in the world, and terrorism has played a major role in that, making areas inaccessible to vaccinators. Shooting security personnel guarding polio teams or the vaccinators themselves is a popular sport for the Taliban, and in January 2016, some fifteen people were killed when a suicide bomber ran towards a van full of guards about to set off with a polio vaccination team. The teams persist despite grave threats to their life. In North and South Waziristan, the TTP head, Hafiz Gul Bahadur, had banned the entry of polio teams since June 2012. In 2013, as a result, nearly three quarters of a million children under the age of five were not immunized against polio, and the virus is thriving in the frontier areas, as well as Karachi. That year (2013), the polio outbreak reported from Syria was traced to Pakistan after the WHO conducted genetic sequencing.

Vaccinating children against polio is a supreme act of heroism in Pakistan. The idea that this innocuous activity needs armed security escort sounds ludicrous at first. The Taliban's retrograde ideology which believes that polio immunization is a Western idea (it is opposed to all ideas that could interchangeably be called Western/American/imperialist, and polio vaccination is, in its scheme of things, similar to women's education) which must be opposed, has led to thousands of children not being vaccinated and polio spreading to other parts of the world from Pakistan. The arrest of Dr Shakil Afridi, who allegedly took part in an undercover vaccination drive to identify Osama bin Laden, has made matters worse.

In November 2013, a young special police force member, Zakir Khan Afridi, was shot in Peshawar for protecting a polio team, a few days before his wedding. The teams were often under attack and even the poor gun-toting security guards would fall victim to determined suicide bombers. Sometimes people refused to be part of this activity as death threats were frequently issued to vaccination team members.

In the capital, 1000 policemen guarded the vaccination drive in November 2013. In fact, the police held a press conference where they were justifiably proud of their role in ensuring that the drive went off smoothly. In probably no other country in the world would one attend a press conference on polio with enthusiastic participation of the police.[36]

Before this, the poliovirus from Pakistan had already been found in Egypt (in 2012) as well as in Palestine and Israel (in 2013), according to the WHO. Pakistan was responsible for the international spread in 2011 and the virus from the country caused an outbreak in western China (according to the WHO).[37] In January 2014, Peshawar had emerged as the largest reservoir of endemic poliovirus in the world, with more than 90 per cent of the polio cases in the country genetically linked to Peshawar. The explosive poliovirus outbreak in FATA, which left sixty-five children paralysed during 2012–13, owes its origins to Peshawar. As much of the population of the area moves through Peshawar, the city acts as an amplifier of the poliovirus (WHO statement, 2014).

The WHO declared the international spread of wild poliovirus (WPV) in 2014 a 'Public Health Emergency of International Concern (PHEIC)'. A WHO advisory made it mandatory for all those travelling from Pakistan to have polio drops and produce a certificate if asked at immigration points. All travellers from Pakistan had to be vaccinated and a certificate produced at the immigration post. I didn't imagine that at this late age, I would need to be vaccinated again for polio. However, despite all the trouble we took, no one checked either my husband or me when we returned to India, though we did have the required certificates.

Drone strikes and other wars

Drone strikes didn't only kill the likes of Hakimullah Mehsud. There was a grave humanitarian aspect to these attacks and that was the killing of civilians. Reprieve, an international human rights organization which worked with several issues in Pakistan, was in the forefront fighting for the cause of the surviving families. There were cases filed in the Peshawar High Court which passed a landmark order in May 2013. A litigation of which little was expected changed the narrative of the drone strikes. It was in 2009 that lawyer Shahzad Akbar decided to challenge the drone strikes; he was not sure where it would lead. There wasn't much noise about them till then, though in 2006, a madrasa had been struck, killing eighty-one people.

Shahzad Akbar, the legal director of the Foundation for Fundamental Rights, which was up against huge odds, championed the cause of the drone attack victims. Lawyers in FATA told survivors that they could not file a case against the drone strikes since in FATA, the courts did not have jurisdiction, according to the Constitution. Akbar said this was misleading and that the courts in FATA could look at cases if they were concerned with fundamental rights. He filed two public interest litigations in the Peshawar High Court in 2011—one on behalf of Noor Khan whose father was killed and one by the foundation. That year, a jirga, or tribal council, was targeted by a missile from a drone. After the historic verdict in May 2013, Akbar proved his academic exercise had legal standing but was disappointed that the Pakistan government didn't take it seriously. The Peshawar High Court had ruled that drone strikes were a blatant violation of 'basic human rights' and were against the UN Charter and other resolutions, and thus, it is held to be a War Crime, cognizable by the International Court of Justice or the Special Tribunal for War Crimes. Thanks to Akbar's petition, the political agents in Peshawar were forced to give data which was physically verified. In North Waziristan Agency, 896 civilian deaths had taken place from 2008 to 2012, with 209 seriously injured. Forty-seven others killed were foreigners. In South Waziristan, the toll was 553 dead and 126 injured in seventy strikes.

In 2010 when Akbar started out, few victims of the drone strikes were coming forward. With some difficulty, he got in touch with Karim Khan whose brother and son had been killed in a drone strike. After Khan, others spoke out as well, and soon it emerged that the drones had killed quite a few civilians. Akbar also decided to involve the US and the CIA in the matter and served a legal notice on behalf of Karim Khan to the CIA station chief in Pakistan, asking why criminal charges should not be brought against him. He found out that under Pakistan law, the CIA station chief can be prosecuted. 'For the first time we named the CIA station chief and my point was to prove there are no holy cows. We also filed murder charges against the station chief saying he was the one giving orders for the drone strikes,' Akbar said. The immediate effect was that sixteen more families who were affected contacted him and there was a protest outside the National Assembly. The CIA station chief had to be replaced as his cover had been exposed, and in November 2013, after a drone strike on Hangu in Khyber Pakhtunkhwa, it was the Pakistan Tehreek-e-Insaf which filed a complaint, naming the CIA station chief in Islamabad and the CIA director. The US embassy frantically tried to get the media not to report their names, even though Pakistan Tehreek-e-Insaf had made it public in the complaint filed at the Tal police station and in a press release. The Hangu strike was aimed at Haqqani members and one of them who was close to the top Haqqani commander, Sirajuddin, was killed. While filing the story, I had to rely on news reports which I could not confirm. In contrast, Imran Khan called a press conference where he was outraged that students and teachers of the madrasa were killed. There were also reports that this was a base for Afghan militants, but Imran brushed aside all this and maintained that innocent lives had been lost and even if they were from some network, they were killed on Pakistani soil where they had a constitutional right to life. I wondered about all the people killed by the Haqqani Network and if they didn't have a right to life. He even promised to show photos of the children killed in Hangu and their names and make it public, something which we waited for in vain.

Till the Peshawar case, no one had been talking about the families of drone strike victims. On 26 October 2013, a week before Hakimullah's death on 1 November 2013, the Brave New Foundation premiered in the capital Robert Greenwald's documentary, *Unmanned: America's Drone Wars*; this was co-produced by Imran Khan's first wife, Jemima Khan. The film-maker spoke to the survivors of drone strikes and for the first time the devastation came to light on screen just as the Pakistan government was mobilizing world opinion. The film interviews a drone operator in the form of Brandon Bryant who worked in the air force who says, 'We kill people and break things.' And he narrates the trauma of seeing on his computer screen while sitting in the US, the people who have been bombed and maimed.

After the case was filed, people from the tribal agencies of Waziristan were mobilized and they attended a jirga in Islamabad. Though later, Tariq, a teenager who attended it was killed in a drone strike, one of the 300 children who have fallen victim. The film has interviews with friends of Tariq who died while preparing for a soccer match. One of the survivors says no one feels safe in North Waziristan any more. Neil Williams, who worked on the film, said he had met Tariq four days before he was killed. Survivors and others took part in a peace march in Waziristan in September 2012. The campaign brought drone strikes into the political debate and parties like the Pakistan Tehreek-e-Insaf benefited from it by eventually forming a government in the Khyber Pakhtunkhwa province.

While the Peshawar High Court order directed the government to take up the matter seriously before the UNSC and file a proper complaint, no progress has been made so far. Akbar was planning to file a contempt petition since the government had not followed the court's orders to prepare a case against drone strikes with the UNSC. The court had asked the government to give complete details of the losses to the UN secretary-general and to constitute an independent War Crimes Tribunal which would have the mandate to investigate and decide if this was a war crime. The ministry of foreign affairs was directed to prepare a draft resolution condemning the drone strikes, and the plan was to get the UNSC and the UN General Assembly to pass it.

In case the US authorities did not comply with the UN resolution, whether passed by the Security Council or by the General Assembly, the Government of Pakistan was to sever all ties with the US, and as a mark of protest, deny all logistic and other facilities to the US within Pakistan, the court ruled.

Drone strikes, even if marginally effective, cannot end terrorism. There is a great cost to civilian life, a collateral damage which cannot be brushed aside lightly. That the US has been reduced to this tactic in collaboration with Pakistan to kill the terrorists speaks volumes for the kind of lawlessness that has been set in action by these groups, some of which were armed and trained by both countries. The death of Hakimullah splintered the TTP, and the secret death of Mullah Omar in 2013 and his successor in 2016 has created leadership issues in the Taliban, though the Haqqanis remain powerful. The talks with the Afghan government are not going anywhere and statements by President Ghani indicate the widening gap between his country and Pakistan.

5

Shooting the Messenger

These are words cast in stone—on a marble plaque at the entrance of the Hyderabad Press Club in Sindh, and they seem even more significant now. On freedom of speech and the press, Jinnah had said, 'I do not wish for a single moment that any culprit who is guilty of sedition, who is guilty of using disaffection, who is guilty of causing race hatred should escape but at the same time I say protect the innocent, protect those journalists who are doing their duty and who are serving both the public and the Government by criticising the Government freely, independently, honestly which is an education for any Government.'[1]

Far from protection, criticism can often end in death, and during the time of Zia-ul-Haq those who crossed the line were whipped. Jinnah was vociferous against the gagging of the press and avowedly against any man's liberty being taken away without judicial trial. Even before Partition, he was against muzzling the press. He was highly critical of the Press Act of 1910 and his speech quoted above was in response to that law.[2]

Journalists were flogged for protests, and in 1978 under Zia's regime, four of them were ordered by military courts to be whipped, leading to public outrage and many journalists courting arrest.[3] General Musharraf, not one for obedience to law, wrote about the press curbs in Bhutto's time. 'Zulfikar Ali Bhutto masqueraded as a democrat but ruled like an autocrat. During his time the press was suppressed more than ever before or since. Many journalists and editors were arrested for dissent and newspapers and journals were closed down.'[4] He was critical too of Nawaz Sharif who told him to take over the *Friday Times* editor Najam Sethi's case and keep him in ISI custody. He told Musharraf that it was legal since it was a case of treason. Musharraf said he refused to do this and finally Sethi was let off.[5] Sethi had been arrested in May 1999 and tortured. Amnesty International called him a 'prisoner of conscience' and he was released a month later after the charges were withdrawn.

The press in Pakistan has been suppressed, with publications shut down and arbitrary actions taken against it, but its journalists remain a fearless and outspoken bunch. On the flip side, the press has been used by rulers with great effect, and as Niazi points out, even during the anti-Ahmadi riots of 1953, inciting articles were carried in the papers with government patronage.[6] There is a long history of censorship as well, and not even the Quaid's sister, Fatima Jinnah, who was critical of Prime Minister Liaquat Ali's government was spared when the critical lines in her speech were faded out on the radio.[7] Later it was Begum Raana Liaquat Ali's turn; her political statement in 1983 demanding to know the truth about her husband's killers, was reduced to insignificance by the press. The notorious press advice system which came into being during the 1965 war with India continued—to the horror of journalists who lived in dread of phone calls telling them what to print and what not to. During the 1971 war, the government-controlled media was reporting that everything was under control and that armed forces had crushed the 'subversive and disgruntled elements in the East'.[8]

Over a year after I returned in 2014, I heard about the resignation of Rashed Rahman, editor of the *Daily Times* founded by Salman Taseer which was a fairly liberal voice in the press pantheon in Pakistan. Rahman was known for his left-of-centre views and used to carry a lot of the stories from *The Hindu*, mainly the op-ed pieces, in his paper, and also ran sharp satirical pieces by Ayaz Amir, journalist and columnist, who was particularly funny. Some of my op-ed articles were featured there, along with those of other Indian writers. I met Rehman once, at the Islamabad Literature Festival, but we never did have that cup of coffee he had invited me to. At the end of 2015, there was pressure to stop two columnists, one of whom was outspokenly vociferous against the army, and Rashed quit, though he did deny that it had anything to do with pressure from the army or security agencies. The Pakistan media is proud of its fearless and free tradition, but journalists are victims of a murky system which can only be exposed at their own peril. The most famous in that line of those who knew too much, investigative journalist Syed Saleem Shahzad, was mysteriously killed, and his murderers are still at large. His book remains one of the best on the deep connections between the various sections of the security establishment and the terror outfits—which he knew well—as well as on the spidery penetration of the al-Qaeda. It is not as if the nexus between the military, the ISI and the terror groups is a secret. In the spirit of a free and vibrant media, there are open discussions about it. If someone is killed, this immediately sparks off rather good guesses on the agency behind it. As Amnesty International found in its report of 2014, the ISI is the most dreaded outfit for the journalists in Pakistan. Though the Amnesty report spoke of a chilling effect, the media, by and large, has stuck its neck out.

It is not uncommon for journalists to be summoned by the ISI officers and asked to explain some story or the other, or sometimes they are invited merely for a chat. There were very strange journalists who hung out outside the Islamabad Press Club, and some were very helpful—they offered to escort you to Peshawar and Quetta, or even to Muzaffarabad. Even a month in advance, they knew my visa would not be renewed. The surprising thing was everyone knew who they were and there was little pretence. I had been warned of such people, but even then, I did almost fall for some of their ploys, which turned out to be quite harmless in the end. Latif Ijaz, the secretary of the club, was friendly and put me on the mailing list, although much of it was in Urdu. Ijaz, with his trademark deerstalker hat, volunteered to teach me the language. I did actually start learning Urdu from my neighbour in Mumbai many years ago and we had got around to reading words, but then, regretfully, I found little time to continue. As a result, I couldn't read a line and had to watch PTV, the only channel in English.

The Islamabad Press Club was so different from the Karachi one. No non-journalists are allowed inside its Victorian facade—the space is fiercely protected. In fact, many Pakistani journalists told me that theirs was a more critical media than India's. The Karachi Press Club (which I visited in 2011), the first such institution in Pakistan, is housed in a stone building with white windows. People had thronged the entrance to welcome us. The large Hussain painting in the club's hall and pictures of Jinnah, along with lace-covered chairs, give the club a quaint, old-world charm. In its proud fifty-year history, no military or police officer has been allowed entry. The Karachi Press Club was held 'to be an island of dissent and a symbol of defiance', and on its silver jubilee in 1985, Justice (retd) Dorab Patel of the Supreme Court congratulated it for holding elections every year for twenty-five years. 'You working journalists have succeeded creditably where politicians and the like have failed miserably,' Patel said.[9]

But the walls outside had a different story. There was a brazen show of support for Mumtaz Qadri emblazoned in graffiti outside the liberal press club: 'We are proud of Mumtaz Qadri [who shot the Punjab governor, Salman Taseer]. We don't like cowards.' This endorsement of a killer who shot Taseer because he spoke up against the country's blasphemy laws and defended Aasia Bibi who was sentenced to death, showed a cold-bloodedness and lack of remorse that was at the very least monstrous. It is not only liberals but newspapers too which have to be on guard.

The *Dawn* office is fortified with high walls, heavy metal doors and CCTVs, an indication that journalism in Pakistan can be life-threatening. An attack had changed the face of a lackadaisical newspaper office. The giant steel door was pushed open for us to spend half a day chatting with the staffers who didn't seem to mind an Indian invasion of curious journalists. Later, the Express group was to come under a series of attacks which led to the paper asking its staff and columnists to go easy on criticizing the Taliban. Yet the press in Pakistan soldiers on, dodging bullets admirably, with a healthy contempt for the establishment and the security agencies.

The Pakistani establishment often points out that the Indian media is the more 'patriotic' one and didn't criticize the government much. Pakistan accuses the Indian media of overreaction, and sadly most of the time it is true. There is a belief that the Indian media is not only 'over-patriotic', but also always overreacts, though I tend to think that's not always the case. For instance, during a TV show in Islamabad, the host asked me if the Indian media had not overreacted during the terror strike of 26 November 2008. I asked him if ten heavily armed men holding an entire city to ransom, never mind where they came from, and shooting randomly, killing at will, was not a good reason to 'overreact'. I later realized that 'overreaction' simply meant that Pakistan was being blamed! I did see enough instances of similar 'overreaction' in Pakistan, when almost every terror attack—apart from the Balochistan insurgency—was blamed on India or the RAW. Every time 26/11 was mentioned, the Pakistan government would bring in the Samjhauta Express case and how details were not shared on the matter despite the statements of Swami Aseemanand who confessed to masterminding the bombing. It is this mutual accusation, lack of empathy and trust which is making any dialogue impossible, but the media alone cannot be blamed for stymieing any progress. It is the lack of political will on the part of both governments and the blame game which is stultifying the process. There is a wariness regarding the Indian journalists—they are capable of doing anything is what I heard after one reportedly tried to sneak into an army bunker in Muzaffarabad. That said, the media in both countries has a certain limitation in covering LoC firing or defence-related matters; it has to perforce rely on government handouts or versions, unless publications are willing to invest time and money for proper investigation. Since these almost always involve the army and going into areas which are restricted, the matter is rarely followed up on an independent level. For instance, while I was in Islamabad, a group of journalists (I was not included) were taken to the LoC villages which had been shelled by the Indian Army—it would be impossible to go there on one's own or without proper escort. Similarly, during the Kargil war, in India while many journalists made it on their own and covered the war on a daily basis in extremely demanding circumstances, there was a point when the coverage was stopped. Later, the army bussed in the media to show how it was winning the war.

Pakistani bureaucrats who lived in India said that they came back as hawks after putting up with a belligerent and jingoistic Indian press. While the Indian media is growing more uncritical by the day of the government and shows its 'patriotic' colours in believing almost everything put out by the army and the government, especially when there is firing on the LoC (same goes for the other side too), in Pakistan and, to some extent, in India, there are other sinister pressures to rein in those who think and write defying establishment curbs. There is little independent investigation or reporting on critical issues involving both countries. In Pakistan, between the terror groups and the security establishment, political parties and religious outfits, the media walks a tightrope. You can always offend someone but not with impunity. Somehow I don't see balanced coverage on either side of the border, despite the few rational voices. As long as there is the peril of 24x7 television, jingoism will rule, and facts will take a beating. The print media is also not blameless in both countries. When the aim is to blame and not understand, recrimination can be the only result.

The press in Pakistan is literally under fire. In December 2013 for the second time since August that year, *Express News* was attacked in Karachi. Armed men fired at the office and threw hand grenades which exploded outside the main gate. It was so simple as terror attacks often are—two men came on motorbikes and started firing, shattering car windows, and hurling grenades. I called up a friend in the office and learnt that there were two groups—one lot was firing from the lane outside the office, while the others covered them from a flyover opposite. The armed men rained bullets which pierced the glass windows of the office. There were reports that the police mobile van was not stationed on the flyover that day. Not entirely a coincidence. Four months earlier, on 16 August, unidentified men had opened fire at the same office, injuring two persons, including a security guard; the CCTV footage showed two blasts outside the office before the firing. The police arrived late, a common drawback in our countries. After this, armed men on motorcycles shot a technician, a security guard and a driver who were sitting in a stationary digital satellite news-gathering van.

The spurt of attacks on the Express News group, the worst of which resulted in three staffers being killed, did have a chilling effect. In other cities, too, staff were targeted and soon the editors decided that they would have to ease up for a while on criticizing the Taliban. There was nothing else that could be done, lives were being lost, one editor frankly admitted to me. So, criticism of the TTP was muzzled for a while, to the chagrin of some outspoken columnists. In Balochistan, the situation was worse, with a number of journalists being killed every year. Security agencies keep a close watch on who is writing what and know exactly which story is being done and by whom, sometimes even before it's published. Mama Qadeer Baloch was given repeated warnings when he launched his epic march from Quetta to Islamabad in 2013 to protest the missing young people of Balochistan, and was allegedly even offered money not to go ahead with his plans. A journalist confirmed that the media was asked to go slow on the coverage. Reporting from Balochistan can be very dangerous for local journalists.

An Amnesty report said that journalists in Pakistan confronted a range of 'red lines', a general term used by media workers to describe the invisible boundaries of public discussion accepted by state and non-state actors in the country's media landscape. During its investigations, it received credible allegations of harassment, abduction, torture and killing of journalists which were perpetrated by a range of state and non-state actors. These included, but were not limited to, the Directorate General for Inter-Services Intelligence, the Muttahida Qaumi Movement, the Lashkar-e-Jhangvi and its associated group, the Ahle Sunnat Wal Jamaat, the TTP, groups with al-Qaeda links, and ethnic Baloch armed outfits, both pro and anti-state.

The report also stated that as much as journalists sought to discharge their professional duties with impartiality, these abuses inevitably had a chilling effect on freedom of expression, pushing the journalists to resort to self-censorship in order to protect themselves. But these allegations against the ISI were refuted, and Colonel Zulfiqar Bhatty told Amnesty International that members of the public could write to the adjutant general of the armed forces regarding any complaints about the ISI or other military institutions. It would be interesting to know how many times action was taken.

Journalists can be shot, kidnapped, threatened and abused. Often, no questions were asked, no one was held responsible. I knew of at least one Pakistani journalist who had been beaten and locked up for twenty-four hours for interacting with Indians. He gave us all a wide berth after that, though he was quite charming. Pakistan counts as one of the most dangerous places to report from.

Biting the bullet

A day before he was shot at in Lahore, journalist Raza Rumi had contacted Amnesty International to say that his name was on a Pakistani Taliban hit list. He said he was not sure if the threat was real or if it was just an attempt at silencing him, and he was very concerned. He came to know the next day, 28 March 2014, that it had not been an idle threat. While he escaped, his driver Mustafa was killed and his guard was paralysed after being shot. Rumi now lives abroad and is a contributing editor to *Friday Times*. Soon after this incident, Geo TV celebrity anchor Hamid Mir was attacked and severely wounded. Reporting these two assaults left me quite shaken. I knew both of them, even if it was for a few months, and while shock didn't register initially due to the frenzy to file the stories, the numbness crept in later and I woke up to the underbelly of reporting Pakistan. Raza was a good host and his Urdu programme on Express TV, *Khabar Se Aage*, targeted the Taliban, the state and its attitude to minorities. We have appeared together on TV talk shows and he was always friendly. He knew it was coming for whatever reason. Crouching behind the car seat after he was fired at in the Raja Market, he tweeted, 'I was dreading this day.'

It was after Rumi was shot at that Amnesty International came out with its report, 'A bullet has been chosen for you', with interviews of 100 journalists, in April 2014. Thirty-four journalists may have been killed as a direct consequence of their work since the restoration of a democratically elected government in Pakistan in March 2008. After Prime Minister Nawaz Sharif formed the government on 5 June 2013, at least eight journalists lost their lives across the country as a direct result of their work, and this included five killed in 2014. Of the thirty-four killings since 2008, nine took place in north-western Pakistan (the Federally Administered Tribal Areas, or Khyber Pakhtunkhwa), thirteen took place in the Balochistan province, and of these, six happened in the province's second town, Khuzdar (Amnesty report, 2014).

The attacks on these high-profile journalists shattered illusions of a free and fair media. Hamid used to come often to Parliament and he would be besieged by people who wanted to be photographed with him. He was clearly in the know about everything the government did, much more than others, and was full of juicy details on the talks with the TTP, which he wrote about later in the *News*. Hamid was earlier the editor of *Ausaf*, a publication which had fundamentalist leanings, and people whispered that he was shot for his past omissions.

Hours after the attack, in a highly unexpected move, his brother, author and journalist, Amir Mir, alleged on TV that the ISI chief, Lt. Gen. Zaheer-ul-Islam was behind the attack. However, many in the media felt that it was improper to make such allegations without proof or proper investigation. Hamid was on his way to his office in Karachi from the airport in the evening. He was sitting in the back seat of the car and the shots were fired into his stomach and pelvic area. It was the presence of mind shown by his driver that saved his life. Hamid's driver, interviewed by Geo TV, said the gunmen were waiting at the Natha Khan flyover a little distance away from the airport; the attack began when he slowed down and was about to turn right on to the main road. He said he saw one man firing at the back of the car but didn't stop to look and sped away to the hospital. Recuperating in the hospital, Hamid's statement which was read out by his brother spoke of threats from both state and non-state actors. He had been told by intelligence officials that he was on a hit list and that the ISI was miffed with his coverage of the Long March from Quetta. He had given the police telephone numbers from which he received threats, but nothing was done. No arrest was made in an earlier case in November 2012 when, in Islamabad, a bomb had been found fitted to his car; this was discovered and defused by the bomb disposal squad. The TTP had taken responsibility for that. Later, he appeared before a judicial commission appointed to inquire into the attack on 19 April 2014. The empire struck back by issuing notices to Geo and later its transmission was suspended for a while.

Hamid openly supported Mama Qadeer's march and was among the few, including the scientist and educationist Pervez Hoodbhoy, who dared to walk with the marchers before they reached Islamabad. Hamid has been awarded the highest civilian honour, the Hilal-e-Imtiaz, and is the popular host of *Capital Talk* on TV. Amir Mir said that two weeks before the shooting, his brother had sent a videotaped message to the US-based Committee to Protect Journalists (CPJ), saying that if there was an attack on him, the ISI chief was to be held responsible. He said his brother was under threat from the time of the ISI chief, Shuja Pasha.

There was an understated element of integrity in Amir Mir's broadcast. He and his brother were the sons of Professor Waris Mir, a Mohajir—a term to describe families that came from India in 1947—and they chose the profession of journalism and no one could stop them from carrying out their mission. Hamid's video to the CPJ had clearly put the onus on Lt. Gen. Zaheer-ul-Islam in the event of an attack on him and he had also told some close friends and associates about this. The ISI was upset with his stand on the Balochistan issue and the trial of General Musharraf, besides his views on the military and its role, Amir said. The attack on his brother was planned and the attackers knew he was going to Karachi and the route he was taking.

Amnesty's report said it was not in a position to assess the claims of the Mir family. However, the CPJ did tell Amnesty that Hamid had frequently contacted them about death threats over the last several years he was receiving from individuals and groups he believed were associated with the ISI. The CPJ said it had not received any video or other message from Hamid to the effect that the ISI or specific individuals should be held responsible if he were to be killed.

Journalists faced a range of threats in Pakistan, including from civil and military state organs such as the police and security forces, according to Amnesty. But no state actor is more feared by journalists than the ISI. Amnesty's investigation of cases shows journalists are particularly at risk of harassment and abuse if they expose security lapses by the military, its alleged links to armed groups, human rights violations by the security forces in Balochistan and north-west Pakistan; or work for foreign media outlets considered by the state to be hostile to Pakistan.

A little over three weeks before Rumi was attacked, a journalist in Mansehra in Khyber Pakhtunkhwa was shot at and he later died in hospital. Abrar Tanoli, a photographer and writer, was also travelling in his car when he was attacked. *Express Tribune*'s partnership with the *International New York Times* could have been another reason for the constant threat. In its edition of 22–23 March 2014, the weekend *International New York Times*—distributed along with the *Express Tribune*—had a huge blank section on its front page. The article that was blanked out was 'What Pakistan Knew About Bin Laden' by journalist Carlotta Gall which had appeared earlier in other editions on the front page and was online. The article (an extract from her book),[10] is continued on page two but in the edition in Islamabad, there was a full-page advertisement for the *Express Tribune*, which is the paper's partner. It is printed in three cities in Pakistan.

Gall's article says:

> Soon after the Navy SEAL raid on Bin Laden's house, a Pakistani official told me that the United States had direct evidence that the ISI chief, Lt. Gen. Ahmed Shuja Pasha,

> knew of Bin Laden's presence in Abbottabad. The information came from a senior United States official, and I guessed that the Americans had intercepted a phone call of Pasha's or one about him in the days after the raid. 'He knew of Osama's whereabouts, yes,' the Pakistani official told me. The official was surprised to learn this and said the Americans were even more so. Pasha had been an energetic opponent of the Taliban and an open and cooperative counterpart for the Americans at the ISI. 'Pasha was always their blue-eyed boy,' the official said. But in the weeks and months after the raid, Pasha and the ISI press office strenuously denied that they had any knowledge of Bin Laden's presence in Abbottabad.

The director general of the ISPR said the allegations of Gall were baseless and ridiculous; there was nothing new and credible, and all speculations had already been proven false. Intelligence sources also said there was no truth in the *New York Times* report.

A week before the attack on Rumi, Kati Marton, the trustee of the CPJ met Prime Minister Sharif and was appreciative of his willingness to listen to the problems of journalists working in Pakistan. Ironically, that was the time our visas were cancelled. The CPJ did a fine job of taking up the issue and issuing strong statements. I did meet Kati Marton, who was married to the late US special ambassador for Pakistan and Afghanistan, Richard Holbrooke, at a reception hosted by the US Ambassador Richard Olson at his residence. She was very optimistic about Sharif's intentions. The CPJ team asked him to review the expulsion of Walsh and also expedite visas for foreign journalists—to which he seemed willing. He also committed to making the country a safe place for journalists. But I knew this optimism would not lead to anything in our case.

The TTP uses its guerrilla tactics with live media as well, and one day it managed to disrupt a show on Express TV where its eponymous spokesperson managed to extract an assurance from the TV anchor that the coverage would be balanced. The hapless anchor, in return, demanded protection for his colleagues. In 2012, the TTP had put up on its website a hit list of media houses and journalists, and after the attack on Rumi, initial TV reports rather pointlessly focused on whether he was on this list or not.

While the killers of Geo TV journalist Wali Khan Babar (in 2012 in Liaquatabad, Karachi) were convicted, the CPJ noted in its 2013 report that Pakistan had one of the world's worst records of impunity in anti-press violence. 'This perfect record of impunity has fostered an ever-more violent climate for journalists. Fatalities have jumped in the past five years, and today, Pakistan ranks among the world's deadliest nations for the press.' It added that the targeted killings of two journalists—Wali Khan Babar in Karachi and Mukarram Khan Aatif in the tribal areas—illustrated the culture of manipulation, intimidation and retribution that led to this killing spree.

Sixty journalists in Pakistan were killed from 1992–2017[11] and in 2014, the country shared number one position with the Democratic Republic of Congo, Afghanistan, Mexico and Ukraine for the deaths of journalists. However, in 2016, it was sixth in terms of journalists killed since 1992, with Iraq and Syria topping the list.[12] On CPJ's Impunity Index, 2016,[13] Pakistan ranked eighth, with twenty-one journalists killed with complete impunity in the past decade. 'In March 2016, a court sentenced one defendant to life in prison and a fine for the 2013 shooting of crime reporter Ayub Khattak. One other case from the past decade, the 2011 murder of television journalist Wali Khan Babar, has met with partial justice. No suspects have been prosecuted in the 2014 attacks on prominent journalists Hamid Mir and Raza Rumi, neither of which were fatal.'[14]

Of the seventy-four cases investigated for the Amnesty report, in only two of these have the perpetrators been convicted; these were for the killing of Wali Khan Babar (in 2011) and the *Wall*

Street Journal reporter Daniel Pearl (in 2002). Police or other authorities carried out an initial investigation in thirty-six cases, and in a handful of incidents, victims or their families received security protection, compensation or other assistance from the state.

Even if the culprits are arrested and the trial gets under way, the obstacles are many. On 1 March 2014, four men were convicted of killing Wali Khan, and were sentenced to life imprisonment. During the trial, eight persons, including two witnesses and a prosecutor, were killed. Two other accused were absconding. This was the first conviction in a journalist's death after Ahmed Omar Saeed Sheikh was convicted of Pearl's murder. The government makes the right noises after a journalist is killed or attacked but there is little follow-up.

Impunity is the norm for attacks on journalists and in the overwhelming majority of cases investigated by Amnesty International, the Pakistani authorities failed to carry out prompt, impartial, independent and thorough investigations into human rights abuses against journalists or to bring those responsible to justice. Pakistan has a reputation for having a fearless and vibrant media. Despite this or perhaps because of it, it is one of the most dangerous countries in the world, judging by the frequency and range of harassment and abuse journalists face, said Amnesty in its 2014 report. (The HRCP said that in 2013 Internet curbs grew and YouTube was not unblocked and other websites were blocked without prior intimation.)

In its 2015 report on attacks on journalists, the CPJ did not list Pakistan as among the top-ten censored countries worldwide; it was upstaged by Eritrea, North Korea, Saudi Arabia, Iran, Cuba and China. After the Lahore bombing in March 2016, which killed seventy-two, the media was openly threatened in a tweet. Jamaat-ur-Ahrar, the Taliban faction that claimed responsibility for the blast aimed at Christians celebrating Easter, warned Pakistani media that they could be the next target.

'Everyone will get their turn in this war, especially the slave Pakistani media,' Ehsanullah Ehsan, spokesperson for the group, tweeted. 'We are just waiting for the appropriate time.'[15]

Facing off with ISI

It is not usual for the ISI to be named publicly in an attack even though fingers point that way. After the attempted murder of Hamid Mir, Zaheer-ul-Islam, the ISI chief, had the ignominy of having his face on TV for hours on end (I think it was seven), while so-called experts indulged in intense haranguing alongside. It was open season and I can be forgiven for thinking that more than the grievous attack on Hamid, it was the allegation made so publicly that caught everyone by surprise. While people privately held the ISI responsible for many barbarous crimes, no one actually had spelt it out so loudly and clearly. The ISPR spokesperson was guarded: 'Raising allegations against the ISI or the head of ISI without any basis is highly regrettable and misleading.'

The stage was set for a confrontation of no mean proportion. The government hit below the belt by suspending Geo's licence for months; it first made sure that the channel was blacked out and the newspapers from the Jang Group were not distributed. There was an abject apology on the front page of the *News* as well two days after the attack on Hamid, on 19 April 2014. The statement said it had not put the blame on any institution or its section. 'The Jang Group values and respects all institutions. All including the accused must be presumed innocent till proven guilty.'

Driving through 'Blue Area' a week after the attack on Hamid, I was surprised to see posters proclaiming great love for the Pakistan Army. Fluttering on each lamp post, the posters had the ISI DG's photo with the slogan 'Pakistan loves Army'. The point they were making was unambiguous. It shouldn't have come as a surprise, especially after protests in major cities in solidarity with the ISI led by the Sunni Ittehad Council (SIC), the

Mohajir Qaumi Movement-Haqiqi (MQM-H), the Ahle Sunnat Wal Jamaat (ASWJ) and others. Geo TV got the flak roundly for its attack on the ISI, and the protestors demanded an apology.

Predictably, Jamaat-ud-Dawa (JuD) was among the groups which put up the posters supporting the Pakistan Army. The Pakistan Tehreek-e-Insaf and other political parties organized a protest, ironically on World Press Freedom Day. I reported that some political parties like the Pakistan Tehreek-e-Insaf, and outfits like the JuD were defending the army and the ISI, and saying that Geo should not have carried such a campaign. I called Mariana Babar, diplomatic correspondent of the *News*, who had worked in the regime of Zia-ul-Haq, for a sane voice in this chaos. A seasoned journalist and keen observer of the Pakistani political theatre, she felt that the ISI taking on the media was not something new. When she started her career under the military rule of Zia-ul-Haq, things had been more or less the same. The situation appeared as if the country had regressed to the 1980s and nothing had changed over the years, she said, adding that the media, especially the electronic one, should show greater responsibility while reporting news.

While everyone thought that other institutions in Pakistan had become strong like the media, judiciary and civil society, Babar said as soon as they stepped on the toes of the army, it hit back to show that it was still a sacred institution. The army remained powerful and possessive about its space, she said.

On the day after the attack on Hamid, I read the morning papers, and was shocked to find that except for the *News* most other English newspapers had played down the incident and the allegations by Amir Mir; instead, in an incredible show of pusillanimity, they had highlighted the ISPR statement. I thought they had decided that discretion was the better part of valour. The defence ministry sent an application to the Pakistan Electronic Media Regulatory Authority (PEMRA) demanding the suspension of licence to the company, Independent Media

Corporation, which runs Geo, and it went off-air in some areas. Vendors stopped distributing the *News* and *Jang* papers. After some reports that Geo had been taken off-air in May, it was actually in June 2014 that the PEMRA officially suspended the channel's licence for fifteen days and imposed a PKR 10-million fine in response to a complaint from the defence ministry. It also warned Geo that if there were more violations, its licence could be revoked.[16] Geo TV was launched in 2002 and is the most-watched channel in Pakistan. Justice was swift in this case, but not so in apprehending Hamid's attackers. I learnt later that Geo paid the fine.

There are few who have not condemned the attack on Hamid but the vindication of the ISI was ferocious. Even a self-confessed critic of the ISI, like Senator Aitzaz Ahsan, said in the Senate, 'Let us not rush to form a judgement and we cannot blame the head of an institution of which I have been a severest critic. The [judicial] commission should complete its inquiry and till then everyone should show some restraint and balance.' Privately many in the media felt that Geo had overstepped its limits and a barely concealed hostility surfaced between Geo and the other channels. The media ranks were in disarray and the hostility to Geo took another turn when the Pakistan Tehreek-e-Insaf Chairperson Imran Khan called for a boycott of Geo for its alleged support for rigging elections. He also gave details of foreign funding (read Indian) to Geo, and demanded an investigation.

The ISPR brazened out the allegations and the ignominy by condemning the attack on Hamid, and called for an independent inquiry to ascertain the facts. I realized that even a powerful group like Jang had no option but to apologize. Many people I spoke to felt that an investigation must first be carried out to determine the facts before going public with accusations.

Squeezed between the Taliban, the army, intelligence and the security agencies, press freedom was not really guaranteed, but the journalists were brave enough to write what they wanted and criticize when necessary and speak out against the Taliban, the ISI and their unholy nexus. Yes, they bowed occasionally to diktats from the Taliban or the ISI, but overall, I think they were a strong, critical force, and as the Amnesty report said, that was also the reason they were under fire. I also like their novelists who have written evocatively about the contemporary situation. Fiction writers like Mohammed Hanif, H.M. Naqvi, Mohsin Hamid, Saba Imtiaz, Jamil Ahmad, Bilal Tanweer and Moni Mohsin give you the real picture, and while truth is often stranger than fiction, in Pakistan fiction has to wrestle with the truth which is in itself unpalatable at times.

Exceptions to the rule

Despite the overall secrecy on defence and nuclear matters, there were occasional bouts of openness for Indian correspondents. Two events stood out for me. First, in 2008, both the Indian journalists were invited for a briefing by the sacred Strategic Plans Division (SPD) which handles the operation, maintenance and security of Pakistan's nuclear weapons programme. And second, the ISPR actually took an Indian journalist, Anita Joshua, to Siachen Glacier after the massive landslide in 2012. It was the then ISPR head, Maj. Gen. Athar Abbas, who took this decision and I learnt later that some of the army officers in Siachen were reluctant to share a presentation in front of an Indian, but Abbas brushed aside their objections.

I barely noticed a cryptic message on 18 December 2013 that announced the change of guard in the SPD, which marked the end of a long and distinguished career of its director general, Lt. Gen. Khalid Ahmed Kidwai, whose name had virtually become synonymous with the nuclear weapons and strategy management of the country. He was replaced by Lt. Gen. Zubair Mahmood Hayat, the corps commander of Bahawalpur, in one of the quieter moves by the Sharif government.

It was Nirupama Subramanian, one of my predecessors in Islamabad and one of the correspondents invited for the SPD briefing in 2008, who egged me on to do this important story, and I wrote an article about the change of guard in this elite and secretive institution. That special briefing where the Indians were invited showed the willingness of the SPD to share and discuss concerns with the media, and going by all accounts, journalists were quite impressed. A lot of doubt had been expressed over guarding Pakistan's nuclear arsenal after Kidwai's exit and even in 2008, when a similar atmosphere of distrust prevailed, Lt. Gen. Kidwai had invited the foreign press for that extraordinary briefing. At that time, he had reassured everyone that the country's strategic assets were in safe hands and that there was 'no conceivable scenario' in which they could fall into the hands of extremists.

Lt. Gen. Kidwai had been heading the SPD since its inception in 1999. 'Within a year of its formation, the SPD had evolved into a true nuclear conclave,' as described by Feroz Hassan Khan in his book, *Eating Grass.*[17] Reports from the US expressed concern over Kidwai's exit after some twelve extensions and the future safety of Pakistan's nuclear arsenal. One of his comments during that briefing had anticipated the fear that the nuclear weapons would fall into the wrong hands. He clearly dismissed this and said there was 'no chance that one day there will be a DG SPD here with a long beard who will be controlling everything'.

Before I left, there was a day-long seminar on nuclear issues where an excited audience bitterly criticized the US and India civilian deal. I met a suave official from the SPD who said I could fix an appointment and visit them, denying that it was out of bounds for an Indian journalist. I didn't get the chance to test this unfortunately.

In a 2014 report by the Nuclear Threat Initiative (NTI), Pakistan was ranked twenty-two and India twenty-three out of twenty-five countries in terms of Nuclear Materials Security

Index conditions; their scores were 46 and 41 respectively. While India criticized the report, the NTI Nuclear Materials Security Index was the second edition of a first-of-its-kind public assessment of nuclear materials' security conditions around the world. Developed with the Economist Intelligence Unit (EIU), the NTI Index was created: (a) to assess the security of weapons-usable nuclear materials around the world; and (b) to encourage governments to take actions and provide assurances about the security of the world's deadliest materials. The report said, 'Among nuclear-armed states, Pakistan is most improved through a series of steps to update nuclear security regulations and to implement best practices, though it ranks 22nd overall.' However, in terms of security control measures, India ranked the lowest below Pakistan among the twenty-five nuclear countries with weapons usable nuclear materials. Pakistan was lowest in the ranking for risk environment, with nineteen points out of 100.

A bloodless coup

It was thanks to A.G. Noorani that I came to know of S. Iftikhar Murshed and *Criterion Quarterly*, a classy magazine with contemporary views. This, along with other magazines like *Herald* and *Newsline*, add a touch of quality and innovation to the Pakistani media. I met Murshed and his son at their home in Islamabad and came back very impressed with their work. The buff-coloured magazine, with its analytical articles, has a steady following. I wrote jokingly that Murshed had, in fact, pulled off a coup with a difference in a country inured to military takeovers. *Criterion Quarterly*, launched in 2005, has gained in stature and is regarded seriously by policymakers. In keeping with the questioning tradition of the media, this is a magazine against religious extremism and terrorism. Murshed was the Pakistani ambassador to Moscow from 2000 to 2005 and the special envoy to Afghanistan from 1996 to 2000. In 2005, he resigned from government to publish *Criterion*, which is funded by committed overseas Pakistanis not looking to make profits. For him, religious extremism and religious terrorism is Pakistan's number one problem, and he feels it is linked to the economy of the country, education, and its history, which singly and collectively have an impact on the ideology of terrorism.

Murshed is as bold as his magazine, telling me he regretted publishing Prime Minister Shaukat Aziz's piece but was proud to get Justice Khalil-ur-Rehman Ramde to take five hours off from court and attend a seminar on terrorism, telecast live; it saw some 'wild views' being expressed, throwing the government into panic and soon after, former Chief Justice Iftikhar Chaudhry was reinstated. Justice Ramde at that time was presiding over the bench which was hearing arguments for the reinstatement of Chaudhry. He compared *Criterion* to Satyajit Ray, not going for the big box office hit but moulding public opinion by not falling for the sex and violence trap. It was an extraordinary interview I had with him, and Murshed took wicked pleasure in his views and criticism of the government. *Criterion*'s articles prompted the Pakistan Tehreek-e-Insaf to aim for revising the Frontier Crimes Regulation in KPK, and that was the kind of policy change he hoped his magazine would crystallize.

Police, protests and media

The police can be just as arbitrary as they are anywhere else, and one day while covering the Musharraf trial, more drama took place outside the court when a young journalist was marched off for no apparent reason. Tayyab Baloch, a staff reporter with a private TV channel, was walking to the courtroom in the National Library when he was rudely interrupted by Jan Mohammed, then inspector general (security) of Islamabad, who asked him who he was before ordering the Rangers officers to check him. Baloch was listening to music on his cell phone which he usually did, and the police asked him why he was carrying his mobile. He tried to tell them that he was going to deposit his mobile at a collection point outside the court but no one listened to him. Mohammed told the police to take him away; he was let off only after some journalists came running and intervened.

While there was a modest gathering to protest against the attack on Rumi, that was not the case for Hamid where I saw a large gathering of media celebrities and senior journalists, all aghast at what had happened. Rumi was shot at a week after Prime Minister Sharif had said he wanted to make Pakistan a journalist-friendly country. And while meeting the CPJ delegation, he had promised a media commission in order to protect the rights of journalists.

The fact that freedom of expression was definitely under threat was brought into sharp focus by the murder of Sabeen Mahmud—a leading human rights activist and founder of The Second Floor (T2F)—a café-cum-gallery-cum-discussion place—in Karachi in 2015. Mahmud was shot dead after she hosted a programme with Mama Qadeer Baloch (who heads the Voice of Baloch Missing Persons) called 'Unsilencing Balochistan' after a public talk at the Lahore University of Management Sciences had been cancelled on government orders.[18] Before that, there was a fracas in the University of Peshawar over a discussion on Malala Yousafzai's book—the Pakistan Tehreek-e-Insaf's Khyber Pakhtunkhwa government stopped a programme organized by the Baacha Khan Trust Educational Foundation, the Area Study Centre (part of the university) and Strengthening Participatory Organization (SPO), where the vice chancellor was the chief guest. I spoke to the director of the Baacha Khan Trust Educational Foundation, Dr Khadim Hussain, who said that a minister from the KPK government from Pakistan Tehreek-e-Insaf, Shah Farman, had called him up and asked him to cancel the function, saying it was a banned book. This was followed up by calls from another minister from the Jamaat-e-Islami, the Pakistan

Tehreek-e-Insaf's coalition partner, who said the programme should not be held.

For a country with a free media, the ban on YouTube for the last two years has been a sticking point. Everyone has found proxy sites to view it on, while the government keeps reneging on its promises of unblocking the site. There have been many protests in the National Assembly, and resolutions passed demanding the unblocking of the site.

YouTube was blocked in September 2012 after a controversial film which provoked protests all over the world was not taken off. A little later, the website Queerpk.com was taken off and made inaccessible. 'The site you are trying to access contains content that is prohibited for viewership from within Pakistan,' a cryptic message said.

The BBC Urdu channel that reported the blocking of the website said it had been set up in July and was the first such website for the gay community. While there is widespread outrage over the banning of YouTube, with the government being repeatedly asked to review the ban, it is unlikely there will be a similar storm of protest over this site. I spoke to a gender studies expert in a university who said the state was increasingly becoming repressive, fundamentalist and that it was theocratic to begin with. There were many forms of violence and this was also one of them—to curtail freedom of expression. The retrogressive laws against homosexuality have not been challenged in Pakistan and there is no public movement to change the law. 'People live out their sexualities in a hidden way,' she said. In June 2011, the US embassy had held a first-of-its-kind lesbian, gay, bisexual and transgender (LGBT) pride celebration in Islamabad which immediately led to protests.[19]

The government and the security empire have the upper hand in Pakistan in many ways. Yet, with all the powers at their command, they have not crushed the free spirit of the people who write and report at will. Many have paid with their blood for writing the truth and will continue to do so. Promises to safeguard the press and media freedom and ensure safety are not credible and remain only on paper. That is the tragic state of affairs with the media, and, journalists who take on the establishment are up against forces which are not necessarily accountable for their actions.

6

No Lines of Control

I found some old connections with India in the field of rural development, and the early days of the Aam Aadmi Party's election in Delhi had inspired many people in Pakistan as it had a David-versus-Goliath ring to it. While Sufi singer Abida Parveen has expressed only feelings of love for India, the textbooks of both countries have depressingly hatred-infusing content to say the least, and there seems to be a curious pride in not knowing the real facts about each other. Ironically, one of the finest breweries in the subcontinent thrives in this country with prohibition, and is run by a Parsi who is keen on launching it in India too. I met MPs from both countries who spoke of peace, and interviewed the late writer Intizar Hussain, survivors of Partition, and Madeeha Gauhar who draws on the forgotten pre-Partition history for her vibrant theatre group, Ajoka.

The man from Pakistan

The house was on Embassy Road and the entrance had a forlorn look. I waited for what seemed like a long time after ringing the bell, forgetting that there was no power. Just when I thought I was at the wrong house, an apologetic man opened the door and showed me into a study which opened out on to a lawn fringed with thick bushes. I was looking at the walls full of photographs and mementos when Shoaib Sultan Khan entered. After pleasantries, he pointed, with a mischievous smile, to one of the pictures behind his large desk and asked me if I recognized the person. I was surprised to see that the face turned towards him was Rahul Gandhi's. Sultan Khan modestly said he was amazed that Rahul had even heard of him and that he was invited to relaunch a programme in India for women. The picture was taken at a workshop for the Rajiv Gandhi Mahila Vikas Pariyojana on 16 July 2008 at Bais in Rae Bareli. Rahul had apparently visited Andhra Pradesh to learn about rural women's initiatives there and heard about the 'man from Pakistan'. Sultan Khan seemed very impressed by 'this young man who has his heart in the right place to do something for the poor'.

People in India were already familiar with this 'Pakistani man' who connected the two countries with his ideas of poverty alleviation. It was his diverse work experience in rural development first as a civil servant in East Pakistan, then in Daudzai and Gilgit Baltistan which he took with him to India as adviser to the United Nations Development Programme's (UNDP) South Asia Poverty Alleviation Programme (SAPAP). He was to test a pilot project in Kurnool in 1994 and that's when Prime Minister P.V. Narasimha Rao's secretary, K.R. Venugopal, became an indispensable part of it. Venugopal made things easy: 'I wouldn't have come to India otherwise and it was he who found Raju for me.' Raju was K. Raju, a former collector of Kurnool, who was the national coordinator of SAPAP from 1996 to 2000.

What led to this was the Independent South Asian Commission on Poverty Alleviation and its report which was adopted by the SAARC heads of nations in 1993. Both Sultan Khan and Venugopal were members. I spoke to Vijay Kumar who was head of the National Rural Livelihoods Mission (NRLM), and met Sultan Khan in 2000. He said the seminal contribution of this report was that social mobilization would be the basis of poverty alleviation. After this, the UNDP decided to implement a pilot project in each SAARC country and that's when it took off in three districts of the then Andhra Pradesh—Kurnool, Anantapur and Mahbubnagar in twenty mandals from 1994.

Sultan Khan's official designation was chairperson of the board of directors of the Rural Support Programmes Network and the National Rural Support Programme in Pakistan, both not-for-profit joint stock companies. He visited India after my op-ed article on him appeared in *The Hindu* in October 2013, and joked that he had become a celebrity, which he was anyway. In a way, the poverty programmes led to the NRLM, and he was keen on knowing their progress in states like Andhra Pradesh and Bihar. Raju and Vijay Kumar looked forward to his visits and going to the field with him. In fact, after the success of the Andhra Pradesh model, the Indian government changed its anti-poverty strategy, and even though there was the inspiring Kudumbashree model in Kerala it was an outlier, Kumar said, since it involved linkages with Panchayati Raj institutions which were not strong everywhere in India. When I spoke to both Raju and Kumar for my articles, they called Sultan Khan a miracle worker, a man who had worked in a difficult place like Pakistan to provide last-mile support services for the poor.

The Andhra Pradesh programme which was later scaled up, now has the involvement of more than 11 million rural women. Many remember the 'Pakistani' with a lot of affection. During Kumar's visit to Pakistan in 2008, the North-West Frontier Province government was keen on support from India, and teams from Pakistan who visited the Andhra projects were struck by the fact that it was entirely dominated by women there. In Andhra Pradesh, it was the women who formed self-help groups (SHG), but it was when Raju visited Gilgit in 1996 that he realized the importance of village-level organizations.

Sultan Khan worked closely with Venugopal to weld a relationship between India and Pakistan and create a model to help the rural poor. While the NRLM is a national programme in India, in Pakistan it has not been scaled up. He has a deep connection with so many Indian bureaucrats and greatly values the over twenty-year friendship with Venugopal, and is especially fond of Kumar and Raju, both of whom learnt a lot from what he was doing in Pakistan.

He was among the first few people I met in Islamabad, in August 2013. When I met Shandana Humayun Khan, the CEO of the Rural Support Programme Network, she insisted I meet the person who really initiated the Aga Khan Rural Support Programme (AKRSP), Shoaib Sultan Khan. I was more keen on meeting the women who were running the self-help groups, but I agreed and I am so glad I did. I didn't expect to hear such a fascinating life story from a bureaucrat.

I thought I would ask him a few questions and leave, but I ended up interviewing him twice on two separate days for almost three hours. There were a few friends with him who had come from Orangi Town in Karachi, and that's how I met one of his old friends, Zafar Altaf, former cricketer and manager of the Pakistan cricket team who had with him some homeopathic medicine for Sultan Khan's cough (pollen allergies were common at that time of the year). I would later meet Altaf for lunch at his house and he gifted me copies of his book on Benazir Bhutto.

In the frenzied coverage about cross-border firing, terror attacks and mutual animosity, a happy cooperation based on poverty alleviation won't make headlines. It's a two-decade-long relationship, the roots of which began when Sultan Khan drove a jeep to his new job in Gilgit to work on the AKRSP in 1982. He started out in East Pakistan as a young civil service officer in 1958. His mentor was Akhtar Hameed Khan who was to play a key role in making young Shoaib a legend in the field of rural development. He met Hameed Khan, then head of the Pakistan Academy for Rural Development, when he was assistant commissioner in Comilla district in what was then East Pakistan.

Hameed Khan perfected what would eventually be known as the Comilla Approach.[1]

He had identified the police thana as a centre of development—the British had demarcated its location by calculating how far the station house officer could go to the farthest point on horseback and return the same day. That symbol of law and order became the symbol of development. Soon a thana training and development centre was set up in all 410 thanas of East Pakistan. Each had twenty-five government departments, and it was a majestic complex, recalled Sultan Khan. People could visit the thana for their needs and return home the same day and the government was able to raise an army of barefoot workers. Later, as director of the Pakistan Academy for Rural Development at Peshawar, he adopted the East Pakistan experience in the Daudzai programme which became a milestone. The Daudzai thana near Peshawar had some 20,000 households and in three years the model of development was so successful that the government wanted to take it to all 110 thanas in the Frontier. However, there were forces at work against the programme and Sultan Khan faced cooked-up charges which were later withdrawn. Then his political patron, former governor of the NWFP and minister, Hyat Sherpao, who was keen on the programme, was killed in a blast in 1975. Disillusioned with the civil service, he quit to work on UN assignments and finally landed up in India in 1994.

It was after a stint as the UNICEF's social development consultant in Sri Lanka in the Mahaweli Ganga project (which earned him a full-page write-up in *Newsweek* called 'A Man Named Khan') that the Aga Khan Foundation asked him to take up a project in Gilgit in Pakistan. The day he was to fly to Gilgit, on 1 December 1982, his flight didn't take off. That's when he got hold of a jeep and drove the 600 kilometres from Islamabad.

The AKRSP has an ongoing programme not only in Gilgit but also in other parts of Pakistan, much of it documented in Sultan Khan's book, *A Journey through Grassroots Development*.[2]

He emerged as a rarity, a bureaucrat who tried to use his powers to do something for the poor, and one who had established strong ties with communities and leaders in both India and Pakistan. His biography is called *Man in the Hat*,[3] but his own memoirs I am sure could fill several volumes.

Instead of some quotes for my story, I ended up doing an op-ed article and a blog on Sultan Khan whom I missed meeting in New Delhi after I returned. He made it to the list of twenty Pakistanis to be proud of in a book published by the Jang Group in April 2016. At eighty-five, he can look back on a more fulfilled life than most people.

Demure yet determined

In a society where women moving around freely aroused suspicions of the worst kind, Shaista's task was tricky. When she and some others first started community work in a tribal area in Haripur, people thought they were American agents or had come to rob them. They started locking up their houses on seeing her, but slowly she convinced them about the need to come out and speak up over issues like water. Women began to realize the joys of mobility by holding meetings and controlling their finances. Over fifteen years ago, Narian village was the first in KPK to have a community organization, and digging bore wells was a priority, which improved the water situation. In the whole process, the women were able to overcome their fear of visiting other mohallas. This freedom often triggered the community's ire—they were called 'shameless' and even got death threats when they first started their organizations.

The women from the self-help groups told their stories casually; they were chilling at times and I got a brief glimpse into their difficult lives which had been transformed by their association with the Rural Support Programme. They were young and older women, demure yet determined, and since I couldn't travel out of Islamabad, some of them came from Haripur and other places to meet me. It was Zubina perhaps who faced the gravest threats to her life when she was trying to train survivors of the massive earthquake in 2005. She was more educated than most girls and had managed to study till the tenth class in Haripur (in KPK) and became a master trainer in handicrafts. When she was sent to Kohistan to teach survival skills to young people, she faced a class full of hostile boys, ready to kill her because she was a woman. Zubina explained to me patiently that women were not allowed to step out of the house or even go into another mohalla. This invited death, and in Besham the young boys were startled to see a woman as their teacher and they reacted in the only way they had been taught. This is an area where a woman can be shot in the name of honour, for looking at a man, for going out to bathe or for any other 'non-reason'. Being a woman, in fact, seemed enough reason for a man to kill you. But Zubina was tough; mere threats were not going to deter her and she told her class to take it or leave it. As part of the Sarhad Rural Support Programme (SRSP), the only development organization working there, she had a distinct advantage and managed to teach tailoring to some boys. The SRSP is part of the Rural Support Programmes Network (RSPN), Pakistan's largest network of NGOs, and its work is based on the approach first implemented in northern Pakistan by the AKRSP in 1982.

The RSPN was set up in 2000 as a network of eleven rural support programmes. Microcredit is a big part of the programme and community groups set up by women run small businesses or shops or even buy taxis for their husbands. Instead of working in other people's houses, they are self-sufficient thanks to the small amounts of money on credit. Fauzia from Nilor said that at first the women started saving PKR 10 and those who couldn't bring money brought something in kind, sometimes even eggs. It was difficult to get loans from banks but the credit from the RSP became a revolving fund and women disbursed money themselves.

More than money or loans, it was the motivation and courage to do something which was a thrill for women like Naheed from a settlement in the Islamabad Capital Territory. Similarly, Shagufta and some other women started their own pickle manufacturing business and she was certainly the first businesswoman in her area. The entire programme taught the women to speak up, and the community groups also started throwing up political leadership—about 300 women have won elections at various levels. In the case of Iram Fatima who contested twice—the second time in the General Elections of Pakistan in 2013—she lost both times but planned to contest again.

After the Indian connection when Shoaib Sultan Khan became adviser to a UNDP project in the SAARC countries, a team from Pakistan visited Andhra Pradesh to see how women were at the forefront, and it had a galvanizing effect. Shandana, the chief executive officer of the RSPN, said that for Pakistanis to see women as leaders was quite startling. After the visit, nearly 50 per cent of the credit groups and community organizations had women working in them, which was less than half of that many years ago. However, the expansion of the Rural Support Programme has been slow—it exists in 111 of the 131 districts of Pakistan, and in two of the thirteen FATAs, covering 5.2 million households. The target is ambitious—17 million poor, rural households. I was invited to visit a successful microcredit programme in Bahawalpur but I didn't even ask to go. I knew what the answer would be.

Soulful and simple

I was introduced to her at one of the Indian high commission parties just as she was leaving and I was entering. I was flaunting my new jeans from Khaadi to friends and I didn't realize it was the Queen of Soul who was looking on. I was so taken aback that I stammered a greeting and she kept bowing. I was puzzled as to what I should do next, as I had already—and I thought effusively—greeted her. She lowered her right hand to her knees lifting it up again and again—thrice in fluid movements—her curls tumbling over her shoulder. I later read somewhere that it was a floor salaam. I had seen courtiers greet the emperor in probably *Mughal-e-Azam* and wondered why I was so deeply honoured. If anything, it was I who should be scraping the floor for her. I stood transfixed till she bowed out of the gate while I heard stifled laughter in the background. I should have bowed deeply as many times in return, explained my wretched friends who were hysterical with laughter, and who had suddenly become sticklers for etiquette. I lacked *tehzeeb*, they stuttered. That was Abida Parveen for you—her love and humility knew no bounds, like her music which melted borders. To my horror, that encounter was narrated many times and it amused some of my friends no end. For a while every time I met them and there was a new person who hadn't heard the story, they would start, 'Do you know what she did when she met Abida Parveen?'

It was a bit comic really. Anyway, undaunted, I fixed up a meeting at her residence, next to a fancy boutique owned by her daughter. I didn't think it would be easy to meet her though. Her new album, *Shah Jo Raag,* had been released in Karachi and that was a perfect peg for my feature. I had to wait for an hour as she was resting, and I was getting nervous that she wouldn't meet me at all. Waiting in AP Gallerie, her boutique, I met some fashion designers from Peshawar who were displaying their well-cut but expensive stuff, and to pass time I looked at a whole wall dedicated to her Sufi albums, and photos (mostly with Indian artistes): Lata Mangeshkar, R.D. Burman, Pandit Jasraj; of her performance in 2008 at the Taj Mahal hotel in Mumbai; there is one of her hugging Shoukat Kaifi Azmi; with her guru, Ustad Salamat Ali Khan; and one of her at Dargah Hazrat Khwaja Moinuddin Chishti in Ajmer Sharif in 2001. There were awards displayed in another section of the gallery which had a motley collection of clothes, jewellery and artefacts.

When I met her at last, she was dressed simply in beige, her hair fell in an unruly mop around her shoulders, and she was warm and effusive as if I was an old friend. To my relief, she didn't mention my lack of tehzeeb. In her mind there was no doubt of the *mohabbat* between India and Pakistan, and her first love was Sufism and her Sufi masters. She was simple and childlike in her answers, and the word '*ruhaniyat*' (soulfulness) was the theme that evening. She took very little credit for her music—it was all a gift from her devotion to her spiritual masters, the many Sufi saints. She was full of the '*jalsa*' in Karachi where the *Shah Jo Raag* album had been launched and the warm feelings from there—the kind of soulfulness that reduced people to tears. She suddenly referred to the politics and the bomb blasts, and said in the midst of these, there was a message of love and peace from Sufism and that message gave an inner strength to people to unite them. It was almost miraculous, she exulted. In this world of love and soul, there was no room for blood, she said.

It was fifteen years ago that she recorded the first *sur* of *Shah Jo Raag*, the verses of Shah Abdul Latif, the eighteenth-century Sufi poet, whose songs have been sung by his disciples, from sunset to sunrise in his mausoleum in Bhit Shah for well over 250 years. It was a colossal effort to compile some of that music for the first time into *Shah Jo Raag*, an eleven-CD album which is accompanied by a beautiful monograph. She started learning music at three, and she giggled as she said that school was everywhere since her father, Ustad Ghulam Haider, ran a music school. Unlike the strict regimen for learning classical music, there was no one place she sat to learn, she said—it was all so casual and fluid, they would fight about notes, he would ask her to sing something, correct her, and so it went on. Music was everywhere, she was learning all the time though she lifted a finger to press home the point that learning was never enough or complete. The real school was dispensable in this charming and informal world she had lived in, and she dismissively said that she had studied up to the twelfth standard (*barah–chaudah*).

Her father was an exponent of the Patiala gharana and a great admirer of the legendary singer Amir Khan whose music he heard on All India Radio. She grew up listening to the songs sung at Bhit Shah and longed to sing them. And she did, after many years of hard work and research. 'Even if you understand a single word, it's a moment of ecstasy, and it shows you how to live your life and what should guide you.' She has sung all the thirty ragas in the album and some of them had not been sung before this way. Her first public performance was also at Bhit Shah and it was not without some trepidation. I couldn't believe that someone who gave herself to so much abandon in her performances, was actually afraid. It was only in 1973 that she auditioned for Radio Pakistan; later, she launched her first album with songs by Bulleh Shah. She has sung at the Taj Mahal hotel in Mumbai a few times and wants more exchange between the two countries. There was so much love across the border among families, artistes, she said, and no one could stop that. For her, India and Pakistan were one country: 'They think the same way and there is sweetness and love. I think this way—please correct me if I am wrong. Love is a force, it's like the sea, it cannot break.'

She has her favourite Indian artistes—Pandit Jasraj, Ustad Amir Khan and Ustad Zakir Hussain Khan. Her favourite in Pakistan was Tari Khan, a celebrated tabla player. Her spiritual guide was Syed Muhammed Najib Sultan Bahu, though she drew inspiration from other Sufi saints as well. She was then busy with a new project translating the compositions of Hazrat Sultan-ul-Arifeen (born in 1631 or perhaps a couple of years earlier, and died in 1691), who wrote in Persian, into Seraiki and she would sing it in both languages. Sultan-ul-Arifeen had said that whoever reads his work will not need to search for a spiritual master. Abida quoted a line by him: 'Where I have reached no one else has.' She closed the interview with that moving line and I thought that along with so many other Pakistanis I met, she had brought an element of sanity and soulfulness into the relationship between our two countries. There was no room for hatred or suspicion here and not even an iota of doubt about the love between the two countries. Abida Parveen's music and performances can take you to a higher realm when the world is being destroyed by violence and she is a very vital part of that narrowing fabric of peace. My favourite album is the one where she has sung the verses by Faiz Ahmad Faiz. I never imagined one day I would meet or interview her. She shows us a way, like Jiddu Krishamurthi did many years ago, to rise above our 'petty tyrannies'.

Voice of the desert

She sang for the first time at the shrine of Lal Shahbaz Qalandar in Sehwan, Sindh. Her family didn't think much of her talent, but at the age of twelve she recorded the song '*Laal Meri*' on Pakistan Radio, but her favourite was '*Badi Lambi Judai*'. When I first heard Reshma I wondered who this woman was, with her full-throated, haunting voice. She was born in Bikaner in Rajasthan in a nomadic Banjara community, and her family moved to Karachi after 1947.

Throat cancer claimed Reshma when I was in Islamabad and I had to write a tribute. In one of the CDs I bought, she speaks before each song and disarmingly attributes her voice to God. She speaks of her family's resistance to her singing and of later acceptance. Reshma was discovered by Saleem Gilani, then a producer with Radio Pakistan who went on to head it as director general. He heard her when she sang at the shrine in Sehwan and called her for a recording to Karachi, according to journalist Murtaza Solangi who had tweeted a photo with Reshma. When I called Solangi, he spoke to me at length about the beginning of her long and stellar singing career.

During his tenure with Radio Pakistan, Solangi launched a series of programmes at different radio stations to pay tribute to living legends, and one of them was Reshma. 'How could I forget Reshma? In my youthful years her voice always enriched me and she connected Rajasthan, Cholistan and Sindh. She was the voice of love and peace. Last year in March, we had an event to pay tribute to her musical journey and contribution, with her contemporaries and young artists. She couldn't resist. I will sing too, she said. And there she was on the stage in unbelievable command, giving instructions to musicians and people on the percussion.' Solangi also described how when she started singing, many eyes went misty. 'When I put a woollen shawl from Sindh on her shoulders, she had an amazing smile. It smells of home, she told me.'

He continued, 'She is not with us, but her voice will always be with us. I will always remember Reshma, the flower of the desert, symbol of love, music and peace!' Her voice which is full of longing, evokes the desert of her origin and always reminds me of wide, open spaces.

Student exchange and Partition memories

If great artistes like Abida Parveen form one end of the spectrum of love between the two countries, there are other attempts to bring the two countries closer. And I came across this Exchange for Change programme quite by accident from an encounter at a friend's lunch party. The Citizens Archive of Pakistan (CAP) was recording oral histories of those who survived Partition and I was lucky to meet some of the people featured in that project. The letters exchange programme, or Exchange for Change, between school students in India and Pakistan since 2010, also set up by the CAP, was one way of sharing and learning about each other. The letters reflected a natural curiosity about food, clothes, monuments and way of life, and the students met at the end of the programme. The CAP is dedicated to cultural and historical preservation, and the letters programme was quite a success with the number of schools and students increasing every year. Untainted by propaganda and stereotypes, the students wanted to visit each other's countries and learn. There was plenty to discover: for instance, that the Taj Mahal is not the only monument in India; Indians eat mangoes and the women wear 'ghaghras'. Some had grandparents born in India and they prayed for unity between the two countries. One student in a letter said that India was a nice place and there were nice people like Gandhi! The third phase connected 5000 schoolchildren from India and Pakistan—2500 from each country.

In a way, both programmes of the CAP were different dimensions of relations between India and Pakistan. One looked to the future and the other wanted to preserve the past, rich with memories painful and happy, but evocative testimonies to the bloody and painful division of a country. The Exchange for Change in collaboration with Routes 2 Roots, an Indian non-profit organization, was for young students while the oral archives documented memories of those who lived around the time of Partition. I interviewed three survivors of Partition and I sensed a feeling of regret because Pakistan didn't turn out the way it was envisaged by Jinnah as a secular state, though for Prof. Naeem Qureshi, the parting was inevitable. 'Partition is a process, where does one begin and where does one end? And the last word on it has not been said.' For others, it was a process that reversed for ever a pluralistic society. It was not what he saw or remembered of Partition that mattered to Khalid Chima, a retired civil servant, it was the aftermath. 'Growing up was a time when religion didn't matter and all you worried about at school was if the new boy was a team player. Your Brahmin scoutmaster ate with you and you had friends staying over. It was a time of long Sunday visits, shikar trips, vacations spent together at hill stations with friends and family,' said Chima. Life changed in the new country, and his father, a government servant in Sialkot, fully intended to go to East Punjab in India during Partition.

He (Chima's father) had come to Lahore in early August to take the family away; he couldn't stand the crowds and felt there should be a mix of people where he lived. But the riots prevented him and so it was a stroke of fate that they stayed back in Pakistan. The Chimas' journey back in time was full of happy memories and their present tinged with sadness and nostalgia. Khalid was deeply affected by what he felt were the other consequences of the political compulsions of Partition and the demand for it. People suffered so much—the murder, rape, looting, the transfer of population (the largest in the world). But what he took as a personal loss was that a cosmopolitan, multireligious, forward-looking, pluralist society was destroyed for all time. 'I think the world is the poorer for that. Though I did not suffer any personal inconvenience but this is what I have suffered.'

Religion, he felt, was something personal and that no one bothered about the other person's religion—until Zia's time. That was when people started wearing religion on their shirtsleeves. Partition was not a footnote in history, and he felt it was important to take stock of it by itself and the social consequences, and inform future generations of its process and the feelings of people who went through it—no one came out unscathed. 'The present generation needs to be informed that things were not what they are told they were—things were different but I doubt if it can ever come back. Because there is a complete absence of any other kind of society or community and the few that are left don't feel very comfortable. Even among Muslims, look at what Taliban is doing—they have their apologists and also their supporters.'

His wife, Nasreen Chima, a former teacher, got increasingly animated as she drew on her memories which went back to the time when she was eight or nine years old in Jhelum. She came from a political family—her grandfather was a member of the Constituent Assembly and her mother Rashida Ahsan was a well-known activist and classmate and close friend of actor Zohra Sehgal.

At the Queen Mary College in Lahore, Rashida had been a staunch member of Congress before she joined the Muslim

League (ML). When Bhagat Singh was tried and sentenced, Rashida and her friends wrote placards in blood, and her uncle who was a magistrate told her not to go out, fearing trouble. He said he would get them distributed—such was the spirit that Bhagat Singh evoked.

Nasreen remembered the transfers and change of schools which became a routine affair, and her parents who became active in politics after they joined the Muslim League. Her parents never forced religion on her. Her mother led processions, and Nasreen as a young girl would sneak into the front without her knowing. It was the men who were jailed first for leading processions till her mother motivated women to step out. One woman was equal to a hundred men, her mother would say. Nasreen enjoyed the marches and the slogans: 'Down with the government'; 'We will make Pakistan even if we have to get our throats slit'. She enjoyed the thrill of defiance, and recalled that everyone was in high spirits before the dawn of freedom.

Immediately after Partition, her house was like a refugee camp. She said if the massacres had not happened, then this migration would not have taken place; if the migration had not happened, Pakistan would have been a plural, diverse, multi-ethnic, multilingual, multireligious and tolerant society. 'Now we are not; we are intolerant, sectarian. We are going through hell—I don't know how it will end.' She also feared for her secular ideals.

Nasreen's friend from a minority community told her one day, 'You are [in] a practical minority; you are more of a minority than we are, because your thinking [is shared by only] a small group.' In Nasreen's view, state and religion should be kept separate—religion was a personal matter and the state should be neutral and secular.

More matter of fact is Dr Qureishi, a professor at Quaid-i-Azam University. He was eleven at the time of Partition and lived in Sargodha where his father was in the police. He was one of the few Muslim students in the Sanathan Dharm High School. Once he went to school wearing a Jinnah badge, and in a jiffy he was mobbed by the older students who saw a potential rebel, and was given what he called a verbal thrashing. Only the intervention of a senior teacher saved him from a beating. Emotions ran high, but luckily Sargodha was spared the Hindu–Muslim riots.

They used to live in the police lines and very near to it there were refugee camps; he could hear the screams when villagers raided them. 'I didn't know if it was kidnapping or if people were robbing the camps. I could see later on that the caravans had moved from the camp—the old and infirm, young boys, women—on carts, walking, or using whatever means of transport they could get. At the same time we saw people coming from India at the airport; the planes would arrive from India with well-to-do Muslims; sometimes planes owned by the Nizam of Hyderabad would come.'

He had a lot of friends among Hindus and Sikhs. 'It never occurred to us that this would happen, but this is a reality—we can't turn our heads from it and I wish it had not happened the way it did. A fallout is that even today we don't have good relations between the two countries . . . There was a feeling [in 1947] that this was an abnormal situation and it would get better. The human casualty—both psychological and otherwise—was staggering.' He thought an objective history of the times has not yet been written either in India or Pakistan, and emotions are still strong on both sides. It would be useful to historians of the future to realize what had happened, he said, suggesting a joint venture by Pakistani and Indian historians to move away from that emotional involvement and write an objective history on what happened to them in later life. It was a trauma, and trauma never goes away, he said.

The CAP Oral History Project, the first of its kind, was started in 2008 by a group of young people documenting narratives of Partition. Swaleha Alam Shahzada, the CAP executive director, was keen on preserving the narratives and diverse oral histories of ordinary people, which would otherwise have been lost forever.

The CAP has more than 2500 hours of audio and over 50,000 images, and the idea was to have a consolidated archive accessible to the public.

Partition and the making of a writer

Partition produced some powerful and iconic writing, and even if he is not as revered as Saadat Hasan Manto, Intizar Hussain carved a place for himself in the pantheon of writers of that period. I was really sorry to hear of his death in February 2016, nearly two years after I had interviewed him when he attended the Islamabad Literature Festival in April 2014. He was a simple man, with a quiet sense of humour; he laughed a lot and was a little uncomfortable talking about his writing—something that came naturally to him. I had read his work translated from the Urdu and from a familiar name, he became someone I could talk to. He confessed that if it wasn't for Partition, he probably wouldn't have become a writer. Fond of literary criticism, with T.S. Eliot being a favourite, he didn't like fiction much, and wrote as a hobby. Words came easily to him and he had studied languages in his BA, including English, Urdu and Persian literature, with a master's in Urdu. He was fond of the Mahabharata and the *Jataka Tales*, and for him the first pain of separation was felt by the Pandavas when they were exiled. 'The first Partition was in the Mahabharata,' he said, 'and then it was me when I was exiled (*laughing*). The pain of leaving one's land, only the Pandavas and I knew. The Mahabharata is such a powerful narrative of that pain.' In his novel *Basti*, he brings in a lot of Hindu stories and myths.

He walked with a stout stick, and after the programme where he launched a collection of his articles, he sat in a corner surrounded by fans, signing his books. He was in the thick of things in June 1947, when he completed his MA. There was tension because of riots, and localities were emptying out fast. Every day a new house would be locked up as residents left in panic. It was this silence and desolation that formed the theme of his first short story.

'I thought I should write about this and I liked reportage as a genre. Striking events were taking place before my eyes and I wrote my first short story, "*Kayuma Ki Dukan*",' he said. The story is about a shop, an adda in his *kasba*. People used to meet there and chat till late into the night, but after the riots the shop was closed.

'As a writer of fiction I was born with Pakistan. In the past I was not very fond of it, but Partition made me a fiction writer,' he said. Hussain was born near Aligarh in a town called Dibai on 21 December 1925. He laughed and said that he wasn't yet ninety as people believed. In 1947, his family, including his five sisters, was not keen on moving to the new country but he and his friends went to Pakistan. Those who went were sure they would come back and it wasn't forever. People packed their things and left, giving their keys to their Hindu neighbours. There is a similar situation in his novel *Basti*.

Hussain wanted to be a teacher and he thought his master's in Urdu had equipped him for that, but when he arrived in Lahore he didn't get a job. Then Faiz Ahmad Faiz was launching a new paper and he went for an interview. He said he felt scared as 'Faiz saab' didn't speak much. He asked a few questions and fell silent. 'He then asked me to wait for a call. I thought I wouldn't get the job and in the meanwhile I got the editor's post in a weekly, but there was some controversy and things took a turn for the worse,' he said.

Then came the call from Faiz offering him a job in Karachi at his paper *Imroze*. But it didn't last long. That was when he decided that he wanted to be a serious writer. His first compilation of short stories, *Streets and Lanes*,[4] was about what he had left behind—the composite culture of Ram Leela, Holi, Id, Moharram. He delved into myth and folklore—*Baital Pachisi*, the story of Shakuntala, *Panchatantra*—and absorbed these elements into his writing.

'I was familiar with Hindu mythology and *Jataka Tales*, and when Alok Bhalla came and visited me he wanted to translate my work and showcase all this. I was one of the few writers in Pakistan who used Hindu mythology,' he said.

The first English translation of his short stories, *A Chronicle of the Peacocks: Stories of Partition, Exile and Lost Memories*,[5] was a result of Bhalla's search for stories on Partition. 'At that time he said to me there is Manto and there is you,' smiled Hussain, pleased with that allusion. He was not overly worried about the translation. 'It is, after all, just that a translation,' he said. He joked that of late he found himself giving more and more speeches. Once he was asked to speak about the writer Nirmal Verma, a man he had met once and who was rather taciturn, but he had read Verma's work and liked it. Nominated for the Man Booker International Prize in 2013, he wrote five novels and seven collections of short stories. He hadn't written a novel after *Aage Samandar Hai* in the 1980s.

The partition of India was hotly debated and the question had now gone beyond writers, and historians had taken over, he felt. 'I am not a historian—*gaya hai saanp ab lakir pita kar* (the snake has gone, now beat the trail it has left behind). What is the point of weeping over Partition? There was no expectation of a deep divide, but the riots changed things, especially in the Punjab,' he said. As a writer, his main interest was in linking the past with the present. His work is evocative of Partition and the dilemma of people in the two new countries.

Uninterrupted dialogue

I met a lot of Indians in Islamabad whom I probably wouldn't have met back home. Soon after I got there in August 2013, there was a visit by a large delegation of MPs led by Mani Shankar Aiyar who sent out very positive signals. They were grilled by the Pakistani media on the hostility to Pakistan in India, and the

MPs in response declared there was a large constituency for peace there. Over fifty parliamentarians from Pakistan and thirteen MPs from India took part in the fifth round of the two-day dialogue facilitated by the Pakistan Institute of Legislative Development and Transparency (PILDAT).

Aiyar said that no one was in favour of Pakistan-bashing, and Shah Mehmood Qureshi from the Pakistan Tehreek-e-Insaf said that the Indian MPs were going back with a clear message that India-bashing was no longer fashionable in Pakistan politics.

Even Kirti Azad of the Bharatiya Janata Party accepted the need for talks, but he said that the terror issue had to be resolved. He joked, 'We enjoy Pakistan-bashing on the cricket field.' Qureshi said that in Pakistan there was no desire for war and though there was a large constituency for peace, there was growing frustration on both sides since the pace of talks was not in step with the desires of the people. The joint statement issued by the MPs urged India and Pakistan to jointly examine issues of climate change and environmental impact assessment, improvement in bilateral trade, activation of gas supplies to Pakistan from India as well as power trading; it also touched on issues such as granting MFN status to India, opening banks of either country in the other to facilitate trade exchanges, improving the visa regime, and expanding existing agreements on handling of humanitarian issues. One of the MPs was Asaduddin Owaisi but he was instructed not to speak, and as a result he didn't even reply to a TV reporter's question asking for his opinion on the lunch! Owaisi grinned and joked, 'I have been warned not to speak since I spew hate speech!'

Soon after this bonhomie, in a video broadcast, Shashi Tharoor accused the civilian government of not being entirely in control in Pakistan. Tharoor, who was then the Union minister of state for human resource development, said that the Mumbai attacks five years ago and the recent LoC incidents had shown a gap between Pakistan's official statement and the military's action, and the civilian government even if sincere, was not entirely in control of the security apparatus.

The video broadcast of his speech threatened to disrupt the Indo-Pak Young Entrepreneurs Bilateral Summit jointly organized by the Islamabad Chamber of Commerce and Industry, Young Indians and the Commonwealth Asia Alliance of Young Entrepreneurs (CAAYE). The organizers were upset that the statement was made on a non-political platform and cut it short.

The young Indian entrepreneurs were just getting used to a different Pakistan, far different from their preconceived ideas. They were shocked by the 'development' that Pakistan had undergone; a young woman was impressed by the motorway from Lahore to the capital, while others marvelled at the presence of food chains such as Dunkin' Donuts, which goes unreported in the Indian media.

Some were amazed at the IT Park in Lahore and felt that Pakistan was not all that different from India. However, back home, the Indian business community felt that Pakistan was a backward country and there were 'negative perceptions about technical, intellectual and economic capacities', according to a Pakistani businessman I spoke to.

Better than Kingfisher

A country with prohibition has one of the best breweries in the subcontinent. A friend said this brewery went to the 'wrong' side! Murree Brewery is a shared legacy and one of the oldest breweries, and it was a pity I couldn't go there. I felt cheated, a bit like Private Job Shepherd Waterhouse who was denied Murree beer over a century ago while on a British campaign.[6] Ian Stephens wrote in 1952 that the 'Murree area during 1946–47 was the scene of wild doings. Hindu, Sikh and some British property had been attacked. Muslim puritans burned down the famous brewery, source of much pleasure for Allied troops during World War II.'[7]

The ruins are all that is left. I met the Parsi owner and its chief executive officer, Isphanyar Bhandara, who was a PMLN member of the National Assembly as well, at a press conference and he agreed to give me an interview later in Islamabad itself.[8]

Back to Private Waterhouse who was climbing up the Murree hill on 28 April 1869. He, like the rest of the 19th foot regiment of the British Army, was hopeful of some beer at the famous brewery. But after a six-mile hike there was disappointment in store. He wrote in his diary, 'I started this morning at 4 am but the column did not leave till 6 o'clock, the road is so steep that the Ambulances had to start a long time first. We had to get out and walk several times . . . before we got to the Brewery which is 6 miles from Murree. This Brewery is a very notable place, sending Beer to all parts of India, while we was [*sic*] at the Brewery the column came up to the Officer in Command, he tried to get each man one pint of Beer but he could not.'[9]

Waterhouse travelled to the Murree hill station nine years after it was established by Edward Dyer with the express purpose of manufacturing beer for thirsty British troops in the subcontinent, instead of getting it all the way from England. In 1889, there were twenty-five breweries in India, and the Murree Brewery had the largest share of production at 37.9 per cent, with units at Murree, Rawalpindi, Ootacamund, Bangalore, Quetta and Ceylon, according to George Watt's *A Dictionary of the Economic Products of India*. Yet today, the brewery has no place in the country of its origin.

Bhandara was very keen on launching Murree in India, and some years ago signed a deal with an Indian businessman. He was disappointed that the venture which gave the rights to a Sikkim-based brewery owned by actor Danny Denzongpa, had not taken off due to 'bureaucratic hurdles and red tape'. Bhandara is not in this for money—it's a dream for him to see Murree beer in India, since it had its roots there and he wants it to be sold there.

He was chuffed though that since the beer is made from Australian barley, it is better than Indian beer. He gets hops from

Germany and has an Indian and German consultant. 'I can say that our beer, without prejudice, is better than Kingfisher's.' Though most people think the brewery was set up by his family, that was not the case. 'It came into my family in 1947. At that time my grandfather, Peshotan Bhandara, was a director when Mr Radcliffe decided to draw the line. My grandparents stayed back on this side but the Hindu partners decided to leave. It was a purchase of convenience and he bought over the British and Hindu stakeholders.'

The brewery's first manager, Edward Dyer, was the father of Colonel Reginald Dyer, the Butcher of Amritsar who had ordered the massacre at Jallianwalla Bagh in 1919. From Ghora Gali on Murree which had low temperatures and ideal conditions for making beer, the brewery moved to its present-day location in 1889 in the plains of the garrison city of Rawalpindi because of space constraints, almost becoming its first occupants.

The history of Murree which was selected as a hill station in 1850 and built by the British soon after the annexation of the Punjab province, is a fascinating account. Till Prohibition in 1977, the company used to supply to the Pakistan Army.[10] Dr Khan writes that the brewery was the largest of its kind, supplying beer all over India. It was given an award for excellence as early as 1876 in the Philadelphia exhibition, and its beer sold for Rs 5 per dozen in the 1880s and at that time it was considered better than imported brands.

I emailed Bapsi Sidhwa, author of the highly acclaimed *Ice Candy Man and Crow Eaters*, in Canada, Bhandara's aunt, for her memories of the brewery, and she sent a very detailed response to my questions. She remembered the brewery and the imposing mansion opposite it.

> My father, P.D. Bhandara, acquired the Murree Brewery in 1947 and he proudly took us from our home in Lahore to Rawalpindi to show us the Brewery Lodge opposite the

> brewery. It was an imposing mansion, and as we walked through its several rooms, furnished in the old British style, my father told us it would be our home in Rawalpindi. Shortly thereafter, the lodge was requisitioned by General Ayub Khan to be used by the foreign office. We moved to Vine Cottage opposite it, which was where one of the British brewers had lived, and this was our home in Pindi ever since. It was spacious and over the years made comfortable and well furnished by my brother Minoo Bhandara. We had many wonderful and happy memories there. The requisition of the Lodge was the only disturbing memory I have.

Every visit she made to the brewery as a child was pure delight. 'I was pampered by the staff and loved the fragrance of straw, barley and hops that pervaded the compound. To this day those memories bring me joy,' Sidhwa said. After her father died, her brother Minoo was called back from Oxford to take over the running of the brewery at the young age of twenty-one, and his son Isphanyar inherited the responsibility at thirty-five after his father's death. The Bhandaras trace their ancestry to a village by the same name in Gujarat.

Parsis in Pakistan are a 'winding down' society in Karachi, Bhandara said, and many of them have migrated. Theirs is one of the few business families left in this country; another family is the Avaris in Karachi. Apart from being one of the first breweries in the subcontinent, it was one of the first commercial ventures to be listed on the Calcutta Stock Exchange. Its branch in Quetta, which was destroyed in the earthquake of 1935, was relocated to Hub in Balochistan and is now run by someone else. The brewery was once the biggest employer in the Punjab but now it has about 1800 workers. Bhandara was proud of his single malts, blended whisky and premium vodka; the only venture that flopped was Irish cream 'as no one likes the concept of liqueurs here and its production was closed'. That was sad since I managed to get some and it was excellent.

There was a time when Murree used to export its fine beer to the US, India, Afghanistan and Europe. Many medals came its way till Zulfiqar Ali Bhutto banned local consumption and exports. 'This was continued by Zia-ul-Haq but my father developed a very good rapport with him and he managed to prevail over him to open the brewery after a gap. Liquor is available on a system of permits to non-Muslims, while exports are still banned,' Bhandara said. The company now has large non-alcoholic exports.

As for Prohibition, it has only made liquor available that much more freely, and the crowds at the permit place and the fact that most people drink, makes the policy look a bit ridiculous. Liquor is also served quietly in some restaurants in the capital, sometimes in teapots or cups if they fear a crackdown. If you knew the owner well, you could even bring your own alcohol.

Mera Rang De Basanti Chola in Bangay

Every 23 March, the day of his hanging, annual demonstrations are held at Shadman Chowk in Lahore which the government had agreed to rename after Bhagat Singh, (though it backed out later). In 2013, the JuD had come to protest. 'We were in for a big shock; the JuD guys defaced our posters. When I asked the man if he was doing this because Bhagat Singh was a Sikh, he said no, it's because he was an atheist,' said Madeeha Gauhar, playwright and director from the Ajoka theatre group. On Bhagat Singh's birthday on 28 September, a small crowd cut a cake in a quiet commemoration. 'It is more about reclaiming a secular narrative and that space is shrinking rapidly,' Gauhar said.[11] Ajoka, wedded to the ideals of secularism, humanism, democracy and tolerance, has been performing plays for the last thirty years in Pakistan, India and all over the world. Madeeha and her group have persisted in keeping the narrative of peace and togetherness flowing through their work.

It was thanks to her that I did stories on the play in Bangay, Bhagat Singh's birthplace, and also on Ajoka's joint theatre ventures with Indian groups. While the renaming of Shadman Chowk didn't come through, the Faisalabad district government was keen on redeveloping his village as a heritage site. Madeeha staged a few popular songs from her play, *Rang De Basanti Chola*, in the now-dilapidated primary school where the young revolutionary studied. The play is based on the exemplary life of Bhagat Singh who was executed by the British in Lahore Central Jail on 23 March 1931. She told me that the one-room government school still stood there with its walls and roof fallen in, but the blackboard and some of the old door frames were intact. Even now a few classes were held in the grounds outside as a mark of respect to Bangay's most famous son. She had planned to stage the entire play and the songs which are part of the Bhagat Singh narrative, and celebrate his heroic life.

The school was kept in its original condition but another one was built elsewhere. There were some very old trees, Madeeha said, and one of them was said to be planted by Bhagat Singh himself. Every November, a free eye camp would be held in the village in his memory. While the play, written by Shahid Nadeem, was performed in India from Kashmir to Kanyakumari, and in Pakistan, it was the first time after Partition that anything on the lines of a commemoration took place in Bangay village, about two hours from Lahore.

Unlike Rawalpindi, I did put in a request to visit Bangay, and I was even told it was possible. It would have been eventful to visit it, but, of course, it was not to be. Instead, I had to be content to speak to Madeeha who took me there with her lively description. 'The play is a small attempt on our part to pay a tribute but the significance of staging it in his village is to reclaim some of the lost historical connections and narrative denied by India and Pakistan. Also the play was an attempt to connect with the peace movement,' she said. Madeeha's mother was from Gujarat and father from Peshawar, and as an artist she felt the need for this connection. History in a sense stopped in 1947 and it was important to rediscover one's identity and sense of belonging and continuity which has been totally broken in Pakistan since 1947 in the way a new discourse/identity was created by the establishment. She wanted to link all these strands—the personal, political and cultural—through her theatre which connected to a deeper, underlying truth.

She strongly felt the need to bring out the story of how relevant Bhagat Singh was still to all of us—he was an atheist and had nothing to do with religion though he was being reconstructed differently in some sections. It was also important to bring back the importance of Bhagat Singh, as many younger people wouldn't even know who he was. Her son, Nirvan, played Bhagat Singh in the play; he was a student of film-making, and has also made a film on how he approached the role. While doing so, he asked students who Bhagat Singh was and the answers he got were varied: that he was a dacoit; he killed Muslims; and one of them even said that Bollywood actor Ajay Devgn had something to do with it. These were students of a premier educational institution, the National School of Arts.

The government had plans to develop Bhagat Singh's village as a heritage site, and his house, which was occupied, would be acquired with the consent of the owners. Both his school and house would be restored to the way they were. The Lyallpur Heritage Foundation was restoring places of importance in five selected villages so that people could visit them. Other than Bangay, Gangapur, the village of engineer and philanthropist Sir Ganga Ram, and Kharal, the home of freedom fighter Ahmed Khan were also selected.

Apart from reviving the importance of Bhagat Singh, in 2014, Madeeha launched a two-year theatre project for peace, collaborating with two well-known groups from India, Manch Rangmanch from Punjab headed by Kewal Dhariwal, and Ranga

Karmi from Kolkata; and along with theatre festivals, seminars were held in Karachi and New Delhi. It was after a six-year gap that Indian and Pakistani theatre groups were collaborating to produce a new play. The proposed joint production, *Ani Mai Da Sufna* (The Blind Woman's Dream), was directed by Ranga Karmi's Usha Ganguly, and written by Shahid Nadeem. She said the script was written in Shahmukhi which was unusual since the Persian script for Punjabi was rarely in use. It had to be transcribed, however, for others to read. The play is based on a true story of a woman who used to live near Lahore and left for Amritsar during Partition. It is set in the aftermath of the terror attacks on Mumbai in 2008 and tells the story of Janki, a woman in her eighties who has never gone back to her home and wants to see it once again. With a contemporary theme in times of terrorism, the play evokes nostalgia, and narrates the main character's longing to see her childhood home and friends. Gauhar said this was the aspiration of thousands of Punjabis who had felt the trauma and violence of Partition the most. The play was also an attempt at talking to younger people, and except for the lead role of Janki which was played by Jatinder Kaur, an actor from Amritsar, the rest of the cast was young and not affected by the events of 1947 and the dislocation.

Earlier in 2004, Ajoka did a very popular play for children called *Border Border* with a cast from Amritsar and Lahore, exposing the 'theatre of the absurd' at the Wagah border. It's about children inadvertently crossing the border, while this current production is a more serious venture. Between 2004 and 2008, there was the Panj Pani Indo-Pak theatre festival in Lahore and Amritsar. While Ajoka had performed for twenty-five years in India, it had never been allowed to visit the Punjab till 2003 when a play based on Sufi poet Bulleh Shah was staged to much acclaim in eight cities. 'It was a turning point in my understanding of history. The connection with East Punjab was so lacking. It was so meaningful and you discover a part of your body which has been brutally cut off. That was the time when news of the ceasefire came on the Line of Control and we were performing there and people said the good tidings came because we brought Bulleh Shah there,' said Gauhar.

Ajoka, now thirty, was the first Pakistani group to perform in Jammu and Srinagar. Travelling to Punjab, Gauhar encountered amazing stories, including one of a boy and his uncles who were forced to convert and become Sikhs. The family was reunited at one of the theatre group's performances. The current play, too, is about the longing to visit Pakistan and she found out that strangely, the visas for senior citizens on arrival didn't work all that well and they could not visit Punjab. The theatre for peace project was aimed at interaction between the audience and artistes, and strengthening cultural diplomacy. For her, it was a journey of getting to know artistes from India and finding a 'part of you that has been lost'. 'Pakistan is an incomplete story where centuries of history have been cut off. Our work is about that memory which has been deliberately lost to us because of some ideological discourse and these historical and personal narratives don't fit in,' said Gauhar. I wonder if the project went off well.

Not all the Indo-Pak connections had happy endings. Often, Pakistani artistes had to go back without performing or the venue of cricket matches had to be changed after protests. I was told about a different art exhibition quite close to my house and that's how I met Arjumand Faisel who ran Gallery 6. A doctor by profession and an artist, he was invited to India to exhibit at least fifty paintings by Pakistani artists in September 2012. He was highly excited by this and seventeen artists were chosen for the event which was a success in Mumbai in February 2013. But Mumbaikars, five years after the terror strike of 26 November, questioned him over that and the killing of Indian Army men. In August, this exhibition was vandalized by Bajrang Dal members in Ahmedabad's Amdavad ni Gufa gallery to protest Pakistan's killing of Indian soldiers on the LoC.[12] Faisel's own paintings were torn down, along with many others. Out of forty-seven works, thirty survived with minor damage, fourteen were badly damaged and three were missing. The International Creative Art Centre (ICAC) which had invited Faisel did not even entertain his calls and pleas to send the paintings back. The ICAC said it couldn't send the paintings back to Pakistan because no courier agency was willing. They sent them to Dubai, and from there, at great personal expense, he got them back to Islamabad. The India Pakistan Friendship Association didn't help either. But undeterred by this experience, Faisel organized 'Resilient Ambassadors', an exhibition of the vandalized paintings. Video footage playing in the background shows young men tearing up the canvases and breaking the frames. Faisel's damaged paintings were cut and repainted on the same canvas but the scars were evident.

Hajra Mansoor, a student of Lucknow Art College and her husband, Mansoor Rahi, had regular exchanges with India where they sold their work and also made many friends. Deeply pained by such incidents where their work was damaged, their love for India persisted and they felt that artists had a unifying role to play.

Not the idea of Pakistan

There is an 'insidious intent' in using school textbooks as propaganda to promote hatred and enmity. That they can be insular, go against the Constitution and have little understanding of history or relation to facts surfaced in a study in 2013 I wrote about. I met the author, Professor A.H. Nayyar, over coffee and we chatted about various aspects that he had analysed. A dedicated academic, his study found that the National Curriculum of 2006 relegated Jinnah's speech to a mere call for freedom of faith. He had studied the content of twenty-seven Urdu textbooks and thirty English textbooks from classes one to ten prescribed for Pakistani schools for the academic year 2013–14, which followed the National Curriculum prepared in 2006.

Textbooks play such a major role in our early understanding of political events and history, and in creating a sense of inclusiveness. Another academician, Professor Krishna Kumar, had made an outstanding analysis of school histories of the freedom struggle in India and Pakistan, which had highlighted the lack of scholarship on each other's countries. 'In general, the power of stereotypes in both countries has proved too strong to allow scope for any serious inquiry and knowledge about each other.'[13]

While Jinnah's domed white tomb in Karachi is a reminder of the man who founded this nation, there was little of his eclecticism and nowhere is it felt more acutely than in the school textbooks. These have been repeatedly analysed and suggestions made, but despite the improvements, flaws remain as Professor Nayyar's study found in 2013.[14] There is also a forcible teaching of Islamic studies to non-Muslim students which clearly violates the Constitution. While there is improvement, especially in English-language books for primary grades, in books on history and geography in the middle grades, and Urdu textbooks for secondary grades, there are continuing problems.

A former professor at the Quaid-i-Azam University in Islamabad, he concludes in his study that two very serious problems with the National Curriculum of 2006 need to be addressed urgently in a resolute manner so as to break from the old ways of using education for indoctrination: one, it must not let religious teachings be included in courses that are to be learnt by students of all faiths; and two, it must refrain from forcing an ideological straitjacket on the idea of Pakistan. But on both counts, the textbooks have failed.

He found that textbook authors were selective in their use of historical facts. Some of the historical distortions that existed in old textbooks persisted and the most glaring are the ones related to the events of 1965 and 1971. In describing the events of 1971, Professor Nayyar said the textbooks entirely blame the Hindus of East Pakistan and omit any reference to the atrocities committed by the Pakistani military and its collaborators. One other persistent old habit is glorifying war and military heroes. Any mention of non-military heroes remains mostly restricted to a few of the founding fathers, which does not help the purpose of including the topic of national heroes in textbooks. The only heroes are either political or military ones, with a few exceptions. Female role models are only two: Mohtarma Fatima Jinnah and Begum Raana Liaquat Ali Khan. One Khyber Pakhtunkhwa text eulogizes Ilm Din as a hero for his extrajudicial, vigilante killing of blasphemers.

On similar lines, Professor Krishna Kumar found that:

> Pakistani textbooks are replete with references to the 1965 and 1971 wars with India. In India, these wars have been the theme of a number of blockbuster films, but we rarely find stories related to them in textbooks. Pakistani school textbooks, on the contrary, use these wars to construct precise knowledge and imagery of battles and heroes. The same applies to war memorial days. For some years, India has been celebrating 16 December as Vijay Diwas (Victory Day) to commemorate the surrender of the Pakistani army in what is now Bangladesh . . . In Pakistan on the other hand, the celebration of 6 September as Defence Day—in memory of the 1965 war—has a larger appeal.[15]

In the past too, textbooks had perpetuated a stereotypical understanding of India, her history and ethos. That made it so much more easy to create an enemy mindset. The myth that Pakistan has not lost any of its wars with India has its genesis perhaps in these textbooks which have influenced young minds, exclusively fed on a diet of military heroes as role models. This study found that some school textbooks in Pakistan even have distorted the speech that the Quaid-i-Azam made on 11 August 1947 to the first Constituent Assembly. Bolitho describes this speech on which Jinnah had worked for many hours as 'the greatest speech of his life'.[16] In that memorable address, Jinnah said:

> You are free; you are free to go to your temples, you are free to go to your mosques or to any other place of worship in this State of Pakistan. You may belong to any religion or creed—that has nothing to do with the fundamental principle that we are all citizens and equal citizens of one state . . . Now I think we should keep that in front of us as our ideal and you will find that in course of time Hindus would cease to be Hindus and Muslims would cease to be Muslims, not in the religious sense, because that is the personal faith of each individual, but in the political sense as citizens of the State.

The 2006 National Curriculum itself commits a serious mistake in killing the true meaning of that speech, says Professor Nayyar after studying some textbooks of Balochistan.[17]

> That is to say, the curriculum relegates Jinnah's speech to a mere call for freedom of faith. Accordingly, the textbook writers have depicted the Quaid's words to only mean that in the new state, religious minorities will enjoy the same rights as the majority, not telling young students that the Quaid did not want religion to have anything to do with the business of the state. It is known that people of a particular school of thought have been very uncomfortable with this vision of the Quaid. They have now found a very ingenious but deceitful way of killing the true meaning of his words.[18]

There is a clear attempt, both in the National Curriculum of 2006 and all the textbooks that have appeared so far, at giving a twist to the meaning of the famous words of the Quaid. The Quaid was clearly separating religion from the state. But the curriculum wants it to only mean that the Quaid was merely asking for protecting the rights of religious minorities. According to them, the Quaid was saying that the religion of a citizen would not affect the affairs of the state, and was not advocating the separation of the state and religion. Professor Nayyar points out, 'This reminds us of another notorious distortion in the words of the Quaid for ideological reasons: Unity, Discipline and Faith were changed to Faith, Unity and Discipline.'

The study criticizes the new curriculum of 2006 for three very serious flaws: it contains instructions that lead to a violation of constitutional protection available to the country's non-Muslim citizens; it demands a narration of the ideological basis of the country and the history woven around it, which leads to several serious problems like distortion of history, creation of irrational hate and blinding prejudice against non-Muslim groups, and takes away from students any capacity to rationally analyse and understand historical events, seek and face realities, and determine their relation with other nations in an unprejudiced manner; and it adds contents to the learning material that is contrary to the facts.

Article 22(1) of the Pakistan Constitution says: 'No person attending any educational institution shall be required to receive religious instructions, or take part in any religious ceremony, or attend religious worship, if such instruction, ceremony or worship relates to a religion other than his own.' The 2006 National Curriculum contravenes this constitutional provision in two ways, the study says, as it makes basic teachings of Islam an integral part of the grade one and two courses called General Knowledge, and it requires inclusion of religious lessons in Urdu textbooks from grade one to grade eight.

In addition, all the prophets are of Abrahamic religions. The lessons exclude non-Abrahamic religions like Hinduism, Sikhism, Buddhism and Zoroastrianism, and violate the constitutional right of children of non-Abrahamic religions. The curricular recommendation of respecting all the faiths gets translated into a one-liner: 'We should respect all faiths,' and no more. This amounts to respecting only the Abrahamic faiths. It is clear that non-Muslim children of grade two are being forced into reciting Islamic ways of greetings and connotations, and to talk of God as Allah.

The study finds that the 2006 National Curriculum is also flawed in its insistence on the narration of Pakistan's identity and history on the basis of the so-called Ideology of Pakistan. Excerpts from the curriculum for classes nine and ten have statements like 'The demand of Pakistan was raised by the entire Muslim nation after a careful deliberation.' This statement fails to inform students that a majority of Muslims did not support this demand until 1946, and that very prominent Islamic scholars, including the leaders of the Jamiat Ulema-e-Hind of Deoband, Abul Kalam Azad, Mufti Mahmood, Abul Ala Maudoodi and Majlis-e-Ahrar remained opposed to the demand for Pakistan. 'There were false statements, for example in the Punjab textbook, p 20: Background of Pakistan Resolution: ". . . Hinduism was constantly trying to merge Islam, like other faiths, into itself."'

There are wilful omissions too in the textbooks. For example, in describing the Indian government's reluctance to pay the due amount to Pakistan out of the joint assets after Partition, no textbook mentions that Mahatma Gandhi went on a hunger strike to press the Indian government to release Pakistan's share. Similarly, while the textbooks describe the Khilafat Movement in a positive light as a movement of the 'Islamic Ummah', they fail to mention that the Quaid-i-Azam was never in its favour, and that Mahatma Gandhi had strongly supported the movement.

There are also statements like 'Because of Akbar's pro-Hindu policies, Hindus became so fearless that they started demolishing tombs and mosques, and constructed temples in their place. Muslims were facing hard times in Hindu majority areas. Muslims were not able to observe their religious obligations freely. Persistence of (*sic*) their faith could cost them their lives.'

The study says this is historically wrong and is aimed at creating hatred against Hindus.

Some of the historical distortions that existed in old textbooks continue to persist in the new ones.[19] The most glaring of these relate to the recent history of Pakistan in the Punjab class nine textbook, especially on the events around 1965 and 1971. The reasons for the 1965 war are given as: 'India committed an open aggression against Pakistan to materialize its expansionist intentions and attacked Pakistan on the night of 6th September.' 'Pakistan was established against the wishes of Hindus, so they never accepted Pakistan from the bottom of their hearts. Wonderful progress and stability of Pakistan constituted a major concern for them. So, they started launching aggressive actions against Pakistan.' 'As punishment for supporting Kashmiri people morally and raising Kashmir issue all over the world, India imposed war on Pakistan in 1965.'

The study said the causes of separation of East Pakistan do not include two crucial things: (a) the refusal of Yahya Khan to transfer power to the majority party as per the Constitution; and (b) the army crackdown on the civilian population and the mass murder, rape and loot the military men committed.

Instead, the reasons the textbook gives include: 'Poor economic condition: East Pakistan had always suffered poor economic conditions. The cause of this economic suffering even before the partition was the Hindu industrialist and Hindu landlord of West Bengal. And now too Hindus dominated East Pakistan's economy.'

Then, 'Negative role of Hindu teachers: Unfortunately, [the] Bengali Muslim was always inferior to the Hindu in education, for which reason a majority of school and college teachers were Hindu, who poisoned the young minds with Bengali nationalism, and instigated it for a rebellion against the Ideology of Pakistan. This is what paved the way for separation of East Pakistan from West Pakistan.' The separation of East Pakistan was also blamed on the big powers like the US, and Soviet Union which signed a treaty with India. The textbook fails to inform students that

Pakistan suffered a military defeat at the hands of India in 1971, and India took 90,000 prisoners of war, Professor Nayyar says.

In the Pakistan Studies for classes nine and ten in Balochistan, the 1965 Indo-Pak war is blamed on India.

> In the beginning of 1965, the freedom movement in Kashmir became so intense that India deployed troops on Pakistan's border with the intent to attack. After facing setbacks in initial clashes, Indian army attacked Lahore from three sides on the night of 6 September 1965. It had hoped to occupy Lahore by the morning. . . . Due to help from Allah, and the bravery of Pakistan's army, India could not sustain the war for even a few days, and its representatives started to request United Nations for cease-fire. Finally the Security Council through a resolution on 20th September called for cease-fire in two days. In order to ensure a safe retreat of its forces, India asked for one more day. Cease-fire became effective on 23rd September.

On the separation of East Pakistan, the text spoke of 'The role of Hindu teachers, and control of Hindus over economy [nearly the same narrative as in the Punjab textbook], and Hindus were already bent upon breaking Pakistan since its creation. The Indian Ambassador in East Pakistan had always been conspiring against Pakistan with the support of local Hindus.'

Extracts from the class ten Pakistan Studies textbooks for the Punjab for the year 2013–14 say, 'In Pakistan, ideology and foreign policy are intertwined. Pakistan is an ideological state, and is based on Islamic ideology. The important objective of Pakistan's Foreign Policy is the defence of ideological frontiers. Pakistan's stability is also implicit in the protection of the Ideology of Pakistan. It can protect its ideology by establishing good relations with Islamic countries.'

The textbooks of compulsory subjects that are to be learnt by students of all faiths include Islamic teachings in two different ways: one, by integrating Islamic studies into the General

Knowledge course for classes one and two; and, two, by including Islamic religious lessons in the Urdu course books for classes one to eight. The General Knowledge textbook for class one in the Punjab mentions only four holy books—Zabur, Torah, Bible and Koran. Though 5 per cent of Pakistan's minorities are Hindu, Christian, Sikh and Buddhist, none of their religious teachings or non-Muslim festivals find a place in textbooks. For the General Knowledge subject for Khyber Pakhtunkhwa, the children have to memorize religious incantations and the questions too have a religious touch; for instance, how many prayers do Muslims offer in a day? Also, students of grades one to three should be able to recognize that Almighty Allah has created them and that everything in the world is created by Allah. Since it's part of the General Knowledge studies, non-Muslim students have to learn all this. And they also have to know all the names of the Prophet, narrate his biography and recite from the Koran.

The new curriculum persists with some of the flaws identified in an earlier study in 2003 which had pointed to the growth of narrow-mindedness and extremism among the youth of the country. *The Subtle Subversion: the State of Curricula and Textbooks in Pakistan*, edited by A.H. Nayyar and Ahmed Salim, and published by the Sustainable Development Policy Institute, finds that social studies have misrepresented events in Pakistan's history, with distortions and omissions, the curricula is insensitive to the religious diversity of the country, and the entire education is loaded with only the teaching of Islam.

Meanwhile, Kumar's analysis of school textbooks of both countries for the period of the freedom struggle points out many shocking acts of omission. 'In the Pakistani representation of Gandhi and the Indian representation of Jinnah, we find serious distortions, but they seem to be rooted more often in the overlooking of certain details than in putative misrepresentation with the help of adjectives.'[20]

Pakistani textbooks assert that the 'Muslims residing in the Indian subcontinent always maintained their distinct cultural identity despite the influential presence of the Hindu religion' and there is an emphasis on the 'Congress being an "Overwhelmingly Hindu body"' and that Sir Syed Ahmad Khan advised Muslims to stay away from it.[21] Gandhi does not have the stature of a hero in the Pakistani textbooks. A few textbooks present him as a major Congress leader, but the characterization is inevitably as a 'Hindu leader'.[22] It is not surprising that the Congress and the leaders are identified as Hindu, as the textbooks speak of freedom from the Hindus.[23] This despite the fact that 'Nehru used to proclaim that he will not be Prime Minister of a Hindu India'.[24] When Mahatma Gandhi was assassinated, Jinnah's response was that a Hindu leader had died.[25]

Gandhi is not identified as the leader of the non-cooperation movement in one state textbook, and Kumar says, 'In Pakistani textbooks there is no mention of Gandhi's personality, the values he upheld and promoted, and the inventive character of his politics. In most textbooks, he is presented as just another Hindu politician. The Indian textbooks, which, do pause for a paragraph to introduce Gandhi to children, also represent his personality and ideas in a sketchy manner.' [26]

Moreover, 'No Pakistani textbook lets the young reader know that the Congress was a party with people from a large range of social backgrounds and ideological positions. Pakistani textbook writers talk about Hindu politicians as if they all had the same viewpoint.'[27]

After 1947, there is little we learn of independent India and Partition. 'As the [Indian and Pakistani] narratives enter the early 1940s, they fulfil our expectations of finding a sharp contrast between the national perspectives embedded in them . . . however, both narratives maintain a selective silence on certain events. Disinterestedness in the "other" grows fast as we hurtle towards the decisive mid-40s. Well before reaching the point at which a formal division had taken place, the memory covering the jointly experienced past gets divided.'[28]

During his visit to Pakistan in 1972, journalist Kuldip Nayar analysed textbooks he brought from there and found that they played up the wars between Hindus and Muslims, with the latter always emerging victorious.[29] He compares textbooks for classes eight and ten, and finds marked differences. The most horrifying distortion is in class eight textbooks which attribute the partition of Bengal to the worship of Goddess Kali. 'Human sacrifices had become the order of the day—a method of slaughtering the Muslims and presenting them at the altar of the Goddess.'[30] The syncretic culture of Hindus and Muslims is not acknowledged in these textbooks though there is evidence that the separation in worship was not so marked. Goddess Kali was invoked by Muslims not so long ago, as M. Mujeeb in *The Indian Muslims* writes of the faint dividing lines between religious beliefs and practices of lower-class Hindus and Muslims in Purnea district. 'In every village could be found a Kali asthan, a shrine dedicated to the worship of Goddess Kali and attached in almost every Muslim house was a little shrine called Khudai Ghar or God's house where prayers were offered in which the names of both Allah and Kali were used.'[31]

While on the one hand, we have moves for peace and for a comprehensive dialogue, perceptions about each other's countries are steeped in stereotypes. 'As a topic of study Pakistan is taboo in Indian schools and the same applies to India in Pakistan.'[32]

Propaganda is detrimental to a positive relationship, and textbooks and learning must foster understanding, instead of enmity. If textbooks distort the image of India and Hindus and the wars that India and Pakistan have fought, little can be expected of people fed on this diet. Professor Nayyar and others must be commended for their surgical analysis and consistent campaign to create quality and inclusive education in Pakistan, a country where privatization of education on the one hand, and the madrasas on the other overemphasize religious education, posing alarming contradictions.

7

Civilian versus Military

A trying time for the general

General Musharraf didn't look like a tyrant about to be indicted. He walked into court briskly, smart in black kameez and coat teamed with a white salwar. For a man diagnosed with three arterial blocks, he looked in the pink of health, with chubby cheeks and his hair had the trademark centre parting. So this is what military dictators look like, I thought as he made his way confidently to the makeshift witness stand, lifting his hand in greeting. Everyone had been waiting in breathless anticipation since 9 a.m. in the cold, cavernous National Library auditorium which was converted into the special trial court for high treason. He was finally there on 18 February 2014, two months after the trial began, after twenty-five hearings and much fuss and bother. Even on that day, there were some glitches and he arrived a little after 1 p.m.

There was only one question on everyone's mind that morning—whether he would actually turn up, and his lawyers, too, kept us on tenterhooks. In retrospect it was amusing. Musharraf, we learnt, had been sitting in his car since 12 p.m. but the Islamabad Police were not willing to take charge of his security. The nine-kilometre route from the Armed Forces Institute of Cardiology

(AFIC) in Rawalpindi was lined with 1100 armed Rangers, and technically he wasn't under arrest, wailed the prosecution. The AFIC commandant apparently asked for a receipt for Musharraf's custody but since he wasn't under arrest, the police couldn't give one. Finally, the judge had to direct the registrar to call the AFIC commandant to get things moving. Musharraf's convoy drove right up to the door of the National Library auditorium, surrounded by Rangers and top police officers, and there was applause from his defence team which stood up to welcome him. He was seated when the three judges entered and Justice Faisal Arab asked him to stand up. It was a token appearance and all over in less than twenty minutes. The doors were locked after he left, but some reporters who moved quickly managed to run out with him and asked him how he was feeling. The answer was a cryptic 'good', and we didn't doubt it. That was the first time we saw jammers in court, placed on either side of the three judges. Musharraf wasn't going to be indicted that day—it was an appearance for form's sake. The charges would be read out once all the applications on the jurisdiction and other matters were disposed of.

When the trial began on 24 December 2013, Musharraf sought exemption on the grounds of security. The former dictator had two near-death experiences in December 2003 when his convoy was bombed. His lawyers used security threats as an excuse for him not to appear and there were some instances when explosives were found on the route. He didn't have a bombproof vehicle which was another reason he couldn't travel safely—or so his lawyers said. On 2 January 2014, when he was to arrive in court, we waited and waited. The day earlier, he hadn't appeared due to a bomb scare. TV journalists popped in and out sending breaking news that he hadn't made it yet. The defence and prosecution squabbled. Musharraf was delayed, we heard. Defence lawyer Anwar Mansoor Khan said he hadn't slept all night as someone kept banging on his door and ringing the bell. Akram Sheikh, the FIA special public prosecutor, an old associate of Nawaz Sharif, said he was intimidated by the eighteen-member defence team led by Sharifuddin Pirzada. Justice Arab watched from the stage and took a dim view of this squabbling which he said took place in 'schools and colleges'. The fact that Musharraf hadn't yet made an appearance didn't hinder this bickering. Pirzada asked for an adjournment—due to the tense atmosphere. Akram Sheikh quoted Shakespeare—a tale full of sound and fury, and it went on till we finally got some news. Anwar Mansoor Khan suddenly said that Musharraf was on his way to court when he had a heart problem and his convoy was diverted to the AFIC.

The police, summoned for clarity by the judges, said he had left his home in Chak Shahzad for court at 12.15 p.m., but he felt ill on the way and went to the AFIC. Exasperation all around. Justice Arab granted him another exemption. Akram Sheikh said a one-time exemption had been granted earlier and even though he had all sympathies for the ailing person, a non-bailable warrant should be issued. It was now clear that Musharraf wasn't coming and the entire morning was wasted for the second day running. We went out to see the Rangers piling on to their trucks and leaving. There was no need for them now. Even the security guards looked miffed.

Musharraf was admitted to the cardiac care unit. The hospital became a refuge till the court which granted him a lot of indulgence since he was a former President and chief of army staff, lost its infinite patience and issued a non-bailable warrant. The defence strategy was to delay matters and they used every trick in the book. They filed myriad applications challenging everything from the constitution of the court to the appointment of the special public prosecutor, and said the trial couldn't go on because the judges and the prosecution were biased, that the Code of Criminal Procedure could not apply to these proceedings, Musharraf must be tried in a military court, and so on. Much time was spent arguing each one of them. At one point in March 2014, Justice Faisal Arab recused himself after the defence lawyer Anwar Mansoor kept objecting and insinuating that he had no confidence in the court and questioned the manner adopted by it while passing orders. However, he was back in court later. Musharraf's appearance in a civilian court was as expected, big breaking news (before that, his non-appearance was causing hysteria). This was unprecedented in a country which deified the military, and everyone went berserk, but for different reasons. There were quick conclusions that Pakistani democracy had finally come of age and that civilian authority could actually triumph over the military. As usual, everyone was wrong—democracy had its Lakshman Rekha in Pakistan. Soon, retired army officers organized meetings to defend Musharraf, and it became obvious that the move to try him wasn't popular. For a former chief of army staff and President to be so arraigned was unthinkable. Some reporters I knew asked me if India had ever tried a dictator for treason. I had to remind them we didn't ever have army rule, though the Emergency imposed by Indira Gandhi was repressive. While trying Musharraf had set a precedent, little else was likely to be achieved, and there was a remote possibility that something like this would be emulated. There were those who said that even if Musharraf was convicted, he would be pardoned. Justice Faisal Arab heading the three-judge bench tried to be as patient and function as best as he could, despite the burden of trying a military dictator in a land where the army was a sacred cow. The government, too, distanced itself at one point, leaving it to the courts to decide. Public opinion was divided on whether it was worth it all to bring him to book. Musharraf, who gave a lot of interviews, asked the army to support him and even said that it was doing so according to his own information. This was naturally and repeatedly denied by the defence minister. The MQM offered support by proclaiming that Musharraf was being tried for being a Mohajir. There was scepticism in some quarters as to whether it made sense to have a trial when the country was battling poor economic growth, terrorism and other challenges.

Akram Sheikh was fond of saying 'let the mills of justice grind slowly but surely'. Every time I asked him about the future of this trial, he would smile and repeat this phrase. He loved trivia—after Musharraf went to hospital, he said, 'Musharraf was not confined to his hospital bed, he had visitors, including his legal counsels, and received over 1500 flower bouquets.' He also referred to an order passed in 2002 by Musharraf himself which said that all cardiac ailments should be treated in the country itself.

The trial was also why I ended up going to the Sharia courts, set up under Zia-ul-Haq's regime to try cases under Islamic law. It was tucked away behind tall trees opposite the Supreme Court, and in the front, was a pretty garden. The courts were small rooms done up in wood and green, and unused for the most part. Few cases came here, I was told, and behind the lavish exterior and the marble steps, nothing really happened. It suddenly became a place the media flocked to since the special identity cards for the Musharraf trial were issued here. The registrar, a kindly sessions judge from Sindh, asked for a photocopy of my ID card which I didn't have. He then graciously got it done with a few extra copies for me. Later, he would read out the many orders in the treason trial in one of the cold courtrooms on the first floor. He was patient with impatient journalists whose phones were recording his orders, and who started breaking the news even before he had finished reading. He would always read it out again for those of us in print who were not in any real hurry other than to lamely tweet.

The court was the auditorium of the National Library with a wooden stage and trappings. The deep, green seats offered marginal comfort in the cold. One of the defence lawyers, Ahmad Raza Kasuri, called the court a Shakespearian theatre and predicted we would all be blown up one day due to the poor security. A comforting thought! The proceedings could easily pass off for a Shakespearian farce. The whole place was crawling with Rangers, and truck containers were placed at strategic intervals to deter potential attackers. Container drivers found themselves out of a job and played cards next to their vehicles. The canteen on the first floor, never used to making more than a few cups of tea, suddenly found itself unprepared for the large demand. The cook invested in a large aluminium vessel and made extra samosas. Cups were always short though.

Here, too, the spooks would question my driver and ask him what I was doing there, as if they didn't know. I would see intelligence guys (my friends said they were) trying to blend in with the large media contingent. No security can stop journalists who want to sneak mobiles into court and every day the police would keep asking if we had deposited our phones at the counter. Once the woman police constable refused to believe me and asked me where my second phone was. It was a trick question and she wasn't convinced. The security staff were bored with the trial. They used to ask us if Musharraf would come to court or if anything really was going to happen at all. I also realized that Musharraf may be vilified for imposing emergency rule, but he was still sought after in the media; in fact, he enjoyed a fair degree of popularity and there was a scramble to speak to him both times he actually came to court.

The National Library is situated on a height and one had to park at the open ground below and walk up to the main entrance, lined with the tall Rangers and plainclothes police in salwar kameez. For the women, there was a small cubicle near the gate for security checks. On 31 March 2014, the day Musharraf rode up in his black SUV for the second time—for his indictment—the tension cut through the morning chill. I thought I was early at 9 a.m., having reached the junction near the Supreme Court, which you cross to go to the National Library, but my car was stopped by the police who said I couldn't go ahead. I argued furiously and made my way to the pavement where more cops tried to turn me back. I said I was from the media and had to make it to court. *'Movement hai, madam, jaldi jaiye,'* a cop grinned. I half ran, half walked to the court and arrived in a dishevelled mess, sweating despite the cold. Who could have guessed that Musharraf would decide to be punctual that day? I was lucky to have even made it. People behind me, including a BBC journalist, were furious. He was stopped and he argued with the police for allowing me, a mere Indian, to pass, while a true-blue Pakistani could not. Apparently, when he told the policeman that he let an Indian pass and stopped him, the cop said he didn't know I was one. I wondered if he would have stopped me. I was a little disconcerted by the event—would he have minded so much if an American or Greek journalist was allowed to pass? The journalists covering the court were friendly for the most part. Some of them who sat next to me in court were questioned by the spooks. 'Why are you sitting next to that Indian? What do you talk about with that Indian girl?' This didn't deter them at all and they, like all the lawyers and police, were always courteous and very helpful.

For the second time Musharraf came to court, a 2000-strong security cover stretched all the way from the AFIC to the National Library building, and he blew in at 9.40 a.m., saluting everyone, again fresh and breezy in a beige salwar kameez with a smart dark blazer. That was the time he wanted to leave the country to meet his mother in Dubai who was ninety-four and unwell. On the day of the indictment, Musharraf's entire legal team led by the redoubtable Sharifuddin Pirzada was replaced with the MQM senator and lawyer Dr Farogh Naseem. After the charges in the high treason case were read out to him, he pleaded not guilty to all five. He then asked the court's permission to speak. 'Thank you very much,' he said in English, 'for giving me the opportunity to address this court. I hold this court and the prosecution in the highest esteem. I am a strong believer with conviction in the supremacy of law and strongly believe in the equality of law.' He had said much the same things in TV interviews. He proclaimed he was not a traitor and had won a gallantry award in the 1965 war and was ready to shed his blood for the country. A traitor, he explained, is one who sells his country and who surrenders before the enemy. He said he was part of the Special Services Group where the motto is '*ghazi ya shahid*' (a living hero or martyr). A traitor is one who loots his country and fills his own coffers and reduces the country to penury, he went on. He said he had not taken a single paisa for himself or accepted a bribe. He gave details of the progress the country made when he was President in terms of debt, poverty alleviation, jobs, improvements in the security apparatus and foreign exchange, and said he could hold forth on various sectors of the economy. Judicial appointments had been made on merit and his tenure was better in every way than previous governments. He even said the development in Balochistan in terms of infrastructure was better than earlier and more funds were made available to that province than the Punjab.

He was not alone, he said, in deciding to impose the Emergency on 3 November 2007 and it involved the then prime minister, the Cabinet and other stakeholders. From a state in default he had raised it to a level of progress and prosperity in every field. There was a lot of respect and honour for the country as a result and he said the treason charge was what he got for his loyalty.

The court was silent on his application to go abroad to seek treatment in the US, visit his mother in Dubai or be taken off the Exit Control List (ECL). On 3 April 2014, the day he left for home from hospital, a bomb exploded on the footpath after his convoy crossed it early in the morning, but he had reached his farmhouse at Chak Shahzad by then. I went to check this out near the Faizabad junction and could barely make out the chipped-off portion of the pavement.

After the non-bailable warrant, Musharraf had no choice but to appear in court. The prosecution said there was nothing in the medical reports to keep him from attending the court, and that he had not suffered a heart attack. Akram Sheikh kept harping that nothing was wrong with the general and he had the blood pressure of a young man and the pulse rate of an athlete, as stated in the medical report. As another diversion, the defence sought exemption for him appearing in court by citing a threat alert issued by the ministry of interior on 10 March 2014 which said that Musharraf could be assassinated; proper screening of the security personnel accompanying him would take six weeks and not seventy-two hours, and Musharraf should be exempted till then. Akram Sheikh was livid and said the government had deployed 2500 personnel and three different routes were worked out for Musharraf's journey to court. His personal security was chosen by him since he was not under arrest. The deployment of security personnel had cost over PKR 20 crore for the last eight hearings and this had never happened in the recorded history of Pakistan.

Musharraf's security became more important than the trial. Threat 'alert 239' cited in a letter dated 10 March 2014 from the National Crisis Management Cell (NCMC) of the interior ministry spoke of a bomb attack by the TTP/al-Qaeda or 'a Salman Taseer incident' (which means one of his security guards could pump bullets into him). Hard-core fighters were placed on the route from the AFIC to the court for this fell purpose, and the threat also said that the terrorists had sympathizers in Musharraf's security cavalcade. This led to fresh delays and a briefing of the judges by the intelligence agencies. The trial was full of these nuggets on a daily basis and provided for much entertainment and news. I faithfully reported everything for the paper as it was important to document the fledgling prosecution of a military dictator in Pakistan.

While covering the trial, I found out that Anwar Mansoor, one of Musharraf's defence lawyers, was held prisoner after the Bangladesh war in 1971. It was an outburst from Mansoor in court in response to something the judge said. The relations between the defence and the prosecution made for more news than the trial itself and slanging matches were common in and out of the court. Mansoor complained of several attacks on him and disturbances at night. He was even robbed once. That morning, an exasperated Justice Arab asked the two teams to be more cordial and this sparked off an unexpected reaction from Mansoor who said it was like asking him to be friends with the Indians which was not possible. He had fought a war with them and could never be friends with Indians since he had been a prisoner of war. Despite this deep-seated feeling, he was friendly to me and always answered all my questions. Later when I spoke to him, he said he had gotten over it but that memory and pain would always stay with him. There were unspeakable tortures and he came back physically and mentally broken. I realized it wasn't something one forgave. That trauma was uppermost in his mind and surfaced at the slightest provocation. This turn of events in court served as one of the many reminders I kept getting that despite all the friendliness, I was reporting from 'enemy' country. We had fought wars, yet we were so courteous on one level. Imagine Mansoor, a 1971 prisoner of war, speaking to an Indian journalist in his own country which had surrendered and lost its eastern wing. It could happen only in our two countries!

Once Musharraf had called all the foreign media for interviews to his farmhouse before the trial began but Snehesh and I, the two Indian journalists posted in the capital, were not invited. In 2013, he was all set to leave the country after he managed to get bail in both the assassination cases of Akbar Bugti and Benazir Bhutto, but he was arrested in the case involving the storming of the Lal Masjid. He was advised by those who knew him, including a former ISI chief, not to return, but blinded by a surge in online popularity, he could only see a glorious comeback and a handsome victory in the elections. He had arrived in Pakistan full of hope but a disappointingly small crowd welcomed him in March 2013. Someone blamed it all on Facebook. As it turned out, not only was he disqualified from contesting the polls but he was to find himself arrested for various cases. It was after an FIA team asked to probe the imposition of Emergency, detention of judges and holding the Constitution in abeyance by Musharraf, submitted its report in November 2013 that the government decided to try the former military dictator for high treason. Nobody thought the government would even attempt this and events showed that it was a mock trial. Justice Tahira Safdar from Balochistan read out the five charges against him: his 'Proclamation of Emergency Order, 2007', holding the Constitution of 1973 in abeyance and subverting the Constitution, thereby committing the offence of high treason punishable under section 2 of the High Treason (Punishment) Act. He had issued a 'Provisional Constitution Order No. 1 of 2007' which empowered the President to amend the Constitution from time to time and he had also suspended the fundamental rights. Thirdly, he issued the 'Oath of Office (Judges) Order, 2007' whereby an oath was introduced in the Schedule which required a judge to abide by the provisions of the Proclamation of Emergency, dated 3 November 2007, and the Provisional Constitutional Order of the same date. This order also resulted in the removal of numerous judges of the superior courts, including the chief justice of Pakistan. Fourthly, on 20 November 2007, as President he issued 'Constitution (Amendment) Order, 2007' whereby Articles 175 (relating to establishment and jurisdiction of courts), 186-A (pertaining to the power of the Supreme Court to transfer cases), 198 (jurisdiction of the high court), 218 (appointment of an election commission), 270B and 270C (relating to elections) were amended and Article 270AAA which reaffirmed and validated all of Musharraf's orders and ordinances, was added to the Constitution.

Fifthly, on 14 December 2007 at Rawalpindi, as President, he issued 'Constitution (Second Amendment) Order, 2007' whereby the Constitution of 1973 was amended.

The statement of charges said that these criminal acts of subversion of the Constitution constituted high treason, and were personal acts of Musharraf for the purpose of 'personal aggrandizement and a consequential vendetta'; at no point of time did Parliament validate these changes in the law.

The trial gave a glimpse of a civilian triumph, momentarily. Though I did cover it till I left, it was muddled in procedure, and it was pretty much not going anywhere. The Supreme Court also dismissed a review petition challenging its earlier order which held that Musharraf's proclamation of Emergency on 3 November 2007 was unconstitutional and void, and which declared him a usurper of power. A full fourteen-member bench of the apex court headed by Chief Justice Tassaduq Hussain Jillani heard the case for three days before deciding to turn down the petition on the grounds that it was time-barred and should have been filed within thirty days of the order on 31 July 2009. The court found no merit in the case and repeatedly ticked off the lawyers representing Musharraf for producing irrelevant arguments. The Supreme Court had in July 2009 already declared Musharraf's decision on 3 November 2007 to impose Emergency as unconstitutional and illegal.

While the government on the face of it looked determined to prosecute Musharraf, his lawyers spoke of a safe passage offered to him even before the trial started. Then there were reports of him being asked to sign an apology by the government which offered to fly in his mother, but was not going to let him out. It came as no surprise that eventually Musharraf went to Dubai in March 2016, promising to return and face the charges, after the apex court struck down his travel ban. Justice Faisal Arab was moved up to the Supreme Court and the trial was moving in a desultory fashion. The limits of civilian rule were clearly set.

Army gets a new chief

The dapper, chain-smoking General Ashfaq Parvez Kayani steered the Pakistan Army for six years after an extension was given to him in 2010 by the then prime minister, Yousuf Raza Gilani, but he was unlikely to get another one. He witnessed the country's first democratic transition and would be remembered for his statements aimed at keeping the army out of the government's hair. Speculation was rife about a post-retirement job but it didn't materialize. In an unusual statement before his retirement on 29 November 2013, he quashed rumours of a new post being created for him. Old soldiers never die, they just fade away, a popular refrain from an old barrack-room ballad—while Kayani may not fade into oblivion he was certainly retiring. Keeping in line with his approach as chief of army staff, where he did not favour interference in the government, his statement clearly indicated the army's support for democracy and civilian institutions. The armed forces of Pakistan fully support and want to strengthen this democratic order, Kayani said. He also stated that the government and the army were on the same page on the question of talks with the TTP and he refuted talk that he favoured a dialogue since army operations had failed to root out terrorism. His retirement came some months after the incident on the LoC when five Indians were beheaded by men dressed in Pakistan Army uniforms. The controversy did not die down for a long time and it was a setback to the already-strained relations after 26/11. While Pakistan has been offering a joint investigation, India has not accepted it and maintains that the five soldiers were killed in August by the Pakistan Army. Pakistan has denied this often enough and Sartaj Aziz while meeting the former Indian high commissioner, stated that the Indian media's 'overreaction' to the LoC incident had also not helped.[1]

When Kayani retired after forty-four years of service, he regretted[2] what he described as 'unfortunate, unfounded and provocative' some statements by the Indian military leadership, particularly the Indian Army chief alleging that the Pakistan Army and the ISI were supporting terrorism. He had backed Prime Minister Sharif's peace overtures to India and said the Pakistan Army was fully supportive of the peace process initiated by the government. He had also said India would be well advised to respond positively to Pakistan's suggestion for holding a joint or impartial investigation into the LoC incidents, preferably by the United Nations.

In 1998 as prime minister, Sharif had chosen General Musharraf, thereby overriding the principle of seniority, and there was speculation that he was not likely to repeat the same mistake. However, Lieutenant General Raheel Sharif, the next chief, superseded two others in rank. We had to clarify in news reports that he wasn't related to the prime minister. General Raheel Sharif, who was principal staff officer to General Kayani, had three years to go before retirement when he took over as chief in November 2013. This was big news and *The Hindu* carried the story on the front page. The new chief came from a traditional military family and was decorated with the Hilal-e-Imtiaz, and is the younger brother of the 1971 war hero Major Shabbir Sharif who was awarded the Nishan-e-Haider. Soon after General Raheel Sharif took over, he visited the headquarters of the Special Service Group (SSG) at Ghazi Base, Tarbela, creating a needless controversy. The fact that Musharraf belonged to this elite cadre and was being tried for treason was not lost on anyone. The visit was probably to underscore the importance of the army and the SSG and also assert the authority of the army at a time when democratic forces were seeking to punish a military dictator. The senior-most army officer Lt. Gen. Haroon Aslam, who was superseded by two of his juniors, tendered his resignation. He was an SSG commando like Musharraf, and the director general of military operations in 1999 when PM Sharif was ousted in a military coup; Sharif could not have had happy memories of another SSG commando who staged that coup, or being under arrest along with his Cabinet.

Apart from creating a security state and ruling Pakistan for most of the time since Partition, the army in the country is flush with funds. It has many tentacles in business, real estate and aviation, as Ayesha Siddiqa has pointed out in her book, *Military*

Inc.[3] Milbus, or 'military capital that is used for personal benefit', is a fact of life and army personnel own large tracts of land and are entitled to decent housing and plots. The military way of life and thinking, to put it mildly, looks down on politicians who are perceived as ineffective and corrupt. While General Kayani may have made the right noises on the ground on enmity with India, he is perceived to be hawkish and things don't seem to have changed much. The threat from terrorism and the enemy within are something the army has to contend with as seriously, if not more so, than the hostility from India. After the Turkish coup in July 2016 that failed to overthrow President Tayyip Erdogan, Imran Khan said that the people of Pakistan would celebrate and distribute sweets if the army takes over.[4] He was scathing about the 'monarchy' of Nawaz Sharif who had further sunk the country into debt. Imran backs the Taliban and calls for peace talks; he backs the army and protests against Sharif. If nothing else, Imran Khan is probably trying to pave his way as Sharif's successor in the next general elections. He seems to have the right credentials. The question, as always, is: can democracy succeed without toeing the military agenda?

8

Reviving a Left-of-centre Politics and Other Stories

It was not only terror, trade or Indo-Pak relations, but other aspects of Pakistan that I wrote about. The left parties were regrouping, only a section of the Left particularly, it was pointed out to me, which was an important development. Whether such a move would leave any long-lasting impression on the political theatre is a big question mark but for those who want to explore a non-neo-liberal, non-right wing option, the Left is there in whatever form. Once strong in the North-West Frontier Province (now KPK), they were ruthlessly exterminated by the Taliban, with the Awami National Party becoming the main sufferer as 500 of its workers, some say, were killed. Does the Left in any form have a future in Pakistan? The ban on student unions has meant that there is no campus politics or elections, and there are councils or religious groupings which have injected a strong dose of fundamentalism. There is a battle between the East and the West on campus; while on the one hand, students struggle for recognition for their organizations, on the other, there is alarm over the power they can wield if allowed the freedom to organize. The other stories in this chapter deal with the Afghan refugees, a sore point in Pakistan with what it calls a 'host fatigue' setting in though 2016 saw a record number of returning Afghans which human rights groups feel is a result of Pakistan forcing them to leave.

The situation of women is precarious: health and food security apart from a lack of decision-making powers, are major concerns. I wrote about two reports which were released, highlighting these aspects, and one of the reports included, for the first time, domestic violence as an issue. On the bright side, women, if given an opportunity can climb the highest mountain—that is mountaineer Samina Ali Baig's message to the world in this gloomy scenario. In the aftermath of the Malala incident and the rather grim situation of girls' education, a Pakistani has produced a path-breaking cartoon series on girl's education called *Burka Avenger*, which uses stereotypes to break them effectively. I interviewed the creator of Burka Avenger, Haroon, for an interesting feature. I also attended a seminar on transgenders and their problems and found that much as in India, they are still not accepted and live on the fringes of society, though there is a progressive Supreme Court ruling in their favour. While I couldn't do much by way of stories on environment, Pakistan is a land of great beauty and has the world's second highest mountain, K2, and the stunning Karakoram range. The Central Karakoram National Park is seeking to become an advertisement for a side of Pakistan we don't see. I wrote on that as well, as also on the horrifying hunting of the houbara bustard. Little did we know that this vulnerable species was the cornerstone of Pakistan's foreign policy. Every year, the bird is hunted in large numbers by Arab royalty whom the Pakistan government cannot afford to displease. So permission to kill it is given with great magnanimity.

A Left revival of sorts

Imagine a trade union in a military unit in Pakistan. Yet that was one of the first unions that Abid Hassan Minto formed when he joined the Communist Party in Pakistan in 1949. It was a workers' association at the Military Engineering Service; the other one was in a multinational oil company at Attock. Such a thing would be unthinkable now, grinned Minto, the president of the Awami Workers Party (AWP), which was formed after a merger of three parties in 2012 (Labour, Awami and Workers' parties). There was a buzz about the new unity of the left parties then. This was a renewed attempt to forge a clearly defined Left in Pakistan, said Minto, a sprightly eighty in 2013 when I met him.

The Communist Party was scattered after the collapse of the Soviet Union and the end of the Cold War, as also due to the resurgence of the global corporate system in the shape of the New World. The disarray of the Left was everywhere, and in Pakistan, the trade union movement was weak and it splintered into many factions. The grouping of parties was based on individuals. For Minto, the key question was what kind of politics the Left had to come up with to deal with new challenges in Pakistan where many things hadn't changed at all.

An opportunity to meet some leftists came up when the Progressive Writers Association (PWA) organized a meeting with communist ideologue Sajjad Zaheer's daughter, Noor Zaheer, who had come from New Delhi to speak about her books. The red-brick building with a small hall was the venue for her speech and when I landed there, my spooks, Beard and a new guy, were there too, and during a break I saw them questioning the organizers. They stayed till tea and when I tried to find my way out of the hall and mistakenly took the wrong staircase, one of them, not Beard, followed me and I asked him to show me the way out. He asked me, cheekily, 'To India?'

But I was glad I had gone there. I met many progressive writers. There was plenty of nostalgia and Noor Zaheer was warmly received. People called her Comrade Noor, in memory of her late father who headed the Communist Party of Pakistan before it was banned in 1954.

I met her early in the morning at the PWA guest house over tea. Zaheer said what was most needed was for splinter groups not only in Pakistan but all over South Asia to come together and challenge the religious and other right-wing forces. Her father had left behind a legacy which should be taken forward and a lot is left to be done. The Left is also seeking a distinct identity from the liberals who hail from a class not interested in social change, according to Aasim Sajjad Akhtar, the secretary general of the AWP, Punjab. He is clear that activism alone won't help consolidate or add up to a coherent movement. Something beyond activism needs to happen and that was one of the aims of trying to bring all the Left groups together.

The Pakistan Communist Party was formed in 1948 by Sajjad Zaheer, Sibte Hasan and Ashfaq Beg after the Calcutta Congress when it was decided to have a separate party, but even at its height it had only 650 or so members—the card holders. The numbers were small but the politics was clear: they were committed to Marxism as a gospel.[1] As soon as the party was banned, since there was no real centre to it, it started breaking up. The deterioration was at the intellectual level—Minto explained there was ideological confusion which took away the commitment, and in Pakistan the party was young. He felt that now it was difficult to bring back that faith.

Minto didn't live in Islamabad and I had to count on the days he visited. But I could make headway thanks to the PWA where I met a few people who were knowledgeable about the Communist Party such as it was in Pakistan. I met Minto at a guest house in Islamabad and he was very forthcoming. He wondered why I took so many notes. 'Are you doing a PhD?' he asked me. But it was a fascinating story and Minto was involved politically in other areas as well and was full of anecdotes.

For the AWP, the challenge is mainly to create an alternative to the neo-liberal economic system. Opting for a social democratic method is the only way out. For the three parties in the merger,

Minto said there is no choice but to revert to the principles enunciated in Left/Marxist politics and they have to adapt to the changing situation. Departing from the earlier internationalist politics that split the communists between China and the Soviets, the new party decided to stick to anti-imperialism and anti-colonialism in some manner, and formulate a joint programme based on Marxist principles. While peasant communities organized in the mid-20th century, and there were some reforms, the ban in 1954 of the Communist Party and its affiliated unions put an end to further struggles. The Left was more of a talking and debating group than a political group, Minto said caustically. There is uncertainty as to whether the Left in a classical fashion will be able to tackle neo-liberal politics. There is an understanding that it needs a new identity which forges links with anti-Taliban and anti-fundamentalist forces. Minto is realistic about the need for a left-of-centre politics.

In the past, the Left had its student, peasant and trade union federations plus the PWA. The AWP feels there is a critical mass for the Left to grow in Pakistan and this could be due to the joint impact of Taliban terror and the onslaught of the middle classes coming up as the partner of the political system. But in this whole mass of civil society, Minto's question is: 'How many want a new politics?'

There are other challenges. Can the AWP take all the principal left groups in Pakistan along? From only talking, it has to work with the peasantry and the working classes, and the methods can be different, but there has to be a commitment to the programme, he said. The idea then would be to put the Left under one political banner and have an anti-feudal, democratic and anti-imperialist stand in the sense that Pakistan should not be governed by the international neo-liberal economy.

The communist forces in Pakistan have been fragmented by international politics and dissensions within, and support of the powers that be, including military dictators. Critics like Fayyaz

Baqir, who was in left student politics in the 1960s, point out that the strength of the communists had been in their strong literary and artistic agenda. Now director of the Akhter Hameed Khan Resource Centre, he said that right from the beginning, the serious shortcoming which persists till today, is that they have no understanding of Pakistan society. The communists didn't produce mass leaders, nor did they throw up non-traditional intellectuals or original research, he said. They were divided between the Soviet and the Chinese camps, and they made no analysis of the class structures or class interests, not to speak of the way the state or the political system worked in Pakistan. They didn't have an understanding of mass politics, and as a result, when the PPP was formed with many elements from the Left, Zulfiqar Ali Bhutto captured power. The Left lacked an understanding of religion and so it couldn't blame the problems only on religious leaders.

The hopelessness is edged with a silver lining. The younger cadre is dedicated, though it is difficult to get students involved in politics. Aasim Sajjad Akhtar got into the left movement by accident, through the study circle route, but that old assembly line, along with the banned student unions, had stopped producing results. While left mainstream politics was a force in other countries, that was not the case in Pakistan. The internal weaknesses came to the fore and there was total collapse; most of the old leadership left the party and the organizational capacity was eroded. The people who stayed on were very junior and they were pushed to the top. There's a lot of dynamism, he said, but no real regeneration in terms of a cadre of younger activists. It will, he said, take a long time to build a cadre to replace the old one.

On the bright side, Akhtar said, there's a lot of impetus coming from the younger cadre which doesn't have the baggage of the Cold War demons. The party also has to find new spaces to work. It is already working with squatters; it's associated with the movement in Okara where the farmers continue to occupy the land grabbed by the army. It's a movement that broke the taboo, especially in the Punjab, where the military is sacrosanct.

He pointed out that you cannot lay claim to an ideology because you own it, you have to build on it; trade unions now are pocket unions. It's about maintaining roots, the ability to be involved and in touch with movements which emerge, while also focusing on building a critical mass, he said. 'The Left is sorely needed for a third perspective. Ideologically, the society shifted to the right, no one is talking of class, gender or social cleavages in society . . . It will take time to make the changes.' I don't know if Minto was questioned by the spooks, but both Baqir and Akhtar had 'visitors' after I left. While Baqir invited them inside and patiently answered their questions, Akhtar gave them an earful.

For the student community to feed into the left parties, there has to be political participation, elections on the campus and the freedom to organize. Young students in Balochistan have already borne the brunt of their independent thinking. Working in the slums and with farmers may be a good start, but under the circumstances it will be a Sisyphean task for the Left to emerge as a serious and dominating stream of thought in the political map of Pakistan. The challenge for the new Left is also to reignite Marxist ideology which most people think is outdated and has little meaning for them.

The ban on student unions

In a large, sunlit football ground, young men performed the *attan*, a slow-moving dance, and the grave teenagers wearing salwar kameez moved rhythmically in large circles, their arms gracefully spread out. There was only one woman and I asked her why no other woman was dancing. She laughed and said she was a PhD student by way of explanation. The Quaid-i-Azam University (QAU), almost on the outskirts of the city, was one of the earliest universities in Pakistan and its campus, with its neatly divided departments, was navigable even for a stranger. I wanted to do a story on the ban on student unions, and when I read about a mela of sorts which had been advertised in the papers, I went there hoping to run into some willing-to-talk students.

There were small stalls that sold trinkets, clothes and pottery, and I wandered around. Phone numbers were exchanged with some students, and one evening I was in the canteen where a small room had been opened for our meeting; there was tea and refreshments too. A huddle of young men explained how things worked in the university bereft of any real campus politics.

They were from the Pakhtun Council and I couldn't meet any others as they had exams, and also since my spooks followed me, it wouldn't be a happy time for them if they were questioned. Salim (name changed) explained that there were six different communities and all had their councils, like the Pakhtun Council. 'We want to ignore political parties and the purpose of the council is to maintain peace and promote culture, and solve problems. For instance, if there is no electricity then we intervene.'

NK, a former general secretary of the Pakhtun Council, said it had around 800 to 1000 members, including 200 women. After political parties were banned during Zia-ul-Haq's time, there was a resistance to organizing on religious or political lines and so the community-based councils came into being. All the councils came together under the umbrella of the QAU Students' Federation. Every council had a Cabinet committee with neutral people who were nominated for not having any political affiliation.

The students didn't have a high opinion of the political system in Pakistan; they wanted to keep that kind of politics out of the campus, as also the hard-core political parties. Unlike other universities where religious parties like the JeI proliferated, the QAU had kept them out. But some private colleges didn't even allow student councils. In some universities, there was no federation of councils. Students said that before admissions, they had to sign an undertaking that they would not be part of any political, religious or ethnic unions. The faculty, too, was in favour of the council system.

There was no official recognition of the council, and in July 2012 students protested that the councils should be made part of the university and they also insisted on representation on the University Disciplinary Committee. Some of the students were rusticated after they disrupted an international conference as part of the protests. The promise to lift the ban on the student unions made by Prime Minister Yousuf Raza Gilani after he was elected in 2008 didn't come through. In January 2016, the Pakistan Senate called the ban unconstitutional and asked a committee to submit recommendations. After Zia ordered a ban in 1984, the orders were rescinded by the Benazir government in 1988. Some three years later, the student unions were challenged in the apex court on the grounds that they were contributing to 'on-campus violence'. Then the Supreme Court imposed a ban on the unions in 1993.[2]

There was a lot of friction with religious student groups like the IJT affiliated to the JeI which had traditionally dominated the campuses, especially in the Punjab. The QAU Students' Federation called itself neutral but they were under powerful political influences. Most students felt the unions should be brought back. But this doesn't even feature as an election issue in mainstream politics. There was some debate in the National Assembly that the federations should be legalized. The Pakhtun Council's sole aim seemed to be to unite all the Pashtun speakers under one umbrella. The council also tried to get the QAU Students' Federation recognized, but the university didn't even do that.

The council took up issues like hostel allotment and quotas since seats are divided by population, with the Punjab getting the lion's share of 50 per cent and KPK 14 per cent. Women are included in the councils, but I didn't get to meet any as the students were busy with their examinations and I was leaving mid-May. A report by Bargad[3] gives a glimpse into the vibrant campus life before 1984 and the dominance of the Islami Jamiat Talaba. It said, 'The student politics was also divided by an intense ideological struggle between the political Islamists and the left-oriented parties in an over-all environment of cold war.' The move to lift the ban on unions had not received much support. 'In an unprecedented move Vice Chancellors of all public and private universities of Pakistan gave a rejoinder to their previous assertions on the student politics (2009). They don't think it appropriate to lift the ban at the present critical situation of the country. They rather support the growth of societies and associations within campuses. They further accuse the student unions of being a source of violence and disruption in studies,' according to the Bargad report.

Student movements were vibrant in Pakistan during Zulfikar Bhutto's time. He drew much strength from their unruly power. But under Zia, madrasas were given more importance and the political vibrancy on the campus was blunted with the union ban. 'Historical evidence proves that before the ban on student unions, much of the street power and larger political assemblies in Pakistan have been attributed to the student politics. After a long lull, the students were again seen on the streets during the lawyers' movement. Nevertheless their organization, thematic training and scale have visibly diluted as compared with previous examples of national movements.'[4]

While students are political in a sense, their organizations, except for the student groups in Balochistan, function more on the lines of welfare groups and are not a part of the broader political picture. There was an incident in 2007 when the IJT opposed the entry of Imran Khan into the Punjab University campus; then there were clashes with the University Students Federation (USF) formed to oppose the Emergency. These incidents had a snowballing effect and the students went on to support the lawyers' agitation against General Musharraf. The fear that students could set a momentum for social change is very real and the curbs may not be lifted fully yet.

The Left also suffered from the ban on this traditional reservoir. The National Students Federation (NSF), one of the first left unions, is faced with a tough challenge. Alia Amirali, the general secretary of the NSF in the Punjab, says the first task is to educate people on what a union is and how it's different from a non-political organization which is allowed on campus. But students are worried about joining the NSF—they fear jails and court cases. There is an antipathy to mainstream politics in the Punjab as opposed to Balochistan where the students' movement has fed so many political groups, like in Khyber Pakhtunkhwa. She says while there is an opportunity to build anew, the real trick is how to achieve this work today in a climate where there is an increasing public–private education divide and also in terms of political consciousness between the Punjab, Khyber Pakhtunkhwa and Balochistan. 'This politicization reflects what is happening in society. The lawyers' movement gave us an impetus that we can be effective and despite small numbers we ended up having more of a discursive impact than we thought,' she says.[5]

But as things stand, in the absence of a free political environment, the NSF is floundering, and raising a dedicated cadre of young students seems difficult.

War and refuge

It was a chance meeting with Professor Anila Daulatzai which got me into writing on Afghan refugees. Speaking at the SDPI on her research based on war widows in Kabul, she was like a breath of fresh air on the Afghan issue. I thought it would be interesting to interview her and get a perspective so different from the usual narrative of Afghans as victims. Outspoken and fiery, Anila was based in the US but was doing her PhD in Kabul. It was a great interview for *The Hindu* op-ed and she raised so many key questions on the US war and humanitarian aid, saying that both were equally culpable. The relationship between Pakistan and Afghanistan is one marked by hostility, and the refugees who have spilled into Pakistan since the Soviet invasion in 1979, don't want to go back to their native country. Somewhere Pakistan feels it has taken on too much, forgetting that when it joined hands with the USA in the war against the Soviets first and again post-9/11, it paved the way for instability and an exodus. Pakistan is appealing to foreign donors to help finance projects for communities which are hosting the refugees. It is also showing impatience with Afghanistan since it was supposed to develop sites for refugees to return home but that was not really done. There is hostility to the Afghan influx and a bitter joke that the language of Karachi, where there are many Afghans, will soon be Pashto.

In 2017, Pakistan continues to host some 1.3 million registered refugees who have proof of registration (PoR) cards issued by Pakistan's National Database and Registration Authority (NADRA), and this gets periodically extended. There are, according to estimates, approximately 600,000 undocumented Afghans living in Pakistan.[6]

The year 2016 saw a twelve-year high in the return of Afghan refugees. More than 370,000 registered Afghan refugees returned home from Pakistan in 2016, compared to just over 58,000 in 2015 under the UNHCR-facilitated voluntary return programme.[7] There was a controversy over the high numbers and Pakistan was accused by human rights groups of forcing the exodus. The majority of those returning are going to Kabul, Nangarhar, Baghlan, Kunduz and Laghman provinces.[8]

The UNHCR says there are a number of related factors which have led to this increase. The rise in return coincides with the introduction, on 1 June 2016, of tighter border management controls at the Torkham border. Afghans now need valid passports and visas in order to enter Pakistan. So many families are now opting to return to join their families in Afghanistan.

Another reason is the increase in the UNHCR's voluntary repatriation and reintegration cash grant which was doubled from $200 to $400 per individual in June 2016, which means $2800 for a family of seven. Moreover, Afghanistan's Ministry of Refugees and Repatriation's campaign launched in July 2016 in Pakistan, encourages Afghans to return home. Besides, in Pakistan, the increase in the number of security operations against undocumented foreigners, including undocumented Afghans, has also impacted the refugees' decision to return. A report by Human Rights Watch in February 2016 was more direct. It indicted the Pakistan government for unlawfully coercing Afghan refugees out of Pakistan, and the UNHCR for remaining silent 'about Pakistan's large-scale refoulement of Afghans, not once stating that many of those returning were primarily fleeing police abuses and fear of deportation and that Pakistan's actions were unlawful'.[9]

One in four refugees in today's world is an Afghan and while the Syrians are about to overtake that, the onus is on Afghanistan to do more to ensure the return of its 5 million refugees back to their country. The theatre of war in Afghanistan has had an impact on its people, the politics of the region and terrorism. While much has been written and researched about the wars, the Taliban and the US as well as ISAF, there is little outcry about the people forced to leave that devastated country and seek refuge elsewhere. In Islamabad, there seems to be little sympathy for the Afghans who are perceived as a criminal bunch. You can see them everywhere in the capital, shabbily dressed, bearded men who collect your garbage for a pittance, or selling French fries at makeshift stalls in the various markets for PKR 30 a helping in crumpled newspapers. Gangs of unkempt Afghan children would roam the streets at times, foraging for food. Once while buying fruit from my usual vendor, there was a group of Afghan children who asked me to get them something. The vendor gave them bananas but they made a face and pointed to a large, red pomegranate. I let them have it, and to my amazement they didn't need a knife to cut it. They chewed it open and tapped it on the pavement to get the luscious seeds to one end and then ate it all up, the red juice streaming down their pink cheeks.

After the anti-Soviet jihad and later the war against terror post-9/11, Pakistan found itself at the receiving end of the problem and had to accommodate the massive influx of Afghans, many of whom blamed Pakistan and the US for their sorry plight. Pakistan has often made it clear that it cannot continue to house the refugees who barely manage to survive despite the grant of land and housing. In Karachi, we were told to avoid the Afghan camps.

I was keen on visiting an Afghan refugee camp, and the UNHCR said there was only one in the capital on the outskirts of Islamabad. It seemed like a mini Afghanistan with a dusty road of sorts leading up to it, full of turbaned men. No grown women were in sight due to the strict purdah system and children milled around playing cricket in the sun or hanging around at a few makeshift stalls. There was a large shed for cattle fodder, stall-fed cows and donkey carts. The only school was shut two years ago. It didn't seem like the rest of the capital at all, with its low mud huts and little strips of by-lanes with stinking gutters all around. My escort and I landed up there in the afternoon and we had to sit in the open, surrounded by the men who spoke of the problems of living in this camp. They were also hounded by the police, and the searches often unearthed many arms and ammunition, which the Afghans said they were used to carrying. I wanted to meet some women and after a long chat with the men, I asked if I could go inside the homes, and they readily agreed, even providing me with a translator.

Afghan hospitality rose above the depressing surroundings and there was hot tea ready and bread which they baked once a day in deep clay ovens in their courtyard. They were trying to recreate their life back home. In Zaituna Bibi's house, a gleaming steel flask occupied pride of place. She proudly told me it was from Kabul and it cost PKR 1500. It kept tea hot for twenty-four hours. She didn't think much of the local flasks as the tea got cold in no time. Like most women in the Afghan refugee settlement in Islamabad, she baked once a day and about thirty of the large 'skateboard' loaves lasted her nine-member family for three meals a day. They all lived and slept in a small room with a shaky roof which doubled as a terrace and sleeping area in the summer heat. The other room was for the cattle—a cow and goats. A small, enclosed courtyard served as her kitchen and seating area. There was a deep mud oven (tandoor) and next to it two broad shelves with aluminium vessels and large cans. There was no gas or power there and firewood cost PKR 3000 a bundle plus another PKR 500 for transport. The only healthcare centre remained closed most of the time and people paid PKR 500 to get to the nearest hospital. But Zaituna Bibi pretended she lived in a palace—her warmth and hospitality, and acceptance of things rose above her sordid existence.

The refugees, most of whom came here in 1979, didn't complain about their homes or the drains or of the lack of basic amenities, but what they dreaded most was the police. In the large gathering, there were many men who have been to jail. Bahadur Khan's son was in jail for twenty days. Originally from Baglan, he came there thirty-five years ago when he was a child. Like most Afghans, he sold vegetables in the market opposite where they used to live earlier till they were allotted this new piece of land.

There were about 3500 people in the camp. Mohammed Isaq came here as a one-year-old baby with his parents who left everything behind in Kunduz. He didn't even know if his home was still there. Isaq sold water or vegetables for a living. There were some electric poles in the vicinity but they didn't get power. The Afghans were caught in a warp—stuck there in difficult conditions and not in a position to go back. If the police caught them, they would tear up the PoR cards and put them in jail.

Some of them had paid PKR 20,000 to be released after begging or borrowing.

The men left for the vegetable market at 5 a.m. and often the police lay in wait to catch them. A search operation had been conducted here before I visited and many arrests were made and some weapons recovered.

Most of them earned PKR 300 to 500 a day, like Ahmad Din. His brother, Azharuddin, had spent five days in jail. Ahmad was afraid to leave for work and constantly feared that he would be picked up. He didn't want any more children as he didn't know how to raise his two young sons. For the Afghans, it was difficult to get SIM cards or open bank accounts. They bought motorcycles in the names of Pakistanis.

Sitting inside their enclosed courtyards, the women often sent little children to fetch water. There was only one functioning bore well. The government had built toilets at the back of the camp. Zaituna said her home in Kunduz might have been beautiful but there was nothing to eat there. She came here when she was three and now had seven children, including four girls. On the single beam holding up the roof, she had tied a battery-operated LED lamp with a ribbon. That was the only source of light in most houses. Her husband plied a donkey cart and earned some PKR 300 a day. Women would step out of the camp for medical check-ups or to visit relatives, always accompanied by men—a way of Afghan culture and tradition.

Since it was not an officially recognized camp, it lacked the basic amenities provided in the refugee villages. In 2009, the Capital Development Authority asked all Afghans residing in a few sectors of Islamabad to vacate the areas in order to initiate some developmental projects. They were offered two options by the UNHCR—they could voluntarily repatriate to Afghanistan or relocate to an alternative site. Some of them did opt to return but around 500 families preferred to stay back and live in this settlement.

There were seventy-six refugee camps, most of them in Khyber Pakhtunkhwa, ten in Balochistan and one in Punjab where they did get free water, light, healthcare and education. Legal assistance was also provided for illegal detentions under the Foreigners Act.

Most refugees came in since 1979 and a census was conducted only in 2005 when about 3 million were documented. However, of this only 37 per cent, or 1.6 million, were in camps. It was after a follow-up census in 2006–07 that the NADRA started registering Afghans who were worried about being thrown out. PoRs were issued to 2.15 million out of the 3 million and the registration process is an ongoing one. The government has an Afghan Management and Repatriation Strategy (AMRS) to facilitate the voluntary return of the refugees.[10]

In May 2012, Pakistan, Iran, Afghanistan and the UNHCR had an international stakeholders' conference in Geneva to formulate a Solutions Strategy for Afghan Refugees (SSAR) and create a conducive atmosphere for their return. Under this, forty-eight sites were identified as potential areas where the refugees could settle, and work had been going well in nineteen of them. However, the numbers of refugees who wanted to return declined each year. In 2013, it was only 31,000.

In Islamabad, I attended the launch of the Pakistan Portfolio of projects under the SSAR which was seeking international funding support. The popular sentiment was that Afghanistan had to do more to bring back the refugees. Pakistan appealed to the donors to provide $367 million for the implementation of projects in refugee hosting and affected areas in the country. The federal minister of states and frontier regions, Lt. Gen. Abdul Qadir Baloch, spoke of how long the government could test the patience of the local population, and how long it would have to wait for the refugee sites to be developed in Afghanistan; he also appealed to the donor community to come forward and reduce the negative impact. I asked the minister what the government's plan would be if the refugees didn't want to leave at all. Off the record, he joked that maybe India should take some of the refugees. In fact at the Afghan camp, some of the refugees asked me in a very serious tone whether I could help them get to India in any way. They loved Indian films and Salman Khan, and said they would love to go to India, and so on. The Afghans have always loved India and that proximity has not exactly been welcomed by Pakistan.

Women and peace

For a region which has always been embroiled in some conflict or the other, women were missing from the peace debate. A regional peace conference I attended with women from the Asian countries, drew attention to the lack of a peace agenda and more so the absence of women in it despite the fact that they bore the brunt of the conflict. Khawar Mumtaz, an activist and head of the National Commission on the Status of Women in Pakistan, said that women had no role in the conflict to begin with and they continued to be marginalized despite being the most affected. Nighat Saeed Khan of the ASR Resource Centre in Lahore said that women were the ones meant to clean up the mess.

Since Afghanistan had recently become part of SAARC, the issues from there were not included in the narrative of South Asia. Khan said that women's groups in Pakistan were against the military supporting the mujahideen fighting in Afghanistan. After so many peace initiatives in the region over a span of thirty-five years, she said the women's agenda did not occupy a place in peace movements or discussions. 'Unless we have ownership, and internalization of the need for women's participation, things will not change,' she pointed out. With reference to Kashmir, she said that she had not been able to convince the men that women needed to be on the peace negotiation committee. It was the challenge to patriarchy more than anything else that was preventing women's participation.

On honour killings

During my first trip to Karachi in 2011, an activist had said that as you go into the interior, you go further back in time. A feudal structure and patriarchy ensured that women were objects to be traded for resolving disputes and killed if they showed any independence. Like the khap panchayats (groups of villagers who take decisions extralegally, much like the jirga) in North India which are above the law and nothing can stop them, the jirga holds sway in some parts of Pakistan. In June 2016, an assistant political agent in Landi Kotal in KPK acquitted two men who had killed their uncle and sister-in-law for having 'illicit relations' after a five-member jirga said it was the local *riwaz*, or custom, to do so and the killers had committed no crime. The jirgas would order the killing of any woman who strayed from the local codes, and in the rural areas, women who wanted to study and not marry a stranger were constantly under threat. Meanwhile, Hindu women were often in danger of being converted and married off, and some of these incidents had been uncovered by the Pakistan Hindu Council. Education for women is a dangerous activity and what happened to Malala Yousafzai and her schoolmates was perhaps the most infamous embodiment of that medieval approach. Schools are under attack and apart from disrupting polio immunization programmes, education of girls is another Taliban bugbear.

On Women's Day, 8 March 2014, I went for a small programme that focused on the situation of girls in Pakistan. Samar Minallah, a human rights activist and film-maker, had made a powerful documentary on the practice of settling disputes by bartering girls. The film showed girls as young as four offered as compensation for a murder. This bizarre practice is called Swara in Khyber Pakhtunkhwa and is known by other names in all provinces of Pakistan. In one case, young Asma's father and brother resisted the resolution of the jirga to hand her over for a dispute involving her uncle. Both were killed for defying the order, and another of her brothers fought to stop this barbarism.

Minallah filed a PIL in the Supreme Court with details of 110 cases of Swara or Vanni, as it is called in the Punjab, or Sang Chatti in Sindh. In a landmark order, the court ruled that the police should take action and stop such incidents and file cases against the perpetrators. The men in some of the families that Minallah met were against the practice of young girls being given away as compensation for a crime committed by male family members. In Sindh, the police and journalists took up the matter and followed up cases. The PPC (Pakistan Penal Code) was then amended to make Swara and similar practices a punishable crime, with a maximum penalty of ten years' imprisonment, but the practice is embedded in customary law. The Prevention of Anti-Women Practices (Criminal Law Amendment) Act 2011 also criminalized practices like Swara and Vanni but reduced the sentence.

Tradition victimized women and apart from customary law, the problem was that women lacked the freedom to take decisions. In some provinces, water and sanitation were lacking. Moreover, even during pregnancy, women had to do a lot of physical work. Pakistan and India have high rates of stunting, and as reported by the National Nutrition Survey 2011 (jointly carried out by the Aga Khan University's department of women and child health, Pakistan's ministry of health and the UNICEF), stunting, wasting and micronutrient malnutrition were endemic in Pakistan. More than 30 per cent of the population lives below the poverty line, the report said, and the poorest 20 per cent of the population earn 6.2 per cent of the country's total income. Most households spend almost half their income on food. Of the SAARC countries, Pakistan has the second highest stunting rate for children under five years of age—43.7 per cent, and higher in the rural areas. About 31.5 per cent of the children are underweight. India, too, has a high rate of stunting among children—43 per cent. The increasing rate of chronic and acute malnutrition in Pakistan is primarily due to poverty, high illiteracy rates among mothers, and food insecurity.

The shelter home

Some institutions in Pakistan have to pretend they don't exist. I was to experience this when I went to a 'place of worship' of the outlawed Ahmadi community in Islamabad, and in Karachi it was the women's shelter home. Nothing gave you an indication of what was inside. The multiple gates and the high security walls, for good reason, hid many vulnerable women who were relieved to be away from the trauma of social ostracism. Honour killings are a major issue, and Uzma Noorani, a trustee of Panah, the privately run shelter for women, is under threat from relatives of the girls. These relatives often waited in the court to take revenge or get the girls back. The brave Noorani and other women risked their lives and reputation to protect these young girls who were often married off to men they didn't like in order to settle some dispute; or were not allowed to marry the men they wanted to. Some years ago, a young girl who married against her family's wishes was tracked down to Lahore and killed; her husband had been from another tribe. The pregnant girl was shot at on her grandfather's order and left for dead. She was taken to a hospital and finally ended up at Panah. The girl, who was five months pregnant when she was referred to them, survived and filed a case leading to two arrests. She remarried and changed her identity for survival.

I met the soft-spoken Mahnaz Rahman, the resident director of the Aurat Foundation, who had helped a young girl who was about to be killed for refusing to marry a person her family had chosen. The girl who wanted to study, escaped to Karachi where she met someone from her village. They ended up getting married but the families found out and she was harassed. Finally, the couple moved to a foreign country.

Money, enmity or land, and a feudal structure are the basis for honour killings. Panah provides free legal aid and help to deal with the trauma, apart from rehabilitation. The majority of women who come here want a divorce or are escaping a forced marriage. Many are also under the threat of honour killing. The women from interior Sindh who want to marry of their own choice face death threats and have nowhere to go. Families come to court and threaten the women and those who are helping them. The earlier shelter home which was less secure was literally under fire often from angry relatives. Noorani and others had had their cars damaged and she was threatened and stalked by an army major whose wife was in the shelter. And the thin security for women is exacerbated by low convictions.

Domestic violence and a survey

For the first time, cases of domestic violence were included in the 2012–13 Pakistan Demographic and Health Survey (PDHS)[11] which reported other shocking findings. The National Institute of Population Studies (NIPS) which did the PDHS found that one-third of the married women, or 32 per cent, had experienced physical violence since the age of fifteen, and one in five women had been victims of physical violence in the last twelve months (the report was released in February 2014). Women in the poorest households were more vulnerable—25 per cent—and the violence in most cases—79 per cent—is perpetrated by the husband. Eleven per cent of women also experienced violence during pregnancy. Almost 40 per cent of women had suffered abuse from their husbands at some point in their life and one-third of them reported some form of physical or emotional violence by their husbands in the last twelve months.

There was huge resistance to including questions on sexual violence, and even the domestic violence questionnaire was inserted with great difficulty, Tanvir Kiyani of the NIPS said. Women don't have the power to make decisions and more than one-third of them had no say on healthcare, or visits to family or relatives or on major household purchases. About 43 per cent of women and one-third of the men agreed that a husband was justified in beating his wife if she argued with him, neglected the children or in-laws, refused to have sex, went out without telling the husband, or burnt the food. About 34 per cent of women agreed that if they argue with their husbands, it is justified if they are beaten.

At a discussion I attended on the report at the SDPI, Dr Abdul Basit Khan, the executive director of the NIPS, said that lack of education, financial constraints, wars and religious extremism had contributed to the situation, and instead of fighting with India, Pakistan should learn from it on the health front. It was one of the few times I heard India not being spoken of in inimical terms.

The report had other shocking findings. One in every fourteen Pakistani children died before reaching the age of one, and one in every eleven did not survive his or her fifth birthday. Infant and under-five mortality rates were at seventy-four and eighty-nine deaths respectively per 1000 live births in the five-year period before the latest report, a far cry from the millennium development goal target of 40/1000 live births. Children in rural areas were more likely to die young with the under-five mortality at 106 per 1000 live births, while in urban areas it was 74/1000 live births, the survey said. Neonatal mortality at fifty-five deaths per 1000 live births had remained unchanged for the last twenty years.

Pakistani households consisted of an average of 6.8 persons and about 39 per cent of the population was under fifteen. Only 11 per cent of the households were headed by women, the survey said. The majority of women, 57 per cent, and 29 per cent of men had no education and only 16 per cent of women and 21 per cent of men had attended primary school. Fertility had decreased from 5.4 births per woman to 3.8 in the last twenty-three years. Women who had a higher education had a fertility rate of 2.5, while for illiterate women it was 4.4. Thirty-five per cent of the women were married at eighteen and more than half—54 per cent—by the age of twenty.

Transgenders in Pakistan

Two of my friends in Pakistan identified themselves as from the transgender community. I met Z at a press conference in a five-star hotel and was introduced by a mutual friend. Dressed casually in baggy jeans and a T-shirt with sneakers, Z looked refreshingly different from the overdressed and made up-to–the-nines women I usually met. After that we hung out together with Z's companion who was equally charming. They made sandwiches as a business and it did well for a while. Often I would be invited for lunch or dinner on their terrace where a large wooden table would be full of food. Crisp French bread with delicious fillings, coffee and sometimes cakes. They cooked well and I enjoyed being there. The funniest time I had was when at a pre-Christmas party for which I landed up late, we played a game, Cards against Humanity, with zany clues and sometimes answers you could have never imagined.

Z had started to undergo a gender transition and had begun taking testosterone. I did notice the excessive growth of hair on the upper lip but I thought little of it till I was told the reason. We often covered events together—and sat together during Musharraf's trial. Other journalists were very curious about Z and would keep asking me was this a boy or a girl, and I would firmly say girl. In a society that finds it difficult to accept transgenders, they had strange experiences. Once, while watching the ceremony that takes place every evening on the Wagah border between

Indian and Pakistani soldiers, they ended up in the section reserved for women!

Life can be difficult for transgenders in the subcontinent, especially in Pakistan, and they braved it out for a while before leaving the country to go to a place where they would be more welcome. We did a lot of fun things together like going to play mini-golf near the Rawal Lake or going bowling to celebrate one of their birthdays. We also watched bad Hindi films together, or ate ice cream at Hotspot, and they were a fun couple, very different from most people in the city. They reminded me of my friends in Mumbai, they were casual and full of beans. When I told Z my visa was cancelled, she immediately called me for a farewell lunch of sorts where we cribbed about the visa problem and I met some of her other friends whose visas were not being renewed and had to leave.

While women suffer from poor social standing and health, for the 1.5 million transgender community in Pakistan, social acceptance—despite court orders—is a long way off. I reported on a discussion at the SDPI and met some members of the community. As Gulnaz, a researcher said, there was a need to be sensitive and understand the community, instead of driving them to the fringes. In one case, Rifee Khan was asked to take private lessons at a premier 'spoken English' training institute in Karachi. Families of other students would object if she studied in class, the institute said. Rifee, a double MA and part of the Gender Interactive Alliance, was one of the three transgenders—the other two being Mahar Anjum and Muskan—to have got jobs in the Sindh government's social welfare department as office assistant, some years after a court order. The situation was very similar to India, though Indian activists said India was better off.

A landmark Supreme Court judgment in 2011 recognized transgenders' right to equality, inheritance, and to be registered as the third gender, or *khwaja seras*, in the National Database and Registration Authority which issues the identity cards, but the community continues to be stigmatized. The court order allows for a third gender category on national identity cards, gives transgenders a legal share in family inheritance, reserves 2 per cent jobs in all sectors, and gives them the right to vote in elections.

The main issue remains social acceptance. Almas Bobby of Transgender Foundation wanted to study beyond matric but couldn't go ahead due to social pressure. She was against separate schools for transgenders as she felt it would isolate them further. Even on the health front, when they went to hospitals, they couldn't stand in the male or female queues. If they stood in one queue, they would be asked to go to the other. So, access to health care was a difficulty.

Rifee called on families to support their children who had a different sexual orientation. She said her family had supported her and so she could study as much as she wanted to. Many families disowned their children and then they had little option but to beg or dance. 'Remember this is a society which persecutes its women, so the transgenders are further marginalized,' she pointed out. Jannat Ali, who is an MBA and heads the Khwaja Sera Society, said she ran a literary project which aimed at teaching skills to young people so that they didn't have to beg on the streets. It was difficult for transgenders to continue in school due to stigma and prevalent attitudes. These children were taunted and many were reluctant to study. However, education remains the only way they can integrate and get jobs.

Samina Ali Baig: Pakistan's first woman Everester

In this gloomy scenario, Pakistan produced its first woman mountaineer of note, and I was happy to meet Samina Ali Baig and her brother, Mirza Ali Baig, at an event just before they went on a seven-summit tour of the world in November 2013. Some months before that, on 19 May 2013, Mirza Ali Baig had stopped 200 metres short of the summit of Mt Everest to let his sister Samina take the last few steps and become the first woman from Pakistan to climb the world's highest mountain.

He wanted to send a message to the world that if he could do this for his sister, others could follow suit and support women in their endeavours. The thirty-year-old Mirza was to attempt Mt Everest in 2014 as part of an Adventure Diplomacy Expedition taking on seven summits in seven continents, along with Samina. A second-year arts student in an Islamabad college, twenty-three-year-old Samina is a native of Shimshal, a remote mountain area in Upper Hunza, which has no phone, power or Internet. The country's only professional woman mountaineer, she started climbing with her brother at the age of nineteen, inspired by stories of women mountaineers who often came to the area. 'My family supported me in this and felt that women too had a right to explore natural resources,' she said. In 2010, they founded a Pakistan Youth Outreach programme to get young people in schools and colleges involved in adventure sports. The Everest expedition was to mainly promote gender equality and to show the world that Pakistani women were also capable of conquering mountains.

'If women can climb mountains, they are mentally and physically strong and they can do anything,' she smiled. She said she would be keen to climb in India too if there was a chance. 'I want to tell women to follow their passion and show the world that no mountain can bend before you.' She was good friends with the Indian twins from Dehradun, Tashi and Nungshi Malik, who reached the summit of Mt Everest together with her.

The seven summits in seven continents are some of the highest in the world: Mount Aconcagua in Argentina, Vinson Massif in Antarctica, Kilimanjaro in Tanzania, Carstensz Pyramid in Indonesia, Everest in Nepal, Denali/McKinley in the USA and Elbrus in Russia.

Of other Malalas

The plump, smiling face of Malala Yousafzai was always in the news and especially at the time she was a contender for the 2013 Nobel Peace Prize. On the day it was announced and she didn't get it, all of Pakistan groaned with disappointment (she was only the second Pakistani after Dr Abdus Salam to be awarded the prize, in 2014, along with Kailash Satyarthi from India). On the International Day of the Girl Child, 11 October 2013, lots of young students came for an exhibition at a five-star hotel and I got a chance to interview some of them for a reaction. The girls spoke of how difficult it was for them to study and it was a signal reminder that deifying Malala was not going to resolve the abysmal situation of girls' education in Pakistan.

On that day, statistics given out on the education of girls were dismal. One in ten children who were not in primary school lived in Pakistan which spends under 2 per cent of its GDP on education. Salman Asif, a gender specialist with the UN, said that Pakistan fared poorly in the Global Gender Gap Index and was ranked 134 out of 135, and 113 out of 120 on the Education Development Index. With 12 million child labourers and high dropout rates from schools, he said it was a 'snatched childhood' for most children.

The present government had made a commitment to raise the percentage of education expenditure to 4 per cent of the GDP. The minister of state for education, Baligh-ur-Rehman, said that while the gross enrolment rate was 92 per cent, the net enrolment rate was way below at 68 per cent. The school dropout rates are among the highest in the world in Pakistan. Only 63 per cent girls were in school while for boys it was 73 per cent. This amounted to at least 3.8 million girls and 2.9 million boys who were out of school, he said. To rectify this, $7 million from the 10-million-dollar Malala Fund would be spent on education in Pakistan.

Many of the students felt Islamabad was a better place to study than some rural area, and demanded more schools for girls and finance for their studies. An eighth class student said it was difficult for girls to travel to school even in cities and there must be some protection of sorts.

Don't mess with the Lady in Black

In a country where terrorists shut down schools in the name of Islam and go to extreme lengths to prevent girls from studying, the Burka Avenger cartoon series was a revolution of sorts. To create a burka-clad superheroine was a master stroke. Its rather modest creator, pop and rock star Aaron Haroon Rashid—simply known by his stage name Haroon—gave me a long interview on his work. It was a Friday and while I was almost late and skipped lunch as it was between interviews, I waited for half an hour and nearly gave up before he arrived, full of apology.

Burka Avenger was launched online first, and he wasn't prepared for the explosion. The first three days after launching the cartoon, the website got 4 million hits, and it was his presence of mind to host the site on an expensive private server that saved the day. When I met him, Burka Avenger was getting 1 million views a week, going from zero to 120,000 fans in a flash. It was after the first episode went online that people took to it in a big way. Not many had seen the launch on 29 July 2013 on Geo Tez channel. After the initial scepticism about the burka-clad woman, people realized she was a schoolteacher with a purpose. The costume was a disguise but a handful of people who were not used to superhero comics were critical. Unwilling to use a Chinese martial art for his superheroine, Haroon invented a new sport called Takht Kabaddi—*takht* is slate in Urdu, and Takht Kabaddi is to do with books and pens and advanced acrobatics. It draws strongly on cultural elements and local themes from the subcontinent. The characters in the cartoon have Asian or Pakistani touches—if you look at the robot Rubot, he's got truck art on him, and Vadero Pajero is the embodiment of the corrupt politician. Haroon said he had a lot of fun inventing the characters and places in the story set in Halwapur—he liked halwa puri—and some of the characters you get familiar with are Tinda, Khamba, Baba Bandook—a very Gabbar Singh-like character—Golu the goat, and Mooli.

The creator of Burka Avenger comes from a mixed background. His mother was an opera singer from New Zealand and father a British Pakistani. After studying for a degree in business finance in the US, he came back to form a popular band, Awaz, which became the first Pakistani group to make it to MTV Asia. Haroon had also been to Hollywood to produce music videos. All of his music has a positive message, and he said he didn't believe in mere entertainment. He got the idea for Burka Avenger on hearing of extremists shutting down girls' schools. He turned the stereotype of a burka-clad woman into a superheroine fighting for education, with pens and books, and showing how the pen is mightier than the sword. He had also realized that a movie would be too large an undertaking and he started with an iPhone game version of Burka Avenger in early 2011. Then he decided to make an animated backstory and once that was done, he got animators, voice-overs and music (the theme music for Burka Avenger is from the original score for the game).

He set up the animation studio Unicorn Black in April 2012 and finished the first episode in July 2012, and in October, the Malala incident occurred. The Malala episode was purely a coincidence, he said, though this was an ongoing issue in Pakistan and one was constantly reading in the press about girls' schools being shut down by extremists. By the time the young schoolgirl was shot at, Burka Avenger had completed six episodes. The similarity is not lost on anyone who has seen the cartoon where a school is shut in the first episode itself.

But Haroon didn't want to cash in on the event and waited for all thirteen episodes to be finished before it was aired publicly on TV in early 2013. One of the ideas behind Burka Avenger was to give children a positive role model. Jiya, the schoolteacher who morphs into the Burka Avenger veiled in a black cape with only her eyes visible and her fist stuck out in a straight line, is in the best traditions of a superheroine. She stands for justice, peace and education for all in her ordinary avatar as a teacher as well, and even without her superheroine persona, she is still fighting for women's rights.

The whole series was made locally with Haroon's staff of thirty-five people who are animators, artists, designers and technicians. There is a lot of interest from people all around the world and he has received many emails from India, including inquiries regarding merchandising, as also offers from one of the largest book publishing companies from India as well as Europe. He was approached by a film agency as well as an Indian film director—they were interested in the rights for a live action movie. Hollywood, too, is keen on rights for the film.

Haroon is keen to work on projects with Indian producers, animators, writers and musicians. He has got a number of emails from India from people who loved the show, and it's heart-warming for him. He believes the way forward for peace is through collaboration with artists, writers, thinkers and philosophers. His dream is to work on animated projects with artistes in India.

Houbara bustard and foreign policy

As a wildlife enthusiast, I was horrified by the hunting of the houbara bustard every year by wealthy Arab princes and leaders. While licences to hunt were issued for ten days, there was little regulation, and I read that the Arabs often left behind their large SUVs and guns, much to the delight of the poor locals who helped in the hunting. The Arabs consider it an aphrodisiac, and also capture it to train falcons. The large number of dead birds in 2014 provoked outrage and condemnation. The big story came after

I left. In August 2015, the Pakistan Supreme Court had banned the hunting of this species classified as vulnerable on the IUCN's Red List, but the government in a bid to reverse the ban came up with an unexpected contention. The bustards—dead ones—were a cornerstone of Pakistan's foreign policy, probably the first bird to be so honoured, and the hunting couldn't be stopped. The *Dawn* in a sarcastic editorial wrote: 'The houbara bustard is a highly regarded bird, but perhaps it too would be surprised to learn that it is a cornerstone of Pakistani foreign policy.'[12]

Indiscriminate hunting is reducing the numbers of these birds in Pakistan and Iran, which is why there have been petitions seeking to regulate this activity. But the Pakistan government has been giving its Arab friends diplomatic licence to hunt as much as they liked. The *Dawn* editorial minced no words: 'A far more sensible approach would have been to submit, along with the core legal arguments, a detailed plan on how the provincial and federal governments would ensure that only limited hunting in strict compliance with licence conditions will be allowed and what fresh conservation steps will be taken to protect the migratory birds. The houbara bustard is a national treasure, not a cornerstone of foreign policy. Perhaps the PML-N needs to rethink its approach to policy, local and foreign—it increasingly appears feckless in both.'

Then in January 2016, the Supreme Court overturned the ban, much to the dismay of conservationists. The apex court order which had one dissenting judge said: 'Examination of the laws clearly shows that permanent ban on hunting of houbara bustard is not envisaged.'[13]

In April 2014, Shireen Mazari of the PTI who, like many others, was outraged by the killing of 2100 bustards, protested against this rampant hunting. The *Dawn* published a report, 'Visit of Prince Fahd bin Sultan bin Abdul Aziz Al Saud regarding hunting of Houbara Bustard', written by the divisional forest officer of the Balochistan Forest and Wildlife Department, Chagai at Dalbandin, in which it was stated that a Saudi prince hunted for twenty-one days—from 11 January to 31 January 2014—and shot 1977 birds, while other members of his party hunted an additional 123 birds, bringing the total houbara bustard toll to 2100.

Mazari in a statement said hunting of the internationally protected bird was banned in Pakistan but the federal government issued special permits to royalty from the Gulf states. Permits, which are person specific and cannot be used by anyone else, allow the holders to hunt up to 100 houbara bustards in ten days in the area allocated, excluding reserved and protected areas, she said.

However, the prince hunted the protected birds in the reserves and protected areas, said the report of 4 February 2014. During the twenty-one-day safari, he hunted the birds for fifteen days in the reserved and protected areas, and poached birds in other areas for six days.

She said this report is a damning exposé of the Pakistan government's complicity in breaking its own and international laws relating to endangered species. She demanded the government end these violations of laws by the Gulf royals and ensure that laws relating to protected species are enforced. She also called for transparency in the issuing of licences for legally permitted hunting so that the houbara bustard is not made extinct simply to pander to royalty or any other hunter. Obviously, her pleas fell on deaf ears and were overtaken by making the poor bustard a morbid ambassador of good relations.

A business card for Pakistan

Even if I couldn't ever visit the lovely Northern Areas, a story was possible sitting in Islamabad. I met Raffaele Del Cima who spoke about developing the Central Karakoram National Park (CKNP) which is the largest protected area in Pakistan spread over 10,000 square kilometres covering four districts in the Gilgit

Baltistan province. It was being promoted as the country's most beautiful and sustainable tourist destination by a community-driven programme of conservation. About 40 per cent of the area is covered by glaciers and it has rare flora and fauna, including the snow leopard, the lynx, Marco Polo sheep and a variety of birds, as well as medicinal plants. The project worked in the villages on the boundaries of the park 'between the earth and the sky'. It has some of the most remote and economically deprived communities living off the land at heights above 3500 metres. Most of the communities are pastoral and travelled during the long winters.

Del Cima, the country operation manager and project director of the Pakistan and Italy government-funded project, Social, Economic and Environmental Development (SEED) for the CKNP, was keen on developing it into a destination not only for mountaineers but also for green industries. He called it a 'unique and beautiful business card for Pakistan'. Well, I wondered if Indians would be allowed there! Friends who visited the area brought back stunning visuals of sweeping landscapes of great beauty.

The park is spread over four of the seven districts of Gilgit Baltistan—Ghanche, Skardu, Gilgit and Hunza Nagar. With the world's second highest mountain K2 as its centrepiece, it has some of the world's highest peaks and largest glaciers, and attracts top mountaineers from all over the world. There are around 230 villages in the buffer zone of the park with a population of 100,000 who benefit from the forests, water, wildlife, medicinal herbs and minerals in the region.

However, the sustainable aspect of the project took some time to establish. Agriculturists and pastoralists from the area were taken into confidence and they mapped the area as a first effort. In addition to providing irrigation, firewood and fodder supplies, introducing stall feeding to minimize predator conflict with domestic cattle which also brought in diseases in wild animals, were other aspects of the programme.

Villages are preventing wildlife and human as well as domestic animal conflict, and also learning the ropes of management. The CKNP authorities are also working closely with communities as partners, and local people are part of the park management as well. By caring for the community which has poor health and water facilities—the area has the highest infant mortality rate in Pakistan at 112 per 1000 live births, and deaths due to poor water quality—the project aims to make a critical difference to the region.

Now, with Italian help, the Karakoram International University is focusing on subjects related to mountaineering, and providing services and support. The project has also established health clinics for the scattered community. It also wants to create a mining sector for semi-precious stones with processing, cutting and polishing. The area is known for its ancient tradition of woodcraft. The International Mountain Research Centre will create a task force as part of the project in which the PhD students of the Karakoram International University will play a pivotal role. Issues related to the park will be top priority and a water-testing facility with a water laboratory and a map showing the quality of water are under preparation.

Another area of focus is cleaning up the glaciers. There is a special campaign for tourism and the first step is to map historical sites and provide GIS maps, apart from setting some protocol for research efforts in the area. There are other trendsetting examples from the region.

The Karakoram International University has the largest solar power system in Gilgit Baltistan as a result of which it has power even in winter. The project also aims to resurrect the image of the area, especially after the brutal killing of eleven mountaineers on 22 June 2013 near the Nanga Parbat base camp which sent waves of terror in the otherwise peaceful region. After my story on the park was published in *The Hindu*, I was encouraged to hear that some readers thought they learnt about an aspect of

Pakistan that was not much written about. It's a pity that this beautiful region is shut off for Indians for the most part, like the rest of the country, and I could only travel vicariously through photographs or by reading accounts of mountaineering exploits and travelogues.

9

Bilateral Ties

I was posted to Pakistan in 2013 soon after the second successive General Elections which was won by the PMLN. That year, there was a series of events provoking outrage in India, starting with the beheading of an Indian soldier in January 2013, and in August, five soldiers were killed on the LoC at a border outpost. First reports said these men were terrorists, and later Defence Minister A.K. Antony said they were dressed in Pakistan Army uniforms, provoking counter outrage from Pakistan which denied it. The national security adviser to PM Nawaz Sharif, Sartaj Aziz, said in Parliament that in the 2013 firing on the LoC, eleven Pakistani lives were lost and an army captain, three soldiers and three civilians were killed, while thirty-one people were injured. Apart from a joint investigation, Pakistan even suggested that the UN Military Observer Group in India and Pakistan (UNMOGIP) be called in, but this was not accepted by India. Military sources in Pakistan always maintain that the Indian firing on the LoC is unprovoked. India has consistently refused to have UNMOGIP investigate the LoC incidents.

There were furious statements made by both sides and yet this was just another regular event in the life of our two nations. Barbaric acts are meant to provoke but despite everything, events didn't escalate to war. Nawaz Sharif was elected prime minister for the third time, and Pakistan was enjoying another rare burst of democracy. He was proud that his election campaign was not full of anti-India barbs and he extended a warm hand of friendship to his neighbour. Great hopes rested on Sharif to tackle terrorism and bring economic stability. The previous government had approved the MFN status for India in 2012, but it was still to be fully granted. The composite dialogue had been disrupted by the 26/11 terror strike, and the trial of the seven accused in this case was dragging along.

Indo-Pak relations can lead to heated debates, and opinions can fly thick and fast. For every expert in India, there is an equal and opposite expert in Pakistan and vice versa. The whole relationship between the two countries is dominated by two streams: a somewhat compulsive peace narrative dented by hostility; and a hawkish line. The peaceniks and well-wishers are part of a small but dogged and vociferous minority, often laughed at for their aim of '*Aman ki Asha*' (literally, Hope for Peace). Among the ordinary people, for the most part, there is a feeling of camaraderie and those with blood relations across the border would like to meet each other, but find it hard to do so. There have been changes over the years and the Indian high commission regularly held briefings on business visas to Pakistan. In fact, the number of visas have been increasing every year and despite all the bad news, there is a lot of people-to-people exchange. There are confidence-building measures, but things tend to get caught in patriotic inertia. We cannot even resolve the question of fisherfolk in each other's jails though there is a judicial commission to address the matter, and it makes periodic visits to assess the situation. Everything seems to be stuck in lethargy and red tape, including the agreements to ease trade and customs clearance. It takes months to verify the nationality of dead fishermen while their families wait for their bodies. If a truck driver is arrested in Kashmir, then the entire cross LoC trade gets blocked for weeks. Our DGMOs meet or call each other as part of a routine exercise, but in case of an extraordinary event, for instance, the beheading of an Indian soldier, things tend to fall apart. In a proxy war, fought precisely for that reason, it is difficult to pinpoint accountability. India and Pakistan agreed to a 'comprehensive dialogue' instead of a 'composite dialogue', in December 2015, and the glass is half-full; we are at least talking to each other on paper and not sulking. Not talking is not an option any more. Besides, as someone said, it's more fun to be an optimist. A joint investigation is going on in the Pathankot terror attack in India in 2016, but whether this will lead to anything is anybody's guess. On the other hand, there is a massive trust deficit, and India and Pakistan appear to be perpetually cross with each other on the question of what it calls 'non-state actors'. The trial of 26/11 is meandering in Pakistan, which is a bugbear with India, and the alleged mastermind of the plot, the founder of LeT, Hafiz Saeed, has only been under house arrest since January 2017. Again, only time will tell if he will be prosecuted in the case. But Pakistan fails to rein in terrorists like Masood Azhar of the Jaish-e-Mohammed, in the limelight after the Pathankot attack who was briefly detained, and others like Mast Gul who escaped the Charar-e-Sharif gun battle and is an active member of the TTP. Anti-Indian hate speech goes on unchecked and unpunished. The BJP has formed a government in Jammu and Kashmir with the Mehbooba Mufti-led Peoples Democratic Party (PDP) but the promised 'healing touch' seems missing so far. This is also a time when the government in Afghanistan is unstable, and the Taliban and ISIS are relentless in inflicting violence in that country. The Taliban is gaining ground in many areas (nine districts as of June 2016);[1] bringing them to the table seems out of question as stated by President Ghani. Pakistan is still aspiring for strategic depth and is not about to give it up at a point when it seems so close to achieving it.[2]

At the end of Attia Hosain's beautiful and haunting pre-Partition ode to a dying Lucknow, *Sunlight on a Broken Column*,[3] Saleem, one of the characters, scoffs at the idea of visas to visit each other in the newly created nations. That Pakistan would be another country and people there would have a different nationality seems incredible. It's something that struck me forcibly when I was reading the book and I realized it must have been unthinkable to have visas to visit a country that was till a while ago, a single entity, now torn apart but retaining so many ties of blood. Those who left for Pakistan, including the Quaid-i-Azam Mohammed Ali Jinnah, seemed to think that they could keep their property and there was this expectation in most people's hearts of returning to visit their old homes. It is this wrenching aspect of Partition that will haunt people forever and visas serve to rub the proverbial salt into the wound.

The division of the Indian subcontinent has left a bitter and antagonistic aftermath. It has created two bickering nations which are vying with each other to increase their military expenditure, with India becoming the largest arms importer in the world in 2014. As Maulana Azad said, 'Partition was a tragedy for India.'[4] And this word has often been used by many to describe Partition and its aftermath. Sardar Patel called it a 'cataclysm', without which 'we would have been much better off'.[5] Jinnah, who had once said 'better a moth-eaten Pakistan than no Pakistan at all',[6] aimed for the moon and got it. We became enemies by design, not destiny, and as Maulana Azad lamented, 'The most regrettable feature of this situation is that the subcontinent of India is divided into two states, which look at one another with hatred and fear.'[7] Both countries are constantly testing newer weapons and stockpiling a formidable nuclear arsenal in the name of deterrence, though that hasn't prevented hostilities. We are not exactly neighbourly. Partition wasn't the beginning of a beautiful friendship. At another level, the separation and the resultant bloodshed has been mind-numbing and the human cost of that divide is staggering.

While Indians need visas to cross the border into Pakistan, and vice versa, the irony is compounded by the ease with which one can walk into Nepal, or Sri Lanka or even Thailand.

The two countries got off to a disastrous start with the war over Kashmir in 1947–48 and there was this fear that India was keen on taking over Pakistan or that it was hoping it would implode at some point. Pakistan's first Muslim army chief and later President, Ayub Khan's prime concern was the defence of Pakistan as 'India's aim is to expand, dominate and spread her influence. In this she considers Pakistan as her enemy number one.'[8] Justifying the reasons for building an army, he said he 'learnt from Sheikh Abdullah that Pandit Nehru told him at the time that Pakistan would disintegrate in a couple of years. He wanted to come to some arrangement with Sheikh Abdullah on the assumption that Pakistan would cease to be a political entity.'[9] He was convinced that 'India was an implacable enemy and wanted to cripple Pakistan at birth',[10] and also created a mindset that while Pakistan didn't want to be India's enemy, India insisted on treating it as one.[11]

Nehru, too, didn't help with statements like 'even if Kashmir were to be handed over to Pakistan on a platter, Pakistan would think of some other way to keep its quarrel with India alive because Kashmir was only a symptom of a disease and that disease was hatred of India'.[12] Sardar Patel referred to Pakistan as a 'diseased limb that had to be amputated'[13] and that it would one day return to the fold. If some Indian leaders thought Pakistan would cease to exist soon, Ayub Khan said, 'India would crumble under the weight of her own problems. It was only a matter of time: all that was required was to leave her to her fate.'[14]

Rhetoric aside, in the Punjab it was clear that the division hadn't hampered mutual affection and there were hopes for better relations. As Rajmohan Gandhi said when he came to launch his book, *Punjab: A History from Aurangzeb to Mountbatten*,[15] in December 2013 in Islamabad, 'The hearts of the people of both sides of the Punjab and in the subcontinent want a coming together of our governments.' The overflowing hall at the Institute of Strategic Studies was a measure of how much Partition and its memory were still festering in the Punjab. People were so wrapped up in their divided history that they launched into their own memories, instead of asking him questions. Gandhi's talk on 'Understanding Pakistan and India through the prism of Undivided Punjab' was lapped up in silence. He was one of the few who called for a 'wide enough consensus' to find a solution between the two countries. His book deals with an under-reported aspect of 1947 which saw the worst killings—there were many in the Punjab who protected each other. The people who protected others from both communities were far more numerous than those who killed, he said, much to the appreciation of his audience. The vast majority helped one another and there were brave and successful attempts. That seems to be a forgotten and little-known aspect in the subsequent war, proxy war and terrorism which form one layer of this mutual lack of admiration.

Keeping the people apart and perpetuating stereotypes about each other becomes another part of the game. In this sabre-rattling and cat-and-mouse play, the mundane visa has become a weapon in the hands of two hostile countries, and as a Pakistan minister said, it is the biggest non-tariff barrier in bilateral relations. It can be an agonizing wait to get one and it can come with strings attached. In my case, it took over eight months and I had almost given up hope, and there were these sarcastic opinions of my colleagues who were quite sure I wouldn't get it. Pakistan issues a city-specific visa for Indians and vice versa. I didn't know this till 2008 after the Mumbai terror attack when I was hoping that Nirupama who was then *The Hindu*'s correspondent in Pakistan, would be able to visit Okara and check on Ajmal Kasab's family. An American journalist managed to get there and do a story. To my surprise, I did come across a few exceptions where people did get liberal visit conditions, but for the most part, there was a dread. Will you get a visa or not was the question.

As a correspondent, I was warned that I could be asked to intervene for visas but the change in rules which directed people to courier their applications directly to the embassy well before I got there, was a relief. The visa issue for correspondents is coloured by the strained relations between the two countries.

Marooned Malayalis

During my travels, I do run into Malayalis in the most unlikely places, (they had even made it to the moon before Neil Armstrong and were ready to greet him with a glass of tea—so runs an old joke), but I didn't imagine there would be a community in virtual exile in Karachi (during my 2011 visit), and it was thanks to 'Mr Kutty', or 'Kutty saar', as he was called, that we met the group of stranded Malayalis in Pakistan. When B.M. Kutty arrived in Karachi on 14 August 1949, there was already a sizeable Muslim community from Kerala there. He described himself as an 'educated shuttlecock' and he came to the port city for no rhyme or reason. As a leading trade unionist and peace activist, he is the secretary of PILER and the secretary general of the Pakistan Peace Coalition. He visits his 'beautiful' home in Vylathur in Kerala's Malappuram district often and by now is a familiar figure in India as well. I did meet him once later in the Delhi Press Club where he was his usual chatty self though not in such good health.

When he left his home in 1949 and inexplicably headed for Karachi, there were no passports. They were welcomed as Mohajirs and in Karachi he found a thriving Malayali community, mostly engaged in small businesses, and running hotels and bidi-making units.[16] In 1986, a survey by the Malabar Muslim Jamaat identified 64,000 Keralites there, mostly those who had fled after the Moplah rebellion in 1921. That number may have dwindled to less than half by now. C.H. Mahmood of the Malabar Muslim Jamaat (formed in 1921) puts the figure at 10,000 Keralite Muslims in Karachi. Kutty married Birjis, a Muslim from Uttar

Pradesh. His language skills were limited but it didn't matter at that point. We met in his modest flat in Karachi, and his room with several black-and-white photographs of his beautiful wife and children, and lots of books, was evocative of his simple yet strenuously active life. He spent two years and eleven months in jail during Ayub Khan's dictatorship.

He mentions in his book that the Jamaat has a small portion of Karachi's old Merva Shah graveyard set apart exclusively for burying Kerala Muslims. He was active in political life in the Awami National Party and a close associate of Baloch politician Ghaus Bakhsh Bizenjo whose autobiography he edited, and later with the National Democratic Party. Despite poor health, he continues to travel and is a strong and sane voice for happier relations between the two countries.

The visa question that perplexed a fictional Saleem would haunt a real-life Keralite nearly thirty years after Partition when he landed in Karachi after being told it was Dubai. Those were the years of the 'Gulf boom' in Kerala and unsuspecting job seekers were deceived by many an agent. Kader, in his late fifties now, is a naturalized Pakistani citizen, but he told us that his visa application was rejected and he couldn't visit his ailing wife in Kerala. On that night in 1976 when he got off the ship in the darkness, he couldn't really tell if it was Karachi. He paid an agent the princely sum of INR 800 to get him on a ship to Dubai. He did go home in 1981 to get married, and has four children, with his eldest son working in his dream destination, Dubai. Though he used to visit his family and spend a month or two in India, he could never bring them to Karachi, and the Indian authorities didn't listen to his pleas that he was not born in Pakistan and to let him return to Kerala.

This was another perplexing fallout of Partition—when a person's nationality is Indian, he has to prove that first and then apply for a visa to go back. There are many like Kader who were deceived into going to Karachi and they have demanded Indian citizenship. After another visa refusal, Kader said in disgust that both countries had one thing in common and that was to torture people. I tend to agree—while there are so many major issues confronting our relationship, not the least of them Kashmir, little is done to resolve them; instead, people are made the target of the tension and mutual discord. The visa becomes a weapon in this discord to harass and intimidate citizens who have a right to travel across borders and visit each other's families. People like Kader, the fisherfolk, ordinary citizens who have relatives—they are some sort of collateral damage to the hostility between the two countries. Most of the Malayalis are shopkeepers in Karachi, and they are spread out in the old Mohajir housing colonies, with their dull buildings, much like Indian middle-class neighbourhoods. They mask their yearning for home with a bravado that has been worn thin by helplessness.

I was to do another story there later when I was posted in Islamabad—of an unfortunate family stuck in Karachi with no hope of ever getting back home. They did eventually go back and credit must go to Kutty for pestering the Indian high commission for their return visas.

Of plebiscite and the right to self-determination

Relations between India and Pakistan, as Ayub Khan once told Nehru, 'had been dictated by drift rather than any rational design. The reason I thought was that neither side had drawn up any plans for neighbourliness.'[17] Ayub felt Nehru wasn't responsive to his various plans and concluded that India would never agree to live as equal and honourable neighbours. 'It was Brahmin chauvinism and arrogance that had forced us to seek a homeland of our own where we could order our life according to our own thinking and faith. They wanted us to remain as serfs, which was precisely the condition in which the Muslim minority in India lived today.'[18] He went on to speak of 'India's deep pathological hatred for Muslims and her hostility to Pakistan stems from her refusal to see a Muslim power developing next door. By the same token, India will never tolerate a Muslim grouping near or far from her borders.'[19]

Like a dark, foreboding cloud which hangs low, there is something ominous about our relations and unlike most dark clouds that proverbial silver lining seems absent. Writers like Stephen Cohen feel the India–Pakistan rivalry will endure up to 2047, making it a century since the two nations were formed.[20] Relations are marked by one-upmanship and defeat any moves to look forward. The two countries drift on a path of enmity and peace, and the two-nation theory seems to have come apart in 1971 itself, much to the despair of Pakistan and its people whose worst fears that India was out to destroy the fledgling Muslim nation, were confirmed. Right from Partition, there were differences in perceptions—for India, freedom from the British came with the sorrow of Partition, or *batwara*, and for Pakistan, it was a celebration of Independence.

There are deep complexities and preconceived notions which colour the relations between the two countries. Ayub Khan in his diatribe against India said that 'Indian nationalism is based on Hinduism and Pakistan's nationalism is based on Islam'[21] which at that time was untrue, but increasingly veering towards accuracy. Before my first visit, I thought Kashmir was the main problem between India and Pakistan. I believed that once this was resolved, everything would be fine. 'Kashmir was the touchstone for Pakistan to test India's sincerity to befriend it'[22] and increasingly, the reason for hostility. In fact, while the various Kashmiri groups in the capital held regular programmes, I didn't see too many others joining in support. That 'beautiful body' which both India and Pakistan desired, to repeat Sheikh Abdullah's unedifying turn of phrase, was still unattainable.[23]

India and Pakistan wanted Kashmir, and the Kashmiris wanted independence, or *azadi*. Three wars, much bloodshed and seven decades after 1947, none of them have got what they desired. Funnily in Pakistan, I met a lot of people who said the Kashmir dispute will go on but that doesn't mean India and Pakistan cannot be friends. The Pakistan government doesn't agree—it cries hoarse that it's about people's aspirations not real estate, and India is not willing to cede an inch. And the issue remains deadlocked. Kashmir figured often in the news while I was there. Visa issues for the Jammu Kashmir Liberation Front (JKLF) leader Yasin Malik's wife and daughter; LeT chief Hafiz Saeed's rallies or abuses; Syed Asiya Andrabi, the Dukhtaran-e-Millat founder-chairperson, spewing anti-India rhetoric over the phone from Srinagar; the late Hamid Gul venting on India; or the Kashmiris in Islamabad who held protests, meetings and press conferences. In informal meetings with Kashmiris, they would speak of how the issue was almost never discussed seriously.

The Pakistani government launched an email campaign, writing to the UN secretary-general on Kashmir Solidarity Day—5 February 2014—demanding that the UN resolutions be enforced. The email said the only solution to the Kashmir issue lay in the appointment of a plebiscite administrator, withdrawal of troops, and a UN-conducted plebiscite to ascertain the will of the people of Jammu and Kashmir before it was too late. That day saw more anti-India speeches and demands for plebiscite. Pakistan kept saying that the UN resolutions would form the benchmark for the rights of the Kashmiris. I stood on the sidewalk near the press club and watched the JuD members accusing India of everything under the sun. The JeI, the Difa-e-Pakistan Council and the JuD held separate rallies to protest against the atrocities in Kashmir by Indian security agencies and demanded self-determination for Kashmiris. '*India ka ek ilaj, al-Jihad, al-Jihad*' (Only one solution for India and that's Jihad), shouted flag-waving members of the JuD while speakers said that Kashmir could only be freed in a holy war. '*India teri maut aayi, Lashkar aayi, Lashkar aayi*' (India, your death has come, the fighters have come), screamed the crowd wearing fluorescent jackets emblazoned with the words 'Falah-i-Insaniyat', the humanitarian arm of the JuD. War cries and calls for jihad against India were common at JuD rallies, and the first one I attended had a long avenue full of young men baying for blood.

Ijaz-ul-Haq of the PML (Zia) took it one step further—he said that Hitler killed Jews one by one but let a few go so that they could tell the world that the rest were dead. In *jannat* (heaven), no Kaffir can live, he bellowed. Kashmir can be resolved only with jihad—now even clean-shaven people are ready for jihad, he roared. Former ISI chief Hamid Gul's son, Abdullah Gul of Anjuman Naujawan-e-Pakistan, said, *'Ye goli aur bandook ka rishta hai'* (This is a relationship between the bullet and the gun). He emphasized that there could be neither trade with India nor any MFN status for it and that it was time for the rise of the Islamist forces. He looked like an affable young man, but his speeches were even more vicious than his father's. Asiya Andrabi gave a speech over the phone in a high-pitched voice. India could capture Kashmir but not the hearts of its people, she said, adding that Kashmir can never be a part of India. She then exhorted Pakistan to free Kashmir from 'impure' India. Andrabi urged the Pakistan government to tell India that Kashmir is an integral part of Pakistan. Kashmir will be part of Pakistan, she screeched, her voice rising higher and higher in anger. Hamid Gul, who has passed way since, was confident that Kashmiris would never go with India. They had to be given the right to self-determination, he said.

Just before Kashmir Solidarity Day, the JeM founder, Maulana Masood Azhar, addressed a large public meeting over the telephone in Muzaffarabad to launch a book by Afzal Guru, on 26 January 2014, India's Republic Day. Azhar issued open threats to avenge the execution of Afzal Guru for the attack on the Indian Parliament in 2001. In 1999, he was one of the militants escorted to Kandahar by the then Indian Foreign Minister Jaswant Singh in exchange for passengers and crew of a hijacked Indian Airlines plane. He formed the JeM in 2000, after he returned to Pakistan.

The JeM was banned, along with the Lashkar-e-Taiba and other groups, by Musharraf but seems to be quite active.

Since there was a weekly foreign office briefing, questions were asked and the foreign office spokesperson, Tasneem Aslam, said in response that the views of an individual who belonged to a proscribed entity should not concern India so much; probably, this was a one-time event. He escaped scrutiny and he did it but his organization is banned in Pakistan and their activities are monitored. She also diverted the question by saying that Pakistan, however, had a position on the provocative statements of the Indian Army chief, an aspect that was being missed.

It was not only Azhar who emerged from the woodwork, but also Hizbul Mujahideen Commander Mast Gul who had escaped after a prolonged gun battle at Charar-e-Sharif in Kashmir in 1995. Gul, now part of the Taliban which claimed responsibility for some bombings in Peshawar, was seated next to the TTP Peshawar chief in North Waziristan, Mufti Hassan Swati, in a front-page picture in the *Dawn*. It was the day after the Kashmir Solidarity Day in February 2014 and not long after Maulana Masood Azhar addressed a rally. Swati had claimed the bombing of a hotel frequented by Shias in the Qissa Khawani Bazaar in Peshawar, saying that Gul had carried out the attack. *Dawn* reported that Gul had escaped an ambush near Peshawar in 2003 and had been underground ever since.

Mutilated by war, terror and repression, Kashmir has become a voiceless entity. It is the raison d'être for Pakistan-trained terror groups calling for a flagrant jihad to claim what they say is rightfully theirs. The Pakistan Army is waging war—whether by proxy or by any another name, it is still war—and believes in the relentless pursuit of Kashmir. Both countries claim inalienable rights over it, often calling it the 'jugular vein', a phrase Jinnah used, though that vein has been slashed and Kashmir is almost bleeding to death. The Indian government, in trying to repress the youth trained and armed by Pakistan, has smothered the place with troops. Kashmir's fate is mired in status quoism and the promised self-determination exercise (in 1947) hasn't taken place after nearly seventy years. The cry for azadi has gone unheard and more than its beauty and syncretic culture, Jammu and Kashmir is remembered for torture camps, brute force, young men being trained in hate and warfare, exiled Pandits, missing young men and their mothers who cannot forget . . . for lost innocence and for the brutalization of women. Its people can't see a way out of the wretchedness, and India and Pakistan lack the will and statesmanship to allow for an honest decision in their interest. Instead, the two countries mindlessly inflict suffering, and blame each other at every step like squabbling, crotchety neighbours, unmindful of the gross tragedy they have wantonly inflicted on thousands of ordinary lives. The massive unrest after the JeM's Burhan Wani was killed in July 2016 reflects the burning resentment and alienation of a people left by the wayside, and pellet guns were aimed at even children who came out to protest. The gun, not dialogue, is India's blinkered solution to a complex problem that hasn't vanished over the years. Kashmir hangs like an unused curtain in the background of our two countries, gathering dust. Everyone knows it's there, but you can sneeze it away.

So, I was surprised that in January 2014, I was invited to the hallowed National Defence University (NDU) in Islamabad for a seminar on Kashmir. Indian lawyer and constitutional expert A.G. Noorani whose writing I greatly admire, was one of the key speakers. I went bright and early to the NDU and my invitation card made sure I was not hassled. I asked one of the organizers why this sudden focus on Kashmir, and one of them said off the record, 'We need to remind these shopkeepers that Kashmir is still a problem.' Noorani spoke well and mentioned the proposed deal between Manmohan Singh and Musharraf which hadn't come through.[24] The two-day programme focused on Kashmir as a matter of the people's right to make a choice and not as a territorial dispute between India and Pakistan.

Noorani was succinct—after the Agra rebuff from the then President General Musharraf, Prime Minister Vajpayee had nothing to offer Pakistan, only sweet words, but in September 2006, Prime Minister Manmohan Singh and Musharraf were ready with a formula which fell apart in 2007. It was a non-territorial arrangement and neither side would give up its stand—the LoC would become lines on a map and people would be free to move: there would be a lot of exchange. The self-rule would extend to the Northern areas and Gilgit Baltistan, and troops would be withdrawn. The chief ministers from both sides would meet and review this interim arrangement for ten to fifteen years and compare notes, and the greatest gainers would be the people. The solution lay in seeking a congruence of interests.

The softening of the Kashmiri border under the Musharraf–Manmohan plan was not a new idea. Way back, Kuldip Nayar had written about John Kenneth Galbraith, then the US envoy to India, who had suggested the reopening of the road between Rawalpindi and Srinagar through Baramulla, Uri and Murree, and the resumption of trade and tourist traffic. But India's military rights in the vale of Kashmir were to remain intact. Nayar writes:

> This was more or less the same proposal that Sheikh Abdullah discussed with me in 1969. His argument was that the border should be soft so that Pakistanis had an easy access to the valley. Strangely enough Bhutto repeated the same thing during an interview with me in March 1971: We can make the ceasefire line a line of peace and let people come and go between the two Kashmirs. After all why should they suffer? Let there be some free movement between them. Then one thing can lead to another. After all, simultaneously we hope that there will be exchange of visits, of officials and non-officials.[25]

The peace narrative reached its zenith during Prime Minister Vajpayee's time, but his memorable bus ride to Lahore in 1999 ended with the Kargil war and the Agra summit was a washout. Dr Singh who very much wanted to visit his village Gah near Chakwal in Pakistan couldn't take a dynamic decision and rise above political compulsions. Calls for peace are now stronger after two successive democratic governments, and friendly overtures from Nawaz Sharif, but paralysed by the usual one step forward, two steps backward disease.

Peace on Siachen

While the main issue of Kashmir festers, there's this tendency to go for the low-hanging fruit, and the Siachen Glacier and Sir Creek are believed to be issues that can be resolved. But events have shown that pussyfooting around other issues, while not resolving the main crux of enmity and wars, will not led anywhere. Siachen is a case in point.

Since the avalanche in the Gayari sector in April 2012, which killed 140, including 129 Pakistani soldiers, General Kayani spoke of the need to withdraw from the glacier. Pakistan was keen on Siachen being demilitarized, and statements would be made to this effect off and on while I was in Islamabad. The foreign office spoke of the environmental dimension of the Siachen Glacier issue. Pakistan said there should be disengagement of forces and demilitarization of the area. Sartaj Aziz, the national security and foreign affairs adviser to the PM, gave an interview to Radio Pakistan saying that Indian forces presented a serious environmental threat to Siachen; that they were damaging the virgin snow on the glacier, a source of drinking water, and Pakistan was a country facing water shortage. He urged a quick pullout of the Indian Army as its continuing presence and waste disposal was damaging the glacier.

I had attended a discussion on the Siachen Glacier in Mumbai some months after the Gayari disaster in 2012 where people from both countries spoke of the need to evolve a consensus on the troop withdrawal. A worrying aspect was also the impact of climate change on Siachen—the snout of the glacier had receded in the past few years. There was also a humane reason for the troops to be removed from the high altitude, and it was a conflict neither country could afford yet they persisted for strategic reasons. At the discussion, only one voice spoke for a solution on Kashmir first. The editor-in-chief of *Kashmir Images*, Bashir Manzar, felt that Siachen could not be looked at in isolation and if Kashmir was not an issue, there would have been no need to militarize Siachen. The two countries were close to signing a deal three times in the past, and for the first time General Kayani was amenable to demilitarizing the Siachen area or cutting down on the troops. Prime Minister Yousuf Raza Gilani had also met his Indian counterpart, Manmohan Singh, in Delhi and things did look optimistic for a while.

The Indian Army has been reluctant to move away despite the colossal price in terms of men and material to hold that snowy defence. Accounts of the Siachen occupation from Indian writers and journalists point to a 'cartographic aggression' by the Pakistanis,[26] while General Musharraf said that India quite frequently intruded into the Siachen Glacier 'which clearly belonged to us'. He then admitted to plans to occupy some of the passes on the Saltoro Range.[27] He also accused the Indian Army of fake attacks and encounters with Pakistan to bump up the need for aggression. By the time the Pakistanis decided to occupy some of the high mountaintops on the Saltoro Range in May 1984, India had launched Operation Meghdoot, and to Musharraf's dismay, the Indians were already there.[28] Indian soldiers, too, were killed in an avalanche in February 2016. Even before and especially after the Kargil war, the Indian Army has been wary of letting go of this high-altitude defence which it has worked hard for over thirty years to keep under its control. That is one more so-called low-hanging fruit out of the running in terms of any peaceful solution.

Hate India for Kashmir

In 2013, the banned LeT seemed to be alive and well in the Pakistani capital. Its bespectacled and bearded founder, Hafiz Saeed, often called Professor (he used to teach earlier), was allowed to masquerade as an NGO activist on behalf of his renamed outfit—a front organization for the LeT, the JuD[29] and its charity arm, Falah-i-Insaniyat. Moreover, Masood Azhar of the Jaish-e-Mohammed, Hafiz Saeed and others seemed to have a carte blanche in making open threats against India. They worked around proxy war limitations to keep up a continuous flow of invective on Kashmir. Saeed, the man wanted in India for the 26/11 attack, enjoyed till his arrest in January 2017, untrammelled freedom of speech and movement. An official once told me that it was the payoff for not sending terrorists to fight in Kashmir across the border. The JuD, in Saeed's words, was recognized for its relief and rescue work after floods and earthquakes, and no court in the land had indicted it. He was also getting invited to speak in universities. He once addressed the Lahore High Court Bar Association on a number of issues, including the Indian elections, the media and the ISI standoff and Kashmir. At that time in 2013, as a strident Opposition in India, the BJP was demanding that no talks be held with Pakistan till Saeed was handed over, but obviously Prime Minister Modi forgot all about that when he dropped into Lahore to meet Sharif in December 2015, on the latter's birthday, fifteen years after Prime Minister Atal Bihari Vajpayee's famous bus ride to Lahore in 1999.

There was a Difa-e-Pakistan Caravan on 6 September 2013, to commemorate the 1965 war, planned from Rawalpindi to Islamabad where there would be a large rally. Giant posters billowing in the wind taunted India: Indian water aggression, LoC attacks, freedom of Kashmir, US drone strikes and terrorism in Pakistan. Since 2010, Saeed has been one of the leading proponents of 'India's water terrorism'.

It was a Sunday and I reached the D-Chowk opposite Parliament and the President's house which is cordoned off with barbed wire and barricades, around 6 p.m. in order to get a place. I needn't have worried. I saw a large crowd exclusively of young men in black shirts and pyjamas, carrying black-and-white flags emblazoned with 'There is no God but one God' in Urdu. The support for Saeed was evident in the huge procession from Rawalpindi to Islamabad. He was not stopped anywhere and allowed to speak in the heart of the city near the National Assembly surrounded by his orderly stick-wielding young men. This all-male procession waving the monochrome Jamaat-ud-Dawa flags swamped the roads as they came in a procession of cars and trucks from Rawalpindi.

And what was so Pakistani and unique were the containers, the kind that go on ships. The stage was three containers parked next to each other, and TV crews were poised precariously on another set of two containers. There was a crude but effective lift in the form of a crate in which we were hoisted up for a bird's-eye view. The only problem was that the empty containers shook with all this movement. I was hoisted on to a Maersk container in a small box attached to a crane, to join scores of TV cameras and journalists, two of whom fell into the space between the containers arranged together like a platform. One of them was knocked out after hitting his head on a camera stand.

From the top, one got a clear view of the crowd which seemed endless. They were strangely quiet and orderly, only shouting at times in support of the speakers' statements which were mostly against India. Apart from me, I met two other women journalists. All the young, bearded men wore black T-shirts and leggings caught up below the shins with elastic. On their T-shirts was written 'Security Jamaat-ud-Dawa'. The main stage was covered with red, patterned carpets, and there was a similar makeshift lift to take the speakers up and down. It was no wonder during his

2013 election campaign, Imran Khan fell off and broke his ribs; the contraption looked highly unstable.

That's when I also met many journalists who translated the speeches for me; one of them even apologized for the vituperative anti-India statements that were coming from the stage. I listened to the accusations that India was drawing all the water from the tributaries of the Indus, and the water treaty was a sham. Hafiz Saeed sat at the centre of the stage smugly smiling. I thought here was a man wanted for the most brazen and biggest terror strike in India, and he was sitting right across from the Pakistani Parliament, in the heart of the Pakistani capital, about to hold forth against the very country he was suspected of terrorizing again and again. Amid calls for India to be torn to pieces and India's *tabahi* (destruction) from other speakers, Saeed was firm that Pakistan should not hold talks with India, backchannel or otherwise, till the Kashmir question was resolved. He said India was using its consulates in Afghanistan as a conduit for terrorism in Balochistan and sending in killers. India was blamed for the violence in Karachi, and flooding Pakistan by releasing waters from the dams. No talks, he thundered, till all this was resolved, and absolutely no need to borrow power from India. Saeed laid down the foreign policy towards India that night before an approving audience which stood out for its lack of variety!

The Pakistani leadership was not spared either. Merely repeating that Kashmir was the jugular vein of Pakistan was not enough, he yelled—that jugular vein had to be got back. He was not for enmity or aggression but at the same time if India insisted that Kashmir was its integral part, then it would be torn from limb to limb. He said it was not terrorism to take away one's right, and if there has to be talks, remember the Kashmiris. He also stated that talks wouldn't resolve issues as in the case of the drone strikes which were ongoing even after talking to the US.

Members from the Difa-e-Pakistan Council were also present: Hamid Gul, the former ISI chief, his son Ayaz, Ijaz-ul-Haq, the son of Zia, and Maulana Samiullah. All of them were competing with each other in their abuse of India. The meeting went on till 10 p.m.

I had often attended Saeed's meetings and listened to his volley of abuse, which seemed quite the norm. He was allowed to visit Balochistan after the earthquake in Awaran, and distribute relief materials alongside the army, and he called a colourful press conference to inform us of the relief work the Falah-i-Insaniyat had been carrying out in Mastung and other regions.

In order to project his humanitarian side, after a report that India and the US were working together to stop funds to terror groups, Saeed conducted a media conference sitting in the middle of sacks of food, plastic water cans, *Star Wars* games and clothes meant to be Id gifts for the people affected by the earthquake in Balochistan. Again, he blamed India for the unrest in Balochistan and said that there were absolutely no problems there otherwise. He said his organization didn't take money from the Pakistan government and his entire funding was from the people who believed in his work; his organizations were registered with the government and the accounts were audited regularly. After the Mumbai attacks, there were US sanctions on his organizations, and bank accounts were frozen. 'We challenged it in the courts and even in the high court I got relief. India had also presented some proof, but the high court cleared me and the JuD . . . and later this also came up before a full bench of the Supreme Court which also cleared me,' he said. Now no one could stop the JuD from doing its humanitarian work, he exulted. The Punjab government, in a fit of generosity, had donated PKR 61 million to the JuD in 2013, and the adviser on national security, Sartaj Aziz, in response to a question I asked him at a press conference, defended the JuD, saying that it was a social work organization. In 2012, the US had announced a $10-million reward for information leading to his capture, and the JuD has sanctions imposed on it by the United Nations Security Council. It is also on the list of banned organizations in Pakistan. However, in 2009, Saeed's detention in the 26/11 case was set aside by the Lahore High Court which did not find any evidence linking him with the terror strike.

Kashmiris throughout the world observe 27 October as Black Day to mark the day in 1947 when the Indian forces entered the Kashmir Valley. The All Party Hurriyat Conference (G) Chairperson Syed Ali Geelani addressed a public meeting in Islamabad over the telephone and said the United Nations had failed to give the right of self-determination to Kashmiris through a plebiscite. He said the Kashmiris did not accept the Indian occupation, and they should be given the right of self-determination.

Protestors also thronged D-Chowk with large placards calling for an end to the bloodshed in the valley. Professor Waqar Ashraf, one of the participants, said that freedom was a right wherever you lived and the Kashmiris should be given that right; they could not be forced to live in a country they did not wish to belong to, and even the United Nations Charter is against it.

The human rights violation in Kashmir was another central issue. Support for the Kashmiris also came from the PTI led by Imran Khan. Dr Shireen Mazari, the PTI central information secretary, said that 27 October was marked as a Black Day when India occupied Kashmir and denied its people their right to self-determination in accordance with the United Nations Charter and the Independence principles that created the two independent states of Pakistan and India in August 1947. I used to meet JKLF founder Amanullah Khan at press conferences and he always remembered my predecessors, including Anita Joshua, fondly. His health was failing even then and he passed away in 2016.

Kashmir is a central issue for both countries, and the rights of the people to determine their status have been wantonly ignored. Training and arming youth or waging jihad has not yielded results just as armed occupation and repression have not. Unrest and unhappiness continue to loom over the region, as a peaceful solution is kept at bay with great determination by the powers that be of both countries. In this monumental mess, other issues like the MFN, Siachen, Sir Creek, LoC trade, and the arrest of fisherfolk, although important, fall by the wayside.

The MFN muddle and the trade deadlock

Just when things were more or less certain on the MFN status and the commerce minister, Khurram Dastgir Khan, was to make a trip to India in January 2014, there was a change of plans. Dastgir granted both the Indian correspondents interviews before his departure, and was full of optimism. In March 2014, Sharif, who for some reason made important announcements when he was not in Pakistan, had us all scrambling when he said in The Hague that Pakistan had postponed granting India MFN status (on 23 March 2014). He was attending the third International Nuclear Security Summit and told the media that there was no consensus on granting India MFN. The federal Cabinet was slated to meet in mid-March 2014 and approve the MFN status to India, but it did not happen. There was a move to rename the MFN and make it non-discriminatory market access (NDMA), as Dastgir had said in his interview to *The Hindu* in January 2014. But this rose by any other name was as much of a problem.

The federal government was prepared to bypass reservations expressed by the local industry and farmers, and give non-discriminatory market access to India which would provide a benefit of PKR 550–600 billion to the country's economy. 'India has given clear indication to accept Pakistan's two main demands of accommodating exportable items and removing additional duties within six months, which has paved the way for Islamabad to grant the NDMA status to New Delhi,' said a top official of the commerce ministry, wishing not to be named.

The local automobile, pharmaceutical industries as well as farmers have serious concerns over the government's decision to grant the MFN status to India. How can India be a favoured, or even worse, the most favoured nation? That sticks in the gullet of many. But there are also real fears on the ground. Thousands of Pakistani farmers had threatened to stage a sit-in at the Wagah border from 31 March 2014 onwards for an indefinite period against Islamabad's decision to grant NDMA to New Delhi. The Pakistan Kisan Ittehad president, Khalid Mehmood Khokhar, said in a press conference that India had already controlled the waters flowing into Pakistan, and now it wanted to control the agriculture of Pakistan. The farmers of the country would not accept this trade, he warned. Farmers' groups felt India would have an unfair advantage as it had subsidies for agriculture, while Pakistan did not.

Trade was currently in India's favour as Pakistan's exports were only $350 million against imports of $1.8 billion. The Indian government granted the MFN status to Pakistan in 1996. But non-tariff barriers remained intact on exports from Pakistan, and both sides did not make much progress towards trade liberalization. Later, Pakistan announced in October 2011 that it would grant the MFN status to India from 1 January 2013 by converting the negative list into a positive one by the end of 2012, a step that would have automatically granted the MFN status to India. However, Pakistan failed to grant it before 31 December 2012.

During my earlier visit to Pakistan in 2011, our group had met a lot of Pakistani businessmen who dispelled the notion that granting the MFN to India would adversely affect Pakistan. They were eager for trade. Importing products from India would be cheaper and better, and one of them was optimistic about the huge volumes of trade. Instead of spending on the army, the government should focus on improving trade and business relations, said another businessman. In Karachi too, there was much discussion on the MFN, and hoteliers like Dinshaw Avari, the director of the oldest five-star hotel there, favoured the MFN status which would help hotels get cheaper and better-quality sanitaryware and lifts, and this would be a good exchange for Pakistani businesses.

But these sane voices seemed to be drowned out by the shrill ones in Parliament. When I was there, I heard strong opposition from political parties to the MFN, with Dastgir Khan, vainly trying to defend his position. Earlier, Sharif had used the General Elections in 2014 in India to postpone the decision since he didn't want to favour any political party. Provisionally, Pakistan was committed to giving India the MFN status in 2012, but the commerce ministry had not come up with a roadmap to see it through. That was also the time when tensions on the LoC were not subsiding.

It was not only tensions on the LoC but also some much-needed groundwork that held up Pakistan completing the process of granting the MFN status. Though trade continued to be normal between the two countries, there was a reluctance, later attributed to the Pakistan Army, to give India the full honours. In the National Assembly when I attended and reported sessions on 26 and 27 September 2013, Pakistani ministers often said that the granting of the MFN status for India would be a top priority and that it had been agreed to in principle, but only after the composite dialogue resumed and tensions on the border were resolved.

While the federal Cabinet had approved the MFN status for India, the ministry of commerce was directed to bring out a summary on how complete normalization of trade could be achieved and how India could create a level playing field, according to sources who were part of this discussion. However, the ministry did not get back to the Cabinet. It should have ideally created a roadmap by February 2014. Apart from the issue of non-tariff barriers, the whole ambit of trade relationships would have to be clarified. Since January 2014, Indian and Pakistani soldiers have been killed on the LoC, creating tension and stalling dialogue.

In the National Assembly discussions, the government also said it wasn't aware that the IMF was putting a condition on the MFN to India for the loan it approved for Pakistan. Many members strongly opposed granting the MFN status to India, fearing it would have repercussions in their political constituencies.

A written reply to a question in the National Assembly in September 2013 was full of details. The federal Cabinet, in its meeting held on 2 November 2011, endorsed the efforts of the ministry of commerce for full normalization of trade relations with India and directed the commerce division to complete the process. On 29 February 2012, the Cabinet approved a negative list of 1209 items for import from India, replacing the positive list. The Cabinet also approved, in principle, the phasing out of the negative list by 31 December 2012, subject to creating a level-playing field for Pakistan's exports to Indian markets. However, the ministry could not meet the timeline as it was consulting the government and private sector stakeholders to evaluate the level playing field enjoyed by Pakistani exports to India, the non-tariff barriers being faced by Pakistani exporters and issues of market access of Pakistani products to India. The elimination of the negative list after the approval of the Cabinet would imply the granting of the MFN status to India.

Once India is granted the MFN status, trade costs will be reduced due to availability of raw materials; machinery will be available at cheaper rates, and freight charges will be lowered. This will help give a positive edge to the overall competiveness of Pakistan. Consumers can buy goods at competitive rates, and Pakistan will gain access to a large Indian market. Also, linkages with the Indian market will improve access to better entrepreneurial, marketing, production and distribution practices, the reply said.

In 2009–10, the exports to India stood at $268.332 million and imports $1225.567, while in 2012–13, it was $271.089 million (exports) and $1568.750 million (imports). The government is keen on increasing this substantially. In 2013, Pakistan and India signed three technical agreements and discussed trade in gas and electricity. The agreements on redressal of trade grievances, mutual recognition and customs cooperation will facilitate bilateral business mechanisms and ease issues relating to certification, licensing and lab testing. The two sides agreed to a number of specific steps and timelines for implementing the agreements. However, the question is if there has been any movement on these matters.

The MFN status is not fully realized yet and will continue to remain another thorn in the fraught relations between India and Pakistan. The Sustainable Policy Development Institute produced a paper[30] on the informal trade between the two countries which totted up to $4.2 billion a year, and trade is conducted through informal couriers in a systematic way. Given the large volumes of informal trade, it is in the interest of the Pakistan government to move fast and adopt measures that lead to formalization. Pakistani producers end up competing with items that are not duty paid and are cheaper in the local market. There is also a loss of revenue to the government as these goods are not subjected to usual customs procedures. Food, herbs and pharmaceutical items are not checked for health and safety standards, posing a risk to human health. The key sectors in which informal flow from India is taking place include fruits and vegetables, textiles, automobile parts, jewellery, cosmetics, medicine, tobacco, herbal products, spices and herbs, paper and paper products, as well as crockery. The major routes from where these goods are channelled into Pakistan include Dubai, Kabul, Kandahar, Chaman and Bandar Abbas. The minor routes include several places in the adjoining border region.

As there's a fascination for Indian clothes, I was not surprised to find that in the wholesale markets in Karachi, Lahore and Rawalpindi, there are around 400 shops which are dealing in Indian cloth, fancy suiting and bridal wear. The price of a sari dress ranged from $50–150 and the price of an Indian bridal dress ranged from $800–1600.

The daily turnover in Indian medicine, as reported in Khyber Pakhtunkhwa province and tribal areas on the Afghan border, was $0.15 million, and the daily turnover in Indian medicine reported in Lahore was $15,000. The monthly turnover from spices was reported at $0.7 million, while the monthly turnover from Indian black tea coming through Afghanistan was calculated at $0.1 million. Even betel leaf comes from India, and on an average the monthly consumption of betel leaf was reported at 0.3 million kilograms in Lahore alone, while the monthly turnover in banned items like gutkha and Pan Parag was reported at $0.40 million. There are a number of shops dealing in Indian auto parts in Karachi, Lahore and Rawalpindi. The average monthly turnover of each shop was $0.1 million in Karachi, $0.25 million in Lahore and $0.12 million in Rawalpindi; the market share stood at around 30 per cent. The total annual turnover in tyres was around $243 million and the market share of retreaded Indian tyres locally was around 70 per cent, i.e. $170 million.[31]

The major engine parts are already imported from China, whereas from India, traders are mainly importing gearboxes of different cars through the Wagah–Attari border. The auto parts imported from India were cost effective and better quality compared to China, the study notes. Cosmetics, herbal products and alcohol too were popular, but on the flip side the study finds that the fear expressed by some Pakistanis was justified. This informal trade in items such as auto parts was crippling the local industry, and while granting the MFN status to India, the SDPI said Pakistan should ensure that both tariff and non-tariff barriers came down to a level where formal trade became more attractive.

LoC trade stalled again

The cross-LoC trade between India and Pakistan came to a standstill after a Pakistani driver was arrested for allegedly carrying brown sugar in a consignment of almonds, on 17 January 2014.

When the driver didn't come back, the Pakistan side of the LoC closed entry and trucks were stranded on either side for nearly a fortnight. Pakistan demanded the release of the driver as he could not be arrested since he enjoyed diplomatic immunity, but India refused to budge. Instead of arriving at a mechanism to resolve this impasse, there was much mudslinging and it took nearly a month for the matter to be ironed out, and I am not sure it was to the satisfaction of both parties. Pakistan raised doubts about the media being present during the arrest and it felt the driver could be innocent. Cross-LoC trade began in 2008 at Salamabad in Uri and Chakan da Bagh in Poonch district with two trade facilitation centres, and it was an important CBM. Reporting this incident included putting together a combination of inputs from Srinagar, where *The Hindu's* Ahmed Ali Fayyaz was best placed to file, and New Delhi, and I could only relay what the Pakistan foreign office was saying. A meeting of the Pakistan–India Joint Working Group (JWG) on Cross-LoC CBMs was held in March in New Delhi and the fact that it met after a gap of nearly one and a half years speaks volumes for the priority such mechanisms have. At a briefing on 6 March 2014, the Pakistan foreign office spokesperson said the meeting was constructive, but raised questions over India's jurisdiction and jurisprudence. It wanted the driver's release and said all such matters should be dealt with at the local level.

It was in the second week of February 2014, nearly a month after the driver was held, that Pakistan resumed trade on humanitarian grounds. Before that, the Indian side had already decided to resume bus services every Monday. Trade and movement of people across the LoC were an important way of ensuring peace, but suspicions cannot die overnight. If a driver has been arrested with contraband, then there must be a mechanism to tackle the situation instead of freezing any movement and leaving people in the lurch. Even a relatively simple situation like this took a month to defuse and there was discussion on the need for a joint mechanism for scanning the vehicles and reviewing standard operating procedures. Banking facilities were also important as the trade presently functions on the basis of barter. At least, a joint scanning mechanism was discussed!

The fisherfolk saga

If you are a fisherman from India or Pakistan and stray into each other's waters even by mistake, you can be arrested and jailed. You may never return home alive and if you die in jail, it can take months for your nationality to be verified while your dead body freezes in a morgue. There has been no civilized mechanism to deal with this, typical of the lethargy, red tape and ill will between the two countries. Apart from the proxy war, the visa mess, the other real horror story is how fishermen from both countries suffer.

Karachi is said to be named after a fisherwoman, Mai Kolachi, and its origins lie in the 400-year-old village of Ibrahim Hydari, right on the sea. On the beach, large nets were being repaired and some fishermen hammered out planks for new boats. Its small, winding lanes buzzed with activity, large cooking pots sat outside an eatery, fish was being chopped at another stall, children were doing odd jobs or driving donkey carts. Its 100,000 inhabitants spilled out on the roads and life was busy and colourful. An old cobbler sat in a corner while opposite him there was a boy dipping dupattas into coloured vats. There was much excitement that day we visited in November 2011 since everyone was setting out for a political rally and piling on to trucks and minivans.

But in this bustling fishing village, many families waited for news of their men, without much hope.

When we met Sugra and her mother, Janna, they were airing large colourful *dhurrie*s or *rilli*s outside their shanty with a single cot outside. Sugra, now a teenager, was a three-month-old baby when her father left on a boat, never to return. She and her mother sell rillis for PKR 200 each and also work as domestic help in the housing colonies nearby. They are fed up with curious visitors who take their pictures and go away. Sugra has seen only a photo of her father. The last they heard of him was that he was in an Ahmedabad jail. He has been gone for over seventeen years now. The Pakistan Fisherfolk Forum, formed in 1998, takes up their cause, and over 200 fishermen have been in Indian jails for nearly fourteen to fifteen years. Meanwhile, more than 300 Indian fisherfolk are rotting in Karachi prisons and dying.

Sugra and her mother keep their hopes alive even though people around them say there is no hope of her father, Achar, ever returning. Janna, who seeks refuge in tears and stitching those dhurries, feels that she has become a tamasha and an object of curiosity.

Some of the other women in a nearby village have husbands or relatives in jails for over a decade and they get letters from them once in a while. It is a dire situation. Janna was married for only two years when her husband went missing. She was thrown out of his house and returned to Ibrahim Hydari. Both mother and daughter are illiterate and the first few letters from Achar were read out by a community representative. Every time there was news of fishermen released from India, Janna's hopes would be raised, only to be disappointed. It is incredible that two ostensibly civilized nations cannot deal with this issue in a more humane manner, but in their short history, though there are exceptions, there is little evidence of humaneness. It is ordinary people who have to suffer the indignities of official hostility and paranoia.

Some 300-odd Indian fishermen and crew members were released in August 2013 after intense lobbying. It was also that time when a report 'Fishing in Troubled Water: The Turmoil of Fisherpeople Caught between India and Pakistan', published by Dialogue for Action, an initiative of Programme for Social Action, New Delhi, was released. The issue of fisherfolk being arrested by the Indian Coast Guard and the Maritime Security

Agency of Pakistan dates back to Partition. The number of people arrested almost reached 1000 in the 1990s.

Under the agreement on consular access signed in 2008, both the countries have to give a list of arrested persons of the other country on 1 January and 1 July each year, which is duly being followed. While an economic cooperation agreement aimed at sharing marine resources and the implementation of 'Release at Sea' is a long way off, the report demanded political will from the leadership of India and Pakistan, and a permanent resolution of the Sir Creek issue.

The other pending matter is the need to release the confiscated boats of fishermen from both sides. There are close to 765 Indian boats in Pakistan and around 200 Pakistani boats in India. All the boats from India are owned by the fisherfolk from Gujarat and Diu, with the boats being bought after taking loans. In Karachi, in 2011, Jatin Desai, an Indian journalist and activist, who has been working for the release of fishermen alongside other campaigners, had met Mai Bhagi whose son, son-in-law and two other relatives were arrested in 1999; their boat was also destroyed. She found out that her son-in-law died in 2012 in the Ahmedabad civil hospital; it took twenty-five days for his body to reach Karachi. Similarly, Rambhai Wala, an Indian fisherman, died in Karachi jail and his body was sent back after forty-five days of wrangling.

In February 2014, an Indian fisherman, Bhagwan, died in Karachi's Landhi Jail. He had been arrested a year earlier with fifty-four others by the Maritime Security Agency. After escaping from jail, he was rearrested in December 2013 when a police patrol found him loitering on the streets near the PIB Colony in Gulshan-e-Iqbal in Karachi. He did not have any identity proof and told the police he was a fisherman who had run away from jail. He used to live on the street and eat at charities. He was a drug addict and had escaped to find some drugs. Jail authorities said it was a natural death from a heart attack.

Thirty-five-year-old Bhikha Lakha Shiyal, an Indian fisherman from Garal village of Junagadh district in Gujarat, passed away in Malir Jail in Karachi on 19 December 2013. He and his other colleagues had been arrested on 25 October 2013 when their boat entered Pakistani waters. A month after his death—attributed to asthma—his body was lying at the Edhi Home in Karachi's Sohrab Goth. His nationality had not been verified till the time of his death. Under the agreement on consular access, within three months of arrest, the fisherman should have at least been allowed to meet an Indian official; but then, paperwork is never-ending in our countries. Finally, the Indian high commission verified that he was an Indian. Shiyal's wife had passed away and he had a son and a daughter.

In 2012, Nawaz Ali, a Pakistani fisherman, died in an Ahmedabad hospital. His body reached Pakistan twenty-five days after his death. In July 2013, Dadubhai Makwana, an Indian fisherman from Junagadh district, passed away in Malir Jail. His body came to India after twenty-one days. The arrests continue and the delay too in solving the issue.

While lists of fishermen arrested are exchanged between the two countries, there is an unconscionable delay in ensuring that they are released. Every transgression is treated with suspicion by both sides and innocent people are forced to suffer. But this is an issue that cannot be addressed piecemeal without the main reasons for our inimical relations being resolved.

10

Voice for Missing Balochis

Rose petals welcomed 'Mama' Qadeer Baloch and his small band of marchers on a rainy evening at Faizabad Junction. The next day he would wheel a small cart with framed photographs of the dead young men and women of Balochistan to the Islamabad Press Club. Rose petals covered their faces. The province which was annexed from the erstwhile Kalat state wants freedom from Pakistan, and the army has been repeatedly crushing the so-called miscreants there in large numbers. The young men are insurgents or rebels depending on which side you are on, and the Pakistan government is fairly convinced that India has a role to play in fomenting trouble in this massive province bordering Iran, and has submitted a dossier to this effect to the UN. The excuse for the many detention camps, and torture and the army being sent out to crush rebellion is fear of another secession. Pakistan is clear that India is doing what it did to support the Mukti Bahini in the war for Bangladesh all over again. The popular belief is that Balochistan and its aspirations are being melded by a RAW conspiracy to unsettle Pakistan. And the arrest in 2016 of Kulbhushan Jadhav, who, the Pakistanis alleged, was an agent of RAW, was shown as proof that its charges were right. I was repeatedly asked on TV about India's role in Balochistan—

it is a recurring theme in the pantheon of accusations. I tried to tell people that I wasn't sending agents into Balochistan and that I worked for an independent newspaper which was not the government. But conveniently, my Indian-ness would morph into being a representative of my government when it suited some, while otherwise I would be just another ordinary Indian to be loved or hated.

The turmoil in Balochistan is often compared to Kashmir. If I as an Indian wrote about Balochistan and its situation and/or interviewed a person like Mama Qadeer, then why didn't I write about the freedom or azadi aspirations of Kashmir and its freedom fighters? If I didn't, I was given to understand that I had no right to write on Balochistan. But we are getting ahead of the story. It was Geo TV anchor Hamid Mir who first compared 'Mama' Qadeer Baloch to Mahatma Gandhi. In fact, Qadeer's arduous exercise was inspired by Gandhi's 390-kilometre Dandi march, only he walked longer than Gandhi—the distance from Quetta to Islamabad is about 3300 kilometres. The cause was just as searing. It was a long march to the capital to demand justice for the thousands of missing persons in Balochistan. Death threats, generous bribes and attacks did not deter Qadeer who founded the Voice for Baloch Missing Persons in 2009, and his small band of followers. He was seventy-two then (March 2014) and the youngest marcher was eleven-year-old Ali Haider.

In the morning when Qadeer started from the Faizabad Junction near Islamabad, the roadside was full of young Baloch men wearing kerchiefs across their faces. If identified, they could be picked up for questioning or worse. Eagle-eyed spooks and police were everywhere and I thought at one point they would outnumber the marchers. I was to see some of them at the site of the suicide bombing in the district court. The march was unique in many ways. It highlighted the problem of the detention camps, and the demands of the people whose family members were missing were amazing—they wanted the UN and even the

NATO to come to their rescue, apart from independence for the province. It looked a little out of proportion at first but they seemed determined, and later, they did meet representatives of the UN and the EU in the capital.

The cases that Qadeer filed led to the Supreme Court establishing that it was the security agencies—the ISI, the Frontier Corps and the military intelligence—that picked up the young men and women. There have been so many orders to produce the missing persons but no one does anything. The security forces defy the orders and it is of no use, Qadeer said. For instance, in the case of one of the marchers, Farzana, the court had ordered her brother, Zakir, to be produced in court. He was picked up in 2009 and his whereabouts were unknown. The twenty-six-year-old was a student leader of a Baloch group, and the family did once get a message from another person who had been released from a detention camp that he was there. But later, there was no news about him.

Farzana said her toenails fell off and she lost weight during the march. A holder of a master's degree in biochemistry with another master's in Baloch literature, her life was disrupted after Zakir was picked up by security agencies some years ago. Among the marchers were nine young women and three children, all of whom have a member of their family missing.

The walk was the least gruelling experience, as another young participant told me. I spoke to them when they were camping outside the Karachi Press Club in December 2013 after walking 700 kilometres. Sixteen-year-old Sammi's father was picked up from a hospital four years ago. She could march again if it meant bringing her father back, she said. Her family was in penury. But the real dread is that many of the missing persons could be dead. People are picked up by security agencies and many of them don't come back for ten years; sometimes they never do; and their bodies are dumped here and there with slips of paper in their pockets.

Most of the children who took part in the protest, like Samina, a seventh-class student, and her younger brother, Ali Haider, had left school to take part in the protest. Their father, Mohammed Ramzan, was missing. During the march, people would abuse and threaten them, and in some instances some people even fired at them from moving vehicles. A truck hit two of the supporters, injuring them.

Qadeer said he had requested a meeting with the UN working group when it visited Balochistan in 2012. 'We were invited to meet them in Islamabad and we decided to walk the over 3000 kilometres from Quetta in a bid to highlight our situation and seek UN intervention,' he said. The group set out on 27 October 2013, and would cover forty kilometres a day; finally, it took them 100 days to get to the capital. Mohammed Ali Talpur, a senior activist, who was part of the march from Karachi, said that this was a message of defiance to the government and by bringing the march to the heart of the establishment, the people of Balochistan wanted to publicize their plight.

I walked with Qadeer from the Faizabad Junction as he said he could give me an interview on the way. There were many people vying for that and my turn came just before we reached Islamabad. Garlanded with roses and wearing a traditional cap, Qadeer, a former bank employee, was friendly and told me he wanted to visit India, a wish that was granted just when I was leaving. He has documented over 19,200 cases of missing persons and recovered 2006 bodies. The issue of missing persons began in 1947 when Balochistan was forced to join Pakistan after it was freed from the Kalat state, he said. His thirty-year-old son Jalil Reki was picked up because he was the Baloch Republican Party's (BRP) central information secretary. His body was dumped in a village bordering Iran. His son's death fired his zeal to set things right and he founded this organization dedicated to focus on the tragedy of the people in Balochistan, wracked by struggles for independence, counter-insurgency, terrorism and action by security forces. He said it was the intelligence agencies who killed his son because they called and said so to someone who was with him at that time. His grandson, too, was part of the march.

In 2012, his organization filed two cases in the Supreme Court on the missing persons; the petitions asked for these persons to be produced in court. He said the conditions in the detention centres were terrible. People could not even stretch their legs, the rooms were tiny, and the prisoners were blindfolded. And in some of the bodies that the group recovered, there were holes drilled in the legs. He said there were also bodies with the vital organs removed. Sana Sangat, a senior leader of the Baloch Students Organization (Azad) who later joined the BRP, was pumped with twenty-eight bullets. And there were women missing from the Marri and Bugti tribes. They had been kidnapped so that pressure could be put on their families to make sure their sons didn't join the various Baloch groups. Among those documented as missing, there were about 170 women. In one instance, a schoolteacher, a mother of a one-year-old son, was picked up. At times, children, too, were taken away.

In another case, after much insistence, the government produced before the Supreme Court some among the thirty-five missing persons who had been reportedly detained at the Malakand internment centre. But none from Balochistan were produced despite court orders. The government had earlier admitted that two among those thirty-five were dead.

According to a 2012 report of the Human Rights Commission of Pakistan's fact-finding mission titled 'Hopes, Fears and Alienation in Balochistan', Balochistan is Pakistan's largest province, its least populous and the most troubled. The most dominant feature of the province is a violent insurgency in the Baloch majority districts that started in 2006 after the killing of Nawab Akbar Bugti in a military operation. From the year 2000 till 2012, the HRCP recorded 198 missing persons from

Balochistan. It also gathered evidence of fifty-seven bodies, some of them unidentified, that were found in the same province.

I met an activist, a former professor, who told me about 'things' happening in Balochistan. Young boys, it seems, were allegedly pressured by Indian agents to go across the border for arms training and they were given lots of money. I was not in a position to verify any of this as it was in Quetta. She, too, had to move out to the capital for her safety and was very critical of India. If this is true, then proxy war is the motto of the two countries and both bleed each other slowly. A grievous tit-for-tat situation.

I honestly don't know if Qadeer is a RAW agent, but the fact remains that young men are missing, there are detention centres and dead bodies are surfacing with great regularity. The highest court in the land has established the wrongdoing and yet its orders are repeatedly flouted. Once, Qadeer called me to say he was going to India. And he called me again the day before I left in May. The spooks didn't leave my side that last day, suspecting a conspiracy; anyway, I didn't have the time to meet him. Alas!

It was after my interview with Qadeer, carried on the op-ed page of *The Hindu* in March 2014, that I was summoned for a grilling at the external publicity office for an hour. Without my asking, Qadeer had denied he was funded by the RAW. (This was one of the sentences highlighted in yellow when I was questioned by the external publicity official.) He said families contributed money and there was no reason to seek funds. Now the tricky quote which became the headline for the interview: 'After I formed my organisation I got a lot of support from people. If there is a referendum in Balochistan, people will vote for independence.' Are you sure, I asked him, a little surprised. He nodded vehemently. The interview with Qadeer was not a secret, subversive activity on my part. I was among the many journalists who walked with him after he entered Islamabad and that was the only time he agreed to give me an interview. In any case, he did say this to others before me, so I didn't see the need for this grilling. The official's take was that I should be writing on art and culture and not on political movements. Did I write on Kashmir, for instance, he snarled at me over tea, which was meant to soften the blow.

I felt they really didn't want Indian correspondents unless we stayed within some harmless plugs or press release writing limits. The officer hadn't read the whole article except for the part where Qadeer denies he is a RAW agent as is popularly believed. All the portions which they found unwholesome were highlighted in bright yellow and thrust under my nose. The dialogue went on these lines: 'Is this what you came here to write?' He accused me of fudging the entire interview and he kept asking me for my notes or recording. I was quite alarmed and hid my notes after I went home. My integrity was in question and the official was crude and nasty. I told him when I was invited to cover the Mohenjo Daro festival, his office didn't respond to my request to go there and that all my requests to travel and write on art and culture were met with radio silence. In Islamabad what art and culture I could write on had already been covered by me. I had by then interviewed Abida Parveen, and written a detailed feature on Haroon the creator of the immensely popular cartoon series Burka Avenger. He then asked me whether I had written on Kashmir and if I supported the Kashmiri movement, and so on. He said it would be difficult to process my visa extension if I did stories like this which was a deliberate attempt to malign the country. He raked up every unpleasant thing he could and it went on in this vein for some time. His subordinate officer whom we usually dealt with later said that Balochistan was an extremely sensitive issue and it usually upset the government no end. It's a paranoia not restricted to Indians, and Carlotta Gall from the *New York Times* was punched in the face and her computer, notebooks and cellphone were taken away in Quetta in 2006.[1]

With the baggage of India's role in East Pakistan, Pakistan constantly harped on India 'destabilizing' Balochistan by funding and supporting the insurgents. Indian journalists were seen as RAW agents, and so this article on 'Mama Baloch' was a no-no. I had gone for a talk given by the author Ayesha Jalal at the Quaid-i-Azam University where she warned the audience about treating the Baloch issue the way matters in East Pakistan were dealt with. She said, 'The lessons of 1971 centred on secession versus power sharing . . . You cannot accuse people who want a share of power at the centre as secessionist or treasonable and by doing so we will go the 1971 way. Power sharing has eluded us over and over again.'

It's a signal warning that is going unheeded; yet, all that matters is whether India and its agents (journalists included) are trying to destabilize Balochistan or infiltrate the TTP.

Some of my Pakistani friends also privately wondered why I had written it and said there was no need for the paper to have highlighted it. I was quite puzzled by this attitude. Correspondents before me had gone to Quetta and written about issues there and there have been phone calls in protest. But they had not been expelled. I knew then, more or less, that it would be difficult to report from this country with all these dos and don'ts. I also told this official that I had written so many positive stories on the country, and how come they were not highlighted in yellow and shoved under my nose? I didn't tell him I knew for a fact that one of my stories was similarly highlighted but in appreciation, and that he had not called me in to praise me then! I realized it was only the so-called 'unpopular' or critical stuff that stayed with them and with most people I knew. However, on this count, even Pakistani journalists were not spared. I spoke to journalists who admitted that the security agencies had asked them not to cover the long march or give publicity to Qadeer.

I really had no intention of courting trouble, nor was it an attempt to destabilize Pakistan, but few believed me. I got a lot of emails appreciating the interview, including from Balochis, which made me feel a little better. Here was a man who marched over 3000 kilometres to draw attention to a serious crisis; it was a great story and I felt it had to be written. Qadeer met the UN and EU officials and demanded NATO intervention to resolve the problem, which was rather brazen. I told the official it was an interview, and I was only reporting it. Nowhere had I said Balochistan must be made an independent state. He couldn't understand or was obtuse about the entire issue. The grilling ended badly; he was a state-of-the-art people shredder.

Epilogue

An Inky Farewell

To enter Faisal Mosque you have to deposit everything you have—mobiles, handbags, cameras, shoes. I had always meant to go inside, but since it was so close to home, I left it for later. I didn't think my visit would happen soon. Both Snehesh, the Press Trust of India's correspondent in Islamabad, and I were having dinner at a friend's when we got the calls. It was a little after 9 p.m. when our usual point man at the external publicity office phoned me first to say that my visa was not going to be extended and I would have to leave in a week. The formal letter would be delivered to my house the next day. He didn't give me a reason. Soon, Snehesh too got the same call. I had expected this sooner or later but when it finally happened, I was annoyed. There was a furious discussion on why this had happened and Snehesh and I listed out our thoughts. My Baloch story was dragged in and other things, and my friends, who were shocked—one of them knew this was to be—tried to commiserate. We rationalized that even nine months in Islamabad wasn't so bad and joked that even a week was a long time in Pakistan.

The kind friend took us out for ice cream; it was the first time we had been out so late on the street. Later we drove to Faisal Mosque, empty of the multitudes and lit by the stars. There was no one in sight. The broad marble steps were chilly under my feet and we climbed up to a massive hall. It was a memorably inky farewell to our nine-month sojourn in the capital. The white minarets glowed in the darkness and the mosque, built on the lines of a spaceship, looked beautiful for once.

The expected letter didn't come the next day though news had spread of our expulsion. There was much speculation about what had happened and the blame game had begun. After a few days when the letter still hadn't come, I spoke to the then head of external publicity, Imran Gardezi, a genial sort of a man. He told me to start packing and said the letter would be delivered shortly. I asked him about future correspondents, since that was the main worry. He said yes, they would be welcome. He agreed to give me a week to leave and I asked permission to leave via Karachi for Mumbai. The rule book says you can only go back the way you came and I didn't see any point in going to New Delhi and the longer route for me via the Wagah border.

Almost everyone I knew back in India was relieved that I was coming back. My friends in Islamabad said I was going back home and it was not such a big deal to be expelled. The visa was not renewed after January 2014, but suddenly the machinery woke up with great alacrity to give us a few days legitimacy in May to return. In a way, I was so glad I wouldn't have to fill more forms for a visa renewal or visit that dank office with its smelly corridors. The external publicity office had its faults but its staff were again nice—tea, biscuits and sympathy were on offer. But they were also puppets doing a job.

With little time left, I went up to visit the Pakistan Monument, located on a little rise above the city. It was Musharraf's idea to showcase the country in a pinkish tableau—a huge lotus with four petals and carvings symbolizing the distinctive provinces of the country. There was a garden of sorts around it and a museum. You could see a lot of the city from the top and the view was worth it. There is nothing that had any history in the capital and the monument perhaps sought to fill that lacuna in a way. But still it was too modern for me. The museums charged extra for foreigners and I paid it, though once at Lok Virsa, the man at the counter was surprised since he thought I was a Pakistani. I told him I was an Indian and he shrugged as if it meant the same thing.

I also made a quick trip to the Bari Imam mausoleum which was under repair. I would often pass the mosque with its shining green domes. Small boys stood outside the barricade selling bright blue plastic bags and there was a row of sweet vendors with orange laddoos. Inside, there was a separate area for women to enter and soon I was besieged with them asking me where I was from. There were the usual smiles of welcome and I can't say it didn't make me feel good, especially since I had less than a week left in the capital. As much of the mosque was under repair, I was allowed to enter briefly into the main hall which was a mess of scaffolding, cans of paint and bamboos propped up everywhere.

In the last few days, more than earlier, the spooks harassed all those who met me and asked for their identity cards. Some of them shouted right back and once outside a restaurant, the traffic was held up thanks to my host refusing to part with his identity card. I was really proud of my friends—they stood up for me and were brave enough to take me out for dinner and meet me despite all this.

I had just paid another year's rent when the news came and I had to call my landlord who was equally taken aback. The packers were efficient and soon the house felt cavernous, emptied of most furniture. My editor asked me to sell everything, including the car, three days before I left on 18 May 2014, and I managed with a day remaining. I found that it was easier than I thought to sell almost anything there. From morning, strangers would wander through the house asking me the price of things and soon I got quite fed up. I had already sold the fridge but a woman who was related to someone's driver came and created a scene and said if she didn't have that fridge, her children would die of thirst that summer. I caved in and gave it to her. She had even brought the money along. My neighbour complained that I hadn't informed her and she would have bought stuff. Anyway, there was a helpful young man at China Market who inspected everything and we decided on a price. We had driven past this flea market kind of place once and since I had no help to do things, my husband suggested I find someone there. He was enterprising and even got someone to buy my car. The buyer was in a big hurry to change the Indian-tainted number plate which began with 27, so I was without a vehicle when I needed it the most.

The spooks stationed outside my house in a last bid to harass people who were going in and out even stopped Sajida while she went off with a tempo-load of stuff. One of my friends came to pick me up for our farewell party and she still remembers that scene of the vehicle full of furniture and knick-knacks, leaving with Sajida sitting in the front—the drama was lost on me then, I was too busy clearing stuff. Beard would be pompously scribbling notes about everyone who came out of the house and when I looked out, he would duck into the trees. I did manage, though, to take my second picture of the man. He finally had something to do and found all this very satisfying. He had a permanent sneer, and looked quite triumphant questioning people who came to my house and, I suspect, writing down the vehicle numbers.

The tempo driver wanted the cold drinks in my fridge and some bed sheets which I let him have. He said his children would be thrilled and the prospect delighted me. I joked that if I wasn't careful, they would have taken me away and found some use for it. I had to leave a few things behind which I was using till the last minute and all I could carry was a suitcase. A little before I had to leave for the airport my suitcase key broke and I had to take a cab to find a Samsonite duplicate which I finally found in a market after searching in many places. I later found out that the spooks hiding behind a tree near my house had told the driver to charge me the earth since I was an Indian. The key didn't work and it was finally my broken one which opened the lock minutes before I had to leave. As if that wasn't enough, the airport security made me open the bags to check on some suspicious object which surfaced in the X-ray—it was an umbrella. The cab I hired to take me to the airport was also told to overcharge me, but he said he couldn't since it was metered. He knew I was an Indian being sent away. It was the spooks' last stand—to be vicious and unkind, for no reason really other than that I was an Indian. They even followed me to the money changer which they hadn't done before. In that small room I found Beard sitting on the only wooden bench, trying to hide behind a newspaper.

Their pettiness was in contrast to the taxi driver—he asked me not to be put off by these men and this government, and that I should have good feelings about Pakistan, as it had nice people like him! I laughed and said I believed that. So, that's how I left the Land of the Pure, with a comfortable overnight stay in Karachi where no one hounded me—at least, I didn't see anyone breathing down my neck. The airport was welcoming and the officials let me out to change my money even after I had passed the security check area. One of them looked at my visa stamp and his eyebrows went up in admonition. 'It's your last day here, madam,' he said. If only he knew, I sighed to myself. I bought some fridge stickers with my remaining Pakistani money, including one of Faisal Mosque, before I boarded the short flight home.

There was much outrage that two Indian journalists were sent back suddenly from Pakistan and I got many calls from people wanting to do stories even before I left. We were in the news for all the wrong reasons. Briefly, I became a minor celebrity of sorts after returning from Islamabad with the tag of 'expelled Indian correspondent', and to my embarrassment, many people congratulated me for being thrown out of Pakistan, so much for that warm feeling and 'Aman ki Asha'. I was on a TV show where the anchor loudly proclaimed I was the expelled journalist from Pakistan. To my embarrassment that became a tag line to introduce me—oh, she was thrown out of Pakistan! My landlord in New Delhi said he was proud of me; I had not realized that to be thrown out of Islamabad would be a badge of honour. For a while I became some kind of an expert on Pakistan and made some TV appearances. Thankfully, this has died down, though I was called on by a TV channel to comment on Sabeen Mahmud's tragic killing in 2015.

The sudden decision to send us back was disruptive to say the least and I wanted to put it behind me. My new job as the environment correspondent in New Delhi kept me busy enough. Many people asked me how it was to live in Islamabad and said that I should write about it. That is one of the reasons for this book. I didn't think it was the Baloch article that got me expelled—it could have been just about anything. We were caught in the crosshairs of official antipathy to Indians and some cheap brinkmanship, and I understood then that democratic forces could only protest, they had no real voice anywhere. Later, I read about the trial and execution of Bhutto with great interest. It showed how the state could completely fabricate a case against none other than a former prime minister and have him executed in the dead of night. It was as if he had never lived or led the country. The trauma that his family was put through and his own treatment as a prisoner spoke volumes about the institutions in Pakistan.

Even in Islamabad, friends had asked me what I had done to be expelled and I really didn't have any answer because I didn't know the reason. So, after both Snehesh and I were asked to leave by 18 May 2014, both sides had no journalists from each other's countries. It was also made out as if future correspondents to replace us would be waved in to the country post-haste. Of course, the Pakistan authorities while accusing us of spying and unfriendly activities had every right to do exactly that.

I should have expected some stories in the Pakistani press about how we were expelled for carrying out 'unfriendly activities' apart from 'activities incompatible with our professional mandate' which was utter nonsense. Whatever these activities were remained undefined, and some reports in the Indian press also made out that we were spies or something on those lines—the basis for this was that we were close to Indian diplomats! To think we had refused—because it was unprofessional—the request from an Indian official to let them know what stories we were filing every day or send copies of stories to them! Apart from these canards planted in the media that we were spies, we had nothing in writing to explain the sudden end to the posting.

Journalists are a critical force; they are not public relations managers; and being posted in another country gives you an opportunity to assess the situation through a magnifying lens and write presciently. That cannot be construed as spying or unfriendly activity. The press in Pakistan has been highly critical of the situation too and they have suffered for that, but some were quick to publish stories which insinuated we were in the wrong. Privately, many people expressed shock and dismay but I didn't see any violent protests in the media there over our expulsion. It wasn't an important issue in the midst of so much blood and terror.

A lot of unnecessary energy has been wasted in the subcontinent by the two countries, and journalists have sometimes been at the receiving end. Before I left for Islamabad, one of the Pakistan high commission officials had told me, 'You have to go with an open mind.' I did, but I was dealing with closed minds out there and that became evident when my visa was not renewed and I was given a week to return. I agree that worse could have happened and one must be grateful for small mercies.

Everyone from the Committee to Protect Journalists, to the press clubs of Mumbai and Delhi, and various organizations both in Pakistan and India, and the Indian ministry of external affairs protested and issued statements, and even if these didn't have any effect, at least they stood up for us. Except for a network of which

I was a founder member and in which I had invested a lot of energy—the Network of Women in Media—which didn't think it was important to raise a protest or even issue a statement in my support.

After Declan Walsh was expelled from Pakistan, the *New York Times* had kept up pressure to reinstate him, and even after the house of its correspondent was searched in Islamabad in 2016, they had protested. My paper was more worried about sending another person, and later after I returned, the then editor, Malini Parthasarathy, didn't allow me to write about a blasphemy issue I had tracked, saying that it was articles like this that had got me out of there. I realized for the first time that I had wasted time trying to file different stories; maybe if I had stuck to press releases, life would have been smoother. However, *The Hindu* did publish almost all of my articles while I was there and Parthasarathy even encouraged me to write a farewell piece after I returned.

The media anywhere, not just in India and Pakistan, but especially in these two countries, has to function in a free atmosphere and using the power of expulsion is arbitrary and imperious. More journalists need to be stationed in each other's countries but it cannot be on restrictive terms—the price for being there cannot be that you are held prisoner in one city with no access to travel, with clods breathing down your neck and suspicion about everything you do. The continuing atmosphere of paranoia cannot die down unless you take a rational approach that journalism is not spying and journalists do not travel to each other's countries for espionage. Each story that you do is not an attempt to denigrate the country but to show up aspects of life and tell stories about people and their lives which is the essence of journalism. As long as governments and establishments control movements across the borders and decide what is kosher in terms of reportage, and have no accountability to anyone, journalists can only protest and defy these norms. That Pakistan was carved out from India and the paranoia that India will always attempt to wreck Pakistan is visible even in the textbooks which are drilling this into children's vulnerable minds. General A.A.K. Niazi in his book *The Betrayal of East Pakistan*[1] talks of the Agartala conspiracy not being a fabricated story to implicate Sheikh Mujibur Rahman. He writes that Indian intelligence activities in East Pakistan had started with the inception of Pakistan. And that they were actively aided by the Hindus settled in East Pakistan. This, Niazi said, has been confirmed by Asoka Raina in his book *Inside RAW: The Story of India's Secret Service*.[2] Every time I had been invited to be a participant in a TV discussion in Islamabad, the very friendly—and mischievous—PTV anchors would suddenly pop the Baloch question out of nowhere and then claim later that I had wriggled out of it. I had to keep telling them that I was not a representative of the Indian government and was an independent journalist working for a newspaper which had no government affiliations. It was an obsession that India is destroying Pakistan once again. I actually heard a question at the foreign office briefing when someone asked if Prime Minister Sharif had said that India and the RAW were responsible for the bombing at the F-8 sector district court in March 2014. The spokesperson flatly denied that the PM had said anything to that effect.

At one level, we, as journalists, function in a quasi or total government mode. While reporting on Kargil, I heard one celebrity Indian journalist say she felt patriotic standing on the LoC, and it was difficult to contain one's passions when one's soldiers were being killed on the front.

When it came to India and Pakistan, we must necessarily let our feelings of jingoism triumph over truth and forgo any rational understanding of events. So, if Indian journalists are expelled, they must obviously be spies. That is patriotism for you, exercised to the fullest in both countries.

There is little change in any understanding between the two countries and the blame game continues with renewed strength. Yet at different levels, from diplomacy down to the common people, there is a call for peace and reason, however faint it may be, and it is coming from an invisible majority which is yet to come into its own. For the ordinary people of the two countries to smash this iron curtain of paranoia and emerge triumphant as true democracies where cooperation and not collateral damage is the norm, may be inevitable, as some have said, but it is certainly taking its time.

In a speech in 1949 on foreign policy, Nehru said, 'There is also no doubt in my mind that it is inevitable for India and Pakistan to have close relations—very close relations—sometime or the other in the future. I cannot state when this will take place, but situated as we are, with all our past, we cannot be really indifferent to each other. We can either be rather hostile to each other or very friendly with each other. Ultimately, we can only be really very friendly, whatever period of hostility may intervene in between.'[3] We seem to be at the 'rather hostile' stage for the longest time.

Like boxers warily circling each other and sometimes jabbing powerfully, but yet to deliver that knockout punch (thankfully—as we are both nuclear powers, and that would mean extinction), the two countries refuse to leave the ring. Ordinary people, the spectators in this game, pay the price.

Notes

Preface

1. Imran Fazal, 'Laden Nagar, Chhota Pak in Nalasopara', http://www.dnaindia.com/mumbai/report-laden-nagar-chhota-pak-in-nalasopara-1784060. Accessed on 26 January 2016.
2. TADA court order, 12 September 2006, http://www.satp.org/satporgtp/countries/india/database/mumbai_blasts_judgement.htm.
3. http://parliamentofindia.nic.in/ls/lsdeb/ls10/ses6/0521049301.htm.
4. Meena Menon, *Riots and After in Mumbai* (New Delhi: Sage, 2012).
5. 'Kargil "misadventure", was "stab" in Atal Vajpayee's back: Nawaz Sharif', 18 February, 2016, http://economictimes.indiatimes.com/news/defence/kargil-misadventure-was-stab-in-atal-vajpayees-back-nawaz-sharif/articleshow/51035959.cms.
6. Raj Chengappa, 'The Kargil War—in search of the truth', 10 February 2013, http://www.tribuneindia.com/2013/20130210/ground.htm.
7. Christophe Jaffrelot, *The Pakistan Paradox: Instability and Resilience* (Gurgaon: Penguin Random House India, 2015).
8. Krishna Kumar, *Prejudice and Pride: School Histories of the Freedom Struggle in India and Pakistan* (New Delhi: Viking, 2001), 3.

Chapter 1: Oh, for a Visa!

1. Piloo Mody, *Zulfi My Friend* (New Delhi: Thomson Press, 1973), 148.

2. Sonup Sahadevan, 'Karan Johar on Ae Dil Hai Mushkil controversy: I will not work with Pakistani talent in future', http://indianexpress.com/article/entertainment/bollywood/karan-johar-breaks-his-silence-i-will-not-work-with-pakistani-talent-in-future-ae-dil-hai-mushkil-3089881/.
3. Mohammad Ayub Khan, *Friends, Not Masters: A Political Autobiography* (Oxford: Oxford University Press, 1967), 12.
4. Khurshid Mahmud Kasuri, *Neither a Hawk Nor a Dove* (Gurgaon: Penguin Random House India, 2015).

Chapter 2: Islamabad, Unreal City

1. Ahmed Rashid, *Taliban: Militant Islam, Oil and Fundamentalism in Central Asia* (New Haven: Yale University Press, 2010), 192.
2. Mohammad Ayub Khan, *Friends, Not Masters* (London: Oxford University Press, 1967).
3. Ibid., 96.
4. Piloo Mody, *Zulfi My Friend* (New Delhi: Thomson Press, 1973), 82–83.
5. Arshad H. Abbasi, Fareeha Mehmood, Ayesha Wasti, Maha Kamal and Zohra Fatima, *Rethinking Pakistan's Energy Equation: Iran–Pakistan Gas Pipeline* (Islamabad: SDPI, 2013).
6. Hector Bolitho, *Jinnah: Creator of Pakistan* (Karachi: Oxford University Press, 2006—first printed in 1954 by John Murray).
7. Piloo Mody, *Zulfi My Friend* (New Delhi: Thomson Press, 1973), 64.
8. A.O. Mitha, *Unlikely Beginnings: A Soldier's Life* (Karachi: Oxford University Press, Karachi, second impression, 2007).
9. Ayesha Siddiqa, *Military Inc.: Inside Pakistan's Military Economy* (London: Pluto Press, 2007).
10. A.O. Mitha, *Unlikely Beginnings: A Soldier's Life* (Oxford University Press, Karachi, second impression, 2007).

Chapter 3: On Being a Foreign Correspondent

1. MFN is a status or level of treatment given by one state to another in terms of international trade—by way of lower tariffs on imported goods or high import quotas.

2. Dilip Mukerjee, *Zulfiqar Ali Bhutto: Quest for Power* (New Delhi: Vikas Publishing House, 1972), 169.
3. Kuldip Nayar, *Distant Neighbours: A Tale of the Subcontinent* (New Delhi: Vikas Publishing House, 1972), 213–14.
4. Ibid., 214.
5. Piloo Mody, *Zulfi, My Friend* (New Delhi: Thomson Press, 1973), 18
6. Raza Rumi, *Delhi by Heart: Impressions of a Pakistani Traveller* (New Delhi: HarperCollins, 2012).
7. Sartaj Aziz, *Between Dreams and Realities: Some Milestones in Pakistan's History* (Karachi: Oxford University Press, 2009).
8. The release of Mullah Abdul Ghani Baradar was criticized by the Afghan government saying he was being kept a prisoner. Pakistani officials kept denying this and said he was a free man and could go anywhere. But the fact remained he was still in Pakistan, reportedly in safe custody and drugged. So the AHPC really couldn't get much out of him when they met him. Baradar, a close associate of Mullah Omar and once the second in command of the Afghan Taliban, was freed in September 2013, to help in the peace negotiations with the Taliban. He was arrested in 2010 by the ISI after the agency found out that he had been mediating between the Afghan President Hamid Karzai's brother and the Taliban without its knowledge a year earlier. In Ahmed Rashid's *Pakistan on the Brink* (Gurgaon: Penguin Random House India, 2012), 114–15.
9. Aitzaz Ahsan, *The Indus Saga* (New Delhi: Roli Books, 2005).
10. Victoria Schofield, *Bhutto: Trial and Execution* (London: Cassell, 1979), 178.
11. Pamela Constable, *Fragments of Grace: My Search for Humanity from Kashmir to Kabul* (Lahore: Vanguard Books, 2004).

Chapter 4: Covering Terrorism

1. Since Ahmadis are not legally considered Muslims, they cannot invoke the name of Allah in any form.
2. Saba Imtiaz, 'Pakistani Police Investigate Fire at Christian TV Station', *New York Times*, 26 November 2015.
3. For a good analysis of the Ahmadi issue as well as the Munir Kayani report on the 1953 anti-Ahmadi violence, please see Ali Usman

Qasmi's *The Ahmadis and the Politics of Religious Exclusion* (London: Anthem Press, 2015).

4. 'The National Assembly of Pakistan Debates Official Report', 30 June 1974 and 7 September 1974.
5. 'The National Assembly of Pakistan Debates Official Report', 30 June 1974.
6. 'The National Assembly of Pakistan Debates Official Report', 7 September 1974.
7. Ibid.
8. Ibid.
9. Ibid.
10. Victoria Schofield, *Bhutto: Trial and Execution* (London: Cassell, 1979), 178
11. 'State of Religious Freedom in Pakistan', Jinnah Institute, 2016.
12. Dilip Mukerjee, *Zulfiqar Ali Bhutto: Quest for Power* (New Delhi: Vikas Publishing House, 1972), 170.
13. A.O. Mitha, *Unlikely Beginnings: A Soldier's Life* (Karachi: Oxford University Press, 2007), 229–30.
14. Khaled Ahmed, *Sectarian War: Pakistan's Sunni–Shia Violence and Its Links to the Middle East* (Karachi: Oxford University Press, second impression, 2013), 7.
15. Ibid., 9.
16. *Diaries of Field Marshal Mohammad Ayub Khan 1966–1972.* Edited and annotated by Craig Baxter (Karachi: Oxford University Press, 2013), 115–16.
17. Gordon Fraser, *Cosmic Anger: Abdus Salam—The First Muslim Nobel Scientist*, Kindle edition, location 4933.
18. Adil Najam, 'Salam Abdus Salam', http://www.thenews.com.pk/Todays-News-9-228553-Salam-Abdus-Salam. Viewed on 26 November 2015.
19. 'Salaam Abdus Salam', http://www.dawn.com/news/674855/salaam-abdus-salam.
20. Gordon Fraser, *Cosmic Anger: Abdus Salam—The First Muslim Nobel Scientist*, Kindle edition.
21. Gordon Fraser, *Cosmic Anger: Abdus Salam—The First Muslim Nobel Scientist*, Kindle edition, location 4912.
22. Computerized National Identity Card is an identity card issued by Pakistan's National Database and Registration Authority.

23. 'State of Religious Freedom in Pakistan', Jinnah Institute, 2016.
24. Ehsan Rehan, 'US Mosque Hosts Celebration In Honor of Pakistani Killer', https://www.rabwah.net/us-mosque-hosts-celebration-honor-pakistani-killer/.
25. 'Religious Minorities in Elections: Equal in Law, Not in Practice', Human Rights Commission of Pakistan, 2013.
26. 'We have suffered 60,000 casualties in this war. This includes 10,000 security personnel. According to the last economic survey, the economic losses so far have been 110 billion US dollars.' From the press briefing of the PM's adviser on national security, Sartaj Aziz, on 26 May 2016.
27. Ahmed Rashid, *Taliban: The Story of the Afghan Warlords* (London: Pan Books, 2001), 93.
28. 'Strategic depth' has been described as the distance between the frontlines or battle sectors and the combatant's capital cities, core industrial areas, military installations, heartlands and population centres. Assessing 'strategic depth' is related to how vulnerable all these are to an offensive, and whether the military can withdraw into its own territory, absorbing the thrust and then enable its own counteroffensive. (Lt. Gen. Prakash Katoch, 23 June 2014, indiandefencereview.com.)
29. Mohammed Yunus, *Persons, Passions and Politics* (New Delhi: Vikas Publishing House, 1980), 6.
30. Aamir Khan, 'Ajmal Kasab "never asked" for mutton biryani, I cooked it up: Ujjwal Nikam', http://indianexpress.com/article/cities/mumbai/kasab-never-asked-for-mutton-biryani-i-cooked-it-up-ujjwal-nikam/.
31. Imran Gabol, 'Govt issues order to place JuD chief Hafiz Saeed under house arrest', https://www.dawn.com/news/1311671.
32. 'India Presses Pakistan to Re-investigate 26/11 Mumbai Attack and Put Hafiz Saeed on Trial', http://www.ndtv.com/india-news/india-presses-pakistan-to-re-investigate-26-11-mumbai-attack-and-put-hafiz-saeed-on-trial-1665060.
33. A covert Pakistani intelligence operation to topple Benazir Bhutto's government in 1989.
34. Syed Irfan Raza, 'Cabinet approves steps for FATA's merger with Khyber Pakhtunkhwa', https://www.dawn.com/news/1318095/cabinet-approves-steps-for-fatas-merger-with-khyber-pakhtunkhwa.

35. I used to go to the court often and being such a small room, I stood out being the only woman. Finally the judge called me in and asked what I wanted. I said I needed the case details and he instructed his clerk to show me the FIR, and he translated it for me as it was in Urdu. Of course, I told him I was an Indian journalist and he was welcoming and helpful. Most judges in India would have thrown me out. As an Indian, I was shown this special courtesy but I didn't see any reporter who I recognized in court during my vigil.
36. Pakistan reported 306 WPV cases in 2014 (compared to ninety-three in 2013), which accounts for 86 per cent of the global case count. In 2015, the figure was fifty-four—a decline by 82 per cent compared to the year 2014. The number of infected districts reduced from forty-three in 2014 to twenty-three in 2015. The majority of WPV cases continue to appear in the known 'reservoir' areas. Although reported cases have risen, access breakthroughs in North and South Waziristan give some cause for optimism. The large-scale displacement of populations afforded opportunities to vaccinate at transit points and in host communities. http://www.endpolio.com.pk/polioin-pakistan. Viewed on 26 June 2016.
37. There were over 20,000 cases of polio before the WHO started its immunization programme in 1994, but after that, the cases were brought down to 2000 (interview with Dr Elias Durry, Emergency Coordinator for Polio Eradication, Pakistan). From 199 cases in the year 2000, it went down to twenty-eight in 2008, and in 2012, it was fifty-eight. But in 2013 till October, fifty-three cases were detected, thirty-seven of them in FATA, a hotspot. The only remaining reservoir of wild poliovirus type 3 in Asia is in Khyber Agency and FATA. http://www.polioeradication.org/dataandmonitoring/poliothisweek.aspx. Viewed on 16 January 2016.

Chapter 5: Shooting the Messenger

1. From his speech on 'The Condition of the Press in India', at the Imperial Legislative Council (19 September 1918).

2. Zamir Niazi, *Press in Chains* (New Delhi, Ajanta Publications, 1987), 28–29.
3. Ibid., 178–79.
4. Pervez Musharraf, *In the Line of Fire: A Memoir* (New York: Free Press, 2006), 159–60.
5. Ibid., 135–36.
6. Zamir Niazi, *Press in Chains* (New Delhi: Ajanta Publications, 1987), 61.
7. Ibid., 68.
8. A.A.K. Niazi, *The Betrayal of East Pakistan* (New Delhi: Manohar Publishers and Distributors, 1998), 127.
9. Zamir Niazi, *Press in Chains* (New Delhi: Ajanta Publications, 1987), 210.
10. Carlotta Gall, *The Wrong Enemy: America in Afghanistan 2001–2014* (Gurgaon: Penguin Random House India, 2014).
11. '60 Journalists Killed in Pakistan since 1992/Motive Confirmed', https://cpj.org/killed/asia/pakistan/.
12. CPJ reports, https://cpj.org/killed/asia/pakistan/murder.php and https://cpj.org/killed/.
13. Elisabeth Witchel, 'Getting Away With Murder', https://cpj.org/reports/2016/10/impunity-index-getting-away-with-murder-killed-justice.php.
14. Ibid.
15. Asad Hashim, 'Pakistan detained more than 5,000 after Easter bombing killed 72', http://www.reuters.com/article/us-pakistan-blast-idUSKCN0WV0FC. Viewed on 29 April 2016.
16. BBC, 'Leading Pakistani Geo TV channel is ordered off air', http://www.bbc.com/news/world-asia-27733077. Viewed on 18 December 2015.
17. Feroz Hassan Khan, *Eating Grass: The Making of the Pakistani Bomb* (New Delhi: Cambridge University Press, 2013), 331.
18. Asad Hashim, 'Pakistani rights activist Sabeen Mahmud shot dead', http://www.aljazeera.com/news/2015/04/pakistani-rights-activist-sabeen-mahmud-killed-150424210251526.html.
19. 'Pakistan: Religious groups condemn US embassy gay event', http://www.bbc.com/news/world-south-asia-14010106.

Chapter 6: No Lines of Control

1. This was documented by the Michigan State University in a book, *Rural Development in Action*, in 1963.
2. Shoaib Sultan Khan, *The Aga Khan Rural Support Programme: A Journey through Grassroots Development* (Karachi: Oxford University Press, 2009).
3. Noel Cossins, *Man in the Hat* (Lahore: Vanguard Books, 2013).
4. *Gulley Kuche*, 1952.
5. Intizar Hussain, *A Chronicle of the Peacocks.* Translated from the Urdu by Alok Bhalla and Vishwamitter Adil. (New Delhi: Oxford University Press, 2004).
6. 'J. S. Waterhouse's Diary, 1864', http://greenhowards.org.uk.gridhosted.co.uk/wp-content/uploads/Job-Waterhouse1.pdf.
7. Ian Stephens, *Horned Moon* (London: Chatto & Windus, 1953), 135.
8. In an interview with the author.
9. http://greenhowards.org.uk.gridhosted.co.uk/wp-content/uploads/Job-Waterhouse1.pdf.
10. Farakh A. Khan, *Murree during the Raj: A British Town in the Hills* (Lahore: Topical Printers, 2013).
11. In an interview with the author.
12. 'VHP activists vandalise art gallery displaying paintings of Pakistani artists in Ahmedabad', http://indiatoday.intoday.in/story/vhp-activists-vandalise-art-gallery-displaying-paintings-of-pakistani-artists/1/300031.html.
13. Krishna Kumar, *Prejudice and Pride: School Histories of the Freedom Struggle in India and Pakistan* (New Delhi: Viking, 2001), 4.
14. *A Missed Opportunity—Continuing Flaws in the New Curriculum and Textbooks after Reforms* (Islamabad: Jinnah Institute, June 2013).
15. Krishna Kumar, *Prejudice and Pride: School Histories of the Freedom Struggle in India and Pakistan* (New Delhi: Viking, 2001), 44–45.
16. Hector Bolitho, *Jinnah: Creator of Pakistan* (Karachi: Oxford University Press, 2006; first printed in 1954 by John Murray), 175–76.
17. 'A most interesting thing to note is that this speech has been distorted with abandon in the Pakistan Studies textbooks of Balochistan.

The English book quotes the Quaid-i-Azam in the following words:

> You are free, whether you want to go to temples, mosques or other places of worship, you are absolutely free. Whatever your religion or caste may be, the affairs of the state shall not be affected. We are heading forward with the basic principle that we are equal citizens of one state. I believe we must adhere to this principle, and you shall see that there would be no discrimination between the Hindus and the Muslims in terms of equal political rights.

18. *A Missed Opportunity—Continuing Flaws in the New Curriculum and Textbooks after Reforms* (Islamabad: Jinnah Institute, June 2013).
19. Ibid.
20. Krishna Kumar, *Prejudice and Pride: School Histories of the Freedom Struggle in India and Pakistan* (New Delhi: Viking, 2001), 76.
21. Ibid., 79.
22. Ibid., 130.
23. Ibid., 200.
24. Mohammad Yunus, *Persons, Passions and Politics* (New Delhi: Vikas Publishing House,1980), 61.
25. Kuldip Nayar, *Distant Neighbours: A Tale of the Subcontinent* (New Delhi: Vikas Publishing House, 1972), 53.
26. Krishna Kumar, *Prejudice and Pride: School Histories of the Freedom Struggle in India and Pakistan* (New Delhi: Viking, 2001), 133, 137.
27. Ibid., 158.
28. Ibid., 195–96.
29. Kuldip Nayar, *Distant Neighbours: A Tale of the Subcontinent* (New Delhi: Vikas Publishing House, 1972).
30. Ibid.
31. M. Mujeeb, *The Indian Muslims* (London: George Allen and Unwin Limited, 1967), 13.
32. Krishna Kumar, *Prejudice and Pride: School Histories of the Freedom Struggle in India and Pakistan* (New Delhi: Viking, 2001), 237.

Chapter 7: Civilian versus Military

1. Pakistan foreign office statement on 3 September 2013.
2. General Kayani's statement on 29 November 2013.
3. Ayesha Siddiqa, *Military Inc.: Inside Pakistan's Military Economy* (Karachi: Oxford University Press, fourth impression, 2011; Gurgaon: Penguin Random House India, 2017).
4. 'People of Pakistan will celebrate if army takes over, says Imran', 17 July 2016, http://www.dawn.com/news/1271411. Viewed on 23 July 2016.

Chapter 8: Reviving a Left-of-centre Politics and Other Stories

1. Interview with Minto in 2013 for *The Hindu*.
2. Zulqarnain Tahir, 'Bilawal Bhutto's initiative may lift ban on students union', http://www.dawn.com/news/1233725. Viewed on 10 February 2016.
3. Iqbal Haider Butt, *Revisiting Student Politics in Pakistan* (Punjab: Bargad Organization for Youth Development, 2008).
4. Ibid.
5. Interview to *The Hindu*, 2013.
6. Personal communication with Duniya Aslam Khan, the public information officer of the UNHCR.
7. Personal communication with Duniya Aslam Khan, February 2017.
8. From personal communication with Duniya Aslam Khan.
9. 'Pakistan Coercion, UN Complicity: The Mass Forced Return of Afghan Refugees', Human Rights Watch, which has interviews with ninety-two refugees who returned to Kabul and twenty-three in Peshawar. The report was released on 13 February 2017.
10. From personal communication with Duniya Aslam Khan of the UNHCR.
11. 'Pakistan Demographic and Health Survey 2012–13' conducted by the NIPS and the ICF International, Calverton, Maryland, USA, in 2013.
12. 'Odd foreign policy priority', http://www.dawn.com/news/1213936/odd-foreign-policy-priority. Viewed on 1 May 2016.

13. 'Supreme Court lifts hunting ban on rare houbara bustard', 23 January 2016, http://www.dawn.com/news/1234663. Viewed on 1 May 2016.

Chapter 9: Bilateral Ties

1. The quarterly report of the Special Inspector General for Afghan Reconstruction (SIGAR) to the United States Congress on 30 January 2017 quotes US Forces Afghanistan (USFOR-A) which stated that approximately 57.2 per cent of the country's 407 districts were under Afghan government control or influence as of 15 November 2016, a 6.2 per cent decrease from the 63.4 per cent reported in late August, and a nearly 15 per cent decrease since November 2015.
2. M.K. Bhadrakumar, 'Why Pakistan feels bold enough to seek "strategic depth" in Afghanistan once again', 16 April 2016, http://scroll.in/article/807161/why-pakistan-feels-bold-enough-to-seek-strategic-depth-in-afghanistan-once-again.
3. Attia Hosain, *Sunlight on a Broken Column* (New Delhi: Penguin Books India, 1992).
4. Maulana Abul Kalam Azad, *India Wins Freedom* (Calcutta: Orient Longman, 1959), 197.
5. Sardar Patel, *For a United India: Speeches of Sardar Patel 1947–50* (New Delhi: Publications Division, Ministry of Information and Broadcasting, Government of India, revised and enlarged edition, 1967), 21.
6. Hector Bolitho, *Jinnah: Creator of Pakistan* (Karachi: Oxford University Press, 2006), 163.
7. Maulana Abul Kalam Azad, *India Wins Freedom* (Calcutta: Orient Longman, 1959), 226.
8. Mohammad Ayub Khan, *Friends, Not Masters* (London: Oxford University Press, 1967), 47.
9. Ibid., 42.
10. Ibid., 48–52.
11. Ibid., 52.
12. Kuldip Nayar, *Wall at Wagah* (New Delhi: Gyan Publishing House, 2003), 11.

13. Sardar Patel, *For a United India: Speeches of Sardar Patel 1947–50* (New Delhi: Publications Division, Ministry of Information and Broadcasting, Government of India, revised and enlarged edition, 1967), 155.
14. Mohammad Ayub Khan, *Friends, Not Masters* (London: Oxford University Press, 1967), 160–61.
15. Rajmohan Gandhi, *Punjab: A History from Aurangzeb to Mountbatten* (New Delhi: Aleph Book Company, 2013).
16. B.M. Kutty, *Sixty Years in Self Exile: No Regrets* (Pakistan Study Centre, University of Karachi, and Pakistan Labour Trust, Karachi, 2011).
17. Mohammad Ayub Khan, *Friends, Not Masters* (London: Oxford University Press, 1967), 123.
18. Ibid., 172.
19. Ibid., 183.
20. Stephen P. Cohen, *Shooting for a Century* (Noida: HarperCollins, 2013), xi.
21. Mohammad Ayub Khan, *Friends, Not Masters* (London: Oxford University Press, 1967), 128.
22. Kuldip Nayar, *Distant Neighbours: A Tale of the Subcontinent* (New Delhi: Vikas Publishing House, 1972), 82.
23. Sheikh Abdullah was fond of comparing Kashmir to a beautiful body which both India and Pakistan desired. (Kuldip Nayar, *Distant Neighbours: A Tale of the Subcontinent*), 108.
24. 'Kashmir: Looking Beyond the Peril' was hosted by the Institute for Strategic Studies Research and Analysis Wing of the National Defence University, Islamabad.
25. Kuldip Nayar, *Distant Neighbours: A Tale of the Subcontinent* (New Delhi: Vikas Publishing House, 1972), 105.
26. Nitin Gokhale, *Beyond NJ 9842: The Siachen Saga* (New Delhi: Bloomsbury, 2015), 11.
27. Pervez Musharraf, *In the Line of Fire: A Memoir* (UK: Pocket Books, 2008), 68, 70.
28. Ibid., 69.
29. It was only in June 2016 that the US State Department added the Jamaat-ud-Dawa and other aliases of the LeT to the list of designated terror organizations. (According to an official statement

of the US State Department, the department has amended Lashkar-e-Taiba's designations to add the aliases: Jamaat-ud-Dawa, the Al-Anfal Trust, Tehrik-e-Hurmat-e-Rasool and Tehrik-e-Tahafuz Qibla Awwal.)

30. Vaqar Ahmed, Abid Q. Suleri, Muhammed Abdul Wahab and Asif Javed, 'Informal Flow of Merchandise from India: The Case of Pakistan' (Islamabad: SDPI).
31. Ibid.

Chapter 10: Voice for Missing Balochis

1. Carlotta Gall, *The Wrong Enemy: America in Afghanistan* (Gurgaon: Penguin Random House India, 2014), xvi.

Epilogue

1. A.A.K. Niazi, *The Betrayal of East Pakistan* (New Delhi: Manohar Publishers, 1998).
2. Ibid., 35.
3. Jawaharlal Nehru, *Independence and After: A Collection of the More Important Speeches of Jawaharlal Nehru, from September 1946 to May 1949*, 247.

Select Bibliography

Ahmed, Khaled. *Sectarian War: Pakistan's Sunni–Shia Violence and Its Links to the Middle East*. Karachi: Oxford University Press, second impression, 2013.

Ayaz, Babar. *What's Wrong with Pakistan?* New Delhi: Hay House Publishers, 2013.

Azad, Maulana Abul Kalam. *India Wins Freedom: An Autobiographical Narrative*. Calcutta: Orient Longman, 1959.

Aziz, Sartaj. *Between Dreams and Realities: Some Milestones in Pakistan's History*. Karachi: Oxford University Press, second impression, 2011.

Barker, Kim. *The Taliban Shuffle: Strange Days in Afghanistan and Pakistan*. New York: Anchor Books, 2012 edition.

Baruah, Amit. *Dateline Islamabad*. New Delhi: Penguin Books India, 2007.

Bhutto, Benazir. *Daughter of the East: An Autobiography*. London: Pocket Books, London, 2008.

Bhutto, Benazir. *Pakistan: The Gathering Storm*. New Delhi: Vikas Publishing House, 1983.

Bhutto, Zulfikar Ali. *If I Am Assassinated*. New Delhi: Vikas Publishing House, 1979.

Bhutto, Zulfikar Ali. *The Myth of Independence*. Karachi: Oxford University Press, 1969.

Bolitho, Hector. *Jinnah: Creator of Pakistan*. Karachi: Oxford University Press, 2006. First printed in 1954 by John Murray.

Brown, Vahid and Don Rassler. *Fountainhead of Jihad: The Haqqani Nexus 1973–2012*. New Delhi: Hachette India, 2013.

Burki, Javed Shahid. *Pakistan Under Bhutto 1971–1977*. London and Basingstoke: Palgrave Macmillan, 1980.

Cohen, Stephen P. *Shooting for a Century*. New Delhi: HarperCollins, 2013.

Coll, Steve. *Ghost Wars*. London: Penguin Books, 2005.

Devji, Faisal. *Muslim Zion: Pakistan as a Political Idea*. Cambridge, Massachusetts: Harvard University Press, 2013.

Fair, C. Christine. *Fighting to the End: The Pakistan Army's Way of War*. New Delhi: Oxford University Press, 2014.

For a United India: Speeches of Sardar Patel 1947–50. Publications Division, Ministry of Information and Broadcasting, Government of India, revised and enlarged edition, 1967.

Gall, Carlotta. *The Wrong Enemy: America in Afghanistan 2001–2014*. Gurgaon: Penguin Random House India, 2014.

Guns and Yellow Roses: Essays on the Kargil War. New Delhi: HarperCollins, 1999.

Haqqani, Husain. *India vs Pakistan: Why Can't We Just Be Friends*? New Delhi: Juggernaut Books, 2016.

Hosain, Attia. *Sunlight on a Broken Column*. New Delhi: Penguin Books India, 1992.

Hussain, Intizar. *Basti*. Translated from the Urdu by Frances W. Pritchett. New Delhi: Oxford University Press, 2007.

Hussain, Zahid. *The Scorpion's Tail*. New York: Free Press, 2013.

Jaffrelot, Christophe. *The Pakistan Paradox: Instability and Resilience*. Gurgaon: Penguin Random House India, 2015.

Jalal, Ayesha. *The Struggle for Pakistan: A Muslim Homeland and Global Politics*. Noida: Belknap Press, 2014.

Khan, Ayub. *Diaries of Field Marshal Mohammad 1966–1972*. Edited and annotated by Craig Baxter. Karachi: Oxford University Press, 2013.

Khan, Feroz Hassan. *Eating Grass: The Making of the Pakistani Bomb*. New Delhi: Cambridge University Press, 2013.

Khan, Mohammad Ayub. *Friends, Not Masters*. London: Oxford University Press, 1967.

Kuldip Nayar. *Distant Neighbours: A Tale of the Subcontinent.* New Delhi: Vikas Publishing House, 1972.

Kumar, Krishna. *Prejudice and Pride: School Histories of the Freedom Struggle in India and Pakistan.* New Delhi: Viking, 2001.

Kutty, B.M. *Sixty Years in Self Exile: No Regrets.* Karachi: Pakistan Study Centre, University of Karachi and Pakistan Labour Trust, 2011.

Mitha, A.O. *Unlikely Beginnings: A Soldier's Life.* Karachi: Oxford University Press, second impression, 2007.

Mody, Piloo. *Zulfi My Friend.* New Delhi: Thomson Press India, 1973.

Mujeeb, M. *The Indian Muslims.* London: George Allen and Unwin Limited, 1967.

Mukerjee, Dilip. *Zulfiqar Ali Bhutto: Quest for Power.* New Delhi: Vikas Publishing House, 1972.

Munoz, Heraldo. *Getting Away with Murder.* New York: W.W. Norton and Co., 2014.

Musharraf, Pervez. *In the Line of Fire: A Memoir.* London: Pocket Books, 2008.

Nayar, Kuldip. *Wall at Wagah.* New Delhi: Gyan Publishing House, 2003.

Nehru, Jawaharlal. *An Autobiography.* New Delhi: Penguin Books India, 2004.

Niazi, A.A.K. *The Betrayal of East Pakistan.* New Delhi: Manohar Publishers and Distributors, 1998.

Niazi, Zamir. *Press in Chains.* New Delhi: Ajanta Publications, 1987.

Noorani, A.G. *The Kashmir Dispute 1947–2012.* Karachi: Oxford University Press, 2014.

Palit, D.K. *The Lightning Campaign: Indo-Pakistan War, 1971.* New Delhi: Thomson Press, 1972.

Rashid, Ahmed. *Descent into Chaos.* London: Allen Lane, 2008.

Rashid, Ahmed. *Pakistan on the Brink.* New Delhi: Allen Lane, 2012.

Rashid, Ahmed. *Taliban: The Story of the Afghan Warlords.* London: Pan Books, 2001.

Roshnai, Sajjad Zaheer. *The Light*. Translated from the Urdu by Amina Azfar. Karachi: Oxford University Press, 2012.

Saleem Shahzad, Syed. *Inside Al-Qaeda and the Taliban*. London: Pluto Press, 2011.

Schofield, Victoria. *Bhutto: Trial and Execution*. London: Cassell, 1979.

Siddiqa, Ayesha. *Military Inc. Inside Pakistan's Military Economy*. Karachi: Oxford University Press, fourth impression, 2011.

Sørenson, Kaare. *The Mind of a Terrorist: The Strange Case of David Headley*. Gurgaon: Penguin Random House India, 2016.

Taseer, Salman. *Bhutto: A Political Autobiography*. New Delhi: Vikas Publishing House, 1980.

Tikekar, Maneesha. *Across the Wagah: An Indian's Sojourn in Pakistan*. New Delhi: Promilla and Co. Publishers, 2006.

Wolpert, Stanley. *Jinnah of Pakistan*. Karachi: Oxford University Press, 1993.

Yunus, Mohammad. *Persons, Passions and Politics*. New Delhi: Vikas Publishing House, 1980.

Zafar, Anjum. *Iqbal: The Life of a Poet Philosopher and Politician*. Gurgaon: Penguin Random House India, 2014.

Index